www.wadsworth.com

www.wadsworth.com is the World Wide Web site for Wadsworth and is your direct source to dozens of online resources.

At www.wadsworth.com you can find out about supplements, demonstration software, and student resources. You can also send email to many of our authors and preview new publications and exciting new technologies.

www.wadsworth.com
Changing the way the world learns®

Girls, Delinquency, and Juvenile Justice

Third Edition

MEDA CHESNEY-LIND
University of Hawaii at Manoa

RANDALL G. SHELDEN
University of Nevada, Las Vegas

THOMSON
™
WADSWORTH

Australia • Canada • Mexico • Singapore • Spain
United Kingdom • United States

THOMSON

WADSWORTH

Senior Executive Editor: *Sabra Horne*
Editorial Assistant: *Paul Massicotte*
Marketing Manager: *Dory Schaeffer*
Marketing Assistant: *Neena Chandra*
Advertising Project Manager: *Stacey Purviance*
Project Manager, Editorial Production:
  Catherine Morris
Print/Media Buyer: *Doreen Suruki*

Permissions Editor: *Sommy Ko*
Production Service: *Matrix Productions*
Copy Editor: *Anna Trabucco*
Cover Designer: *Yvo Riezebos*
Cover Image: © *Getty Images*
Compositor: *Pre-Press Company, Inc.*
Text and Cover Printer: *Webcom*

For more information about our products,
contact us at:
**Thomson Learning Academic
Resource Center
1-800-423-0563**
For permission to use material from this text,
contact us by:
Phone: 1-800-730-2214
Fax: 1-800-730-2215
Web: http://www.thomsonrights.com

Library of Congress Contol Number: 2003104975

ISBN 0-534-55774-0

Wadsworth/Thomson Learning
10 Davis Drive
Belmont, CA 94002-3098
USA

Asia
Thomson Learning
5 Shenton Way #01-01
UIC Building
Singapore 068808

Australia/New Zealand
Thomson Learning
102 Dodds Street
Southbank, Victoria 3006
Australia

Canada
Nelson
1120 Birchmount Road
Toronto, Ontario M1K 5G4
Canada

Europe/Middle East/Africa
Thomson Learning
High Holborn House
50/51 Bedford Row
London WC1R 4LR
United Kingdom

Latin America
Thomson Learning
Seneca, 53
Colonia Polanco
11560 Mexico D.F.
Mexico

Spain/Portugal
Paraninfo
Calle/Magallanes, 25
28015 Madrid, Spain

Contents

Foreword

Girls are not supposed to be "bad." There is something about "bad girls" that embarrasses us, makes us want to change the topic. The image of a "bad girl" is threatening and naughty, maybe even sexually dirty or unspeakable. For boys, breaking the rules can be seen as a part of growing up— we say that such boys are "precocious," and when they get particularly rambunctious, they are "feeling their oats." Girls are supposed to be different. They are supposed to be nice, to be a joy to their parents and an example of correctness in the way they act.

This is all a stereotype, of course. Girls are different in some ways from boys, but they have a young person's capacity for misbehavior that is not so dissimilar from that of boys. More than one-fourth of juvenile arrestees are girls, and that rate is rising. Any crime for which boys sometimes get in trouble is a crime for which girls are also sometimes arrested. Boys who get in trouble with the law have always been an important theme in social science, and today we can increasingly say that girls provide the same kind of social science material.

It is just as clear that we cannot profitably study girls as if they were boys. Although we need to recognize that girls can cause as much trouble as boys, the profile of the trouble girls get into is, on the whole, different from that of boys. Girls get in trouble for getting caught running away when boys are seldom in trouble for their running away. Boys are more likely to be violent, and the crimes for which they are arrested are on the whole more serious than girls' crimes. Both boys and girls who break the law have suffered high rates of abuse by adults, but whereas boys are beaten, girls are both beaten and sexually molested. Boys often act out by hurting others; girls by running away.

The differences between girls and boys raise an important challenge to social science. How do we know that delinquency theory, most of which was developed by studying boys, fits girls, too? Can we apply general delinquency models that are dominated by studies of boys to the smaller number of girls who are entering the system? And, perhaps most important, should the juvenile justice system take account of girls' misbehavior differently than boys'?

The answer to these questions is neither obvious nor simple. That is one of the reasons why, as editor of the *Wadsworth Series on Contemporary Issues in Crime and Justice,* I am delighted to announce the publication of *Girls, Delinquency, and Juvenile Justice* by Meda Chesney-Lind and Randall G. Shelden. The *Contemporary Issues* series is devoted to furthering our understanding of important issues in crime and justice by providing an in-depth treatment of topics that are neglected or insufficiently discussed in today's textbooks. *Girls, Delinquency, and Juvenile Justice* is an excellent example of the kind of work the series was designed to foster.

This book brims with important facts, findings, and other insights about girls and juvenile justice. The studies tell us important particulars about how the juvenile justice system affects girls who enter it. The stories of accusation and adjudication, punishment and incarceration provide weighty insight to the dynamics of justice for girls. We find ourselves confronted with a system that seems close to incapable of taking these girls' lives into account, a system that is built on bad assumptions and failed strategies. This story is not an easy one to read, and the facts of this book should surely make us uncomfortable about the system we have developed to deal with troublesome girls.

The authors have provided for us not only a critique of "what is," but also a precious opportunity to think about "what if." What if girls' life experiences became the basis under which the justice system treated them? And what if the inequalities that affect girls today were reduced, what might happen with regard to those girls' misbehavior? Thinking in terms not just of the current world, but the possibilities for a new kind of justice, will open doorways to new thinking about social and criminal justice strategies. An opportunity to think creatively about new ways of building societal responses to misbehavior is a major contribution of this volume.

But that valuable contribution, important as it is, is not what makes this book special. You will appreciate the cool, analytical critique of the juvenile justice system, of course, offered by two of the most talented analysts of justice writing in social science today. But what will affect you even more is the voices of the girls themselves. For nobody can critique the juvenile justice system more effectively, nobody can describe what is wrong with more insight, than the girls themselves. We see the lives of girls in the full richness of their stories. We begin to see how the events of a young girl's life can translate into the challenges of youth, and we can begin to understand the paradox that girls are so often being processed by the justice system because the only choices they could see were the very acts that the justice system condemns.

This is a revolutionary book, in a way. It asks you to stop thinking about justice as a quality of penal system action, and begins to show how justice is a quality of "fit." Girls who violate the law may understandably engage our concern, and their acts may give us pause. But when we consider their lives in a more holistic way, we come to see that the juvenile justice system is like a vast and complex instrument capable of playing only one note, when a symphony is desired. Reading this book will, I hope and expect, bring each of you closer to the point of writing a part of a new symphony of justice.

Todd R. Clear

Preface

I t has been about fifteen years since we began work on the first edition of this book, culminating in its publication in 1992. As we write the preface to the third edition, the world we inhabit has been dramatically changed. The dramatic events of September 11, 2001 made certain that the world, as we know it, might never be the same. As these words are written (February 2003), an invasion of Iraq seems inevitable. The country is divided, as it was during the later years of the Vietnam War, with world opinion standing firmly against the United States' position against Iraq.

It might at first glance seem that the issue of girls and the juvenile justice system is far removed from these outside events. Yet the issues we cover in this book cannot be separated from such events, as if anything in our lives can be so separated. Indeed, if anything has an impact on the lives of girls and the juvenile justice system that responds to their problems and misdeeds, the "war on terrorism" and the conflict over Iraq certainly should. Among other reasons, these events will drain much-needed funds that could be set aside to assist troubled girls and their families. In fact, the Bush administration cancelled several very ambitious plans to address the issue of girls and the juvenile justice system, including a National Girls Institute to be housed within the Office of Juvenile Justice and Delinquency Prevention, saying the withdrawal of funds for this program was due in part to "recent world events." Moreover, the continuing economic woes facing the country, plus the growing deficits, must necessarily impact millions of families, especially the nation's poor and marginalized populations. Perhaps more important, the spending on the "war on terrorism" and the conflict in Iraq has already resulted in a budgetary crisis in virtually every state in the nation. The inevitable cutbacks that will certainly follow will naturally have the most negative impact on the lives of ordinary people, but especially the poorest of our citizens. Girls in trouble will, of course, be further victimized.

It should come as little surprise to find that states undergoing such crises find themselves strapped for money for reasons other than the "war on terrorism" and the Iraq conflict. This is because the "get tough" legislation that has dominated crime policies during the past two decades has resulted in the largest increase in prison construction in the history of this country (Austin and Irwin, 2001; Shelden, 2001; Shelden and Brown, 2003). For both adults and juveniles, imprisonment is becoming more of a reality, as incarceration rates continue to go higher and higher. Girls, including those charged with status offenses (including those "bootstrapped" into the "delinquent" category by being referred to juvenile court on violations of court orders, such as probation violations), will also experience this increase in the drop off rate. Expenditures on prisons and juvenile detention centers have not been receiving the legislator's axe in recent years. There appears to be plenty of money available for the construction of these "edifices" but little money for education, health care, and much-needed treatment and prevention programs for girls (Shelden, 2002).

In this third edition we have added many new features and updated all the statistics, to the extent that new data were available. To Chapter 3 we have added a new section on girls and violence, while challenging the allegation of a "new breed" of "violent" girls. In this new section we address the personal and social context of such "violence." In Chapter 10, where girls tell their "own stories," we have replaced the original Hawaii study with a new one in which researchers from the University of Hawaii Youth Gang Project (YGP) and the University of Hawaii Girls' Project conducted focus groups and small group interview sessions with both girls and boys of varying ethnic backgrounds. Finally, we have added some new material to Chapter 11 on girls programming.

We do not have to reiterate most of what we said in the preface to the second edition, especially about the declining economic situation, growing inequality, and the continuance of male domination. We regret to say that nothing much has changed—in fact, things have become worse. We continue to receive notifications that this book has been helpful to many individuals and organizations and we are thankful for the kudos we have received over the years for the work we have assembled here. We know that this book has become a reference point for those engaged in activism in the field of juvenile justice, especially as it impacts girls. We sincerely hope that the third edition will continue to have such a positive impact.

ACKNOWLEDGMENTS

We would both like to acknowledge all of the people associated with Wadsworth publishers for their assistance in getting this third edition completed. Special thanks to Sabra Horne who kept prodding the authors to "get this done." Many others at Wadsworth, too numerous to mention, should also be thanked. Thanks go out also to all the anonymous and not-so-anonymous reviewers who have shown us our errors and made valuable suggestions for each of the three editions. For the third we wish to thank Kevin Thompson, North Dakota State University; Candice Batton, University of Nebraska; Cyndi Banks, Northern Arizona University; Daniel Ponstingle, Lorain County Community College; and Verna Henson, Southwest Texas State University. We would also like to extend our appreciation to all of those scholars, teachers, students, and practitioners who helped make the first two editions of this book so popular. We are continuously amazed at the success we have had with this book. We both have received more than our share of kudos from many different people. Our respective "significant others" have our gratitude for their unyielding support. Special thanks and love to Ian and Virginia.

1

Introduction:
Why a Book on Girls and
Juvenile Justice?

"I ran away so many times. I tried anything, man, and they wouldn't believe me. . . . As far as they are concerned they think I'm the problem. You know, runaway, bad label."

STATEMENT OF A SIXTEEN-YEAR-OLD PART-HAWAIIAN GIRL WHO, AFTER
HAVING BEEN PHYSICALLY AND SEXUALLY ASSAULTED, STARTED RUNNING
AWAY FROM HOME AND WAS ARRESTED AS A "RUNAWAY" IN HAWAII

Crying is not going to get me home. The outside tears are nothing but water. I'm crying on the inside where no one can see it.

A 14-YEAR-OLD GIRL IN A CALIFORNIA JUVENILE HALL
(AMERICAN BAR ASSOCIATION, 2001: 1)

You know, one of these days I'm going to have to kill myself before you guys are gonna listen to me. I can't stay at home.

STATEMENT OF A SIXTEEN-YEAR-OLD TUCSON RUNAWAY WITH
A LONG HISTORY OF PHYSICAL ABUSE (DAVIDSON, 1982: 26)

Police have arrested a thirty-eight-year-old Waikiki man on a possible third-degree rape charge after a seventeen-year-old California girl told police he assaulted her last night. The girl, a San Carlos resident, was arrested for being here without parental supervision.

POLICE/FIRE/RESCUE SECTION, *HONOLULU STAR BULLETIN,* JULY 5, 1984

"Juvenile Hall strip search of girl spurs questions;
DA begins probe of incident where man was present"

SAN FRANCISCO EXAMINER, FEBRUARY 16, 1996

Fifteen-year-old Kathy Robbins' offense against society was running
away from home. She paid for it with her life in a Glenn County Jail cell.

LOS ANGELES DAILY JOURNAL, MARCH 30, 1987

Historically, female juvenile delinquency has been "ignored, trivialized or
denied" (Chesney-Lind & Okamoto, 2001: 3), while girls in the juvenile
justice system were once "dubbed" the "forgotten few" (Bergsmann,
1989). This response has gradually changed, as statistics consistently illustrate the
increasing involvement of female youth in the juvenile justice system (Budnick
& Shields-Fletcher, 1998). Throughout the past decade, an increasing amount of
literature has focused on the etiology, prevalence, and treatment of female juvenile delinquency (Belknap, Holsinger, & Dunn, 1997; Chesney-Lind &
Okamoto, 2001), and has highlighted the unique patterns of female juvenile offending (Poe-Yamagata & Butts, 1996). The "invisibility" of female delinquency
has also lessened because of dramatic changes in the arrests of girls during the
last decade of the twentieth century. In fact, increases in girls' arrests dramatically
outstripped those of boys for most of the last decade. In 2000, girls accounted
for 27 percent of juvenile arrests, up from 22 percent at the beginning of the last
decade (Sourcebook of Criminal Justice Statistics, Federal Bureau of Investigation, 2001). Attention is being drawn to the fact that their arrests for nontraditional, even violent, offenses are among those showing the greatest increases.
These shifts and changes all bring into sharp focus the need to better understand
the dynamics involved in female delinquency and the need to tailor responses to
the unique circumstances of girls growing up in the new millennium.

Who is the typical female delinquent? What causes her to get into trouble?
What happens to her if she is arrested? These are questions that few members
of the general public could answer quickly. In contrast, almost all citizens can
talk about "delinquency," by which they generally mean male delinquency.
They can even generate some specific complaints about the failure of the juvenile justice system to deal with such matters as the "alarming" increase in serious juvenile crime and the leniency of juvenile courts on juveniles found
guilty of offenses (Males, 1999; Elikann, 1999).

This situation should come as no surprise. Even the academic study of
delinquent behavior has, for all intents and purposes, been the study of male
delinquency. "The delinquent is a rogue male," wrote Albert Cohen in his influential book on gang delinquency in 1955 (Cohen, 1955: 140). More than a
decade later, Travis Hirschi (1969), in his equally important book, *The Causes
of Delinquency,* relegated women to a footnote: "in the analysis that follows, the
'non-Negro' becomes 'white,' and the girls disappear."

This book is our effort to begin to rectify the long history of neglect in delinquency research, an effort begun in the first two editions of this book. Feminist poet Adrienne Rich (1976) suggested that the feminist enterprise is best undertaken by asking, "But what was it like for women?" In this book, we will be asking, What is it like for girls? We seek to put girls—their lives, their problems, and their experiences with the juvenile justice system—at the center of our inquiry. Fortunately, interest in women's issues has meant that many notable studies on this topic are beginning to appear, and we will be drawing on them, as well as on our own work, in the chapters that follow.

Chapter 2 shows that although there are many similarities between male and female delinquency, there are also significant differences. First, and most important, girls tend to be arrested for offenses that are less serious than those committed by boys. About half of all girls arrested are arrested for one of two offenses: larceny–theft (which for girls is often shoplifting) and running away from home. Boys' delinquency also involves many minor offenses, but the crimes boys commit are more varied.

One of the two major "girls' offenses"—running away from home—points up another significant aspect of female delinquency. Girls are quite often arrested for offenses that are not actual crimes like robbery or burglary. Instead, the offenses are activities such as running away from home, being incorrigible, or being beyond parental control. These are called "status offenses" and, as we see in Chapter 2, they have long played a major role in bringing girls into the juvenile justice system. (In fact, in the early years of the juvenile justice system, most of the girls in juvenile court were charged with these offenses.) As we shall see, status offenses (particularly running away from home and ungovernability) continue to be major factors.

Why are girls more likely than boys to be arrested for running away from home? There are no easy answers to this question. Studies of actual delinquency (not simply arrests) show that girls and boys run away from home in about equal numbers. There is some evidence to suggest that parents and police may be responding differently to the same behavior. Parents may be calling the police when their daughters do not come home, and police may be more likely to arrest a female than a male runaway.

Another cause of different responses to running away speaks to the reasons that boys and girls have for leaving home. Girls are much more likely than boys to be the victims of child sexual abuse, with some experts estimating that roughly 70 percent of the victims of such abuse are girls (Finkelhor & Baron, 1986; National Clearinghouse on Child Abuse and Neglect Information, 2001). Not surprisingly, the evidence also suggests a link between this problem and girls' delinquency—particularly running away from home. Chapter 3 also reviews several studies indicating that an astonishing fraction (often two-thirds to three-quarters) of the girls who find their way into runaway shelters or juvenile detention facilities have been sexually abused. The numbers of girls who experience serious problems with physical abuse are also high. The relationship among girls' problems, their attempts to escape these forms of victimization by running away, and the traditional reaction of the juvenile justice system is a unique aspect of girls' interaction with the system.

Chapter 4 explores a relatively recent development in research on delinquency and girls, specifically the involvement of girls in youth gangs. Though girls have traditionally been less involved in gang behavior than boys, their numbers tended to be underestimated by researchers who focused exclusively on male gang life. Current research is correcting this impression and documenting the social and economic changes that have propelled girls into gang life as a survival mechanism. Research clearly shows that although girls join gangs for many of the same reasons that boys do—for status, for protection, for a sense of belonging and identity, and to meet basic human needs that are not being met by such major institutions as the family and the school—their experience of gang life and the streets is deeply affected by their gender. Reviewed in this chapter are several case studies that include interview data reflecting what gang girls have to say about their lives.

Chapter 5 surveys existing delinquency theories, which were admittedly developed to explain male delinquency, to see if they can be used to explain female delinquency as well. Clearly, the theories were much affected by notions that class and protest masculinity were at the core of delinquency. Will what some have rather flippantly called the "add-women-and-stir" approach be sufficient to create a theory that can explain girls' delinquency as well as boys'? This book argues that the issue is not quite that simple and that far more needs to be understood about the lives of girls, particularly young women of color and young women on the economic margin, and about girls' victimization before a comprehensive theory of delinquency is written.

In Chapter 6, we attempt to piece together what life is like for girls who enter the juvenile justice system. The early insights into male delinquency were largely gleaned by intensive field observation of delinquent boys. This chapter looks at the few studies that use a similar approach to the understanding of girls' definitions of their own situations, choices, and behavior. Research on the settings, such as families and schools, in which girls find themselves and the impact of variations in those settings is also reviewed, in addition to the work of those seeking a fuller understanding of how poverty and racism shape girls' lives.

In general, the first half of the book establishes that girls undergo a childhood and adolescence that is heavily colored by their gender (a case can also be made that the lives of boys are affected by gender roles). It is simply not possible to discuss their problems, their delinquency, and their experiences with the juvenile justice system without considering gender in all its dimensions. Girls and boys do not inhabit the same worlds, and they do not have the same choices. This is not to say that girls do not share some problems with boys (notably the burdens of class and race), but even the manner in which these attributes affect the daily lives of young people is heavily mediated by gender.

In one sense, thinking about girls' lives and troubles as they relate to female delinquency sidesteps some important questions that must ultimately be answered if we are to build a truly inclusive delinquency theory. First, there is the issue of why girls commit less delinquency (the "gender-ratio" issue). And there is the related but independent matter of whether theories generated to explain the behavior of boys can be useful in explaining the behavior of girls (the "generalizability" issue) (see Daly and Chesney-Lind, 1988). The first question asks, "What is it about girls' lives that produces less delinquency than is found among boys?" The second asks, "If girls were exposed to the same opportunities, had the same personality characteristics as boys, and so on, would their delinquency rate mirror that of boys?"

It is our opinion that too little is known now about the development of girls to answer either question unequivocally. This can be seen from the complexity of the findings that are emerging as research is conducted on girls' lives; sometimes the traditionally male theories seem to work, but more often their applicability to the delinquency of girls is a "yes, but. . . ." Yes, getting youth together in groups generally causes delinquency, but if we are talking about girls, it may not have that effect because girls spend time in small, intimate groups. Yes, school failure is important in the delinquency of boys, but sometimes it figures more largely in the delinquency of girls. We simply need to conduct more research on girls' lives before we can sketch out answers to either of the basic questions identified here. We also must consider the role played by other social institutions, particularly the institutions charged with the social control of youths (the juvenile justice system), in the lives of girls.

This discussion sets the stage for consideration of what the juvenile justice system is and has been for the girls who encounter it. Chapter 7 reviews its history. Of particular importance in our understanding of the juvenile court's response to girls is a review of the court's evolution as a sort of judicial parent (*parens patriae*) as well as a more traditional court of law. This orientation, for example, justified the arrest and incarceration of youths for noncriminal status offenses, many of which refer to failure to obey parents, to be amenable to their control, to avoid sexual experimentation, and in general to act in ways that parents might want daughters to act. Chapter 8 documents the ongoing judicial paternalism addressed to girls, many of whom have been at odds with their parents. Indeed, the chapter establishes that the juvenile justice system has a continuing concern with girls' obedience to family authority over and above a concern for girls' criminal behavior.

The judicial "double standard," or sexism, was so deeply ingrained in the system that girls' attempts to explain their problems with their parents or even provide accounts of abuse were often ignored. Instead, the girls were seen as the problem. Chapter 9 documents the method the juvenile justice system has historically employed to handle defiant and/or desperate girls: institutionalization in detention centers, adult jails, or training schools.

Unfortunately, contemporary judicial responses to girls in trouble still leave much to be desired. Despite over fifteen years of federal efforts to encourage deinstitutionalization of status offenders, for example, there are still many girls who are inappropriately detained and incarcerated.

A recent study of the nation's detention centers revealed that in 1999 only 2 percent of the boys in these facilities were being held for status offenses, but

8 percent of the girls were being held on these charges. Also, in 1999, among those placed in public residential facilities (mostly training schools), only 1 percent of the boys, but 8 percent of the girls, were in for status offenses. Among those in private facilities, however, the gender differences were stark: 7 percent of the boys, but 24 percent of the girls, were there for status offenses. Many other girls are incarcerated for violating the conditions of their probation or parole or for simple nonviolent property crimes. Specifically, in public facilities 12 percent of the boys, but 24 percent of the girls, are in for this reason; in private facilities these percentages are 10 percent for boys and 15 percent for girls (see Chapter 9). Moreover, the gains signaled by the deinstitutionalization movement have occasioned a strong parental and judicial backlash, which has most recently expressed itself in congressional efforts to undo some of the most important of the federal efforts to remove noncriminal youth from institutions.

In Chapter 10 we listen to the girls themselves as they talk about their lives and their experiences with the juvenile justice system. The interviews (taken from two separate studies, one in Hawaii and another in California) make clear that one major problem that girls currently encounter in the system is a product of their difficulties with their parents. Typically, when a boy is arrested or detained, his parents may be upset with him but will generally support him in court. In contrast, girls charged with status offenses have been in court precisely because circumstances at home led them to try the streets. In such situations, parents are not allies and may, in fact, be prosecutors. Moreover, courts are often left with few choices other than incarceration because placements have historically been in very short supply and woefully inadequate for dealing with the psychological problems of troubled young people. The net result was that girls often ended up in juvenile institutions for noncriminal behavior and their male counterparts did not.

National efforts to deinstitutionalize status offenders have resulted in some progress; for example, the past decade showed a dramatic reduction in girls' incarceration in certain states, but recall that these efforts have been under almost constant fire in Congress since the passage of the Juvenile Justice and Delinquency Act of 1974. Of even greater concern is the recent jump in the detention rates for girls (with rates of increase far greater than those seen for boys).

Fortunately, renewed interest in girls' issues nationally means there is renewed interest in programming for girls, and some of the most promising programs are examined in Chapter 11. Programs such as therapeutic foster homes, group living situations, homes for teen mothers and their children, and independent living arrangements have proven superior to locking up troubled and victimized girls.

Readers will likely notice that this book is really two books: one about the girls in the juvenile justice system (e.g., the actual behavior that brings them into the system) and another about the juvenile justice system's history and practices toward girls. We believe that these perspectives are inseparable if we are to understand girls and their delinquent behavior.

An appreciation of a young woman's experience of girlhood, particularly one that attends to the special problems of girls at the margin, is long overdue.

The early years of life set the stage for girls to experience their gender as identity, as role, as rule, and, ultimately, as an institutional web of expectations that defines women, especially young women, as subordinate to men. Despite its importance, astonishingly little research has been done on the development of girls—and this is particularly true of girls of color. We do know from the pioneering work of Gilligan and others (Gilligan et al., 1990) that even privileged girls emerge from adolescence with poor self-images, relatively low expectations of life, and much less confidence in themselves and their abilities than do boys. How this occurs, or how young women undergo a process that might be dubbed "training girls to know their place," must be understood if we are ever to come to grips with girls' delinquency and its meaning.

One central but neglected element in the enforcement of girls' place, and ultimately women's place, has been the juvenile justice system. This book documents the role of the system in the enforcement of girls' obedience to a special set of expectations about their deportment, their sexuality, and their obedience to familial demands. Its historic concern with adolescent morality, and particularly girls' morality, has been at the heart of the definition of female delinquency both past and present. Many girls, we argue, are still being arrested, detained, judged, and institutionalized for behavior that is overlooked when boys do it. Likewise, girls' genuine problems with families are being ignored because the judicial system that was established ostensibly to "protect" them has not really been interested in their physical or emotional safety. Instead, it has served to shore up the boundaries of a girlhood that shaped and forced young women into being future second-class citizens.

In sum, we see this book as one way to answer the question, What is it like for girls? For us, this question has two facets: first, what elements of girls' lives might bring them into the juvenile justice system, and second, what is the quality of justice meted out to young women in police stations, detention centers, halfway houses, and training schools? We know that we are relying heavily on the efforts of many others who share our concerns. We also greatly appreciate the fine but largely unappreciated work done by scholars in earlier generations. Our hope is to develop an understanding of the lives of girls in the juvenile justice system and, at a minimum, to begin to imagine ways of responding to their troubles that do more than add to their problems.

2

The Extent of Female Delinquency

Like all criminal and delinquent behavior, female delinquency encompasses a very wide range of disparate activities. Girls can be labeled as delinquent for the commission of crimes (e.g., burglary, larceny, assault), but they also can be brought into the juvenile justice system, and in many states treated as delinquent, for committing what are called "status offenses." These are offenses for which only juveniles can be taken into custody and include an array of behaviors (running away from home, being a truant, violating a curfew, being incorrigible or "beyond control"). Status offenses play a major and controversial role in female delinquency.

The purpose of this chapter is to explore the question "What is female delinquency, and how much is there?" This chapter examines data from a variety of sources to determine not only how much female delinquency exists, but also its manifestations. Throughout this discussion, many comparisons are made. We lay out differences between the dimensions of girls' offending as measured by anonymous, self-report studies and those that emerge from portraits drawn by official agencies such as the police and the juvenile courts. We also look at gender differences in delinquency and trends in girls' delinquency over time.

RECENT TRENDS:
NATIONAL ARREST DATA

Each year the Federal Bureau of Investigation (FBI) compiles crime data from over ten thousand law enforcement agencies in the United States and publishes these figures in *Crime in the United States: Uniform Crime Reports*. The report includes information on characteristics of persons under the age of eighteen arrested for a variety of offenses. The 2000 arrest figures (Table 2-1) reveal that there are considerable gender differences in official delinquency (that is, the picture of delinquency derived from statistics maintained by law enforcement officers). Most obvious is that far fewer girls than boys are arrested for delinquent behavior. Although 399,444 arrests of girls occurred in 2000, arrests of males outnumber female arrests by more than a 2:1 ratio, meaning that more than two boys are arrested for every girl arrested.

Boys are also far more likely than girls to be arrested for violent crimes and serious property offenses. The male-to-female ratio for violent index crimes (homicide, forcible rape, robbery, aggravated assault) is about 5:1, and the ratio for the most serious index property crimes (burglary, motor vehicle theft, and arson) is about 2.5:1. Males are also far more likely to be arrested for such offenses as possession of stolen property, vandalism, weapons offenses, and "other assaults." Because of these sorts of arrest patterns, serious violent and property offenses have traditionally been considered "masculine" offenses.

Girls, in contrast, are more likely to be arrested for running away from home and prostitution. Over half (59 percent) of those arrested for running away are girls (about a 1.4:1 ratio). The male-to-female ratios are also much closer for such offenses as larceny–theft (2:1), forgery (2:1), fraud (2:1), and embezzlement (roughly equal at just over a 1:1 ratio), although, with the notable exception of larceny–theft, very few youths are arrested for any of these offenses.

The number of girls is also more likely to approach that of boys in the commission of other "deportment" and status offenses. For instance, the male-to-female ratio for both curfew violations and liquor laws is greater than 2:1. However, boys do outnumber girls by a considerable margin among those arrested for drug law violations (almost 6:1).

Arrest statistics also can provide a portrait of the character of both female and male official delinquency. The distribution of arrests within each sex cohort (Table 2-1) shows that the bulk of offenses for which both males and females are arrested are relatively minor and that many do not have a clearly defined victim. For example, larceny–theft dominates both boys' and girls' delinquency, but most of these arrests, particularly for girls, are for shoplifting (Cameron, 1953; Steffensmeier & Steffensmeier, 1980; Shelden & Horvath, 1986). One out of seven arrests of boys and one out of five arrests of girls were for this one offense. In contrast, only 4.8 percent of boys' arrests and 2.7 percent of girls' arrests in 2000 were for serious violent crime.

Table 2-1. Arrests of Persons under 18, by Sex, 2000

	MALE		FEMALE	
	Number	Percent	Number	Percent
Total	1,010,186	100.0	393,444	100.0
Index Crimes				
Homicide	610	*	73	*
Forcible Rape	2,588	*	29	*
Robbery	17,742	1.5	1,535	*
Aggravated Assault	30,229	3.0	9,049	2.3
Burglary	50,535	5.0	6,890	1.8
Larceny–Theft	140,363	13.9	82,594	21.0
Motor Vehicle Theft	23,344	2.3	4,804	1.2
Arson	4,574	0.5	600	*
Total Violent	51,169	4.8	10,686	2.7
Total Property	218,816	21.7	94,888	24.1
Total Index	269,985	26.5	105,574	26.8
Part II Offenses				
Other Assaults	95,602	9.5	42,790	10.9
Forgery/Counterfeiting	2,591	*	1,301	*
Fraud	3,642	*	1,799	*
Embezzlement	650	*	582	*
Stolen Property	14,377	1.4	2,718	*
Vandalism	59,211	5.9	8,523	2.2
Weapons	19,875	2.0	2,204	*
Prostitution	336	*	443	*
Other Sex Offenses	9,666	1.0	732	*
Drugs	98,514	9.8	17,695	4.5
Gambling	389	*	34	*
Offenses Against the Family	3,199	*	1,911	*
DUI	9,928	1.0	2,017	*
Liquor Laws	62,719	6.2	28,585	7.3
Drunkenness	10,652	1.1	2,570	*
Disorderly Conduct	64,663	6.4	26,755	6.8
Vagrancy	1,440	*	432	*
Curfew and Loitering	69,268	6.9	31,559	8.0
Runaway	36,255	3.6	52,061	13.2
All Other Offenses	180,224	17.8	63,159	16.1

*Less than .1%

SOURCE: U.S. Department of Justice, Sourcebook of Criminal Justice Statistics Online—2001, Table 4.9.

Status offenses play a more significant role in girls' arrests than boys' arrests. The status offenses of running away and violating curfew/loitering accounted for about 21 percent of all girls' arrests in 2000, but only about 10 percent of boys' arrests—figures that remained relatively stable during the past decade (and over previous decades as well), although as we shall see, there has been a downward trend in the last few years. Arrests of girls for one status offense alone, running away, account for almost 13 percent of all girls' arrests, compared with less than four percent of boys' arrests. The arrest figures for two status offenses include only running away and curfew violation in the FBI report. This understates the extent of status offense arrests because the category "all other offenses" (which includes other status offenses, such as "incorrigibility," "unmanageableness," and truancy) is an important component of both male and female delinquency: 16.1 percent of girls' arrests and 17.8 percent of boys' arrests fall into this category. Hawaii data suggest that about three-quarters of girls who are arrested for this offense are actually arrested for incorrigibility or "injurious behavior," compared with only one-third of the boys (Chesney-Lind, 1987: 210).

Both girls and boys are arrested in large numbers for alcohol-related offenses, but burglary and vandalism (which account for about 11 percent of boys' offenses) are relatively unimportant in girls' delinquency (accounting for only 3 percent of their arrests). Generally, official delinquency is dominated by less serious offenses, and this is particularly true of female delinquency. A ranking of offenses that account for the greatest number of girls' and boys' arrests over time (Table 2-2) shows this clearly. For the past two decades, boys were most likely to have been arrested for larceny–theft and "all other" offenses. Larceny–theft ranks first among girls' arrests for both 1990 and 2000, accounting for over a quarter of all girls' arrests in 1990 and just over one-fifth in 2000. Running away also dominates girls' arrests, constituting just over one-fifth in 1990 and about one out of six in 2000 (as noted in previous editions of this book, this offense has consistently been ranked in the top two or three since at least 1970). In recent years, drug offenses have jumped into the top five for boys' arrests, accounting for just under 10 percent in 2000. Thus, running away and larceny–theft continue to dominate girls' delinquency arrests, as has been the case since 1970, and together these two offenses have accounted for more than one-third (46 percent in 1990) of all female arrests. For 2000, however, note that the category "other assaults" jumped into the top five for the first time; for girls this offense accounted for just over 10 percent of all of their arrests. This might be explained by the greater willingness of school officials and police departments to arrest girls for minor forms of fighting on and off school grounds. More will be said about this later.

The delinquency of boys does not show a similar degree of concentration. For example, the top five arrest categories in 2000 accounted for more than two-thirds (69 percent) of all the arrests of girls but less than 60 percent (57.9 percent) of the total for boys.

This discussion brings up other salient questions: What are the trends in female delinquency? Are there more female delinquents today? Are they more likely than their counterparts of a previous time period to commit "masculine offenses"? FBI data for the past few decades reveal some interesting patterns. First, the number of girls arrested rose dramatically during the 1960s and early 1970s—between 1960 and 1975, for example, by around 250 percent (Federal Bureau of Investigation, 1976: 183). Statistics like these, particularly when coupled with increases in the arrests of girls for nontraditional

**Table 2-2. Rank Order of Arrests for Juveniles, 1990 and 2000
(Figures based upon percent distribution within each sex cohort)**

	MALE		FEMALE	
	1990	**2000**	**1990**	**2000**
(1)	Larceny–Theft (19.5)	All Other (17.8)	Larceny–Theft (25.9)	Larceny–Theft (21.0)
(2)	All Other (14.2)[1]	Larceny–Theft (13.9)	Runaways (20.0)	All Other (16.1)
(3)	Burglary (7.5)	Drugs (9.8)	All Other (13.0)	Runaway (13.2)
(4)	Vandalism (7.2)	Other Assaults (9.5)	Liquor Laws (8.6)	Other Assaults (10.9)
(5)	Other Assaults (6.8)	Curfew/Loitering (6.9)	Other Assaults (7.0)	Curfew/Loitering (8.0)

	MALE		FEMALE	
	1990	**2000**	**1990**	**2000**
Arrests for Serious Violent Offenses[2]	5.9	4.8	2.7	2.7
Arrests for All Violent Offenses[3]	12.7	14.3	9.7	13.6
Arrests for Status Offenses[4]	8.1	10.5	24.6	21.2

[1]"All other" refers to a variety of offenses, usually state and local ordinances. Among the most common are public nuisance, trespassing, failure to appear on warrants, contempt of court, and, for juveniles especially, violation of various court orders (e.g., probation, parole) and certain status offenses. This category does not include traffic offenses.

[2]Arrests for murder, robbery, rape, and aggravated assault.

[3]Also includes arrests for other assaults, a Part II crime.

[4]Arrests for curfew and runaway.

SOURCE: U.S. Department of Justice, Sourcebook of Criminal Justice Statistics—1991. Washington, D.C.: U.S. Government Printing Office, 1992, p. 443; Sourcebook of Criminal Justice Statistics Online—2001, Table 4.9.

offenses, such as a 503.5 percent hike in the arrests of teenage girls for serious, violent crimes, encouraged many to believe that the women's movement had triggered a crime wave among young women (Adler, 1975). The controversy—both theoretical and empirical—that emerged around what some have called the "liberation hypothesis" or the "equality" hypothesis is an important one. The impact of this perspective on theories about girls' crime will be discussed later in this book. Here, we examine the arrest trends in further detail to determine what the data actually show about the amount and character of girls' delinquency since 1970.

Examining the data in Tables 2-3 and 2-4, we see several trends. First, although for some offenses the rate of increases for girls has been higher than that for boys, such increases are due in part to the relatively low base rate for girls in 1970. Further, for the most part, as arrests for girls have gone up, so too have arrests for boys. In other words, the patterns appear to be similar for both sexes. Second, while it could be argued that for some crimes girls are "catching up," the fact of the matter is that boys clearly outnumber girls for most major crimes, with the exception of larceny–theft.

Table 2-3. Girls' Share of all Juvenile Arrests, 1990 and 2000, Index Crimes and Selected Part II Offenses

	1990	2000
Part I Crimes		
Homicide	6.3	7.5
Rape	2.0	1.9
Robbery	8.1	8.8
Aggravated Assault	14.9	22.0
Burglary	8.1	11.2
Larceny–Theft	26.9	34.8
Motor Vehicle Theft	10.5	17.0
Arson	9.5	10.7
Total Violent	11.8	16.8
Total Property	20.5	28.3
Total Index	19.4	26.5
Selected Part II Offenses		
Other Assaults	23.0	30.7
Fraud	34.7	33.2
Stolen Property	8.9	12.4
Vandalism	8.8	12.1
Weapons	6.4	9.4
Drugs	11.6	13.4
Liquor Laws	26.6	30.1
Disorderly Conduct	19.4	27.7
Curfew	24.9	30.3
Runaway	56.3	58.4
All Other	21.3	24.3
Total Arrests	21.9	26.6

SOURCE: Sourcebook of Criminal Justice Statistics Online—2001, Table 4.9.

What must be explored in some detail here are the trends concerning girls' arrests for violent offenses. As noted in both Tables 2-3 and 2-4, both in terms of rates per 100,000 and the proportion of arrests accounted for by girls, arrests for these kinds of offenses increased in the 1980s, but have shown a noteworthy decline since then, especially since the mid-1990s. The increases during the 1980s and early 1990s were greatest for two specific offenses in particular: aggravated assaults and "other assaults." However, almost equally high increases occurred for boys. The arrest rates for girls for aggravated assault increased by 118 percent between 1970 and 1980, but only by 10 percent between 1980 and 1998 (the largest increases came between 1980 and 1990), and by 125 percent from 1970 to 1998. For boys, though, the arrest rate increased by 103 percent between 1970 and 1980, followed by an increase of 79 percent

Table 2-4. Juvenile Arrest Rates (per 100,000 population aged 5–17), 1970, 1980, 1990, 2000

	FEMALE				MALE			
	1970	1980	1990	2000	1970	1980	1990	2000
Part I Crimes								
Homicide	*	*	*	*	5	6	10	2
Rape	*	*	*	*	11	17	18	10
Robbery	8	12	12	6	99	160	119	67
Aggravated Assault	11	24	29	36	64	130	168	114
Burglary	25	58	37	27	498	819	395	191
Larceny–Theft	298	466	424	328	818	1265	1030	531
Motor Vehicle Theft	14	25	33	19	240	212	255	88
Arson	1	4	3	2	18	30	24	17
Total Violent	19	36	41	42	179	313	315	193
Total Property	338	553	497	376	1574	2326	1704	827
Total Index	357	589	538	418	1753	2639	2019	1020
Part II Crimes								
Other Assaults	40	73	115	170	149	261	359	362
Forgery	5	12	9	5	18	26	18	10
Fraud	3	9	12	7	12	22	27	14
Embezzlement	*	1	1	2	*	3	2	2
Stolen Property	5	13	13	11	62	128	122	54
Vandalism	20	39	34	34	262	431	379	224
Weapons	3	6	8	9	59	61	120	75
Prostitution	3	9	3	2	1	3	2	1
Other Sex Offenses	8	3	4	3	29	42	50	37
Drugs	65	70	30**	70	216	431	227**	373
Gambling	*	*	*	*	6	7	3	1
Offenses Against Family	*	3	3	8	2	5	6	12
DUI	*	13	9	8	16	108	53	38
Liquor Laws	47	134	141	114	210	442	341	237
Drunkenness	20	25	12	10	123	150	68	40
Disorderly Conduct	79	90	83	107	363	401	306	245
Vagrancy	9	3	2	2	41	13	9	5
Curfew	80	67	76	126	292	207	187	262
Runaway	335	355	327	251	300	243	239	137
All Other	209	244	212	251	631	948	743	682
Total	1288	1758	1632	1608	4545	6571	5280	3831

* Less than 1 per 100,000.

** 1990 arrest figures represent a significant drop from 1989 figures, according to the FBI report. In subsequent years the arrest rates increased for both sexes. In 1989, the male arrest rate was 287 and the female arrest rate was 41. Total arrests between 1989 and 1990 decreased by 21% for males and 27% for females. The data on drug arrests for 1990, therefore, should be looked at skeptically.

SOURCES: 2000 figures from Sourcebook of Criminal Justice Statistics Online—2001, Table 4.9; other years are taken from the FBI's annual report for those years.

from 1980 to 1998, with an overall increase of 290 percent between 1970 and 1998. Thus, both girls and boys showed rather large increases for this crime, but with boys clearly rising much faster since 1980 (Table 2-4). For the offense "other assaults," girls' arrest rates increased by 83 percent between 1970 and 1980, by 61 percent between 1980 and 1998, and by 182 percent between 1970 and 1998. For boys, these increases were 75 percent, 167 percent, and 388 percent, respectively. In other words, arrests for violent crime have increased rather dramatically during the past two decades for juveniles in general, both boys and girls. But these conclusions should be tempered by noting that the largest increases for "violent" crime have been for relatively minor assaults and boys have clearly been in the lead. The male of the species still has a considerable lead in committing violent acts.

There are several possible explanations for the increases in arrests for these two violent offenses. First, many of these increases could be attributed to the increase in girls' involvement in gang-related offenses. However, at the same time, the increase in actual *arrests* could also be an artifact of increased police attention to the gang problem, rather than a real increase in violent behavior. Second, some of the increase could be attributed to increasing attention toward the problem of domestic violence, which has resulted in more arrests for both males and females. Third, and perhaps more important, there is evidence to suggest that in recent years many of the arrests on these charges may be because of greater attention to normal adolescent fighting and/or girls fighting with parents.[1] In the past, such aggression was ignored or dealt with informally. Fourth, some of this increase is undoubtedly a reflection of a real increase in violence, which may be a reflection of larger and more structural problems in modern society that are causing greater violence among both male *and* female youth (e.g., poverty, violence at home, lack of hope, poor educational and occupational opportunities, the increase in the amount and sophistication of modern weaponry, and the increasing acceptance of carrying and/or using weapons in our society).

Labeling girls as "violent" or "more violent" than at some point in the past is a process of social construction. Feminist criminologists have criticized traditional schools of criminology for assuming that male delinquency, even in its most violent forms, was somehow an understandable if not "normal" response to their situations. Girls who shared the same social and cultural milieu as delinquent boys but who were not violent were somehow abnormal or "overcontrolled" (Cain, 1989). Essentially, law-abiding behavior on the part of at least some boys and men is taken as a sign of character, but when women avoid crime and violence, it is an expression of weakness (Naffine, 1987). The other side of this equation is that *if* girls engage in even minor forms of violence, they are somehow more vicious than their male counterparts. In this fashion, the construction of an artificial, passive femininity lays the foundation for the demonization of young girls of color, as has been the case in the media treatment of girl gang members (see Chapter 4). Also, from the media we often get the interpretation that when there are increases in male violence the response is something like "so what else is new?" but when there is an increase in girls'

violence something fundamental is wrong or there is a "new breed" of "violent women" roaming the streets and threatening the social order.

If we consider the girls' share of all juvenile arrests, a more complex picture emerges. As noted in Table 2-3, the share has risen from about 22 percent
to just over 26 percent between 1990 and 2000. There were gains made in
most of the Part I crimes, although their overall contribution to these arrests
increased by about 7 percent between 1990 and 2000. Perhaps the most significant increases came with the categories of "larceny–theft" and aggravated assault. Whereas girls constituted just over one-fourth of all arrests for
larceny–theft in 1990, they accounted for more than one-third in 2000; as for
aggravated assault, their share went from about 15 percent in 1990 to 22 percent in 2000. Their share of all Part I property crimes went from just over 20
percent in 1990 to just over one-fourth in 2000. Their share of violent index
crimes went from just under 12 percent to almost 17 percent, accounted for
largely by increases in aggravated assault.

A very slight increase occurred in girls' share of arrests for drugs, going
from just under 12 percent to just over 13 percent between 1990 and 2000,
reversing a downward trend that began in the mid-1970s. This no doubt stems
from the continuing "war on drugs" that has resulted in tremendous increases
in arrests for both adults and juveniles. Between 1990 and 2000 the girls' share
of arrests showed growth in seven Part I crime categories (for an overall increase of 7 percent) and in 10 categories of Part II offenses, but in all but three
categories (other assaults, disorderly conduct, and curfew) the increase was less
than 5 percent.

More important, the increases seen during this past quarter of a century in
the traditionally female areas of crime were not signaling an upward spiral in
girls' illegal activities. As an illustration of this, consider larceny–theft. In 1970
about 26 percent of all juveniles arrested for this offense were females; by
1980, about the same percentage were female. By 2000, the percentage went
up by only about 7 percent. For the crime of fraud, the female share increased
by about 5 percent from 1970 to 1986, then decreased by 1.5 percent between
1990 and 2000.

Turning to consideration of arrests of girls for nontraditional, "masculine"
offenses, girls under eighteen constituted 11.8 percent of all those arrested for
violent index offenses in 1990 and 16.8 percent in 2000. This means the
change that did occur in the female share of index offenses is largely explained
by increases in girls' arrests for property crimes, notably larceny–theft. Indeed,
arrests of girls made up 26.9 percent of all the index property crime arrests in
1990 and 26.5 percent in 2000. So girls' share of all index crimes went from
19.4 percent in 1989 to 26.5 percent in 1998, but not much of the increase is
explained by arrests for serious violent offenses (see Table 2-3). It should be
noted, at least in passing, that arrest figures often tell us more about the
changes in law enforcement policies, both nationwide and locally. Indeed,
much of these increases may be explained by the almost obsessive attention
paid to drug use and gangs.[2]

During the same period, girls' share of arrests for curfew violation climbed steadily, while their share of runaway arrests remained virtually the same. The shift occurred during a period when various national and state legislative initiatives encouraged the diversion from official processing of youth suspected of committing status offenses.

Still another way of looking at arrest trends is rates per 100,000 population (aged five to seventeen). Because there are more males than females within this cohort, rates can provide a more reliable comparison of differences between female and male delinquency. Table 2-4 gives arrest rates for each offense category for the years 1970, 1980, 1990, and 2000 and reflects much the same pattern seen in the raw arrest data, although the shifts in girls' delinquency are far less dramatic because the rates control for changes in population size. Arrest rates for both males and females increased significantly between 1970 and 1980 for almost all offenses, but then either leveled off or decreased after 1980. The relative gap between males and females has narrowed for several offense categories during the past twenty-five years; however, most of the narrowing began to take place after 1965 and continued until the early 1980s. During most of the 1980s the rates remained fairly stable, but beginning in the latter part of the decade (around 1988) an increase was observed for both males and females. Between 1980 and 1995 the arrest rates for girls increased for most index crimes, with the exception of burglary, yet similar patterns can be seen for boys' arrest rates. Despite these changes, male arrest rates continue to be considerably higher than female rates for most offenses, especially the most serious offenses (e.g., homicide, rape, robbery, aggravated assault, burglary).

A similar but more detailed analysis of arrest trends of young people was undertaken by Steffensmeier and Steffensmeier (1980), although for an earlier period of time (1965–1977). They, too, noted that female rates rose in most offense categories, with large increases occurring in the categories of larceny–theft, liquor law and narcotic drug law violations, and running away. However, male arrest rates also rose during the same period, showing a pattern generally similar to that of the female arrest rates. The trend continued well into the 1980s and early 1990s. In other words, patterns of both male and female arrests have, with few exceptions, paralleled each other; when one goes up, so does the other.

In general, what the Steffensmeiers noted (and what our more recent data show) is that the offenses that have accounted for large increases in female arrests are "traditionally female" and are in areas where changes in enforcement practices have also been occurring. For example, the authors remarked that store managers today are more likely to insist on the arrest of people whom they suspect of shoplifting than they were in the past. With respect to the arrests of young women for specific violent "masculine" crimes (murder, aggravated assault, robbery, other assaults, and weapons offenses), there was a slight contraction of the gap between males and females; however, much of the apparent female gain was due to an increase in the arrests of girls for "other assaults" that are "relatively nonserious in nature and tend to consist of being bystanders or companions to males involved in skirmishes" (Steffensmeier & Steffensmeier, 1980: 70). Juvenile crime, like its adult counterpart, is still mainly a male issue.

By way of summary, although the number of youths arrested in the United States swelled remarkably during the 1970s, the increases did not signal major changes in the character of official delinquency. Patterns of female juvenile arrests. have remained the same during the past twenty-five years, except that the relative gap between males and females has diminished for some offenses. Females have typically been arrested for the following offenses: running away, larceny–theft (mostly shoplifting), liquor law violations, curfew violations, disorderly conduct, other assaults, and the catchall category "all other offenses" (which, for girls, may include many arrests for certain status offenses). Males, in contrast, have been less likely to be arrested for status offenses and more likely to be arrested for property offenses (especially burglary and vandalism) and drug offenses.

Taking the decade of the 1990s as a whole, we see a huge contradiction between media representations and the "law and order" rhetoric of most politicians, and reality. Despite media images of "wild youths" and "superpredators" preying on citizens everywhere, during the past decade we have witnessed a significant *decrease* in youth crime for both sexes. With significant decline in almost all categories of offenses, there is little data to support belief in a general rise in these so-called "superpredators" (for a good representation of this belief, see Bennett, DiLulio, and Walters, 1996; for an excellent critique, see Elikann, 1999). What the arrest figures may demonstrate more than anything else is changes in official crime control policies which, among other consequences, have resulted in the targeting of certain kinds of youthful behaviors (e.g., involvement with drugs, schoolyard fights, or domestic disturbances). As Mike Males has observed, the real "superpredators" (if we want to use this value-laden term) are adults, as their crime rates have steadily increased during the past decade (Males, 1999). These figures also belie the myth of rising female violence, which is still another artifact of the media.

Arrest statistics, though, tell only part of the story, for several shortcomings characterize the reports published annually by the FBI. An obvious problem is that the FBI's figures are based upon police contacts that result in an arrest. However, the police do not arrest all of those who have committed an offense (see Hagan, 1987: 29–31, and Barlow, 1987: 88–111). Further, as Chapter 7 makes clear, police officers "contact" many more youths than they arrest. These two facts make it possible that arrest statistics are as much a measure of police behavior as they are of criminal behavior. For a more complete picture of the extent of female delinquency, it is also necessary to examine a very popular alternative source of information on the volume of delinquency: self-report surveys. In such surveys people respond anonymously to questionnaires or participate anonymously in interviews about their delinquent activities, especially about acts that never come to the attention of the police.

SELF-REPORT SURVEYS

Researchers have long used self-report surveys to attempt to gain information about the extent of juvenile delinquency. Typically, the surveys reveal that female delinquency is more common than arrest statistics indicate and that there are more similarities than official statistics suggest between male and female juvenile delinquency. They also show that males are more involved in delinquency, especially the most serious types of offenses. These findings point to some possible gender biases operating within the juvenile justice system because the picture of female delinquency that emerges from the self-report data shows about as many boys as girls committing status offenses.

Concerning the volume of unreported female delinquency, Cernkovich and Giordano (1979) found that although the ratio of male to female arrestees was approximately 4:1 in the late 1970s, that ratio was twice as large as the mean ratio of 2.18:1 that they found in their self-report data. Similar findings have also been reported in other self-report studies (Canter, 1982: 374).

In a comprehensive review of self-report studies published between 1955 and 1977, Steffensmeier and Steffensmeier (1980) noted that male–female differences tend to be greater for crimes of violence and serious property crimes. Males and females report similar rates (especially in more recent surveys) for such offenses as truancy, driving without a license, running away from home, and minor forms of theft. The fact that males and females are about equally likely to admit running away is interesting because females are much more likely to be arrested (as already indicated) and to be referred to the juvenile court for this offense (a point that will be covered in more detail in Chapter 7). This interpretation is underscored by a study conducted by Teilmann and Landry (1981), who compared girls' contribution to arrests for runaway and incorrigibility with girls' self-reports of these two activities. They found about a 10 percent overrepresentation of girls among those arrested for runaway, and an astounding 31 percent overrepresentation in arrests for incorrigibility.

These findings were confirmed and amplified by a reanalysis of National Youth Survey data (Canter, 1982) that indicated that both male and female delinquency did rise during the 1967–1977 decade—especially in the offense categories of marijuana use, truancy, and alcohol use—but the increases were similar for both males and females. In other words, there was no evidence that the character of girls' delinquency changed during a decade characterized by considerable discussion of women's roles. Instead, reports from this national probability sample of 1,725 youths aged thirteen to sixteen showed parallel increases in involvement in certain delinquent behaviors but stability in the sex differences in delinquent behavior.

It might be useful to consider in some detail a picture of female delinquency drawn from self-report surveys. One good example is the just-mentioned National Youth Survey reanalysis by Canter (1982). Examining categories of offenses over time, the study found much similarity between female and male delinquency and found that there was no behavior in which girls were significantly more involved than boys—even in offenses traditionally ascribed to girls (such as prostitution and running away from home).

These findings might lead one to the conclusion that delinquency is almost exclusively a male problem, but that is not really the case. For example, no statistically significant differences appeared in boys' and girls' involvement in 40 percent of the behaviors examined. Even when differences did appear, they were such that, in the author's words, "their statistical significance overstates their practical significance" because there was considerable overlap between male and female distributions and "males and females display comparable patterns of offenses in terms of proportions as well as means" (Canter, 1982: 380). What this suggests is that, as in many other areas of research into gender differences, emphasis on the ways in which male and female behavior differs often obscures the fact that the behaviors engaged in by most youths are actually very similar; it is only at the extremes that a gender difference emerges.

This perspective on gender differences should be kept in mind as we review more closely a self-report survey of midwestern youths by Cernkovich and Giordano (1979) that provides details on female delinquency and how it differs from male misbehavior. By examining behaviors in which boys clearly dominate and those in which girls and boys are involved to like extents, we can more rewardingly discuss differences and similarities in self-reported delinquent behavior. Cernkovich and Giordano's study divided self-reported delinquency into three categories: one in which the proportion of males admitting commission of the offense exceeds the female proportion by a considerable margin, one in which the proportion of males only moderately exceeds that of females, and one in which almost equal numbers of girls and boys admit having committed the offense.

Regarding male-dominated offenses, boys are more likely to report involvement in gang fighting, carrying a hidden weapon, strong-arming students and others, aggravated assault, hitting students, and sexual assault.

Boys are also disproportionately involved in serious property crimes; they are much more likely to report involvement in thefts of more than $50, and they are somewhat more likely to report lesser thefts (between $5 and $50). However, other property crimes show fewer gender differences than one might expect: motor vehicle theft shows a male-to-female ratio of 2.6:1; burglary, 3.88:1; and joyriding, 2.37:1 (all based upon the proportion of youths ever committing the offenses). These gender gaps are certainly of a smaller magnitude than those found in official statistics. Of interest, too, is the male dominance in some offenses that are considered traditionally "feminine," such as prostitution and sexual intercourse.

Concerning offenses in which differences in the proportions of males and females involved are less marked, some surprises appear. For example, vandalism is often seen as a "male" offense, but if one considers damaging family property, almost as many girls commit that offense as do boys (male/female, 1.5:1). The strong-arming of teachers (1.8:1) and even hitting of teachers (1.9:1) show less gender difference than one might anticipate. Finally, boys dominate slightly in the selling of drugs and the procurement of alcohol (although when frequency is considered, boys tend to commit more of these acts than girls do).

In regard to offenses in which the gender difference is minimal, girls are about as likely as boys to have used a variety of drugs (alcohol, marijuana, barbiturates, amphetamines, and cocaine). They are also about as likely to have run away from home, skipped classes, and engaged in disorderly conduct, as well as to have hit their parents.

The unexpected similarity in girls' and boys' violence against parents highlights another problem with some of the offense categories used in arrest statistics: categories can obscure significant differences in specific behaviors and in responses to these behaviors. Consider, for example, property damage. The National Youth Survey found that girls damage family property and males tend to damage other kinds of property (e.g., school property). A similar pattern appears in the area of assault, with girls closing the gender gap when simple assault against parents is considered. This pattern suggests that the setting in which delinquent behavior occurs and the relationship between victim and assailant differ for males and females in many offenses. These differences may have important implications for reporting, and for reactions of juvenile justice officials.

Cernkovich and Giordano also found that for certain offenses there were almost no gender differences. Two of these were status offenses, such as running away from home (male/female ratio, .99:1) and defying parental authority (.97:1), which often result in a charge of "incorrigibility" or "unmanageability" in the juvenile court. These offenses are interesting because they focus on the critical role of family relationships in the generation and labeling of female and male delinquency. As will be seen in later chapters, although both boys and girls commit these offenses, many "delinquent" acts that bring girls into the juvenile justice system are the result of problems, conflicts, and disagreements between girls and members of their families. Boys, although they admit these behaviors, appear less likely to be officially arrested and processed for them.

Cernkovich and Giordano also found that various sex offenses, drug (including alcohol) use, minor forms of theft, disturbances, and school-related offenses tend to be about equally committed by male and female adolescents. As does the National Youth Survey, the data in their study show how similar males and females are in offense patterns. For twenty-four of the thirty-six delinquent acts included, the male/female ratio was less than 2:1. More recent surveys confirm the lack of gender differences in most drug and alcohol use. For instance, the most recent annual survey of high school seniors conducted by the Institute for Social Research (University of Michigan) found that in 1993, 87 percent of the males and 87.2 percent of the females said that they had used alcohol. Males were slightly more likely to say they had smoked marijuana (38.9 percent vs. 31.2 percent of the females), used cocaine (7.5 percent of the males and 4.6 percent of the females), and used heroin (1.5 percent of the males and 0.7 percent of the females) (Maguire & Pastore, 1994: 325–326).

The Cernkovich and Giordano survey also focused on frequency of delinquency. For males, offenses committed more than once were most likely to be skipping school, disobeying parents, sex with the opposite sex, use of alcohol and marijuana, gambling, and disturbing the peace. For females, an almost identical list appears: skipping school, disobeying parents, sex with the opposite sex, and use of alcohol and marijuana. The authors stressed that for both males and females, the most serious offenses were committed only once.

Other studies confirm the overall pattern found in the two studies discussed so far and add additional details about male dominance among the more serious offenses. In one study, a sample of 1,735 fifteen-year-olds in a Midwestern county showed that males were about four times as likely as females to commit burglary and auto theft, six times as likely to commit a theft of between $50 and $500, and about three times as likely to commit an aggravated assault (Figueira-McDonough, Barton, & Sarri, 1981). Similarly, Kratcoski and Kratcoski (1975) found that males were five times as likely to commit a theft of $50 or more, six times as likely to commit a burglary, and three times as likely to commit a robbery. However, both surveys found great similarity when it came to minor offenses.

More recent self-report data tell the same basic story. Table 2-5 shows data collected from the annual survey of high school seniors by the University of Michigan. As shown here, males are far more likely than females to commit most of these offenses, with the exception of "argued/had fight with parents," for which females had the edge, however slight (such an offense could no doubt result in a referral to juvenile court on a charge of "unmanageable" or "incorrigible" or some similar status offense). According to this survey, males are far more violent in their actions than females, in addition to being involved in more serious property offenses. Aside from arguing and/or having fights with parents, girls were most often involved in minor property offenses. Curiously, relatively few of these youths were ever arrested and taken to the police station, especially the girls.

What is interesting to note about this particular annual survey is that we have access to data going back to 1981. Comparing 1981 data with 1998 data shows that, with a small number of exceptions, there have been few changes in the percent of seniors reportedly engaging in such behaviors. In fact, for *every* one of the offenses noted in Table 2-5 there have been *decreases* in the proportion of both boys and girls engaging in such behavior since the year 1981!

Self-report studies, then, suggest that female delinquency is more prevalent than official statistics lead one to believe. The content of female delinquency is similar to male delinquency in that most instances are of minor seriousness, but girls commit offenses far less frequently than do boys. Some researchers (Hindelang, 1979) have suggested that it is frequency rather than character of delinquent behavior that explains the dominance of boys in the arrest statistics. That might account for the prominence of boys among those arrested for violent offenses, but not for the overrepresentation of girls among youths charged with status offenses and prostitution.

**Table 2-5. High School Seniors Reporting Involvement
in Delinquent Activities in the Last 12 Months, 1998,
by Gender (percent engaging at least once)**

	Male	Female
Argued/had fight with parents	85.9	90.5
Hit instructor/supervisor	4.7	1.4
Got into serious fight in school or at work	21.4	11.4
Took part in fight with group of friends against another group	25.8	15.3
Hurt someone badly enough to need bandages or doctor	22.8	6.1
Used gun or knife or other weapon to get something from a person	6.7	1.9
Took something not belonging to you worth under $50	38.5	24.6
Took something not belonging to you worth over $50	16.7	6.7
Took something from a store without paying for it	33.5	26.1
Took car not belonging to you or someone in your family	6.5	2.9
Went into some house/building when you weren't supposed to be there	30.6	19.0
Set fire to someone's property on purpose	4.2	1.0
Damaged school property on purpose	20.5	8.3
Was arrested and taken to police station	15.3	4.6

SOURCE: K. Maguire and A. L. Pastore (eds.), Sourcebook on Criminal Justice Statistics, 1998 (Washington, D.C.: U.S. Department of Justice, Bureau of Justice Statistics, 1999): 209–211.

DELINQUENT CAREERS

The past several decades have witnessed considerable interest in delinquent "careers." Most of the research has been longitudinal, which means that a sample of youths is examined over a given period to explore the extent of their involvement in delinquent behavior. Most studies have measured delinquency by using contact with police or courts (Visher & Roth, 1986), which, as we have seen, may exaggerate the gender difference in delinquency; nonetheless, they provide an important perspective on girls' official delinquent careers.

Longitudinal research has revealed not only that adolescent males are more actively involved in delinquent behavior (in terms of number and seriousness of offenses that bring them to official attention) but also that their "careers" go on longer than those of females. In one of the most comprehensive studies, Tracy, Wolfgang, and Figlio (1985) examined the arrest records of all youths born in Philadelphia in 1958 who resided there between their tenth and seventeenth birthdays, a total of 28,338 youths. (See Wolfgang, Figlio, and Sellin, 1972, for an earlier study of an all-male Philadelphia birth cohort.) They found that, whereas 32.8 percent of the males had at least one police contact before their eighteenth birthday, this was true for only 14.1 percent of the females. Male delinquency, as measured by arrest, was also more serious. The male offense rate overall was four times greater than that for females, but the ratio was almost 9:1 for index offenses and 14:1 for violent index offenses. Girls were also one-and-a-half times more likely to be "one-time delinquents" (Tracy, Wolfgang, & Figlio, 1985: 6).

Other studies use data from the National Survey of Health and Development (Mulligan et al., 1963; Douglas et al., 1966; Wadsworth, 1979), which followed 5,362 children drawn from a cohort born between March 3 and March 9, 1946, in England, Wales, and Scotland. These studies found lower arrest rates for both boys and girls than was the case in the Philadelphia cohort; 18 percent of the males but only 3 percent of the females were "convicted or cautioned by the police" by their eighteenth birthday. The national survey also followed both male and female offenders into their adult years; Wadsworth reports (1979: 103) that by age twenty-one only 2 percent of the girls, compared with 15.3 percent of the boys, had an adult arrest. Some years later, Ouston (1984), using a later (1959–1960) inner-city London birth cohort, found figures closer to those of the Philadelphia researchers: 29 percent of the males and 6 percent of the females had arrest records (see also Edwards, 1973).

Shannon (1982) gives us a sense of changes in delinquent careers, as measured by arrest, over time by using data from three birth cohorts (1942, 1949, and 1955) in Racine, Wisconsin. In the 1942 cohort, 41.0 percent of the males and 8.7 percent of the females had at least one arrest; in the 1949 cohort, 47.3 percent and 15.1 percent, respectively; in the 1955 cohort, 44.1 percent and 22.2 percent.

These studies have found that boys' delinquent careers (usually as measured by police contact or arrest) are longer than girls' careers. Moreover, males are more likely to extend their delinquent careers into their adult lives and are more likely to begin their careers at an earlier age. There is also some indication that studies done with more recent cohorts show larger numbers of girls being contacted or arrested by police. However, there may be a problem in sketching out the shape of delinquent careers by using official contacts as a measure of delinquency because arrests are, in a sense, measures of police attitudes and practices as well.

Fortunately, the dynamics of self-reported female delinquency have also been explored using the National Youth Study data. Ageton (1983) followed a sample of girls aged eleven through seventeen through the years 1976 to 1980 (when they were between fifteen and twenty-one) and ascertained diminished incidence of offending as they matured. The decline was particularly marked in connection with assaultive crimes: the proportion of females involved fell from 36 percent to 12 percent. One particular item is noteworthy: hitting other students was by far the most common kind of aggressive offense engaged in by the girls (this behavior is also one of the most commonly included in the FBI category known as "other assaults" that has shown an increase in recent years) (Ageton, 1983: 562).

Although the National Youth Study does not enable us to examine status offenses in any great detail, a study by Datesman and Aickin (1984) gives us a look at this important subgroup. The two researchers examined offense specialization and escalation among status offenders by means of a sample of offenders referred to a Delaware family court. Some persons, especially juvenile court officials, have argued that court intervention with status offenders is justified because without it, these youths will "escalate" into more serious offenders.

Datesman and Aickin also investigated both self-report and official delin-quency data in this sample ($N = 634$) and followed up with the offenders three years later. Both kinds of data indicated that it would be reasonable to create a "specialized status offender group," at least among those whose first referral to court was for a status offense; this was particularly true for girls (Datesman & Aickin, 1984: 1273). Further, the researchers discovered that status offenders rarely returned to court (between 60 percent and 80 percent did not, depend-ing upon the specific offense); when they did return, it was almost always for another status offense. This was, again, particularly true for female offenders. Almost identical findings were reported in a longitudinal study of juvenile court referrals in Las Vegas (Shelden, Horvath, & Tracy, 1989).

In total, these studies suggest that girls' official delinquent careers are shorter and involve less serious offenses than do the careers of boys. Even in areas having to do with typically "female" offenses, such as status offenses, girls appear to desist after one referral to court rather than continuing to commit offenses. There is also some indirect indication that in recent years more girls have been contacted by police. Because self-report delinquency studies point to no great change in girls' behavior, such arrests may be a result of changes in police behavior. This idea is explored more fully in Chapter 7.

RACIAL DIFFERENCES

There are many important racial differences in female delinquency. Rates of involvement in delinquent activity (as measured by both official and self-report data) show black males with the highest level, followed by white males, black females, and white females. Some studies indicate a rate of involvement for black females very close to that for white males. For instance, Tracy, Wolf-gang, and Figlio (1985) found that 18.5 percent of the black females had at least one arrest, compared to 22.7 percent of the white males. In contrast, about 9 percent of the white females had at least one arrest. They also noted that 6.0 percent of the black females had at least one arrest for an index crime, compared to 8.9 percent of the white males. For nonindex offenses, the per-centages were 15.7 percent and 19.9 percent, respectively. Data from this most recent Philadelphia birth cohort to be studied have been used in two unpub-lished dissertations (Facella, 1983; Otten, 1985).

The most recent figures from juvenile court data reveal that in 1997 there were significant differences when comparing blacks and whites according to gender. For instance, black youths of both genders are overrepresented based upon their percentages in the general population. Black males, for example, constituted 31 percent of all the male delinquency cases, while black juveniles constituted 30 percent of the female cases. Both black males and black females were most likely to have the highest percentages for "person" or violent crimes, with black females having a slightly higher percentage within their re-spective gender group: black females constituted 39 percent of all females charged with "person" crimes and black males comprised 36 percent of all males charged with a person crime. During 1997 there was a noteworthy difference as far as drug offenses are concerned. Whereas black males comprised 35 percent of the males referred for drug offenses, black females constituted only 15 percent of all females referred for this offense (Sickmund, 2000).

One of the most interesting findings was that among both white and nonwhite females, running away from home and a category called "missing person" constituted almost one-half of all offenses (46.3 percent for white females, 46.5 percent for nonwhite females). Both white males and females were proportionately much more likely than their nonwhite counterparts to be arrested for victimless and public-order offenses, such as drug offenses and public disturbances (Otten, 1985: 105–106). Finally, there were differences between white and nonwhite females concerning delinquent careers. Among the nonwhite females, 8.1 percent were "chronic recidivists" (five or more arrests); among white females, 4.9 percent (Facella, 1983: 218–219).

An analysis of delinquent careers based upon a longitudinal study of 863 youths first referred to juvenile court in 1980 in Las Vegas found significant racial differences, but slightly less evidence that those differences override gender differences (Shelden, 1987). Specifically, the total participation rates per 1,000 population aged ten to seventeen in Clark County were highest for nonwhite males (40.1 percent), followed by white males (20.8 percent), nonwhite females (14.1 percent), and white females (9.9 percent). A reasonable inference is that nonwhite females are closer to white females than they are to nonwhite males.

Self-report studies shed additional light on this subject. For instance, Jensen and Eve (1976) reported that 2 percent of the black females committed theft of $50 or more, compared with 1 percent of the white females; for auto theft, however, there was no difference, with 4 percent of each group reporting the offense. Hindelang, Hirschi, and Weis (1981), in their self-report study, found that black females were much more likely than white females to admit committing theft of $50 or more, auto theft, aggravated assault, and robbery, but that both black and white girls were about equally involved in burglary. For two major offenses, robbery and aggravated assault, black females were very close to white males.

In the self-report study by Cernkovich and Giordano cited earlier, there were several interesting differences in the types of delinquency admitted by white and nonwhite girls. The researchers found statistically significant differences in the types of delinquent acts.

The patterns noted here are obvious: nonwhite females seem, in this study, to be more likely to engage in personal crimes, and white females are more likely to be involved in drug- or alcohol-related offenses (some very serious) and status offenses. However, note that white girls engage in more delinquent behavior. Additionally, and perhaps more important, the study found that there were no significant differences for 50 percent of the acts surveyed. In other words, white females engage in more delinquent activity, but much of this is a function of their higher levels of involvement in drug-related offenses and some status offenses (Cernkovich & Giordano, 1979).

The National Youth Survey also reviewed racial differences in female delinquency. Its findings, too, suggest caution in interpretation of data. First, NYS researchers discovered that no racial differences existed between 1976 and 1980 when delinquent behavior as a whole was considered. Blacks tended to report more violent offenses, but there was a marked decline in both incidence (percentage committing at least one offense) and prevalence (total offenses committed over time) in girls' commission of such offenses. Frequency of theft increased for whites and decreased for blacks during this period, showing a 2:1 white-to-black ratio. Moreover, the racial differential was strong in 1976 but not in 1980. Indeed, although black girls always displayed the higher scores, the white/black ratio dropped from 1.4 in 1979 to almost 1.1 in 1980 (Ageton, 1983: 577). The study also found, in following a specific cohort over time, that black girls initially reported greater involvement in theft offenses, yet by the middle of the study years, white girls surpassed black girls on almost all theft items.

The association of race with assaultive offenses is also slight, with "the overriding trend for decreasing or relatively stable involvement in assaultive crimes" as both black and white girls matured (Ageton, 1983: 565). Also, although the proportions of blacks involved in these offenses are generally higher, white girls are significantly more likely to report the hitting of parents.

Cautions about racial differences in female delinquency, particularly violent delinquency, are raised by another study. Laub and McDermott (1985) examined 1973–1981 national victimization data for personal crimes, looking for trends in crimes committed by young black women. They were specifically interested in evidence of what they called the "convergence" theory of black male and female offending—the notion that the big differences between white male and white female delinquency are not found between black male and female delinquents. Their findings did not support the notion. Despite much fluctuation during the years Laub and McDermott studied, the highest personal crime rates (per 100,000 population) were consistently for black males, followed by white males. White females had the lowest personal crime rates for all years; black females had a higher rate than white males only for 1973. The rates for black females dropped significantly between 1973 and 1977, but have since risen steadily. In contrast, white female rates have changed very little, ranging from a low of 1,062 in 1975 to a high of 1,359 in 1979. The rates for white males rose after 1975, and those of black males after 1977, following a period of significant decrease from 1973 to 1977.

Laub and McDermott also discovered considerable differences in rates for specific personal offenses: rape, robbery, aggravated assault, simple assault, and personal larceny. The highest rates for both black and white girls and for white boys were for the simple assault category; the highest rate for black males was for the robbery category; and the lowest rate was for the personal larceny category. Over time, the data showed the greatest convergence between black and white girls concerning assault, not theft crimes. Divergence from the male pattern was clear: white females had not engaged in more delinquent behavior, but white males had done so. Among blacks, the decline in female delinquency was steeper than the decline in male delinquency.

Laub and McDermott concluded that there is a convergence occurring in delinquency, a convergence of white and nonwhite female delinquency. The convergence is explained largely by a substantial decline in black female offending for the nine-year period they examined compared with stability in white female offending. Black girls, according to this study, do commit more personal crimes than do white girls, but even here there was considerable variation within offense categories, and the gap is shrinking.

The most recent data on gender and racial differences comes from the aforementioned national self-report survey. As noted in Table 2-6, there are some noteworthy differences for some offenses. White and Hispanic females are about equally likely to have consumed alcohol, both having considerably higher rates than black females. A similar pattern exists for using marijuana. For more serious offenses, such as property destruction, theft, and carrying a handgun, few differences exist. However, black girls are more likely than either whites or Hispanics to have committed assault and engaged in sexual activities. As for males, whites are slightly more likely to carry weapons and destroy property, whereas blacks and Hispanics are more likely to commit assault. Incidentally, what needs to be underscored is the fact that only a small percentage of all youths are engaged in serious criminal activity, regardless of race or gender.

Thus, race differences in girls' offending are not as marked as some might expect. Especially questionable are notions that black girls are far more delinquent than their white counterparts and that their delinquency is far more "masculine" in content. In fact, although there are some differences between black and white girls in delinquency content, the differences tend to be less marked as the girls mature. More to the point, black girls, like their white counterparts, are still quite likely to be arrested for traditionally female offenses.

SUMMARY

This chapter has reviewed the extent of girls' involvement in delinquency. Careful measures of girls' delinquency reveal that it is more varied than official statistics indicate. Girls commit a variety of offenses but are less likely than boys to engage in serious, violent delinquency. In general, although female delinquency differs from male delinquency, some research, particularly that derived from self-report studies, suggests that there are more similarities than previously imagined in male and female delinquency. In essence, most delinquency is quite minor and the differences between boys' and girls' misbehavior are not pronounced. Discussions of delinquency that focus on very serious violent offenses tend to exaggerate the gender differences in delinquency because males are more likely to commit these offenses.

Evidence also indicates that female delinquency has changed little in the past three decades. Both official arrest statistics and self-report data suggest that

**Table 2-6. Recent Participation (within past 12 months
or 30 days prior to interview) in Delinquent and
Deviant Acts, by Race and Gender (ages 12–16), 1999**

Behavior	MALES			FEMALES		
	White	Black	Hispanic	White	Black	Hispanic
Smoked cigarettes						
Last 30 days	22%	14%	19%	23%	9%	15%
Drank alcohol						
Last 30 days	23	13	22	23	13	20
Before or during school or work in last 30 days	6	4	6	4	3	6
Used marijuana						
Last 30 days	10	9	9	9	5	9
Before or during school or work in last 30 days	4	4	5	3	2	3
Carried a handgun						
Last 12 months	10	8	8	2	2	2
Last 30 days	5	5	4	1	1	1
Had sex						
Last 12 months*	17	38	26	20	26	19
Belonged to a gang						
Last 12 months	2	6	5	1	2	2
Destroyed property						
Last 12 months	21	18	17	11	10	11
Stole something worth over $50						
Last 12 months	7	7	8	3	4	4
Committed assault						
Last 12 months	15	21	13	7	12	10

* Only youth 14 and older were asked about their sexual activity.

SOURCE: Snyder and Sickmund (1999: 60).

the changes we have seen in girls' misbehavior have been in minor and traditionally female offenses—despite all the attention given to increases in girls' arrests for violent offenses. Girls are still arrested and referred to court for large numbers of minor property offenses and status offenses. There is some evidence from cohort studies that more girls are being arrested, but there is little or no evidence that during a period characterized by much discussion about the need for changes in girls' and women's situations, there was any major change in girls' delinquent behavior.

There is also less support than some imagine for the notion that black girls are markedly more delinquent than their white counterparts. Certainly, differences exist, but they tend to appear more often in official statistics; when self-report studies are consulted, white girls are slightly more delinquent than their nonwhite counterparts, although there are differences in the types of delinquency that the two groups commit.

In sum, studies of female and male delinquency, like studies of other forms of gender difference, tend to make more of dissimilarities than they do of similarities. Both are interesting from a theoretical standpoint, but to date only the gender difference in violent crime has attracted attention. Also of interest is the fact that although girls commit many offenses, only some of the offenses, notably status offenses, tend to result in arrest. The succeeding chapters will help us further examine the crimes that typically bring girls into the juvenile justice system and what happens to them there.

NOTES

1. Although we have no hard data on this, both authors have learned from several sources inside the juvenile justice system about the following trend that appears to be occurring. Because juvenile courts have been restrained in recent years from responding vigorously to cases of runaways, some police and probation officers are suggesting to parents the following: When a girl threatens to run away, the parent should stand in her way; if she runs into the parent or pushes the parent out of the way, then the parent can call the court and have the girl arrested on "simple assault" or "battery" or some other "personal" crime that would fit into the FBI category "other assaults." We have no idea how often this happens or how this could shape arrest figures that are reported to the FBI. We bring this up to illustrate that these FBI categories are just that: "categories" representing a wide variety of behaviors and different social contexts. Therefore, official arrest statistics like those discussed in this chapter should be interpreted cautiously.

2. For documentation about the "war on drugs" see, for instance, Reinarman and Levine (1997) and Baum (1997); for gangs see Shelden, Tracy, and Brown (2001).

3

The Nature of Female Delinquency

The picture of the girl in trouble that emerges from the official statistics and self-report studies reviewed in Chapter 2 is somewhat cloudy and one-dimensional. Accordingly, this section of the chapter will further explore female delinquency by considering in more detail behaviors of girls that may land them in the juvenile justice system. We will focus on a range of offenses; some, like status offenses and shoplifting, bring large numbers of girls into the system. Other offenses that represent unique forms of girls' delinquency (gang delinquency) will be considered in another chapter. It is hoped that these descriptions will begin to illuminate the relationship among girls' lives, their troubles, and their crime.

GIRLS AND SHOPLIFTING

As we saw earlier, girls are frequently arrested for what is known as larceny–theft, principally for shoplifting. We also saw that arrests of girls for this single offense account for about a quarter of all girls' delinquency. However, the knowledge we have about this offense is rather sketchy, which is surprising because of its great incidence and immense annual cost to retailers, estimated to be as high as $8 billion (Hagan, 1987: 271). The most recent data come from a 1995 survey of 171 retailers who reported 171,141 shoplifting incidents, with an estimated loss of $7.94 billion. It was found that the largest age group was between 13 and 17 years of age, which accounted for just over 30 percent of all incidents (Hayes, 1996). The few studies of shoplifters have focused more on adults (e.g., Cameron, 1964) and on the decision of store personnel to prosecute than on shoplifters' motives. As noted in the previous chapter, shoplifting is typically one of the most common offenses within the "larceny–theft" category, as documented in a recent study in New Mexico of those appearing in a "teen court" program (Harrison, Maupin, & Mays, 2001). One recent survey in England found that there are more than 4 million shoplifting incidents reported to the police each year and about 1.3 million arrests (Farrington, 1999).

Morris (1987) cites evidence from England that indicates that women, in contrast to men, tend to shoplift fewer and less costly items. Further, they tend to be less sophisticated or professional (i.e., less likely to be "boosters," as noted by Cameron, 1964). In regard to juveniles in magistrates' courts during 1985, of the cohort aged ten to fourteen, 53 percent of the girls were sentenced for shoplifting, compared with only 20 percent of the boys; of the cohort aged fourteen to seventeen, the percentages were 44 and 14, respectively (Morris, 1987: 29).

According to self-report studies, however, males are more likely to shoplift. An English self-report study found they outnumbered females by a 2:1 ratio. Another study also found males to be more likely than females to shoplift, but the male/female ratio for youths "cautioned by the police" or actually sentenced was only 1.7:1 (Morris, 1987: 31). Morris suggests that females are more often detected by store personnel because the latter expect women to shoplift more than men and therefore watch women more closely (Morris, 1987: 30). She cites research that found that British police believe more girls shoplift than boys, and that items stolen are different. Yet official statistics revealed that in 1985, females constituted only 36 percent of those cautioned or found guilty of shoplifting (Morris, 1987: 196).

A similar pattern emerged in a study of serious delinquency in Florida. In comparing girls' self-reports of delinquency with official arrests, Horowitz and Pottieger (1991) found that police tended to arrest fewer girls than boys for major felonies, but more girls than boys for petty property crimes. The researchers suggested that this might have been a product of police bias because shoplifting is seen as a "stereotypical female crime" (Horowitz & Pottieger, 1991: 19).

Explanations of male and female shoplifting have generally been simplistic and gender biased. A common explanation for female shoplifting, according to Morris (1987: 65), is that it is "a result of subconscious motivations (kleptomania), depression (for example, resulting from the menopause) or poverty (for example, mothers on welfare who steal food)." A common explanation of male shoplifting is that it results from " peer-group pressure" and "excitement and thrills" (Salmelainen, 1995). One recent English study concluded that shoplifters suffer from both personal and physical stress, tend to be depressed, and have low self-esteem and various personality problems (Day, Maltby, & Giles, 2000). A study in Buffalo, New York, cited lack of "self-control" as the principal cause (Deng & Zhang, 1998).

One consideration that rarely appears in studies of shoplifting is that young people, especially girls, may be inordinately sensitive to the consumer culture: they steal things they feel they need, or indeed may actually need but cannot afford. For example, Campbell (1981) notes that women—young and old—are the targets of enormously expensive advertising campaigns for a vast array of personal products. They also constitute a large proportion of those who shop, spend more time doing it as a pastime, and consequently are exposed to greater temptation (Campbell, 1981: 122–123; see also Lo, 1994). Perhaps this may partly explain the fact that, according to one recent study, about one in every 10 to 15 shoppers has shoplifted at least once in their lives (Lo, 1994). Temptation is probably most pronounced for girls, whose popularity is tied very much to physical appearance and participation in fashions and fads.

Participation in the teen consumer subculture is costly, and if a young woman cannot afford participation, she is likely to steal her way in. It is no surprise, then, that girls are more likely than boys to shoplift cosmetics and clothes. Boys, in contrast, are much more likely to steal electronic items (Campbell, 1981: 122–123; Sarasalo, Bergman, & Toth, 1998). Moreover, because girls spend more time shopping, they undergo more scrutiny by store detectives, who report they are suspicious of young people in groups, particularly if they are not dressed well (May, 1978). In short, the teenage subculture may be particularly hard on girls from poor families. They are bombarded daily with the message that they are acceptable only if they look a particular way, yet they do not have the money necessary to purchase the "look." These pressures can be seen in the comments of one delinquent girl to one of the authors:

> I took everything. I mean from pins to makeup, and fingernail polish and fake fingernails. Even toothbrushes [laughs]. We went over there to go shopping, but I told them, "Nah, I shop for you guys," and what I went away with . . . was almost $300. I had two packages full.

In general, shoplifting by girls must be placed within the context of girls' lives in a youth- and consumer-oriented culture. Here the drawbacks of not having money are evident, and for girls, as we shall see in subsequent chapters, there are few avenues to teenage success. Shoplifting, then, is a social cost attributable to the bombarding of young people with images of looks and goods attainable only with money many of them do not have.

STATUS OFFENSES

One of the distinguishing characteristics of female delinquency is the role played by status offenses. Arrest statistics, reviewed in Chapter 2, consistently show that running away and curfew violation constitute a major portion of official female delinquency and that they are far less prominent in male delinquency. These two offenses alone generally account for approximately a quarter of all arrests of girls.

There are other uniquely juvenile offenses that also fall into the status offense category, and some of these have played, if anything, a more significant historical role in girls' official delinquency. These include truancy and offenses known variously as "incorrigibility," "unmanageability," and "being beyond control." In many jurisdictions the offenses have been combined under such categories as PINS, CHINS, and MINS (referring to persons, children, and minors "in need of supervision") (Bearrows, 1987: 194).

Almost all states now differentiate in some way between status and delinquent offenses (including specifying different procedures for the handling of status offenses). Only eleven states classify delinquents and status offenders within the same category, and six of these provide for differential handling (Bearrows, 1987: 194). States also tend to specify in some manner which behaviors are prohibited under the status offense categories. For instance, Montana state statutes say this about a YINS ("youth in need of supervision"): "habitually disobeys the reasonable and lawful demands of his [or her] parents or guardian, or is ungovernable and beyond their control" (Bortner, 1988: 96). In some states a child who "is in danger of leading an idle or immoral life," who is a "wayward child," who "endangers the morals of himself or others," or "who associates with vagrant, vicious or immoral persons" can be brought before the juvenile court (Bortner, 1988: 98–100).

Current attempts to differentiate between status and delinquent offenses are somewhat ironic because, as we shall see, the early juvenile justice system developed the concept of delinquency to include status offenses and to avoid the notion that delinquent behavior and criminal behavior were the same (Platt, 1969: 138; Sutton, 1988: 162–163; Feld, 1988: 822–825).

Some of the most common definitions of delinquency and status offenses, originating with the 1899 Juvenile Court Act in Chicago, are listed below (Bartollas (2003: 11)).

Violates any law or ordinance

Violates juvenile court order

Associates with criminal or immoral persons

Engages in any calling, occupation, or exhibition punishable by law

Frequents taverns or uses alcohol

Wanders the streets in the nighttime

Grows up in idleness or crime (breaking curfew)

Enters or visits a house of ill repute

Is habitually truant

Is habitually disobedient or refuses to obey reasonable and proper orders of parents, guardians, or custodians

Is incorrigible or ungovernable

Absents himself or herself from home without permission

Persists in violating school rules and regulations

Endangers welfare, morals, and/or health of self or others

Uses vile, obscene, or vulgar language (in a public place)

Smokes cigarettes (in a public place)

Engages in dissolute or immoral life or conduct

Wanders about railroad yards or tracks

Jumps a train or enters a train without authority

Loiters, sleeps in alleys, begs, or receives alms (or is in the street for that purpose)

Clearly, each of us has engaged in one or more of these behaviors at one time or another. In large part, the separation of status offenders from other delinquent youths has emerged in response to concerns about the rights of youths charged with status offenses. These legal and legislative challenges are discussed in Chapter 7; here we can simply say that status offense laws have been objected to on constitutional grounds. One of the most common grounds is "void for vagueness"; it is difficult to determine precisely the meaning of "habitual disobedience," "lawful parental demands," or "being in danger of leading an idle or immoral life." Another concern is that status offense laws violate the Eighth Amendment in that punishment ensues from status rather than behavior. Still another argument is that such laws deny children equal protection because the laws apply only to children. Further, it is argued that status offenders are denied due process in that they are deprived of liberty "in the name of treatment" (Bearrows, 1987: 184–185).

Legislation to curb the courts' authority was enacted in 1974. The *Juvenile Justice and Delinquency Prevention Act* (JJDPA) requires that states receiving federal delinquency-prevention money begin to divert and deinstitutionalize youth arrested and/or referred to court for status offenses (42 U.S.C. 5633 (a) (12) (A)). Proponents of the act argued that community agencies rather than police departments and juvenile courts are more appropriate entities to deal with youths who are not guilty of criminal behavior. The JJDPA and its impact on the juvenile justice system are treated at length in later chapters, but here we discuss why status offenses, and federal efforts to divert and deinstitutionalize status offenders, have a special meaning for girls.

Girls are more likely than boys not only to be arrested for status offenses but also to be referred to court in consequence. Official court statistics in Australia (Hancock and Chesney-Lind, 1982; Adler, 1998), Great Britain (Smith, 1978; Cain, 1989), Canada (Geller, 1981), Venezuela (Castro, 1981: 222), Belgium (Cain, 1989), and the United States show that many young women arrested and/or referred to court are charged with status offenses. In the United States, for example, approximately 35 percent of the girls but only 10 percent of the boys referred to juvenile court in 1985 were referred for these offenses (Snyder et al., 1989: 11, 31); similar figures were reported for 1977 (Black & Smith, 1981). One analysis of national statistics in the late 1970s revealed that girls were 170 percent more likely than boys to be referred to juvenile court for status offenses; the highest percentage was for ungovernability and running away (Smith, 1980: 4–6). Recent studies continue to find females being far more likely to be referred to court for status offenses (Rhodes & Fischer, 1993). The most recent juvenile court data (1997) show that nationally 60 percent of those referred to court for running away are females (Sickmund, 2000). As we move further into the juvenile justice system, we find girls receiving harsher punishments for status offenses than their male counterparts. As we shall see in Chapter 8, more than one-fifth (23%) of girls in residential placement are in for status offenses, compared to only 4 percent of the boys. Further, 7 percent of the girls placed out of home are runaways, in contrast to only 1 percent of the boys; 9 percent of the girls and only 2 percent of the boys are in for incorrigibility (Sickmund & Wan, 1999).

For many years statistics showing large numbers of girls arrested and referred to court for status offenses were taken as representative of the different types of male and female delinquency. However, as we have seen, self-report studies of male and female delinquency do not reflect the large differences in misbehavior found in official statistics. A persuasive explanation for the differences between official and unofficial rates of female delinquency is that the juvenile justice system's historic commitment to the notion of the state as parent has encouraged abuse of the status offense category (Teitelbaum & Gough, 1977). The language of status offense provisions invites, in the words of one critic of the system, "discretionary" application that "allows parents, police, and juvenile court authorities, who ordinarily decide whether PINS [status offense] proceedings should be initiated, to hold girls legally accountable for behavior—often sexual or in some way related to sex—that they would not consider serious if committed by boys" (Sussman, 1977: 183).

A major source of the bias in contemporary juvenile courts is undoubtedly parental use (some might say abuse) of the status offense category. Ketchum (1978: 37) reports that 72 percent of status offenders are turned in by relatives. Recent national data, while slightly less explicit, also show that girls are more likely to be referred to court by "sources other than law enforcement agencies" (which would include parents, schools, and so on). In 1983, 23 percent of girls but only 16 percent of boys charged with delinquent offenses were referred to court by non-law-enforcement agencies. The pattern among youths referred for status offenses, predictably, was even more pronounced: well over half (56 percent) of the girls and 45 percent of the boys were referred by sources other than law enforcement agencies (Snyder & Finnegan, 1987: 21; see also Pope & Feyerherm, 1982).

Because parents are likely to set different standards of obedience for their male and female children, and because there are few legal guidelines concerning what constitutes a reasonable parental request, parents are able to refer their children to court for a variety of activities. Andrews and Cohn (1974) found that in New York these parental concerns varied from serious problems (like running away from home) to "sleeping all day" and "refusing to do household chores." Despite the petty nature of some complaints, court personnel routinely failed to make independent determinations about youthful behaviors and typically responded to parental wishes (Andrews & Cohn, 1974: 1404).

That parents are often committed to two standards of adolescent behavior is one explanation for the overrepresentation of girls charged with status offenses in court populations—and the standards should not be discounted as a major source of tension even in modern families. Despite expectations to the contrary, gender-specific socialization patterns have not changed very much, and this is especially true of parents' relationships with daughters (Katz, 1979; Block 1984). It appears that even parents who oppose sexism in general feel "uncomfortable tampering with existing traditions" and "do not want to risk their children becoming misfits" (Katz, 1979: 24). Clearly, parental attempts to follow these customs will continue to be a source of conflict between girls and their elders.

Thorne, in her ethnography of gender in grade school, found that girls were still using "cosmetics, discussions of boyfriends, dressing sexually, and other forms of exaggerated 'teen' femininity to challenge adult, and class[-] and race-based[,] authority in schools." She also found that "the double standard persists, and girls who are overtly sexual run the risk of being labeled sluts" (Thorne, 1994: 156).

Contemporary ethnographies of school life echo the validity of these parental perceptions. Orenstein's observations also point to the durability of the sexual double standard; at the schools she observed that sex "ruins girls" but "enhance[s] boys" (Orenstein, 1994: 57). Parents, too, according to Thorne, have new reasons to enforce the time-honored sexual double standard. Perhaps correctly concerned about sexual harassment and rape, to say nothing of HIV/AIDS if their daughters are heterosexually active, "parents in gestures that mix protection with punishment, often tighten control of girls when they become adolescents, and sexuality becomes a terrain of struggle between the generations" (Thorne, 1994: 156). Finally, Thorne notes that as girls use sexuality as a proxy for independence, they sadly and ironically reinforce their status as sexual objects seeking male approval—ultimately ratifying their status as the subordinate sex.

Whatever the reason, parental attempts to adhere to and enforce the sexual double standard will continue to be a source of conflict between parents and their daughters. Another important aspect of girls' troubles with parents that has received attention only in more recent years is physical and sexual abuse. It is increasingly clear that childhood sexual abuse is particularly salient for girls and may well propel girls into behaviors such as running away from home or other status offenses. As already noted, girls are much more likely than boys to be the victims of childhood sexual abuse: it has been estimated that roughly 70 percent of the victims are female (Finkelhor & Baron, 1986: 45). Girls' sexual abuse usually starts earlier than boys' (Finkelhor & Baron, 1986: 48); is more likely to be perpetrated by family members (usually the father or the stepfather); and consequently lasts longer than that of boys (DeJong, Hervada, & Emmett, 1983; Russell, 1986). All these factors are associated with more severe trauma, causing dramatic short- and long-term effects in victims (Adams-Tucker, 1982). The effects often noted by researchers include "fear, anxiety, depression, anger and hostility, and inappropriate sexual behavior," as well as behaviors of greater familiarity to criminologists, such as running away from home, difficulties in school, truancy, and early marriage (Browne & Finkelhor, 1986: 69).

Herman's study of incest survivors in therapy found that they were more likely to have run away from home than a matched sample of women whose fathers were "seductive" (33 percent compared with 5 percent) (Herman, 1981). Another study of women patients found that half the victims of childhood sexual abuse, but only 20 percent of the nonvictim group, had left home before the age of eighteen (Meiselman, 1978). Not surprisingly, then, studies of girls on the streets or in court populations show high rates of both physical and sexual abuse.

National research on the characteristics of girls in the juvenile justice system clearly shows the role played by physical and sexual abuse in girls' delinquency. According to a study of girls in juvenile correctional settings conducted by the American Correctional Association (1990), a very large proportion of these girls—about half of whom were of minority backgrounds—had experienced physical abuse (61 percent), with nearly half saying that they had experienced this eleven or more times. Many had reported the abuse, but the results of this reporting were sobering, with the majority saying that either nothing changed (30 percent) or that the reporting just made things worse (25 percent). More than half of these girls (54 percent) had experienced sexual abuse, and for most this was not an isolated incident; one-third reported that it happened from three to ten times, while another 27 percent said that it occurred eleven or more times. Most were nine years of age or younger when the abuse began.

Given this history, it should be no surprise that the vast majority of the girls surveyed had run away from home (81 percent), and of those that had run, 39 percent had run ten or more times. Over half (54 percent) said that they had attempted suicide, and when asked the reason for this they said it was because they "felt no one cared" (American Correctional Association, 1990: 55). Finally, what might be called a survival or coping strategy is criminalized; girls in correctional establishments reported that their first arrests were typically for running away from home (21 percent) or for larceny–theft (25 percent) (American Correctional Association, 1990: 46–71).

Detailed studies of youths entering the juvenile justice system in Florida have compared the "constellations of problems" presented by girls and boys entering detention (Dembo, Williams, & Schmeidler, 1993). These researchers have found that female youth were more likely than male youth to have abuse histories and contact with the juvenile justice system for status offenses, whereas male youth had higher rates of involvement with a variety of delinquent offenses. Further research on a larger cohort of youth ($N = 2,104$) admitted to an assessment center in Tampa concluded that "girls' problem behavior commonly relates to an abusive and traumatizing home life, whereas boys' law violating behavior reflects their involvement in a delinquent life style" (Dembo et al., 1995: 21).

Still another study found that 60 percent of the street prostitutes interviewed had been sexually abused as juveniles (Silbert & Pines, 1981: 409). Girls at an Arkansas diagnostic unit and school who had been adjudged guilty of either status or delinquent offenses reported similarly high levels of sexual abuse in addition to physical abuse: 53 percent indicated they had been sexually abused, 25 percent recalled scars, 38 percent recalled bleeding from abuse, and 51 percent recalled bruises (Mouzakitis, 1981). A survey of girls in the juvenile justice system in Wisconsin (Phelps et al., 1982) revealed that 79 percent had been subjected to physical abuse that resulted in some injury, and 32 percent had been sexually abused by parents or persons closely connected to their families. Moreover, 50 percent had been sexually assaulted ("raped" or forced to participate in sexual acts) (Phelps et al., 1982: 66). Even higher figures were reported by McCormack and her associates in their study of youths in a runaway shelter in Toronto (McCormack, Janus, & Burgess, 1986): 73 percent of the females and 38 percent of the males had been sexually abused. Finally, a study of youths charged with running away or truancy, or who were listed as missing persons in Arizona, found that 55 percent were incest victims (Reich & Guitierres, 1979). More recent research has continued to arrive at the same results, linking running away with negative home environments consisting of both physical and sexual abuse (Warren, Gary, & Moorhead, 1994; Kurtz, Kurtz, & Jarvis, 1991; Whitbeck et al., 1997; Sullivan & Knutson, 2000; Kaufman & Widom 1999; Gilfus, 1992).

A study of the backgrounds of adult women in prison underscores the important link between childhood victimization and later criminal careers (Chesney-Lind & Rodriguez, 1983). Chesney-Lind and Rodriguez's interviews revealed that most female offenders were victims of physical and/or sexual abuse as youngsters: over 60 percent had been sexually abused, and about half had been raped. Their situations prompted them to run away from home (three-fourths had been arrested on this and other status offense charges) and to engage in prostitution and petty property crimes for survival. Many also began what became lifetime problems with drugs. As adults, the women continued these activities because they possessed little education and almost no marketable occupational skills (see also Miller, 1986).

Confirmation of the consequences of childhood sexual and physical abuse for adult female criminal behavior has also come recently from a study of 908 individuals with substantiated histories of abuse. Widom (1988) found that abused or neglected females were twice as likely as a matched group of controls to have an adult criminal record: 16 percent compared with 7.5 percent. The difference among men was not as dramatic: 42 percent compared with 33 percent. Men from abusive backgrounds were also more likely than members of the control group to contribute to the "cycle of violence," with more arrests for violent offenses as adults. In contrast, when women with abusive backgrounds entered the criminal justice system, their arrests tended to involve property and public order offenses, such as disorderly conduct, curfew violation, and loitering (Widom, 1988: 17). Another, more recent, study by Widom found that child sexual abuse victims are more likely to be arrested for prostitution as an adult than both nonsexually abused juveniles and those who were just abused and neglected (Widom & Ames, 1994). Similar conclusions were found in a study of adolescent runaways and homeless women by Simons and Whitbeck (1991).

In summary, girls may well have several legitimate reasons to differ with their parents—reasons that may bring them into court as status offenders. Because of its history and structure, the juvenile justice system, as we shall see in subsequent chapters, has tended to ignore children's rights in favor of judicial support for family authority and power over offspring. (For a discussion of recent court rulings that have reduced children's rights in favor of parents and/or the state, see Minow, 1987.) Girls who may in fact be victims find themselves arrested and referred to court for noncriminal offenses. One of the most common of the status offense charges, and one that merits further discussion, is running away from home.

RUNAWAYS

Between 1.3 and 1.4 million youths run away from home each year and more than 12,000 run away from juvenile facilities (Kaufman & Widom, 1999; Swaim & Bracken, 1997; Finkelhor, Hotaling, & Sedlak, 1990); over half are girls (Finkelhor, Hotaling, & Sedlak, 1990: 186). Moreover, over 100,000 children are on the streets as "throwaways": children told to leave home by parents, or children whose parents make no effort to recover them (Finkelhor, Hotaling, & Sedlak, 1990; Swaim & Bracken, 1997). One recent report estimated that as many as 500,000 youths are by themselves on the streets of large cities (Trumbull, 1995). Girls constitute over half of this group. Most youths who run away remain within ten miles of home (usually staying with friends nearby), and about 60 percent return home within three days (Nye & Edelbrock, 1980: 148). Most runaways have experienced severe problems at home; however, those who run away more than once have the most severe problems (Olson et al., 1980; Swaim & Bracken, 1997). Running away from home typically follows a lengthy period of intense family conflict. What usually occurs is abuse or overly strict discipline or, in many cases, both. Runaways often feel unwanted, abused, neglected, and rejected by their parents. Many believe their parents have unrealistic expectations of them and use excessive punishment. Also, as we shall see, the programs available within the juvenile justice system do not seem to work for runaways; one estimate is that roughly half the hard-core runaways have fled from foster homes, group homes, correctional institutions, or some place other than their own homes (Sullivan, 1988b: 32).

Further, many have experienced poor relationships outside of the home, often characterized by ostracism from both teachers and peers. They have also experienced failure at school, often being placed in lower tracks, and many have had to repeat grades. In-school problems and habitual truancy are also common. Not surprisingly, most have very negative feelings toward school in general (Swaim & Bracken, 1997: 397).

It is clear that many young women are on the streets in flight from sexual victimization at home. Once there, they often resort to crime in order to survive, but they do not have much attachment to their delinquent activities. Angry about being labeled delinquent, most still engage in illegal acts. The Wisconsin study (Phelps et al., 1982) found that 54 percent of the girls who ran away found it necessary to steal money for food and clothing. A few exchanged sexual contact for money, food, and/or shelter (Phelps et al., 1982: 67). In Toronto, McCormack, Janus, and Burgess (1986: 392–393) discovered that sexually abused female runaways were significantly more likely than their nonabused counterparts to engage in delinquent or such criminal activities as substance abuse, petty theft, and prostitution. No similar pattern was found among male runaways. Not surprisingly, girls tend to exhibit more negative physical self-concepts than males (Swaim & Bracken, 1997; Crain, 1996).

Sexual abuse, then, appears to be the most common element in the lives of girls who run away. A fourteen-year-old runaway illustrates this problem in what she had to say about her father (Roberts, 1987: 53): "He started sexually abusing me. . . . It's been happening since I was eleven years old. . . . My father taught me if I told, he would kill me. When I did bad in school he would keep me in at night and beat me. He kept hitting me in the stomach." Besides experiencing abuse, many runaway girls come from families characterized by an unusual amount of parental control. An illustrative instance is a fifteen-year-old girl in Roberts's study who reported that she ran away because she had been grounded for an indefinite period of time and was in fear of additional physical abuse from her father (who had been arrested for wife battering). Her parents were divorced, but she remained with her father because her mother and stepfather did not want her. Her father refused to let her date until she was eighteen, and each time she fled he would find her, bring her home, and beat her. After the fourth runaway episode she was placed in a foster home (Roberts, 1987: 54–55).

A study of Canadian runaways by Janus and his colleagues found that girls are far more likely than boys to cite physical and sexual abuse as the main reason for running away. Specifically, the first time they ran away, almost half of the girls (49 percent) but only one-third of the boys cited physical abuse as the reason, whereas the girls were *six times more likely than the boys to cite sexual abuse as the reason for running away* (24 percent vs. 4 percent). These differences were more pronounced the last time they ran away: 42 percent of the girls cited physical abuse compared to 26 percent of the boys, whereas about one-fifth of the girls *but only 1 percent of the boys* cited sexual abuse (Janus et al., 1995).

In another study, Brennan (1980) placed girls who run away in a category he called "rebellious and constrained middle class drop-out girls." They tend to be angry, refractory, and alienated, to have delinquent peers, to have been rejected by their parents, and to have been abused. Edelbrock (1980) looked at the incidence of running away in matched samples of "normal" and "disturbed" children aged four to sixteen. The "normals" were random selections from the Maryland, Virginia, and Washington, D.C., area; the "disturbed" were drawn from youngsters referred to a mental health agency. It was found that running away was more common among disturbed girls than among disturbed boys, especially relative to the twelve-to-sixteen age cohort. How Edelbrock defined disturbed (other than being referred to a mental health agency) was not made clear. It could be that one reason that girls fell into the "disturbed" category was because they had run away and had subsequently been referred to an agency for doing so. After passage of the JJDPA in 1974, increasing numbers of youths who had previously been processed as status offenders were appearing in the mental health system and, more specifically, in mental hospitals and private treatment facilities (Schwartz, 1989: 131–148). In any event, the girls in the Edelbrock sample were found to have more behavioral problems, including the use of drugs and alcohol, "poor behavior with parents," suicidal talk, being "disobedient" at home, feeling unloved, and experiencing "sexual problems" (which were undefined). Edelbrock made no mention of sexual abuse at home—an omission until recently typical of studies of runaways. Indeed, this is one reason for the space devoted here to this piece of research, for it typifies the genre: runaway behavior is explained away, blamed on the youths, and sexualized.

A higher rate of suicidal behavior has been found to exist among girls who run away. Rotheram-Borus, in a study of predominantly African American and Hispanic runaways in a New York City runaway shelter (1993), found that girls, more often than boys, had attempted suicide and were also classified as depressed. Specifically, 44 percent of the girls but only 29 percent of the boys had attempted suicide. Almost two-thirds of the girls (62 percent) were classified as depressed, in contrast to 44 percent of the boys.

Another analysis of the same data noted in the Rotheram-Borus study found extensive drug use, unprotected sexual behavior, and other behaviors that placed these youths at extremely high risk of contracting the AIDS virus (Koopman, Rosario, & Rotheram-Borus, 1994). Few gender differences were found as far as drug use and sexual behavior were concerned, except that males had more sexual partners than females. The authors noted that national data from the National Institute on Drug Abuse indicate that runaways are far more likely to abuse a wide range of drugs than are nonrunaway adolescents. Specifically, runaways are about seven times more likely to use crack and four times more likely to use heroin.

Consider, though, the higher rate of runaway behavior found among girls twelve to sixteen in the Edelbrock report. For sexually abused girls, the abuse begins somewhat early in their lives, and when they reach puberty and early adolescence they begin to question the behavior. They come to the realization that it is not "normal" (as they have been told by their father or stepfather) and hence fall prone to guilt and shame, which eventuates in attempts to escape.[1]

Most runaways have fled homes where abuse was an everyday event; several studies have noted that a preponderance of girls referred to juvenile court have been sexually and/or physically abused (Andrews & Cohn, 1974; National Institute of Mental Health, 1977; Rush, 1980; Phelps et al., 1982; McCormack, Janus, & Burgess, 1986; Koroki & Chesney-Lind, 1985; Janus et al.,

1995). Yet their lives on the streets are almost always even more abusive in nature because they often become trapped in the sordid trafficking of children for sexual gratification. Campagna and Poffenberger (1988) estimate that this business involves around 1.2 million children, with 150,000 or so involved in prostitution alone. The highest profits are realized from prostitution with adolescent girls, many of whom are runaways or "throwaways." Noting the relationship between sexual abuse and runaway behavior, the researchers comment on the irony for many of these girls: " . . . prostitution was an exit from an intolerable home life and a practical option to the alternative of institutionalized care in foster homes or state juvenile facilities" (1988: 65). Pimps often place young girls in brothels, truck stops, sex rings, and child pornography rings, and sometimes in what is known as a "circuit," "a string or series of working sites scattered across a dozen or more states" where they "work the streets" or work in brothels or "out-call" services (1988: 59–70). For some but not necessarily all girl runaways, then, prostitution becomes a way to survive in the absence of few other earning skills (Miller, 1986: 139).

PROSTITUTION AMONG GIRLS

As the preceding section suggests, running away from home for any length of time often leads girls into prostitution. Among the common methods of entering into that desperate existence, running away is the most common, followed by being abandoned (Boyer & James, 1982: 77).

Accurate data on the number of active prostitutes are difficult to obtain. As noted earlier (see Table 2-1), only 779 juveniles were arrested for prostitution in 2000, of whom about 57 percent were girls. It was estimated by the U.S. Department of Health, Education and Welfare in 1978 that there were about 900,000 juvenile prostitutes in the United States, most of them girls (Boyer & James, 1982: 77). A 1981 survey estimated roughly 600,000 prostitutes under the age of sixteen (reported in *USA Today,* January 13, 1986). Another estimate is that of the nearly one million youthful runaways, about 25 percent are "hard core" and half of them (perhaps 125,000) have worked as prostitutes (Sullivan, 1988b: 32). Still another, more recent, estimate is that there are around 1.3 million prostitutes in America, around 500,000 of them children (Cugini, 1997). The figures vary widely, but they are all sizable enough to indicate a social dysfunction of considerable proportions.

How is it that thousands of teenage girls end up "turning tricks" as prostitutes? Research suggests several interrelated reasons. The first was discussed in the previous section: it is a form of survival. Consistent with the research cited earlier, Boyer and James (1982: 79) report that between 40 percent and 75 percent of teenage prostitutes have been the victims of physical and/or sexual abuse. A study of 138 female prostitutes by James (1976) found that over a third had been molested, about half had been raped, and almost two-thirds had been physically abused. A more recent estimate in Atlanta suggests that as many as

90 percent of prostitutions were abused as children and 85 percent experienced incest (Reid, 2001). As Boyer and James (1982: 79) state, "The imposition of adult sexuality on children disrupts psychosexual development," and among its effects are promiscuity, rebellion, feelings of shame and guilt, and a loss of self-esteem. Once girls reach puberty, they often come to the realization that their experiences are different from those of their peers and begin to withdraw. Many "hold a distorted image of their own bodies," which may "lead them to expect that their worth will only be acknowledged when they permit sexual access" (Boyer & James, 1982: 80). Further, the girls may learn "that the most effective way to communicate with adults is through sex" (Campagna & Poffenberger, 1988: 66) and view themselves as "salable commodities" (Boyer & James, 1982: 80).

The most common form of teenage prostitution today may be what some have called "survival sex." This differs from the more "commercial" variety "in that it is sex in return for that which one needs immediately: warm shelter for a night, drugs or perhaps a few Big Macs" (Beyette, 1988). The director of Children of the Night, an agency in Hollywood, California, that tries to help teenage prostitutes, decries the descriptor as a sort of "1980s yuppie term" that softens or renders acceptable what is in reality "sexual exploitation" and a criminal offense (Beyette, 1988). Whatever one calls it, teenage prostitution is widespread, and according to the director of the Children's Hospital High Risk Project in Los Angeles, its practitioners are getting younger (in Los Angeles in 1987, about 40 percent were under the age of fifteen). Most have come from dysfunctional families characterized by alcoholism or drug abuse, physical abuse, and neglect. Many can be classified as "chronic homeless" (three or more months on their own). They often live in so-called squats or crash pads in abandoned buildings with no bathrooms or utilities. One estimate is that in Hollywood alone there are as many as four thousand runaways on any given day, and about ten thousand in Los Angeles County; most ply the prostitution trade (Beyette, 1988).

Campagna and Poffenberger say several additional factors may play a role in a girl's taking up prostitution (1988: 65–66). She may be coerced, tricked, seduced, or even blackmailed by a pimp. Or through conditioning within the family she may develop very low self-esteem and believe that she deserves to be a prostitute. Further, a lack of shelters may conduce entry into prostitution. In Atlanta, girls as young as 10 years of age are "being recruited into prostitution by their peers and by older men who are pimps." Many have either run away or been "kicked out of their homes." Some are enticed with promises of careers in music videos or as models. They fall prey to the illusion of "easy money" and then "end up at the mercy of their pimps or johns" and abused (Reid, 2001).

The problem is compounded by the fact that so many are contracting the AIDS virus. One estimate is that about half of all street prostitutes are HIV infected. For teenagers, an estimated two out of every five are HIV infected. One teenage girl interviewed by Cugini said that one of the dangers of this life is that of getting HIV. One stated that "Everyone always uses a condom, but they can break. I know plenty of people who have gotten something from doing this. Condoms are not 100%" (Cugini, 1997).

The girl or young woman who is becoming a prostitute has moved from turning a few tricks now and then or from having done so a few times in the past while carrying out a more acceptable role such as housewife or student to being a person who is not given access to more acceptable roles. In other words, being a prostitute becomes her major role. Boyer and James (1982: 93) write that "typically, the adolescent does not at first recognize her acts as constituting prostitution. At some point, however, she begins to realize that the behavior she has adopted signifies that she is a prostitute."

Detailed information on the lives of these girls is often available only in journalistic accounts. The following story about Sheri (not her real name), a twelve-year-old white girl, appeared in the *Los Angeles Herald Examiner* (Yorkin, 1982):

> At a time when most twelve-year-olds are worrying about their first crushes, Sheri has been raped many times, once by five men in a station wagon who deserted her up in the Hollywood Hills. She was threatened with a gun by a "trick" and jumped from the car to escape. One street pimp tried to kidnap her, another threatened to kill her.

Sheri preferred the streets to living with her bartending mother; her mother's boyfriend, who worked as an electrician; her twin sister; and an older brother and his wife. One of nine children, she was born after her mother and father separated. Her father was an alcoholic who was very violent when drunk. When they were nine, the twins went to live with their father in Alabama for the summer. Sheri recalls, "He molested both of us and he raped my sister—who looked like she was about five."

Sheri said that she had had a speech impediment when she was younger and was always teased about it. She was very quiet and shy; her sister was popular and outgoing. There was a great deal of conflict in the home, and when her mother moved in with her boyfriend (who, incidentally, was black), "Sheri faced merciless jeering by schoolmates, who she said always made fun of her anyway."

At the age of eleven, when she was forced to give up her kitten because a landlord prohibited pets, she ran away and ended up at the corner of Hollywood and Vine. Her first night there a man befriended her, shared a marijuana cigarette, and tried to rape her. She escaped but eventually came into contact with a pimp, who bought her some new clothes; after a great deal of coercion, she began "turning tricks" for him. About a year later she came under the aegis of Children of the Night and eventually was placed in a foster home.

One recent account tells the story of a pimp named Roy and his three "workers" (Cugini, 1997). They work an "escort service" in the Washington, D.C., area. Roy claims he has about 300 "workers." When asked why they do it, one girl (under 18) said that the main reason is "fast cash." "You get a minimum of $100 an hour here. The customer pays $150, Roy gets $50, you get $100." Continuing, this girl said:

With that kind of money, you can make as much as a person with a college degree and a professional type job. . . . The problem is that prostitution is addictive. Once you get used to having hundreds in your pocket at all times, and you set your standard of living to that, it's nearly impossible to live otherwise. I have another job assembling waffle irons. I make six dollars an hour. I feel completely ridiculous leaving after an eight-hour day, knowing I've made about fifty dollars, before taxes. I could have made more than twice that here in one hour! I just do it so my parents will think I'm working. I dropped out of school. Plus, you get tips, anywhere from $20–50 (Cugini, 1997: 2).

Prostitution among girls, then, is not so much a choice as a survival mechanism for those who have few other options once forced onto the streets. Despite the obvious need, programs such as Children of the Night are the exception rather than the rule. For many young people who cannot stay at home, there is little help from the social service and criminal justice systems.

International Prostitution

Most of this book deals only with the situation of girls in the United States and other developed countries, but no account of teenage prostitution can be considered complete without a discussion of the dimensions of the sexual exploitation of girls internationally. Here, numbers are even more difficult to come by. The explosion of prostitution in Asia is startling and undeniable. It is also clearly and ironically linked to the expanded presence of Western military and economic interests, especially in Thailand, Korea, India, and the Philippines. Anne O'Reilly (1993) notes that estimates of the extent of child prostitution worldwide range from 10,000 to more than 2,000,000. One of the most recent estimates is that there are about one million children trafficked into prostitution each year in Southeast Asia alone, with about 10,000 children from 6 to 14 "enslaved in brothels in Sri Lanka" (Blaylock, 2001, quoting Meier, 2000).

One reason often cited to explain the increase of child prostitution is a mistaken assumption that these young girls are free of sexually transmitted diseases. More important, however, is the existence of widespread poverty among less-developed countries. One result is that many poor families often have to resort to the "selling" of their children, especially young girls, to the "sex industry." A report by Sachs (1994) goes even further and argues that child prostitution is a growing "commodity" as there exists a multibillion-dollar industry in which children are treated like "mass-produced goods." Sachs further suggests that the rapid increase of this problem "has been attributed to the world's materialistic orientation, where society willingly surrenders unfortunate children for both economic and sexual gratification." A recent study found a thriving "sex market" in the United Kingdom (May and Edwards, 2000).

Messerschmidt (1986) notes that when U.S. corporations dramatically increased their investments in East Asia, the impact, particularly on women in Thailand and the Philippines, was immediate. Eighty to ninety percent of those corporations' light assembly workers are women, and they are subjected to "crowded and unsanitary boarding houses, extremely low wages and severe health hazards" (Messerschmidt, 1986: 94). And speaking of the Phillipines, one recent United Nations estimate is that there are more than 60,000 child prostitutes, some as young as nine years of age. One of the most "robust economic sectors is that of providing sexual services" (Blaylock, quoting Satchell, 2000).

The role of U.S. agribusiness corporations in exacerbating the impoverishment of rural areas in these countries must not be overlooked (Lappe et al., 1977), because widespread economic crisis provides the impetus for families to send their daughters to the city for employment. For example, Messerschmidt (1986: 95) states that in Thailand, one-third of the families have no land, and three-quarters have less than the two acres needed for subsistence. The economic marginality of girls and women in the cities means that even employment is not necessarily an alternative to prostitution but, instead, possibly a gateway to that activity. For example, Fuentes and Ehrenreich (1983: 26) discuss the fact that when girls and women are sent from the impoverished countryside to work in factories, expenses are far more than they imagined. Further, they are expected to send money home. Consequently, some factory girls become prostitutes and others supplement their factory salaries with prostitution. Sometimes, as happens in Thailand, girls arrive in cities to be prostitutes after having been sent or sold (some for as little as a few dollars) by desperate poor rural families (Lenze, 1979).

The numbers of girls and women who are involved in prostitution in Thailand are truly staggering. Gay (1985) estimates that there were 20,000 prostitutes there in 1957; in 1982 there were 700,000 (500,000 in Bangkok), about 10 percent of all Thai women between the ages of fifteen and thirty. Obviously not all of these are girls, but many accounts stress the extreme youth of Asian prostitutes (Moselina, 1981; Sturdevant, 1988). For example, Kunstel and Albright (1987) report that the Anti-Slavery Society has estimated that 30,000 prostitutes aged fifteen and under worked in Bangkok alone in 1984. They interviewed one who had been sold to a whorehouse by her father: "My father was depressed because he was in very huge debt. My mother was sick" (Kunstel & Albright, 1987: 9). She was somewhat fortunate to have escaped from the whorehouse, which was owned by a prominent business leader; the house catered to tourist clients, "mostly men from Arab countries and Asia neighbors, with a smattering of Europeans and a few Americans" (Kunstel & Albright, 1987: 10).

More recent reports document that the problem of girl prostitutes in Thailand and throughout Southeast Asia continues. Gooi (1993) reports that about 5,000 young girls from the province of Yunnan in China have been induced to cross into Thailand, where pimps have forced them to work in a "thriving sex industry." Tasker (1994) notes that parents continue to sell their daughters because of their extreme poverty. Lillian Robinson (1996) reports that in Thailand an estimated 6 to 9 percent of the country's female population has been, at one time or another, in that country's "sex industry." She also notes that about half of the child prostitutes are HIV positive. Another report found that about 15,000 were "sold into slavery in Cambodia between 1991 and 1997, and the Thai government reports that 60,000 Thai children are sold into prostitution." The total in all of Southeast Asia is estimated to be between 200,000 and 800,000 (Blaylock, quoting Satchell, 2000).

Other parts of Southeast Asia also have a thriving "sex industry." In India, notes Lisa McArthur (1996), an estimated 200,000 prostitutes are from Nepal, around one-third of whom are between the ages of twelve and sixteen. Enforcement of the laws is lax, with only a 10 percent conviction rate. A report from *WIN News,* appropriately called "Rape for Profit" (Staff, 1995), confirms McArthur's findings and notes that many young girls from Nepal are being recruited to work in the brothels of Bombay. This report estimates that about half of India's "sex slaves" are from Nepal. These girls are promised jobs or marriage, but are usually reduced to facing extreme physical abuse, imprisonment, and AIDS. In China, reports note a big increase in child prostitution, with many poor families selling their children to sex rings. This has been because of increasing demands for young girls, usually from Western visitors (Sherry, Lee, & Vatikiotis, 1995; see also Simons, 1994). Finally, in Dacca, Bangladesh, there are around 5,000 girls "working" in one small section alone. In a nearby village there are another estimated 2,000 girls. The choices of these girls are limited (as is the case all over Southeast Asia), for many are employed as domestic workers but are subjected to abuse. If they leave these jobs, the only option is the "sex industry" (Magee & Sherwell, 1996).

In the Philippines, the role of both tourism and militarism in the creation of a market for prostitution is also clear. Accounts documenting the explosion of prostitution in the islands note that in the 1960s and 1970s it was fueled by the Vietnam War (Moselina, 1981). However, the continued presence of the U.S. military in Southeast Asian outposts, along with expanded tourism, supports the ongoing sexual exploitation of girls and young women in the area. According to Sturdevant (1988), the United States has approximately 190,000 military personnel stationed in Korea, the Philippines, Japan, and Okinawa or on duty with the Seventh Fleet. When these men are not on base, they seek rest and recreation (R and R) in towns that have grown up around the installations.

One of the most notorious of such towns was Olongapo City (population 143,279), which exists almost exclusively to serve the R and R needs of the U.S. Naval Base in Subic Bay, now closed. It was described by its mayor as a "camp follower city" (Golley, 1983). Sixteen thousand registered "hostesses" and an estimated eight thousand streetwalkers (many underage) serviced the estimated six thousand to seven thousand American military and civilian personnel who came to it every day. Most of the women were from impoverished rural areas and either had been sent by their families to the city with the hope of possible employment or were escaping sexual abuse, rape, or abandonment at home (Moselina, 1981: 6–23). Families often send their daughters to cities in the company of adults, who promise that they will be trained for income-producing jobs. The girls may begin by working as domestic servants while hoping for places on the assembly lines, but they usually end up on the streets of Manila (Enloe, 1983).

"Sex tours" are a third element in child prostitution in Asia. Estimates are that between 70 and 80 percent of male tourists from Japan, the United States, Australia, and Western Europe traveling to the Philippines and Korea "do so solely for the purpose of sexual entertainment" (Gay, 1985: 34). In Korea, prostitution is big business, with annual revenues of close to $270 million. *Kisaeng* or brothel tours cover two or three days, cost roughly $200, and are very popular with foreign businessmen, U.S. military personnel, and government officials (Messerschmidt, 1986). Underage prostitution is illegal in Korea, but it is only the girls and not their clients who are punished during occasional sweeps of establishments. Girls found guilty of prostitution are held for a year in detention centers; most return to prostitution (Sturdevant, 1988).

In the Philippines, child prostitution is not illegal. In the 1980s, social workers in that country estimated that roughly a hundred thousand children live on the streets and that twenty thousand under age eighteen are fully employed as prostitutes (Ryan, 1988). One thirteen-year-old girl told a reporter that her "uncle" (a mid-thirties Caucasian) had taken her to a seaside resort, bought her a "ladies drink" (white wine), and given her a new bikini: "He gives me a lot of money and buys me clothes and jewelry, and takes me places. He really loves me" (Ryan, 1988). She was telling her story to obviously desperate and envious "street youths" at the time of the interview. A more recent report says that after the U.S. military left in 1992, there was "aggressive marketing by Philippine red-light entrepreneurs"; the report describes the area as one of "two of the Pacific region's most rancid fleshpots." Among the factors cited as causing this development are "poverty, the rise of criminal Mafias in Russia and Eastern Europe, the spread of sex tourism, and the Internet pornography boom" (Blaylock, 2001 quoting Satchell, 2000).

The problem of child prostitution has not escaped other parts of the world; the Brazilian Center for Childhood and Adolescence has estimated that there are around 50,000 girl prostitutes in that country. Not surprisingly, they are lured into this business because of their extreme poverty. The average age of these girls has been decreasing in recent years, and the younger ones are subjected to far more inhumane treatment than their older counterparts. These young girls are almost totally ignorant of basic information about pregnancy and AIDS (Dimenstein, 1994).

Tokyo is also a child prostitution problem area (Blaylock, 2001). One recent report noted that Japan, a country "with the second strongest economy and highest academic standing in the world, is facing a major problem with wide-spreading and popular after-school activity of its young female students." The report noted the increasing number of these students "soliciting their bodies for entertainment" and for extra "pocket money." It was noted that several "image clubs" exist where men pay as much as $150 an hour "to live out their wildest fantasies about schoolgirls." Such clubs "solicit women by advertising in magazines and newspapers, on subway trains, and by direct mail." Even Kleenex™ tissues that have the club's phone number are available at train stations! One recent estimate claimed that in 1995 almost 6,000 girls were involved in "telephone club liaisons or other sex-related activities." About one-quarter of these girls were in junior high school. A 1996 government survey of 110 schools found that 4 percent of high school and 3.8 percent of junior high school girls had acted as "paid escorts" (Nguyen, nd; also noted in Blaylock, 2001).

South African countries also have a thriving child prostitution business, as noted in a recent UNICEF report (Perschlet-Desai, 2001). Citing chronic poverty, a breakdown of family support systems, and growing gender inequality, among other causes, the report notes that 98 percent of the children involved are females, with 26 percent being between 10 and 14 years of age. Most (69%) have dropped out of school. Twenty percent of the girls interviewed for the study said they had been sexually abused, mostly by members of their own family, by neighbors, or people at school. About half had contracted a sexually transmitted disease, usually gonorrhea. In Mozambique, the rate of HIV/AIDS has reached epidemic proportions: of a population of 17 million, about 1.5 million are infected. Around 600,000 children have been orphaned as a result.

One sees clearly in these countries the wretched interface between sexual and economic exploitation. In an increasingly global society, young Asian women are being reduced to expendable, sexual commodities to feed the jaded appetites of prosperous males. They are the international victims of what one critic called "the playboy mentality . . . which has reduced sex to a mere physicality . . . and the prostitute . . . to a mere object for sexual gratification" (Moselina, 1981: 24).

GIRLS AND VIOLENCE

If we are to believe the news media and some politicians, girls are getting progressively more violent each year. Hardly a week passes without there being some feature story about girls committing some "violent" act or statements to the effect that girls are getting just as violent as boys. Indeed, there has been a veritable flood of these news stories with essentially the same theme: today, girls are in gangs, they are "meaner" than girls in earlier generations, and, as a consequence, their behavior does not fit the traditional stereotype of female delinquency.

On August 6, 1993, for example, in a feature spread on teen violence, *Newsweek* had a box entitled "Girls Will Be Girls" which noted that "some girls now carry guns. Others hide razor blades in their mouths." Explaining this trend, the article noted that "The plague of teen violence is an equal-opportunity scourge. Crime by girls is on the rise, or so various jurisdictions report" (Leslie, 1993:44). Exactly a year earlier, a short-subject film appeared on a CBS program, entitled "Street Stories." "Girls in the Hood," a rebroadcast of a story first aired in January 1992, opened with this voice-over:

> Some of the politicians like to call this the Year of the Woman. The women you are about to meet probably aren't what they had in mind.

These women are active, they're independent, and they're exercising power in a field dominated by men. In January Harold Dowe first took us to the streets of Los Angeles to meet two uncommon women who are members of street gangs (CBS, 1992).

These stories are only two examples of the many media accounts that have appeared since journalists launched the second wave of the "liberation" hypothesis. Where did this latest trend come from? Perhaps the start was a *Wall Street Journal* article, "You've Come a Long Way, Moll," published on January 25, 1990. This news piece noted that "between 1978–1988 the number of women arrested for violent crimes went up 41.5 percent, vs. 23.1 percent for men. The trend is even starker for teenagers" (Crittenden, 1990:A14). But the trend was accelerated by the identification of a new, specific version of this more general revisiting of the liberation hypothesis. The *New York Times'* front-page story, entitled "For Gold Earrings and Protection, More Girls Take the Road to Violence," opened in this way:

> For Aleysha J., the road to crime has been paved with huge gold earrings and name brand clothes. At Aleysha's high school in the Bronx, popularity comes from looking the part. Aleysha's mother has no money to buy her nice things so the diminutive 15 year old steals them, an act that she feels makes her equal parts bad girl and liberated woman (Lee, 1991:A1).

This is followed by the assertion that "[t]here are more and more girls like Aleysha in troubled neighborhoods in the New York Metropolitan areas, people who work with children say. There are more girls in gangs, more girls in the drug trade, more girls carrying guns and knives, more girls in trouble." Whatever the original source, at this point a phenomenon known as "pack journalism" took over. The *Philadelphia Inquirer*, for instance, ran a story subtitled "Troubled Girls, Troubling Violence" on February 23, 1992, that claimed:

> Girls are committing more violent crimes than ever before. Girls used to get in trouble like this mostly as accomplices of boys, but that's no longer true. They don't need the boys. And their attitudes toward their crimes are often as hard as the weapons they wield—as shown in this account based on documents and interviews with participants, parents, police and school officials. While boys still account for the vast majority of juvenile crime, girls are starting to catch up (Santiago, 1992:A1).

This particular story featured a single incident in which an African American girl attacked another girl (described as "middle-class" and who appeared white in the photo that accompanied the story) in a subway. The *Washington Post* ran a similar story, entitled "Delinquent Girls Achieving a Violent Equality in D.C." on December 23, 1992 (Lewis, 1992), and the stories continue to appear. For example, about two years later (December 12, 1994), the *San Francisco Examiner* printed a story with the headline, "Ruthless Girlz" (Marinucci, Winokur, & Lewis, 1994).

Another example was a lead article in the *Boston Globe Magazine* (Ford, 1998). In large bold red letters, the title of this article tells it all: "BAD GIRLS." On the front page we are told the following:

> Until about 10 years ago, teenage girls seldom fought each other, even with fists. They did not carry knives and razors and box cutters. They did not form roaming packs and attack other girls. They did not fight with sticks, bats, and bricks. Though most of them still aren't likely to carry guns, girls are moving into the world of violence that once belonged to boys.

The writer presents cases that, although true, are caricatures of girl offenders. The story would suggest that we are, once again, being confronted with a "new breed" of "violent" female offenders that are getting just as wicked and evil as their male counterparts. We say "once again" because such sensationalistic accounts in newspapers have appeared on many occasions throughout the years. In fact, if one searched newspaper archives one could find similar accounts of female lawlessness (including violence) dating back as far as the early years of this century.

In virtually all stories on this topic, the issue is framed in a similar fashion. Typically, a specific and egregious example of female violence is described. This is followed by a quick review of the FBI's latest arrest statistics showing what appear to be large increases in the number of girls arrested for violent offenses, as well as quotes from the "experts," usually police officers, teachers, or various social service workers, but occasionally criminologists. Much of the "evidence" cited is anecdotal and the focus is almost always on a few isolated and exceptional cases (otherwise it would not be "news") followed by gross generalizations.

How should we respond to such exaggerated news stories? Are girls really getting as violent as boys? In this section we will explore this topic in great detail. Before we do this we must caution the reader that the use of words like "violence" and "assault" are value laden and cover a wide variety of behaviors, most of which are relatively harmless. For instance, both authors have examined juvenile court reports showing the number of referrals during a given year and, within the body of these reports, offenses are broken down according to several rather broad categories. Typically, one of these categories is "person crimes" (sometimes called "crimes against the person" or "personal crimes") and always the largest single category is that of "other assaults" (which do not involve the use of a weapon or result in serious injury). As we shall show below, the term "violent crime" lumps together assaults with deadly weapons leading to serious injuries and minor fist fights on high school campuses or, increasingly, fights between children and their parents.

Contrary to arrest data, self-report data of youthful involvement in violent offenses suggests that girls' violence and aggression is decreasing at a substantially greater rate than that of boys. For example, data collected by the Centers for Disease Control over the last decade support the decrease in girls' aggression. The CDC has been monitoring youthful behavior in a national sample of school aged youth in a number of domains (including violence) at regular intervals since 1991 in a biennial survey entitled the Youth Risk Behavior Survey. Data collected over the 1990s reveal that, whereas 34.4 percent of girls surveyed in 1991 said that they had been in a physical fight in the last year, by 1999 that figure had dropped to 27.3 percent (a 21 percent decrease in girls' fighting). Boys' violence also decreased during the same period but only slightly—from 44.0 percent to 42.5 percent (a 3.4% drop; Brener, Simon, Krug, & Lowry, 1999; Centers for Disease Control, 2000). Further, the number of girls who reported carrying weapons and guns declined substantially. Summarizing these trends, Brener, et al. (1999) concluded that, although there was a significant linear decrease in physical fighting for both male and female students, females seemed to have had a steeper decline. These findings are consistent with earlier research that revealed significant decreases in girls' involvement in felony assaults, minor assaults, and hard drugs, and no change in a wide range of other delinquent behaviors—including felony theft, minor theft, and index delinquency (Huizinga, 1997).

For this reason, self-report data, particularly from the 1970s and 1980s, has always shown higher involvement of girls in assaultive behavior than official statistics would indicate. As an example, Canter (1982) reported a male-versus-female, self-reported delinquency ratio of 3.4:1 for minor assault and 3.5:1 for serious assault. At that time, arrest statistics showed much greater male participation in aggravated assault (5.6:1; Federal Bureau of Investigation, 1980) and simple assault (3.8:1; Canter, 1982). Currently, arrest statistics show a 3.54:1 ratio for "aggravated assault" and a 2.25:1 ratio for "other assaults" (Federal Bureau of Investigation, 1999). Taken together, these numbers suggest a closing gap between what girls have always done (and reported, when asked anonymously) and arrest statistics rather than a course change in girls' participation in serious violence.

The trends in girls' lethal violence illustrate even more dramatic decreases over time. While girls' arrests for all forms of assault skyrocketed in the 1990s, girls' arrests for robbery fell by 45.3 percent and murder by 1.4 percent between 1991 and 2000 (Federal Bureau of Investigation, 2001). Further, recent research on girls' violence in San Francisco, which utilized vital statistics maintained by health officials (rather than arrest data), found that there has been a 63 percent drop in teen-girl fatalities between the 1960s and the 1990s, and that girls' hospital injuries were dramatically underrepresented among those reporting injuries, including assaults (Males & Shorter, 2001).

Relabeling Status Offenses

Why is it that arrest data suggest an increase in female juvenile delinquency, while self-report data suggest a decrease in it? Research suggests that it is likely that changes in enforcement practices have dramatically narrowed the gap in delinquency between girls and boys. Specifically, behaviors that were once categorized as status offenses (noncriminal offenses such as "runaway" and "person in need of supervision") and domestic violence have been increasingly relabeled into violent offenses, potentially accounting for increases in girls' arrest trends.

More specifically, changes in police practices with reference to domestic violence have resulted in an increased number of arrests of girls and women for assault. For example, a recent study of domestic violence arrests in California that included both juvenile and adult arrests revealed that over the past decade, girls' and women's share of these arrests nearly tripled (going from 6.0 percent in 1988 to 16.5 percent in 1998). African American girls and women had arrest rates roughly three times those of white girls and women in 1998: 149.6 compared to 46.4 (Bureau of Criminal Information and Analysis, 1999).

Girls' case files in various states highlight a similar trend of relabeling domestic violence into more serious offenses. Mayer (1994) reviewed over two thousand cases of girls referred to Maryland's juvenile justice system for "person-to-person" offenses. Although virtually all of these offenses (97.9%) involved "assault," about half of them were "family centered" and involved such activities as "a girl hitting her mother and her mother subsequently pressing charges" (p. 2). Similarly, Acoca (1999) examined nearly 1,000 girls' files from four California counties and found that a majority of their offenses involved assault. However, a close reading of these girls' case files revealed that most of their assault charges were the result of "nonserious, mutual combat situations with parents" (p. 8). Case descriptions ranged from self-defense (e.g., "father lunged at [daughter] while she was calling the police about a domestic dispute. [Daughter] hit him.") to trivial arguments (e.g., girl arrested "for throwing cookies at her mother").[2]

In Hawaii, there has been an increase in arrests of youth for serious crimes of violence coupled with a recent decline. In Hawaii, murder, rape, robbery, and aggravated assault increased 60 percent from 1987 to 1996, then declined 8.6 percent between 1996 and 1997 (Criminal Justice Statistics Center, 1999). Most of the change can be attributed to increases in the number of youths arrested for two offenses: aggravated assault and robbery. Between 1994 and 1996, for example, the number of youths arrested for robbery doubled.

Likewise for "violence" in schools. In Canada, for instance, Artz and Riecken (1999) reported that 20.9 percent of 703 adolescent girls surveyed in schools and 51.9 percent of 763 adolescent boys reported having "beaten up another kid" at least once or twice in the year in which the survey was conducted. This suggests a ratio of 2.5:1 for males over females and supports the notion that the gender gap is growing smaller.

Detailed comparisons drawn from supplemental homicide reports from unpublished FBI data also hint at the central, rather than peripheral, way in which gender has colored and differentiated girls' and boys' violence. In a study of these FBI data on the characteristics of girls' and boys' homicides between 1984 and 1993, Loper and Cornell (1996) found that girls accounted for "proportionately fewer homicides in 1993 (6%) than in 1984 (14%)" (p. 324). Additionally, they found that, in comparison to boys' homicides, girls who killed were more likely to use a knife than a gun and to murder someone as a result of conflict (rather than in the commission of a crime). Girls were also more likely than boys to murder family members (32%) and very young

Table 3-1. Actual and Potential Involvement in Physical Violence

	Females %	Males %	Source
Involved In:			
Physical fight in the past year	34	51	Adams et al.
	32	51	Kann et al.
Four or more physical fights in the past year	9	15	Adams et al.
Fought With:			
Stranger	7	15	Adams et al.
Friend	24	46	Adams et al.
Date/romantic partner	8	2	Adams et al.
Parent/sibling	34	9	Adams et al.
Other	4	6	Adams et al.
Several of the above	24	26	Adams et al.
Carried a Weapon:			
In the past month	7	17	Adams et al.
	9	34	Kann et al.

SOURCES: Adams et al. (1995: ages 14–17, 1992 data) and Kann et al. (1995: grades 9–12, 1993 data) in Girls, Inc., 1996.

victims (24 percent of their victims were under the age of three compared to 1 percent of the boy's victims). When involved in a peer homicide, girls were more likely than boys to have killed as a result of an interpersonal conflict and were more likely to kill alone, while boys were more likely to kill with an accomplice. Loper and Cornell concluded that "the stereotype of girls becoming gun-toting robbers was not supported. The dramatic increase in gun-related homicides . . . applies to boys but not girls" (p. 332).

Reitsma-Street (1999) notes that although the number of overall charges against girls in Canada in 1995/96 was at an all-time high, the absolute numbers for serious charges like arson, break and enter, fraud, robbery, major theft, and trafficking or possession of drugs were low and have remained constant.

To further support this notion, other research on trends in self-report data of youthful involvement in violent offenses also fails to show the dramatic changes found in official statistics. Specifically, a matched sample of "high risk" youth (aged 13–17) surveyed in the 1977 National Youth Study and the more recent 1989 Denver Youth Survey revealed significant decreases in girls' involvement in felony assaults, minor assaults, and hard drugs, and no change in a wide range of other delinquent behaviors—including felony theft, minor theft, and index delinquency (Huizinga, 1997). Further, a summary of two more recent studies on self-reported aggression (see Table 3-1) also reflects that while about a third of girls reported having been in a physical fight in the last year, this was true of over half of the boys in both samples (Girls Incorporated, 1996).

**Table 3-2. Canadian Boys and Girls Charged
with Homicide and Attempted Murder 1992–1996**

Type of Offense	Actual Number Charged by Year				
	1992	1993	1994	1995	1996
Homicide					
Boys	49	33	48	49	47
Girls	4	3	4	12	3
Attempted Murder					
Boys	66	61	103	81	81
Girls	12	9	9	4	6

SOURCE: DeKeseredy, W. (2000). *Women, Crime and the Canadian Criminal Justice System.* Cincinnati, OH: Anderson.

Table 3-3. Male and Female Youth Charged with Violent Crimes

Violent Crimes	Actual Number Charged by Year							
	1992	1993	1994	1995	1996	1997	1998	1999
Boys	15,734	16,381	16,753	17,288	17,206	16,556	16,534	15,787
Girls	4,294	5,096	4,903	5,153	5,315	5,616	5,661	5,294

SOURCE: Statistics Canada (2001). Youths and adults charged in criminal incidents, Criminal Code, federal and provincial statutes by sex. Ottawa, ON: CANSIM, Matrices 2198 and 2199 and Catalogue no. 85-205-XIB. www.statcan.ca/english/Pgdb/State/Justice/legal14.htm.

In Canada, DeKeseredy (2000) states that Canadian girls are not becoming more violent, although highly publicized freak, albeit horrific, events give the impression that violence among girls is increasing. The number of girls in Canada who commit homicide is so low that it makes it difficult to draw firm conclusions about differences between boys and girls. Although the typical female youth involved in violence is not profiled in the media, the public is horrified by the perspective on violent youth conveyed by the media's repeated recycling of "isolated incidents of extreme violence" (Corrado, Cohen, & Odgers, 1998: 13–14). Further, girls who kill their parents often do so for revenge against or escape from their abuse (DeKeseredy, 2000). Table 3-2 shows the number of boys and girls charged with homicide and attempted murder in Canada between 1992 and 1996. Table 3-3 shows the number of boys and girls charged with violent crimes in Canada between 1992 and 1999.

In viewing the tables above, one will note that actual numbers are presented, rather than rates of charges. Due to the low base rate among females who commit violent crimes, it is important to view actual numbers in order to avoid presenting a distorted picture. Corrado, Cohen, and Odgers (1998: 12) provide a good example: in Canada in 1986, 1,728 females were charged with violent crimes, as compared with 5,096 in 1993, while charges against males during the same period rose from 7,547 to 16,735. The increase for females was 3,368, while the increase for males was 8,828; however, if reported in terms of rate increases, the percentage increase for females would be much higher (approximately 295%) than the percentage for males (approximately 221%).

Aggression and Gender

What distinguishes girls' aggression from boys' aggression? Some studies have found very few observable differences between the two genders in manifestations of aggressive behaviors such as conduct problems (Tiet, Wasserman, Loeber, McReynolds, & Miller, 2001) and bullying (Gropper & Froschl, 2000). Nonetheless, much attention has been given in the research literature to the unique aspects of girls' aggression. This section will discuss two of these aspects—relational aggression and the effects of trauma.

The psychological literature that considers forms of aggression other than physical aggression (or violence) is also relevant here. For example, results from a large ($N = 16,038$) national longitudinal survey of children and youth (aged 4 to 11 years) in Canada indicate that although boys exhibit higher levels of physical aggression at all ages, girls demonstrate higher levels of indirect aggression (defined as "behavior aimed at hurting someone without the use of physical aggression"; Tremblay, 2000: 20) than do boys at each age from 4 to 11. This literature generally reflects that, while boys and men are more likely to be physically aggressive, differences begin to even out when verbal aggression is considered (yelling, insulting, teasing; Bjorkqvist & Niemela, 1992). Further, girls in adolescence may be more likely than boys to use "indirect aggression," such as gossip, telling bad or false stories, or telling secrets (Bjorkqvist, Osterman, & Kaukiainen, 1992). Tremblay (2000) contends that the use of indirect aggression increases with age for girls and boys. When this broad definition of "aggression" is utilized, only about 5 percent of the variance in aggression is explained by gender (Bjorkqvist & Niemela, 1992).

Research has suggested the presence of gender-specific forms of aggression in childhood and adolescence. These studies support the hypothesis that boys' aggression tends to be more "overt," such as hitting or pushing others or threatening to beat others up, whereas girls' aggression tends to be more "relational," or focused on damaging another child's friendships or feelings of inclusion by the peer group (Crick & Grotpeter, 1995; Lagerspetz & Bjorkqvist, 1994). Research has suggested that relationally aggressive youth experience more difficulties with social adjustment, as they are significantly more disliked and lonelier than nonrelationally aggressive peers (Crick & Grotpeter, 1995). These findings suggests that girls' aggression is rooted in significant relationships within childhood and adolescence, and, unlike boys, is less likely to focus on typical male behaviors such as physical dominance and intimidation. It also highlights the historically patriarchal context of the conceptualization of aggression, and the need to acknowledge its gender-specific manifestations.

Research suggests that trauma, particularly in the form of physical and sexual abuse, has a profound impact on the development of female juvenile delinquency. Artz (1998), for example, found that violent girls in Canada reported significantly greater rates of victimization and abuse than their nonviolent counterparts, and reported great fear of sexual assault, especially from their boyfriends. Artz found that 20 percent of violent girls reported they were physically abused at home (compared to 10 percent of violent males, and 6.3 percent of nonviolent girls) and that roughly one out of four violent girls had been sexually abused compared with one in ten of nonviolent girls. Dembo, et al. (1995) concluded, ["girls' problem behavior commonly relates to an abusive and traumatizing home life, whereas boys' law violating behavior reflects their involvement in a delinquent life style"] (p. 21).

Some research done in Australia is noteworthy here because the researchers look at gender differences in aggressive behavior (Owens, 1996, 1997) and distinguish between children's aggression toward same- and cross-sex targets (Russell & Owens, 1999). The results of their most recent study suggest that girls direct more physical aggression toward boys than to girls, but more verbal and indirect aggression toward girls than to boys. Thus, they indicate that "in the case of some forms of aggression, girls' aggression is directed more at other girls than to boys" (Russell & Owens, 1999: 374).

Those who study aggression in young children and young adults also note that girls' aggression is usually within the home or "intra-female" and, thus, likely to be less often reported to authorities (Bjorkqvist & Niemela, 1992). The fact that these forms of aggression have been largely ignored by scholars as well as the general public also means that there is substantial room for girls' aggression to be "discovered" at a time when concern about youthful violence is heightened. The historical lack of attention to girls' aggression can largely be explained by the small numbers of girls involved as represented by official statistics and the fact that violence has traditionally been viewed as masculine, thus, the girls who use it have not been deemed representative of female behavior (Artz, 1998).

Finally, girls' behavior, including violence, needs to be put in its patriarchal context. In her analysis of self-reported violence in girls in Canada, Artz (1998) has done precisely that, and the results were striking. In addition to noting that girls who had problems with violence had extensive histories of victimization, both at the hands of parents and boyfriends, follow-up interviews with a small group of violent girls to probe their behavior further found that these girls had learned at home that "might makes right" and engaged in "horizontal violence" directed at other powerless girls (often with boys as the audience). Certainly, these findings provide little ammunition for those who would contend that the "new" violent girl is a product of any form of "emancipation."

DeKeseredy (2000, p. 46) supports the contentions of Artz (1998) in noting that the "ideology of familial patriarchy . . . supports the abuse of women who violate the ideals of male power and control over women." This ideology is acted out by those males and females who insist upon women being obedient, respectful, loyal, dependent, sexually accessible, and sexually faithful to males (DeKeseredy, 2000). Artz (1998) suggests that violent girls more often than not "buy in" to these beliefs and "police" other girls' behaviors, thus serving to preserve the status quo, including their own continued oppression.

In their case studies of the life experiences of girls in custody in British Columbia, Canada, Artz, Blais, and Nicholson (2000: 31) found that the majority of girls were largely male-focused in that they wanted very much to have boyfriends and always made sure that they had at least one, both in and out of jail. One girl strongly identified with the boys and saw herself as "one of the guys," also admitting that she had "always wanted to be a boy." Only one girl spoke little about boys; at 18 years of age she was the oldest girl in the center. All the girls used derogatory terms to describe other girls, and when they spoke about girls, their words reflected views of females as "other." Many girls saw other girls as threats, particularly if they were pretty or "didn't know their place" (i.e., thought they were better than other girls). A "pretty" girl, or a girl to whom the boys pay attention, was a primary target for girl-to-girl victimization because she had the potential to unseat those who occupied the top rung on the "pretty power heirarchy" (Artz, Blais, & Nicholson, 2000: 124). An "ugly" or "dirty" girl (a girl designated a slut) was also a primary target for girl-to-girl victimization because she "deserved" to be beaten for her unappealing looks and for her "unacceptable" behavior.

However, what needs to be understood about girls' delinquency, particularly from a programmatic and policy standpoint, is the clear link between victimization, trauma, and girls' delinquency. The other major theme that must be addressed is the fact that most often this trauma produces not violent offenses but rather what have long been regarded as "trivial" or unimportant offenses such as running away from home.

Speaking of violent crime, the crime of robbery has traditionally been included within this broad category. Though typically a masculine crime, in recent years increasing numbers of women and girls have been charged with this offense, further leading to sensational reports of "violent girls and women." The next section explores this important topic in more detail.

Girls and Robbery

Although robbery arrests have declined during the past couple of years, these decreases came after years of steady increase, prompting some observers to note that the number of juvenile arrests for serious crimes of violence (murder, forcible rape, robbery, and aggravated assault) still remains considerably above levels recorded a decade earlier. Juveniles have accounted for about 30 percent of all robbery arrests in recent years, suggesting that a focus on juvenile robbery is important, both nationally and locally.

But what of girls' participation in the traditionally male offense of robbery? Here, the arrest evidence seems less easily explained. Are girls, in fact, engaging in nontraditional criminal behavior? Are girls getting more violent?

To answer this question, robbery itself must first be understood. Steffensmeier and Allan (1995) found that offenses such as robbery fit the low-yield, criminal mischief category of offenses—a category that also shows the youngest peaks and sharpest declines. They contend that because of the increased risk and relatively low yield involved in robbery, its appeal decreases to maturing youth. Such a decrease is particularly sharp as peer support for such behavior declines and bonds to society are strengthened.

Popular youth culture, which stresses the importance of name brand clothing, gold jewelry, and expensive electronic gear, often visibly separates the "haves" from the "have-nots" and appears to play a major role in robbery, particularly juvenile robbery. Youth status, then, coupled with the economic marginality of some urban youth, creates a fertile environment for robbery; in short, at least some youth resort to victimizing their peers in order to obtain material goods they could not otherwise afford.

Other research has amplified these findings, noting that youth also commit robbery offenses for reasons less related to economics. The thrill and excitement associated with street robbery, coupled with a desire to target individuals who are perceived as "show-offs," motivates some youth to participate in robberies (Sommers & Baskin, 1993; Miller, 1998b). Existing research also indicates that juvenile robberies are not sophisticated and planned offenses, but rather are impulsive and spontaneous events. Juvenile robbers are less likely to victimize the elderly and most likely to victimize their peers. And although gang involvement was not consistently mentioned in the literature, it is clear that juvenile robberies are generally committed by two or more people.

The literature also establishes that robbery is a particularly gendered offense. Boys tend to commit the vast majority of offenses, perhaps because the robbery setting provides the ideal opportunity to construct an "essential" toughness and "maleness" (Katz, 1988; Messerschmidt, 1993; Miller, 1998). Typically, male-on-male robberies occur on the streets and entail more physical violence. Female robberies are less frequent, and, although occurring on the streets, do not usually involve serious physical violence; they can, however, involve physical contact such as hitting, shoving, and fighting with the victim.

Although females commit fewer robbery offenses than do males, both males and females express similar reasons for engaging in robbery. In a significant qualitative review of the role of gender in robbery, Miller analyzed interviews with youthful robbers in St. Louis, Missouri (1998b), and concluded that the acquisition of money and "status-conferring goods," such as jewelry, is the primary motivation for committing the offense for both males and females.

Males are most likely to use weapons when committing a robbery. In Miller's study, for example, all of the males in the sample reported using a gun. Males use physical violence and weapons as a way of accomplishing gender and displaying masculinity (Simpson & Ellis, 1995: 50). Female robberies tend not to include weapons because females typically prey on other females, and female victims tend to be more submissive and less likely to fight back (Miller, 1998b).

Qualitative research, however, cannot fully address the changes that have been observed over time in the offense of juvenile robbery. For this reason, to help answer some of these questions, research was conducted by the senior author (Chesney-Lind) and Paramore in 1998. This study utilized City and

County of Honolulu Police Department juvenile robbery incident files, which contained extensive details of actual robberies in which juveniles were arrested for two time periods: 1991 and 1997.

By way of background, Hawaii, like the rest of the nation, had seen an increase in the arrests of youth for serious crimes of violence, in the last decade, coupled with a more recent decline. Specifically, arrests of youth for the violent crimes of murder, rape, robbery, and aggravated assault increased 60% from 1987 to 1996 coupled with an 8.6% decline between 1996 and 1997 (Crime in Hawaii, 1996, 1997). Most of the change could be attributed to increases in the number of youth arrested for two offenses: aggravated assault and robbery. Between 1994 and 1996, for example, the number of youth arrested for robbery doubled in Honolulu.

These increases prompted a study of the actual dimensions of juvenile robbery in Honolulu (see Chesney-Lind & Paramore, 2001). In this study, police files from two time periods (1991 and 1997) that focused on robbery incidents resulting in arrest were identified. According to these data, in 1991, the vast majority of those arrested for robbery in Honolulu were male—114 (95%) versus 6 (5%) female. However, a shift occurred in 1997—83.3% were males. Thus, the proportion of robbery arrests involving girls more than tripled, between 1991 and 1997.

Taken alone, these numeric increases, along with anecdotal information, are precisely why the "surge" in girls' violence has been made. However, in this study, we were able to carefully characterize of each of these "robberies" during the two time periods. Essentially, the data suggested that no major shift in the pattern of juvenile robbery occurred between 1991 to 1997 in Honolulu. Rather it appears that less serious offenses, including a number committed by girls, are being swept up into the system perhaps as a result of changes in school policy and parental attitudes (many of the robberies occurred as youth were going to and from school). Consistent with this explanation are the following observable patterns in our data: during the two time periods under review, the age of offenders shifts downward, as does the value of items taken. In 1991, the median value of the items stolen was $10.00; by 1997, the median value had dropped to $1.25. Most significantly, the proportion of adult victims declines sharply while the number of juvenile victims increases. Finally, while more of the robberies involved weapons in 1997, those weapons were less likely to be firearms and the incidents were less likely to result in injury to the victim. In short, the data suggest that the problem of juvenile robbery in the City and County of Honolulu is largely characterized by slightly older youth bullying and "hi-jacking" younger youth for small amounts of cash and occasionally jewelry and that arrests of youth for these forms of robbery accounted for virtually all of the increase observed.

It does appear that gender matters in juvenile robbery. Most of the victims of girls arrested for robbery were other girls from whom they took small amounts of cash and personal items. Artz (1998), in her research on violent girls, has suggested that girls' aggression is much like the "horizontal violence" found in other powerless groups. Here girls mimic the oppressor's behavior (male violence) and beat up similarly situated girls, often on the most specious of pretexts. Such behavior may give the girl who commits the act a fleeting sense of power, but it ultimately does little to advance her status (since she can never be a boy). Artz contends that such female-on-female violence does little to challenge the sexual status quo and becomes a form of tension release that affirms rather than challenges the sex/gender system in high schools. Moreover, as virtually all of Artz' girls demonstrate, today's victor is tomorrow's victim; the girls she interviewed were staying away from school because of fear of future violence and victimization, often at the hands of former girlfriends or acquaintances. One girl even told her that she was getting really mad at another girl "because she reminds me of me" (Artz, 1998: 124). Artz also found that violent girls, but not necessarily violent boys, had more serious histories of physical/sexual violence at home, although the same was not found with violent boys (who were more impacted by violent neighborhoods); violent girls were also more fearful of assaults from boyfriends than were nonviolent girls.

SUMMARY

In this chapter we have examined several forms of female delinquency. Despite dramatic differences in the types of offenses and crimes in which girls become involved, there are certain similarities. First and foremost, girls' delinquencies are shaped by the unique problems they face in a society that gives women, particularly girls, very little power, few options, and even fewer civil rights. These burdens become even heavier when girls' problems are compounded by poverty, abusive families, and membership in a minority ethnic group.

Status offenses have always been closely identified with female delinquency. Running away from home and being unmanageable or incorrigible have long been seen as typically female offenses. The prevalence of status offenses in girls' delinquency, we have argued, stems in part from the parental desire to control the behavior of girls. Gender bias is suggested in comparisons of referrals to juvenile court with self-report studies that show that boys and girls are about equally likely to commit these types of offenses. The bias is even more troubling when one considers that persistent status offense behavior, notably running away, in girls appears to be linked to abuse, especially sexual abuse, within the home.

Running away very often leads girls to commit a variety of crimes in order to survive, among them engaging in prostitution. Girls who join the ranks of street youth often end up in the world of prostitution, where their abuse continues at the hands of pimps and customers alike. Even more tragic is international prostitution, wherein the extreme powerlessness of girls in impoverished Asian societies has resulted in overt commodification.

Shoplifting has consistently been the most common property offense committed by girls. From the few available studies, it appears that girls and boys are about equally likely to shoplift, but girls are more likely to be detected by store personnel, arrested by the police, and referred to juvenile court. Items stolen by girls are of lesser value than those stolen by boys, and girls are more apt to be amateurs. Most of the items girls steal are for personal use and may be linked to their desire to conform to a standard of female beauty and appearance that is otherwise inaccessible to poor girls.

Robbery, a non-traditional girls offense, suggests a newer trend in girl's arrests. Basically, as the societal concern about youth violence more broadly increases, and more minor forms of violence are now not ignored but instead criminalized, we can expect to see more girls brought into the juvenile justice system for offenses that were once thought to be typically male. Even in these incidents, though, gender plays an important role. Girls tend to rob other girls, not boys; and on the rare occasions where they do rob males, girls typically rely on their gender to entrap the victim rather than relying on physical strength and intimidation as do boys and men who rob.

Our understanding of girls' delinquency is sketchy at best. Very little is known about the few girls who commit serious, violent crimes. Also, little is known about girls and property crime, aside from shoplifting (and even here the evidence is scanty). Even in areas extensively researched, as in the case of status offenses, a review of the literature reveals the need for objective inquiry. In essence, investigation of girls' lives and their troubles, uncluttered by stereotypical thinking, has begun only within the past few decades. Studies that have been done suggest that girls' unique situations in communities deeply divided by race, class, and gender have a definite impact on the character of girls' crime, whether trivial or serious.

NOTES

1. Bottcher's study of ten girls in the California Youth Authority illustrates these problems well (Bottcher, 1986). Her study will be discussed in more detail in Chapter 9.

2. We should note at this time that despite what this research indicates, recent statistics have identified the rising use of detention with girls and the disproportionate representation of girls of color in detention. These issues will be discussed in Chapter 8.

3. Robbery refers to the taking of another person's property, through either the use or threatened use of physical force.

4

Girls and Gangs

eginning in the early part of the 1990s, there was a resurgence of interest in female offenders who engage in nontraditional, masculine crimes—particularly their involvement in gangs. The purpose of this chapter is to critically assess whether girls are becoming more like their male counterparts in relation to gang activities.

Girls' involvement in delinquent gangs has never been of the same magnitude as boys'. Indeed, the stereotype of the delinquent in general is that of a male. The subject of girl delinquents in general, and girl gang members in particular, has been largely ignored. When girls and women are mentioned, it is often through media stereotypes of bad, evil, or even overly masculine girls, ignoring the social context, especially that for young minority women (Joe & Chesney-Lind, 1993: 3; see also Chesney-Lind, 1993). Traditional discussions of gang delinquency, from Thrasher's work in Chicago in the 1920s (1927) to more recent accounts (Cohen, 1955; Cloward & Ohlin, 1960; Short & Strodbeck, 1965; Keiser, 1969; Dawley, 1992), stress the image of girls as playing auxiliary roles to boys' gangs, if they are involved in gang activity at all. In fact, in his study of over 1,000 gangs in Chicago, Thrasher discovered only six female gangs, and only two of these he called true gangs. The stereotypical gang role for girls was "to conceal and carry weapons for the boys, to provide sexual favors, and sometimes to fight against girls who were connected with enemy boys' gangs" (Mann, 1984: 45). Most of the earlier accounts of girls' roles in gangs were based on data given by male gang members to male researchers and then in turn interpreted by male academics, which no doubt reinforced traditional stereotypes (Campbell, 1990: 166). More often than not, girl gang members have been portrayed "as maladjusted tomboys or sexual chattel who, in either case, are no more than mere appendages to boy members of the gang" (Joe & Chesney-Lind, 1993: 8).

Such impressions are often reinforced by male studies of girl gang members. Walter Miller's nationwide study of gangs in the mid-1970s, for example, found fully independent girl gangs to be rare, constituting less than 10 percent of all gangs. He also noted that about half the male gangs in the New York area had female auxiliary groups and that, of all the gangs known to exist in the Bronx and Queens areas of New York City, there were only six independent female gangs. Further, he reported that the crimes committed by girl gangs were far less serious than those committed by boy gangs and were no more violent than in the past (Miller, 1975). In contrast, Joan Moore's research on gangs in East Los Angeles estimated that about one-third of the gang members were female (Moore, 1991: 8).

 Given the range of estimates, one might wonder whether girls and their involvement with gang life resembles the involvement of girls in other youth subcultures, where they have been described as "present but invisible" (McRobbie & Garber, 1975). Certainly, Moore's higher estimate indicates that she and her associates saw girls that others had missed. The long-standing "gendered habits" of researchers has meant that girls' involvement with gangs has been neglected, sexualized, and oversimplified.[1] So, although there have been a growing number of studies investigating the connections between male gangs, violence, and other criminal activities, there has been relatively little parallel development in research on female involvement in gang activity. The recent excellent study by Jody Miller (2001) is a welcome exception. As with all young women who find their way into the juvenile justice system, girls in gangs have been invisible.

This pattern of invisibility was undoubtedly set by Thrasher and carried on by many subsequent, mostly male, researchers. Jankowski (1991), for instance, sees gangs as a distinctly male phenomenon, and females are discussed in the context of "property" and "sex." Curiously, when female researchers have studied female gang members, a different perspective emerges, one which suggests that girl gang members do *not* fully accept such conceptions of their roles and positions. Miller notes that many scholars have argued that "gender is no longer relevant on the streets" (Miller, 2001: 5). This will become evident when we review some of these studies below.

Taylor's (1993) work marks a complete reversal in themes: girls are the central focus, but from a male-centered perspective. His work, like Thrasher's and Jankowski's, is a reflection of a general tendency to minimize and distort the motivations and roles of female gang members, and is the result of the gender bias on the part of the male gang researchers, who describe the female experience from the male gang member's viewpoint or from their own stance (Campbell, 1990). Taylor himself, throughout his study, repeats some of the same tired stereotypes of girl gang members as sexual property of gang boys or as ruthless, degendered tomboys.

Taylor's study provides a facade of academic support for the media's definition of the girl gang member as a junior version of the liberated female crook of the 1970s. It should be noted that it is difficult to determine exactly how many girls and women he interviewed for his book (and there are many methodological shortcomings that seriously call into question his findings), but his introduction clearly sets the tone for his work when he writes: "We have found that females are just as capable as males of being ruthless insofar as their life opportunities are presented. This study indicates that females have moved beyond the status quo of gender repression" (Taylor, 1993: 8).

Other studies of female gang members stress the image of girls as having auxiliary roles to boy gangs (Miller, 1975, 1980; Rice, 1963; Brown, 1977; Flowers, 1987). Miller (1980) also conducted an in-depth analysis of a Boston gang known as The Molls. This gang consisted of a core membership of 11 girls whose ages ranged from 13 to 16. They were white and Catholic (mostly Irish). These girls seemed to fit the stereotype of inner-city working-class girls, as they spent most of their time "hanging out" around street corners and looking and talking tough. They were known in the neighborhood as "bad girls." Their illegal activities included truancy, theft, drinking, property damage, sex offenses, and assault, in order of decreasing frequency. Truancy was by far their most common offense, occurring about three times as often as the next most common offense, which was theft (predominantly shoplifting).

Similar findings have been reported in Philadelphia (Brown, 1977) and in New York City (Campbell, 1984). In general, although there have been some changes and some indications that girls are becoming more independent and aggressive, overall these studies portray girls who are part of gangs as either the girlfriends of the male members or "little sisters" subgroups of the male gang (Bowker, 1978: 184; Hanson, 1964). Further, they suggest that the role for girls in gangs is "to conceal and carry weapons for the boys, to provide sexual favors, and sometimes to fight against girls who were connected with enemy boys' gangs (Mann, 1984: 45).

Girl gangs typically emerge after a male gang has been established and it "often takes a feminized version of the male name" (Campbell, 1990: 177). Examples of the latter include the Egyptian Cobrettes (related to the male gang called the Egyptian Cobras), the Lady Rocketeers (affiliated with the male Rocketeers), and the Vice Queens (related to the Vice Kings) (Bowker, 1978: 144). One group was known as The Dagger Debs, a female Puerto Rican gang in New York City, and was associated with a male counterpart known as the Daggers. This group, consisting of about 14 full-time members, was described as a tough gang that exhibited typical "male" behavior. It was observed that they were aggressive and took an active role in gang wars (Hanson, 1964; see also Prothrow-Stith, 1991 and Fishman, 1988).

According to Campbell (1984: 9), in New York City there are as many as 400 gangs with a membership of about 40,000. About ten percent of the gang members are female. Their ages usually range from 14 to 30. Some are married with children and all are from working or lower class backgrounds. The earliest gangs in the New York City area date back to 1825 to a gang called the

"Forty Thieves" located in lower Manhattan (Campbell, 1984). This gang consisted mainly of Irish youth and originated from a drinking spot owned by a woman. Soon other gangs formed; again, mostly Irish. The earliest gang wars lasted two or three days without interference by the police. Women were not excluded from the fighting. Gangs were diversified even then, with some members fighting for the group and some who were only interested in financial gain. Women were involved in each type of gang. They were usually viewed as instigators of activities. They were generally seen as auxiliary to the male gangs. They functioned as weapons holders, alibi givers, spies, and lures, and to provide sex for the male members.

The area of East Los Angeles provides a fascinating glimpse of how gangs emerge and change with the times. Gangs in this area first emerged during the late 1930s and early 1940s; girl gangs came along with male gangs. Many gangs started in an area known as El Hoyo Maravilla (translated roughly as "the hole" in Spanish). The girl gangs in Maravilla (going by such names as Black Legion, Cherries, Elks, Black Cats, and others) were small groups not tightly bound to the boy gangs and not as closely bound to a specific barrio as were the boys. They often partied with boys from different gangs (Moore, 1991: 27–28).[2]

In the mid-1940s there were some girl gangs that were auxiliaries to the boy gangs (for example, Jr. Vamps, who were associated with the Cut-downs). The girl gangs from the White Fence area were more like the traditional auxiliary girl gangs. Many offshoots of these gangs continue to flourish today, some 70 years later. The fact that they have existed so long may contribute to the media's continued fascination with girl gangs. It is unfortunate that the vast research on these and other girl gangs (showing the incredible diversity of these groups) is usually ignored by the mass media. Instead, we are too often presented with stereotypic images (for a fuller treatment of the media's treatment of girl gangs, see Chesney-Lind and Shelden, 1998: 45–47).

TRENDS IN GIRL GANG MEMBERSHIP

Media portrayals of young women suggest that they, like their male counterparts, are increasingly involved in gang activities. Several sources of information are available to look at this issue.

Girl Gang Membership and Crimes

Official estimates of the number of youth involved in gangs have increased dramatically over the past decade, as noted in Chapter 1. But what is the role of gender in gang membership? Let us look more closely at the characteristics of youth labeled by police as gang members. One report in the early 1980s noted that in New York City police estimated that about half of all gangs had female members (Dolan & Finney, 1984). In Los Angeles, for each male gang, there is one or more female group. However, these claims may be highly exaggerated. According to the "GREAT" database program (Fall, 1991), only about

6 percent of all gang members in Los Angeles County were female (Reiner, 1992: 111). A 1992 survey showed the exact same percentage (Howell, 1998). Esbensen and Huizinga (1993) found in their Denver gang study that 25 percent of all gang members were females; Moore estimated that gang membership in Los Angeles included one-third females (Moore, 1991). Some self-report studies put the percentages much higher, such as the 38 percent figure reported in an 11-city survey of eighth graders (Esbensen & Osgood, 1997).

Bjerregaard and Smith (1993) found that in every offense category, female gang members had a higher rate of delinquent offenses than nongang females. Fagan (1990) also found high levels of involvement in serious delinquency among female gang members in Chicago, Los Angeles, and San Diego; in fact, in all delinquent categories, including violent acts, female gang members committed more offenses than nongang males (Howell, 1998). Curry and his associates found that girls are three times more likely than boys to be involved in "property offenses" and about half as likely to be involved in violent offenses. Looking at these statistics differently, only girls' involvement in property offenses exceeded one percent of the total number of offenses tracked nationally. Contrary to popular conceptions about "violent girls," only 8 (0.7%) of the 1,072 gang-related homicides in this data set were attributed to girls. Homicides by girls differ significantly from those committed by boys. According to one study, girls' homicides are more likely to grow out of an interpersonal dispute with the victim (79%), while homicides committed by boys are more likely to be crime related (57%); that is, occurring during the commission of another crime, such as robbery (Loper & Cornell, 1995).

Many argue that law enforcement agencies tend to minimize female gang membership. Curry (1998: 20) has suggested that law enforcement might not view female gang involvement as serious enough to be considered a problem. As noted earlier, researchers and law enforcement personnel have had "gendered habits," and as a result, females have been invisible as gang members, as they had historically been invisible as potential crime- and fire-fighters (see also Sikes, 1997).

A study by Curry, Ball, and Fox (1994) noted that some cities reported that as a matter of policy, females were not counted as gang members; a few cities counted them as "associate gang members"; of those law enforcement agencies with gang problems, no statistics on females were kept and nine more felt confident in reporting no female gang members.

Sikes (1997) posits that investigating females in gangs is of low priority to law enforcement agencies. Many gang girls are minors; thus, police have less inclination to deal with these girls because they believe that the juvenile justice agencies will simply ignore the problem or release the girls immediately. They view females as less a threat than males and so, Sikes believes, this preserves an attitude that "leads to both an over[]identification of those boys only on the fringes of gang activity as bona fide gang members and an under[]representation of girls" (Sikes, 1997: 66).

A more detailed look at differences between male and female gang members in police databases can be obtained from a study that analyzed files maintained by the Honolulu Police Department (HPD). Examining the characteristics of a sample of youth ($N = 361$) labeled as gang members by the HPD in 1991 (Chesney-Lind et al., 1994), this study specifically examined the total offense patterns of those labeled as gang members, and it also compared a juvenile subsample of these individuals with nongang delinquents.

The study found patterns consistent with the national data. For example, only 7 percent of the suspected gang members on Oahu were female and, surprisingly, the vast majority of these young women were legally adults (70%); the median age for the young women was 24.5 and 21.5 for the men in the sample.

Virtually all the youth identified as gang members were drawn from low-income ethnic groups in the islands, but these ethnic differences were also found between male and female gang members. The men were more likely than the women to come almost exclusively from immigrant groups (Samoan and Filipino); the women, by contrast, were more likely to be Native Hawaiian and Filipino.

Most important, women and girls labeled as gang members committed fewer and less serious offenses than men did. Indeed, the offense profile for the females in the gang sample bears a very close relationship to typical female delinquency. Over one-third of the "most serious" arrests of girls (38.1%) were for status offenses (19%), and drug offenses (9.5%) follow property offenses (mostly larceny–theft). For boys, the most serious offense was likely to be "other assaults" (27%), followed by larceny–theft (14%). In essence, this profile indicated that although both the males and females in this sample of suspected gang members were chronic but not serious offenders, this was particularly true of the girls. These offense patterns correspond closely to overall national arrest patterns, especially for the girls (see Chapter 2). Serious violent offenses accounted for 23 percent of the most serious offenses of males suspected of gang membership, but *none* of the girls' most serious offenses.

Finally, it is important to note that once police identified a youth as a gang member, that person apparently remained in the database regardless of patterns of desistance; for example, 22 percent of the sample had not been arrested in three years and there was no gender difference in this pattern.

These patterns prompted a further exploration of the degree to which young women labeled by police as "suspected gang members" differed from young women who had been arrested for delinquency. To do this, a comparison group was created for those in the Oahu sample who were legally juveniles. Youth suspected of gang membership were matched on ethnicity, age, and gender with youth who were in the juvenile arrest data base, but who had not been labeled as gang members. A look at offense patterns of this smaller group indicates no major differences between girls suspected of gang membership and their nongang counterparts. The modal most serious offense for gang girls was status offenses, and for nongang girls it was other assaults.[3]

These quantitative data do not provide support for claims of the rise of a "new" violent female offender. Yet we still have an inadequate understanding of the lives of girl gang members. There have been a small but growing number of excellent ethnographic studies of girls in gangs, which suggest a much more complex picture in which some girls solve their problems of gender, race, and class through gang membership. As we review these studies later in this chapter, it will become clear that girls' experiences with gangs cannot simply be framed as "breaking into" a male world. They have long been in gangs and their participation in these gangs, even their violence, is heavily influenced by their gender.

Types of Female Gangs

There are three types of female gang involvement: (1) membership in an independent gang, (2) regular membership in a male gang as a coed, and (3) as female auxiliaries of male gangs. Most girls are found within the third type.[4]

Auxiliaries usually form after a male gang comes into existence and, as noted earlier, usually take a feminized version of the boys' gang name. They often reflect the age grouping found in male units. They have no formal leader but usually have some members with more clout than others. Girls are not coerced to join. Rather, they come into the gang through regular friendships and families. "Wannabes" are informally screened for acceptability. Initiation usually involves an intense fistfight with a regular (girl) member of the gang to prove the wannabe's courage. Initiation ceremonies are not unlike those conducted by sororities or fraternities or even country clubs (Campbell, 1993: 136). "The gang will not accept just anyone, and this fact alone augments the members' self-esteem, which has taken such hard knocks from teachers, social workers, police, and families. The gang rejects 'prospects' whose aim is merely to avail themselves of the gang's fighting ability for their own ends" (Ibid.).

Even these auxiliary gangs are more than mere appendages of the male gangs, for many of the girls have some control over their own gang. They collect dues, hold meetings, expel members for violating rules, and so on. Strong normative control is exerted over members of the gang. For instance, once a girl becomes involved with a boy, she must remain loyal while the relationship lasts. Remaining loyal to the boy is important because suspicion and jealousy are extremely disruptive, and a norm of fidelity seeks to prevent this. Girl gangs usually fight other girl gangs (sometimes even boy gangs). However, girls generally do not use guns but, rather, fight with fists or knives. There is recent evidence that this may be changing for some gangs as more and more guns become available and as fewer legitimate opportunities become available for underclass women.

Many of these young women are becoming less attached to male gangs. Campbell's study (1984a) of independent female gangs in New York illustrates this. She found that these gangs exist as their own unique subculture in an attempt to survive within the larger capitalist society. Similarly, Taylor's most recent study of Detroit gangs focused on female gangs, which he describes as much more independent and more willing to use force than did earlier girl gangs. Much of the violence, especially utilizing weapons, is an effort at survival in a difficult and cruel world. Taylor quotes one gang member: "Look, it's easy for somebody that lives in some quiet place to talk 'bout violence. But, come and live with us and you'll be carrying a gun or two yourself." Another stated: "Call it violence if you want, but I say it's just taking care of yourself" (Taylor, 1993: 100). Kitchen (1995: 43) notes that many female gang members "are rejecting the roles as mere extensions of male gangs, and working for males as drug runners and prostitutes. These females see the only way out of the ghetto life, while keeping their self-respect, is through the creation of their own crews, with their own rules and values."

Many recent scholars have suggested that severe economic and social changes within the inner cities have lessened the importance of gender, at least on the streets within the gang context. Jody Miller notes that the "convergence of economic marginality and the growth in drug markets have resulted in a lessening of social control over young women, who have developed role models on the street that guide them toward increased participation in these contexts" (Miller, 2001: 5). She also notes that some scholars have argued that many young women on the streets within the inner cities have created, in some instances, greater autonomy, partly reflected in greater participation in the drug trade. On the other hand, critics of this position note that those who suggest that gender has less relevance confuse the activities of women with equality. Miller observes, rightly, that "gender inequality remains a cornerstone of the urban street scene," which contradicts the claim that the women's movement has created equality on the streets (Miller, 2001: 7).

MOVING BEYOND THE STEREOTYPES: THE SOCIAL CONTEXT OF GIRL GANGS

During the past two decades several firsthand accounts of girl gangs have been conducted in a wide variety of settings, literally covering the breadth of the United States, from Hawaii to New York. Several themes emerge from these studies: (1) the importance of class and race; (2) crimes and drug use; (3) reasons for joining the gang (including some benefits); (4) their relationship with male gangs and males in general (including being victimized); (5) family-related issues; and (6) school and work issues. We will cover each of these themes in the following sections.

Class and Race

Kitchen's study in Fort Wayne, Indiana, revealed some strong feelings about race and racism. Her respondents had some very strong feelings about the society they lived in, expressing the belief that racism was fundamental. One gang member expressed her feelings this way: "I think people are racist, because they always stop and look at me funny, and think I'm going to rob them or beat them up. Everyone is scared of you if you black." Another complained that "every time I go to the store with my friends the managers, or security, are always following us around. Like they think 'cause we black we couldn't afford to buy nothin' so we must be stealing" (Kitchen, 1995: 100).

Kitchen's study demonstrates the dual problems faced by African American women: racism and sexism. The world they inhabit does not afford many legitimate opportunities to succeed. It is a world filled with poverty on the one hand and the ready availability of drugs on the other hand. Selling drugs becomes an accepted part of an informal economy that has become institutionalized over many years. It is capitalism in its purest form—a product is in demand, and there are many willing to provide the goods. Whereas African American women face many barriers in the legitimate world of work, including the consternation of males who do not approve of women who are in any way tough and assertive, they find acceptance and respect in the world of drug dealing.

Miller's study of Columbus and St. Louis gangs found that both class and race were of paramount importance. Both race and class was even more crucial in St. Louis, as there were more living in poverty than in Columbus and almost all of the girls were African American (89%), while the rest were other racial minorities. In Columbus, where the poverty level was not quite as high as in St. Louis, about one-fourth of the gang members were white (Miller, 2001: 93).

A study by Joe and Chesney-Lind of girl gang members in Hawaii found that these gang members come from many different ethnic backgrounds from those normally found on the mainland. Honolulu, its major city, currently has around 171 different gangs, with an estimated membership of 1,267. The majority of the girls were either Filipino or Samoan, whom the authors describe as part of the "have-not" ethnic groups (Joe and Chesney-Lind, 1993: 14).

A study of 65 female gang members in San Francisco (Lauderback, Hansen, & Waldorf, 1992) found that race was of critical importance, as the majority of the seven gangs studied were Latinas (78.5 percent), with African Americans (15.4 percent) and Samoans (6.2 percent) comprising the remainder. Some noteworthy differences were found when comparing Latina and African American gang members. The African Americans were less likely to be affiliated with male gangs, while Latinas were more likely. Latina gang members were also more likely to be involved in activities with their male counterparts, while the African American female gang members were more likely to engage in activities (for example, drug sales) on their own. All of the African American gang members were actively involved in selling drugs. For the total sample, however, less than one-half were involved in selling drugs.

A study of Hispanic girl gangs in southern California shows that there are few economic opportunities within the barrio. As a result, families are disintegrating and do not have the capability of providing access to culturally emphasized success goals for young people about to enter adulthood. Not surprisingly, almost all activities of young people occur within the context of gang life, where they learn how to get along in the world and are insulated from the harsh environment of the barrio (Quicker, 1983).

Harper and Robinson (1999) demonstrated the importance of social class in a study. Those girls who identified themselves as current (7.1%) or past (14.3%) gang members had the following characteristics: 96 percent of their families were receiving unemployment or welfare benefits; 56 percent were receiving food stamps; 71 percent received reduced-cost or free lunches at school; 48 percent were from single-parent families.

The economic context of gangs in general, both male and female, cannot be ignored, especially given the occupational structure of America. A quote from a "crew" member by Taylor (1990: 57) illustrates this. She flatly stated that: "Better paying jobs ain't in this world for bloods, especially young bloods. I been kicking it with a crew since I was thirteen. . . . Some of the fellahs after that got busted, had to join job training fake-ass programs. Train you for what? A cook? Bullshit janitor job? A security guard that pays $3.65 an hour?" Kitchen's study provides additional documentation of the economic deprivation underclass women, especially African American women, face today. The specific area she studied (South Central Fort Wayne) had a poverty level that was higher than that of the city as a whole and higher than the national average (almost 40 percent of all persons and 27 percent of all families were below the poverty level). For African Americans the percentages were even higher (38.5 percent of all African American persons and 39.5 percent of all African American families). African American females in this part of Fort Wayne fared even worse: over half (54.2%) of African American female-headed households lived under the poverty level (Kitchen, 1995: 84). The gang members Kitchen studied had some job experience but most were in low-paying, service industries.

A study by Laidler and Hunt (1997) found that most of the girl gang members either grew up in the same housing project or knew a relative associated with their group. The majority of these females were immigrants. Thirty-five percent of the fathers were absent; others were semi-skilled or unskilled laborers. Their mothers were in the service industry or in unskilled jobs; 25 percent were homemakers/babysitters.

It is important to emphasize the social context of poverty within which girl gangs exist and to examine what it means to be a young girl growing up in such an environment. Campbell notes that female gang members "seek to resolve the intractable problems of class by simultaneously rejecting and opposing some aspects of community and mainstream values while incorporating and internalizing others. Their resulting identity is often apparently contradictory or incoherent" (1990: 172). Campbell argues that, at least for the young female gang members she studied in New York, there are five major problems such poverty-class girls face and to which they seek answers within the gang (Ibid.: 172–173):

(1) "A future of meaningless domestic labor with little possibility of educational or occupational escape." Indeed, most are from welfare families and have dropped out of school and thus have few marketable skills.

(2) "Subordination to the man in the house." Especially within the Hispanic culture, the woman must submit to the man and has no say in the matter.

(3) "Responsibility for children." This job is hers and hers alone and this further restricts her options.

(4) "The social isolation of the housewife." She becomes trapped within the home with, at best, a few friends who are also housewives.

(5) "The powerlessness of underclass membership." As a member of this class, she is not only removed from the social and economic world, but is potentially a victim of crime within her own neighborhood.

Crime and Drugs

Most studies of gangs show that gang membership tends to increase individuals' rates of delinquency, which tend to decrease after they leave (Shelden, Tracy, & Brown, 2001). The research is also clear that male gang members commit far more crimes than their female counterparts. A study by Esbensen, Descheses, and Winfree (1999) found that gang girls, though involved in a much lower number of incidents, are very similar to gang boys in the types of illegal acts they commit. These researchers concluded that their findings did not support the idea that gang girls are only ancillary members or that they are excluded from the illegal and violent activities in which male gang members are engaged. "They are involved in assaults, robberies, gang fights, and drug sales at substantial rates" (Esbensen et al., 1999: 48).

In Miller's study of girl gang members in St. Louis and Columbus, it was found that for most kinds of offenses, girls in gangs committed far more offenses than girls not in gangs, especially serious crimes. Likewise, the use of both alcohol and drugs was far greater for the gang members than the nongang members. Drug sales were especially more prevalent among the girl gang members, as they were almost six times more likely to sell marijuana and nine times more likely to sell crack cocaine. Miller also found significant differences between the St. Louis gang members and their Columbus counterparts as far as the frequency of participation in delinquent activities. The Columbus girls were more likely than the girls in St. Louis to be involved in minor, moderate, and serious delinquency, while the St. Louis girls were far more likely to be involved in drug sales (Miller, 2001: 124–128). What is truly unique about Miller's findings about gang crime is that, when comparing male and female gang members, there were no significant differences in their levels of crime: girls were about as likely as boys to steal things, joyride in stolen cars, damage or destroy things, intimidate or threaten people, attack people with the intent to seriously hurt them (62 percent of the males and 55 percent of the females participated in this offense), and sell drugs (Miller, 2001: 133). Consistent with prior research, most of the girls' crimes were "spur of the moment" with little advanced planning.

Miller also found that making money by selling drugs was more pronounced in St. Louis than in Columbus. Most of the proceeds of drug selling were used to "party." Also, the drug selling was sporadic rather than a daily event. One girl told Miller that "I ain't never really made it a career or nothing like that" (Miller, 2001: 144).

Being "bad," "crazy," or "wild" earns respect and status within the gang. Harris found that there were four motives for engaging in gang violence: honor, local turf defense, control, and gain. "Machismo, even for girls, is involved in the value system that promotes the ready resort to violence upon the appearance of relatively weak provoking stimuli" (Harris, 1997: 158).

The same "macho themes" emerged in a study of the female "age sets" found in a large gang in Phoenix, Arizona (Moore, Vigil, & Levy, 1995). In these groups the girls, as well as the boys, use fighting to achieve status and recognition. Even here, though, gender and culture mediate the violence. One girl recounts that she established her reputation by "protecting one of my girls. He [a male acquaintance] was slapping her around and he was hitting her and kicking her, and I went and jumped him and started hitting him" (Ibid.: 39). Once respect is achieved, these researchers found girls relied on their reputations and fought less often. One interview conducted by Sikes (1997: 21) concluded that: "In this world, the strongest . . . (gangbanger), the one 'crazy' enough to take the dare—snipe at the cop, deal the big bucks, wipe out the enemy—survived. So you found a guy who was crazy or became crazy yourself."

Most females, researchers (e.g., Sikes, 1997 and Harris, 1997) have noted, don't seek out violence; it is simply a part of the girls' existence, as acceptable as any other behavior, such as drinking, or taking or selling drugs, in their society. Sikes, for instance, found that many girls had become ruthless and able to act violently without limits. This behavior was prompted by the overarching need to survive in the environment in which these girls saw themselves. "The more you could feel, the more you cared, the greater chance of self-destruction. It was not coincidental that many of the kids in gangs took drugs or drank. Drugs helped protect them from things that would, if fully perceived, drive them crazy. . . ." (Sikes, 1997: 27).

Kitchen (1995) explored the issue of violence and the question of whether female gang members were as tough and aggressive as their male counterparts. All of her subjects stated that the use of violence was often necessary if one was going to sell drugs. One respondent flatly stated that, "Anyone who sells drugs has to be violent, even if they female. It is part of doin' business." Another stated that people would take advantage of the female not willing to use force. "Someone think you weak, they goin' take from ya'. Even if you female you got to be willing to shoot." And another responded that these women "fight each other, they fight guys, sell drugs, wear colors, they do everything the guys do." Another stated that, "Females who are soft won't make it" (Kitchen, 1995: 93). Another researcher noted that: "Being 'bad' provides an outlet, a diversion from the monotony of her life and that of her friends. Possessions and partying are major preoccupations. Authority figures provide opportunities to prove toughness and control in challenging situations" (Davis, 1999: 254).

Kitchen noted that joining a gang seemed to be fueled by the desire to make money and by the lack of good jobs in the area. Selling drugs was the main method of obtaining money for gang members, both male and female. One of her subjects expressed the problem this way: "They ain't no jobs out here. No one goin' hire someone like me. I ain't never had a job, and ain't no one goin' to give me a chance. Most people around here have to collect welfare or sell drugs, or both." Another female gang member stated: "I don't have enough education or experience to get nothing but a minimum wage job. That's bullshit workin' for minimum wage. It ain't worth it. That's why these cats are out there sellin' drugs" (Ibid.: 90). The selling of crack cocaine was the most lucrative business in this area. As another female gang member put it: "Most are selling crack cocaine 'cause that is where you make the most money. You can find crack on any corner. You have to ask who sellin' marijuana, but both males and females can be found selling crack on any street corner in this area" (Ibid.: 90–91). Another female stated that by selling drugs more money can be made than by working at minimum wage jobs. She said that "there's a lot of young people around here who are living on their own and takin' care of their mothers only because of selling crack. They couldn't make that kind of money workin' no minimum wage job. . . . It's sad that you can make more money selling drugs, but that's the way it is" (Ibid.: 91).

Kitchen notes that toughness, meanness, and aggressiveness are qualities that women must possess in order to succeed in the informal economy. On the other hand, when African American women possess these qualities within the formal economy, they "are seen as too aggressive and threatening to the male structure." However, such qualities "are necessary, and contribute to your success in business and respect from peers in an underclass community, whether you are operating legitimately or not" (Kitchen, 1995: 93). It is clear that most of Kitchen's respondents believed that in order to succeed they had to take on certain masculine characteristics or behaviors. One responded, "Most women if they actin' like men get the same respect as men. It's the same as in legitimate businesses. Those women who act aggressive and will do anything to get to the top, get to the top, and get respect. Those who sleep their way to the top, or are too soft, ain't goin' to get the same respect" (Kitchen, 1995: 108).

Sikes (1997: 12) found that the female gang members in Los Angeles were "hypnotized by the equating of money with power and fashioned gang hierarchies on things like clothing, gold-plated AK-47 pendants, and expensive Nike™ air shoes." (By equating money with power, these girls demonstrate that they have internalized the American culture itself, not unlike most others who grow up in this society. In their case, unfortunately, the opportunities to achieve cultural goals have been largely blocked. This idea is consistent with "strain" theories of crime, to be discussed in the next chapter.) Like the girls engaged in shoplifting, the new youth culture's emphasis on materialism creates a tension that ultimately results in crime. This "tension exists not only between deviance and respectability but also between old-fashioned and modern values, between poverty and glamour" (Harris, 1997: 131).

Laidler and Hunt, who note that female gang members are often characterized as being "wild, hedonistic, irrational, amoral and violent," present a somewhat different interpretation. These girls challenge the traditional gender roles and are therefore deemed to be more troublesome than male gang members. They suggest that there exists a "punitive policy response to the grimness of street life, like the stiffening of sentences, criminalizing drug addiction among pregnant women, remanding juveniles to adult courts, and reducing monies for diversion" (Laidler & Hunt, 1997: 148).

Laidler and Hunt found that "gang[]banging is an ideal arena for studying the way in which gender is accomplished because the streets—like mainstream society—are typically organized along patriarchal lines" (Messerschmidt, 1993; Joe & Chesney-Lind, 1995). As Messerschmidt (1995: 174) succinctly put it, "gender is a critical organizing tool in gangs" (quoted in Laidler & Hunt, 1997: 149).

An African American female gang known as the Vice Queens provides yet another glimpse of the relationship between gangs and criminal behavior. This gang was a female auxiliary gang to a male gang, the Vice Kings, that existed in Chicago during the early 1960s (Fishman, 1988). As other studies have found, the bulk of their time was spent hanging out on the streets with the Vice Kings, which usually included sexual activities and the consumption of alcohol. Contrary to popular opinion, most of their time was not spent in delinquent activities. Their delinquent activities, however, were quite varied. They committed such traditional female crimes as shoplifting and running away from home, along with such minor offenses as driving without a license, disturbing the peace, and loitering. They also committed traditional male crimes, such as auto theft and grand larceny, although these were not as frequent.

Drug use is quite common among girl gang members, as it is for males. In the San Francisco gang study (Lauderback et al., 1992), drug use was reportedly widespread among these young women, although marijuana was the most popular drug. They are not generally bothered by the police (half of those interviewed had no arrest record), primarily because they do not wear the usual gang attire. One member stated, "Basically we just wear our little beads and braids and stuff so they [the police] just think we are some girls hanging out." Another member stated, "We not in the gang bang shootings and all of that" (Ibid.: 63). The Potrero Hill Posse gets its supply of drugs from its own homegirls (usually senior members of the gang), while the Latina gang members get their drugs from both homegirls and homeboys. Most of their crack sales are conducted in rock houses. These houses are usually a neighbor's residence that is rented in exchange for drugs.

In the Hawaii study, the majority of both male and female gang members had extensive arrest records, with about one-fourth of each group having 10 or more arrests. Their offenses were mostly property offenses, but many (about one-third of the girls) had been arrested for violent offenses. Not surprisingly, girls were about equally likely to have committed status offenses[5] as any other type of offense. Peer pressure was cited by both groups as a reason for their criminal behavior, but boys were more likely to cite economic reasons (for example, they needed money) (Joe & Chesney-Lind, 1995).

It is important to note, once again, that the bulk of a gang member's time is not spent committing crimes. Furthermore, most crimes happen rather spontaneously, often because of just plain boredom. In the Hawaii study, Joe and Chesney-Lind found that gang members join together to hang out and have fun and develop makeshift strategies to fill the time void. They engage in sporting activities and various activities on the state's many beaches. The girls, in contrast to the boys, handle the boredom of their lives somewhat differently. Many of their activities correspond to traditional gender roles—the girls often engage in singing, going to dances, and learning the hula from their families, while the boys spend a lot of their time cruising. This cruising is not unlike similar teenage activities in any city or town in America. As is typical for males, such activity often includes such expressions of masculinity as drinking, fighting, and petty theft (for example, ripping off the tourists). A typical day of a male is described as follows by an 18-year-old Samoan:

> After school there is nothing to do. A lot of my friends like to lift weights, if there was someplace to lift weights. A lot of my friends don't know how to read, they try to read, but say they can't, and they don't have programs or places for them to go. . . . There are no activities, so now we hang around and drink beer. We hang around, roam the streets. . . . Yesterday we went to a pool hall and got into a fight over there (Joe & Chesney-Lind, 1995: 20).

In contrast, girls are not usually involved in much drinking or fighting, although this occasionally happens. When it does happen, it is due either to unsubstantiated rumors (for example, that someone in a rival gang threatened a girl gang member) or to the boredom in their lives. A 15-year-old Samoan girl explained it this way: "Sometimes we like cause trouble, yeah, 'cause boring, so boring, so we like make trouble eh, to make a scene" (Joe & Chesney-Lind, 1995: 21).

The Hawaii study found significant gender differences in the nature and extent of crime. Generally speaking, the girls were found to be much less involved than the boys in most areas of criminal behavior. It is interesting to note that one of the major activities of the boys was fighting, but when the girls were in their presence, they did not engage in much violence. Drug dealing was another major difference between the boys and the girls. The involvement among the boys in drug using and selling was far more frequent than among the girls. However, even among the boys, only a few were involved in selling drugs. Mostly it was using drugs and drinking that occupied the time of both boys and girls.

For girls, arrests for running away and other status offenses (for example, staying out beyond curfew) were more common. Usually such arrests stemmed from the double standard of enforcement—boys were allowed to engage in this sort of behavior.

Moore's study of girl gangs in East Los Angeles reveals that drugs are a major problem. She noted that heroin has been a consistent feature of Chicano life for many years. Moore commented that in the 1980s there was a heroin epidemic that was barely noticed in the press, no doubt because of the focus on crack cocaine. The lifestyle that revolved around the use of heroin was known as the *tecato* lifestyle. As the life history of one gang member revealed, this was a life filled with a sporadic work history and characterized by frequent jail and prison terms. By the age of 20 about half of the male gang members studied, but less than 25 percent of the females, were using heroin. By this age most had already been labeled tecatos by their gang and had withdrawn into their own subculture. To give an idea of the importance of heroin in their lives, Moore reported that 39 percent of the men and 16 percent of the women mentioned "heroin, drugs, narcotics" as being "the major happening during their teens" and "it was during their teens that they were initiated into the world of heroin and its usually disastrous life consequences" (Moore, 1991: 107).

These individuals did not differ significantly from nonheroin users so far as family characteristics were concerned. However, they were significantly more likely to have grown up in a family in which an addict lived in the home. Also, they were significantly more likely than nonusers to answer yes to the question, "Are you all for your barrio now?"

There were significant differences between men and women tecatos. Men were more likely to begin heroin and to continue the tecato lifestyle within the context of the gang. Also, the men were more likely to spend a greater part of their lives in and out of jails and prisons.

The women were more likely to be preoccupied with their children, while the men tended to lose contact with their children, a not altogether surprising finding. Also, the women were more likely to grow up in a family with another addict in the home and were most likely to begin using heroin with a boyfriend or husband. The world of the streets dictated that "a tecata's next boyfriend will also be a heroin user" (Moore, 1991: 109). The women tended to continue using heroin for longer periods of time than did the men. Being arrested was a common occurrence, and most grew up in households where other members had an arrest record. Men were more likely than women to have been arrested, however (Ibid.: 111).

Reasons for Joining the Gang

Girls in gangs are not generally "recruited" in the normal sense of the term, nor are they pressured or coerced. Members come from normal friendship groups in the neighborhood and through family ties (Harris, 1988). The reasons girls join a gang are much the same as those of their male counterparts: a sense of belonging (familylike), power, protection, respect, fear, and, sometimes, paranoia. In addition, with membership comes prestige and identity, guidance, and ample access to drugs and cash. Sikes notes that:

although most girls in gangs are poor and members of minorities—being cut off from mainstream society is among the reasons kids join gangs—I met white girls from middle class homes who packed 9-millimeter semiautomatics. It's precisely the gang girl's similarity to other teenagers that makes their cruel behavior so haunting (Sikes, 1997: xxiv).

The Hawaii study by Joe and Chesney-Lind illustrates a common theme among both male and female gang membership: many, if not most, gradually "grow into" gangs rather than merely "join." For the Hawaii youths, gangs had been a constant presence in their neighborhoods while growing up, and the majority of both boys and girls had another family member (usually a sibling) who had belonged to a gang. Girls tended to join at an earlier age (12) than boys (14). Few reported having been jumped in or otherwise initiated into the gang. The boys' gangs were generally larger than the girls' (45 percent of the boy gangs had 30 or more members, whereas about half of the girl gangs had between 10 and 20 members).

The need for "protection" should not be dismissed lightly, for this has always been one of the most common reasons cited to explain male gang membership, and it may apply equally to girls. Jody Miller notes that young women join gangs partly "as a means of protecting themselves from violence and other family problems and from mistreatment at the hands of other men in their lives. Within the gang, girls' friendships provide an outlet for members to cope with abuse and other life problems" (Miller, 2001: 13).

The gang becomes a sort of "family." Indeed, Brown (1977) found that friendships with fellow gang members were of utmost importance for girl gang members. Giordano's study (1978) arrived at the same conclusions, with an additional reason that gangs also provided opportunities for mate selection, with many boys and girls in the same gang (i.e., boys in the main gang and girls in the auxiliary gang) eventually marrying and having their own families (Flowers, 1987: 137; Campbell, 1984). Girls in gangs observed by Campbell very often engaged in the same behavior as the boys, such as smoking pot, drinking, fighting, committing theft, and "partying." Also, most of the fights the girls got into arose from domestic or romantic disputes (Campbell, 1984: 33).

The "pseudo community" of a gang "provides a haven for sexually abused and battered girls who [have] no genuine sense of safety, of being significant, or of the promise for a better life away from their neighborhood or community" (Davis, 1999: 257). However, in joining the gang, she risks being subjected to cruel treatment, injury, or death. Expected to do the bidding of the gang, activities that are, for the most part, criminal, she may find herself even more isolated if she is arrested and incarcerated.

The current generation of girls started to join gangs in the late 1980s and early 1990s. Some were steady girlfriends of gang members, says Sikes, adding that "almost any pair of kids who stuck together for more than six month informed me they had a 'common-law marriage'" (Sikes, 1997: 102).

Females, like males, generally go through some form of initiation, not unlike initiations into other groups in society (e.g., fraternities and sororities, military boot camps, etc.). Some of these initiations may include being beaten and kicked by gang members, participating in a robbery or drive-by shooting, getting tattoos, having to fight 5 to 12 gang members at once, or having sex with multiple male gang members. In addition, stealing sprees, muggings, or mental tests administered by other gang members are common requirements for initiation.

Laidler and Hunt found that one other type of initiation was that girls might be required to fight with a male, unlike the independent female gang. They were also targets for violence by other male gangs and/or the females in similar gangs (male-dominated). The Latinas self-reported fighting among themselves usually because of disrespect from another girl or because of a male; much of the conflict arose after drinking heavily. These fights were fist-fights and did not include weapons (Laidler & Hunt, 1997: 160).

Some gangs have what are called *roll-ins,* in which a female initiate rolls a pair of dice and whatever number appears determines how many males have sex with her. In addition, there is a rumored "HIV initiation" in which females have sex with an HIV-infected male—there is, however, no data to support this claim; all reports and tests have been negative. Sex is one of the ways to use and/or abuse girls in an auxiliary or coed gang (Sikes, 1997: 102–103). Psychiatrist Robert Jiminez of Los Angeles told Sikes that of the many girls he has interviewed, only 15 were gang-raped as part of an initiation. Females are most often psychologically coerced. "A girl wouldn't have sex if she had a choice, but if it means being left out, she'll do it—giving in to her boyfriend for as much sex as he wants, when he wants it, and how he wants it—sodomy or whatever." More common is gang sex, "pulling a train" on a drunken girl at a gang party: "the boy's rank in the gang determined whether he was the engine, the caboose, or somewhere in between . . ." (Sikes, 1997: 103).

Moore found that a clear majority of the males (89%) lived in the gang territory and sort of drifted into the gang through friends in the neighborhood and at school. For the girls, whereas 65 percent lived in the neighborhood and naturally drifted into the gang like the boys did, a significant number got into the gang through relatives and close friends, including boyfriends. One of the most common differences between the male and female gang members was the existence of problems within the home, which served as a major reason for joining a gang. One of the major problems that the girls had that the boys did not was the experience of being sexually abused (Moore, 1991).

Fishman's study of the Vice Queens (in Chicago) noted that they lived in a predominantly African American, low-income community characterized by poverty, unemployment, deterioration, and a high crime rate. Joining the gang came quite naturally and participation in the gang functioned to give them companionship, status, and protection (Fishman, 1988). Fishman concluded that the Vice Queens deviated somewhat from the traditional female gang that has been portrayed in the literature. The key to understanding this difference may be that this group was African American and had experienced socialization practices distinctly different from those of their white counterparts. Specifically, they were "socialized to be independent, assertive and to take risks with the expectations that these are characteristics that they will need to

function effectively within the black low income community . . . As a consequence, black girls demonstrate, out of necessity, a greater flexibility in roles."
The girls in this study used their participation within this gang "as a means to
acquire some knowledge of such adaptive strategies as hustling and fighting in
order to be prepared to survive as independent adult women within their
community" (Fishman, 1988: 26–27).

Harris's study of female gangs in Southern California found that females
join gangs much the same as they would any other group of their peers, but
that the gang becomes a way of life, "a total institution, much like a commune
or military unit completely absorbing the individual into the subculture"
(Harris, 1997: 151–152). She found that certain values become internalized in
a gang girl and any girl who exhibits the qualities of being willing to fight, to
be "bad" and/or "crazy," to have great stamina and fortitude, and to use drugs
is a welcome addition to the group (Harris, 1997: 152). Also, in Mexican
American female gangs, which are perhaps the most uncommon within the
varied ethnic groups, the requirements for joining a gang are to be of Mexican
American descent and to live in, or near, the barrio (Harris, 1997: 152–153).

Harris found that the reasons for joining a gang centered around belonging and seeking an identity. Members' perception of the gang was that with
these other girls, they had "a common destiny . . . a need for group support and
cohesiveness, and a need for revenge. . . ." (Harris, 1997: 154–155). The violent
nature of their own lives also appeared as a commonality among the Mexican
American female gang members. The abusive relationships they had witnessed
or experienced themselves created the necessity for an outlet for their emotions—often their anger and their rage.

As a member of the gang, the girl is willing to exhibit risk-taking behavior
in order to maintain her status and to prove her loyalty. "Supporting the 'hood'
and identification as a gang member are two norms of great consequence, with
strong sanctions applied if a girl is shown to be disloyal"(Harris, 1997: 156–157).

The everyday lives of girls gang members and the neighborhood context
of marginalization made joining or forming gangs an answer to their problems. Joe and Chesney-Lind put it this way:

> At one level, the boredom, lack of resources, and high visibility of
> crime in their neglected communities create the conditions for turning to
> others who are similarly situated, and consequently, it is the group that re-
> alistically offers a social outlet. At another level, the stress on the family
> from living in marginalized areas combined with financial struggles cre-
> ated heated tension, and in many cases, violence in the home. It is the
> group that provides our respondents with a safe refuge and a surrogate
> family (Joe & Chesney-Lind, 1993: 17).

These young people lived in areas with very limited recreational activities, no
jobs, no vocational training opportunities, no money to pay for what entertainment was available, and "nowhere to go and nothing happening for long stretches
of time." Many of the respondents said, "here is nothing to do" (Ibid.: 19).

For both the boys and the girls, the gang serves as an alternative family. Some of these youths come from families in which the parents are overemployed (working at two working-class or service jobs) just to make ends meet in an area with an extremely high cost of living. Many youths are on their own much of the time, without any supervision, mostly due to being in a single-parent household with that parent (usually the mother) working full-time. In other cases there are family stresses due to frequent periods of unemployment or underemployment. Thus the gang takes the place of members' families in terms of having someone to share problems with and give support. One girl, a 15-year-old Samoan, stated it this way: "We all like sistas all taking care of each other." Another girl belonged to a group called JEMA, which stands for Just Every Mother's Angel. She describes the origins of this group as follows: "We chose that because all the girls I hang out with, yeah, all their mothers passed away, and during elementary days, we all used to hang and all our mothers were close, yeah, so that's how we came up with that name" (Ibid.: 23).

Campbell's study of a Hispanic gang in New York concluded that for these girls the gang represents "an idealized collective solution to the bleak future that awaits" them. These girls have a tendency to portray the gang to themselves and the outside world in a very idealized and romantic manner (1990: 173). As it does their male counterparts, the gang offers girls solutions to two important needs noted by Maslow: acceptance and safety (Campbell, 1993: 136). These girls develop an exaggerated sense of belonging to the gang. In reality, they were loners prior to joining the gang, having been only loosely connected to schoolmates and neighborhood peer groups. The gang closeness, as well as the excitement of gang life, is more fiction than reality. Their daily street talks are filled with exaggerated stories of parties, drugs, alcohol, and other varieties of fun. However, as Campbell notes:

> These events stand as a bulwark against the loneliness and drudgery of their future lives. They also belie the day-to-day reality of gang life. The lack of recreational opportunities, the long days unfilled by work or school, and the absence of money mean that hours and days are whiled away on street corners. "Doing nothing" means hanging out on the stoop; the hours of "bullshit" punctuated by trips to the store to buy one can of beer at a time. When an unexpected windfall arrives, marijuana and rum are purchased in bulk and the partying begins. The next day, life returns to normal (Campbell, 1990: 176).

Instability in these girls' lives plays an important part in understanding their membership in street gangs. Frequent moves and failure to form real ties to school friends make rebelling easier and more attractive. Perhaps because of this instability, female gang members bond so strongly that they will risk their own safety to help another female. Gilligan (1982) believes that female adolescent crises pose difficulties for girls through the sacrifice of childhood idealization (in relationships) in exchange for stronger self-identity. Their aspirations, when elicited, are typically unrealistic, with the girls expressing desires to be rock stars or professional models. Campbell cites recent data revealing a very bleak future indeed, as 94 percent will have children, and 84 percent of these will have to raise their children without a husband. Most will be dependent upon some form of welfare (Gilligan, 1991: 182). Their lives, in effect, reflect all the burdens of their triple handicaps of race, class, and gender. "Gang life becomes girls' religion, giving courage and faith and teaching one how to live. It gives the sense of something greater than the individual, of some higher purpose" (Sikes, 1997: 37).

The most recent study conducted by Jody Miller (2001), who compared girl gang and nongang members in two cities (Columbus, Ohio and St. Louis, Missouri), found three underlying themes in the lives of the girls who joined gangs. First, the neighborhood contexts of these girls contributed to their joining gangs (and most of them joined the gang before age 14). These contexts included important peer and other friendship networks, the presence of gangs, plus the extreme poverty in their neighborhoods.

Secondly, Miller found that there were serious family problems (a theme mentioned in virtually every other study of gang contexts, especially for girls), including violence and drug abuse, all of which led them to avoid their homes whenever possible.

Finally, Miller found that for most girls a strong influence came from gang-involved family members (such as older siblings and cousins). Each of these three themes typically overlapped in the lives of the girls Miller studied.

Reference should be made to Miller's discussion of the "neighborhood context" of the girls who joined gangs. Most telling is the extreme poverty. In Columbus, for instance, while the median income of the entire city was $26,651, within the gang members' neighborhoods it was $19,625; while about 17 percent lived in poverty in the general Columbus area, 29 percent lived in poverty where these girls lived; and while the unemployment rate in the greater Columbus area was 5.9 percent, in the girls' neighborhoods it stood at 13.2 percent. In St. Louis, the situation was even worse, as just over 40 percent lived in poverty and 18 percent were unemployed (Miller, 2001: 39).

Miller also found that for girls who joined gangs, there was a significantly greater amount of gang activity around the neighborhood and more gang members who lived on the same street than for girls who did not join gangs. In other words, gangs were a constant presence in the lives of these girls (Miller, 2001: 41). Not surprisingly, the girls in her study who joined gangs typically "hung out" with gang members for "some time"—often for as much as a year—before finally making a commitment to actually become a regular member (Miller, 2001: 35).

Girls not only "age in" but also they "age out" of gangs at earlier ages than do boys. According to Harris, girls are most active in gangs between 13 and 16 years of age. She suggests that "by 17 or 18" interests and activities of individual members are directed toward the larger community rather than toward the gang, and girls begin to leave the active gang milieu (Harris, 1997: 300). Others "mature out" of gang activity when they have children or go to jail. Miller (2001: 35) found that the majority (69%) of the girls in her study joined the gang when they were under 14 years of age.

However, for many girls, leaving the gang life constitutes much the same activity as initiation into the gang. It is not uncommon for female gangs to "beat out" members, with other members taking turns beating each girl who has asked to quit the gang. In some instances, members kill those who want out or force the girl to kill a member of her family in order to leave the gang, but these instances are rare (McNaught, 1999).

McNaught (1999) suggests that some girls who are drawn into gangs through sexual relationships and become pregnant are especially oppressed. Often the children's fathers are incarcerated and cannot provide assistance and their fellow gang members, their only friends, indeed, their family, often reject them. In addition, these girls have no skills or education to help themselves and their children. These girls realize that their gang membership can no longer help them and so they drift away from the gang.

In the Laidler and Hunt study, the girls joined gangs for the "familylike" relationships; however, they found that such feelings were different for girls in the independent female gang and the other female gangs. In the independent gang, the group "served as a surrogate family; providing a fictive kinship network and resource to draw upon for emotional and economic support." The females also joined together to make money. This was done largely through drug sales and shoplifting; they viewed their actions as a way to make life better for themselves and their children (Laidler & Hunt, 1997: 153–154).

The conclusions reached by Joe and Chesney-Lind echo the words of Thrasher and many others (see Chapter 5) and can be used to summarize the other studies noted above. They state that, for both the girls and the boys:

> The gang is a haven for coping with the many problems they encounter in their everyday life in marginalized communities. Paradoxically, the sense of solidarity achieved from sharing everyday life with similarly situated others has the unintended effect of drawing many gang youth— both boys and girls—into behaviors that ultimately create new problems for them. . . . The gang provides a needed social outlet and tonic for the boredom of low income life. The gang provides friends and activities in communities where such recreational outlets are pitifully slim. Gender, though, shapes these activities. For girls, the list of pro-social activities is longer than [for]boys. For boys, getting together in groups quickly moves into cruising instead of hanging out and that, in turn, leads to fights and confrontations with other groups of boys (1993: 29–30).

For the girls, the abusive relationships within their families and in their communities lead them to seek protection within the gang, which in turn gives them skills for fighting back. But the violence the girls do engage in, which violates traditional notions of femininity, is hardly evidence of any sort of liberation from patriarchal controls. As Joe and Chesney-Lind note, the life of girls in gangs is not an expression of liberation, but rather "reflects the attempts of young women to cope with a bleak and harsh present as well as a dismal future" (1993: 32).

Relationship with Males and Male Gangs

Sexism was a topic that Kitchen explored with her respondents. Women (especially African American women) do not appear to get much respect within the legitimate business world, but in the informal economy of drug dealing, they command respect as long as they are tough and do not sell themselves. As one put it, "The only girls not respected around here are the ones that are givin' it up for drugs, or are sellin' themselves to buy. Most women get respect if they sellin' drugs, but not if they using. It's OK for guys to use, but not us" (Ibid.: 104). This double standard did not go unnoticed among some of the female gang members Kitchen interviewed. One commented, "I think it is harder for girls to earn respect than guys. Guys just beat someone up, or carry a gun, and they got respect. But girls, if they mess up, they get treated like a ho [whore] . . . ." Another stated that, "Guys get more attention, and women do not get the same amount of respect on jobs. Males have better opportunities. The bosses think 'cause they guys they will do a better job." Still another said that, "Guys around here don't respect women much. I think it is because of all the rap music bashin' women. I listen to some of this music calling women bitches and ho's and it upsets me. I think the guys around here think sex is all we're good for" (Kitchen, 1995: 104).

Quicker's study of Chicana gang members in East Los Angeles found evidence that these girls, although still somewhat dependent upon their male counterparts, were becoming more and more independent. These girls identified themselves as homegirls and their male counterparts as homeboys, a common reference to relationships in the barrio (Quicker, 1983).

Campbell (1995: 70) states: "These types of roles tend to suggest a no-win situation for gang girls. As Sex Objects, they are cheap women rejected by other girls, parents, social workers, and ironically often by the boys themselves. As Tomboys, they are resented by boys and ridiculed by family and friends who wait patiently for them to 'grow out of it.'"

Fishman's study of the Vice Queens (1995) found that the relationship these girls had with the boys in the Vice Kings was primarily sexual. "Vice Queens had sexual relations with members of the gang in the process of 'going with' the boys and they bore the boys' illegitimate children." Moreover, their relationships were very open and lacked the subtle discretion consistent with middle-class values. That is, rather than engage in flirtatious behavior, they "unabashedly placed themselves at the boys' disposal and openly encouraged them to fondle and to have sexual relations with them." There was little actual dating in the usual sense, and the boys tended to pay attention to the girls only when they wanted sex. Typically, the males tended to "handle them, curse them and beat them." Although they did "go steady," neither "perceived each other as future marriage partners." The Vice Kings viewed the Vice Queens "as useful for premarital sexual relations but not as steady girlfriends."

Females are increasingly encouraged to consider themselves equal to males, yet most of their experiences with males are those of abuse, both physical and sexual, and violence (Davis, 1999). One survey, conducted in Seattle's juvenile detention center, found that 98 percent of the females incarcerated were sexual abuse victims (Mendez, 1996: A7). Similarly, Sikes (1997) found that the girls she studied had many problems of this nature. She found that they were victims of physical brutality in gangs and in domestic situations as well.

According to a U.S. Department of Justice report, "Many female groups are no longer simply extensions of male gangs. Female gang members manage their own affairs, make their own decisions, and often engage in a system of norms that is similar to that of male gangs" (U.S. Department of Justice, 1998: 14).

Harris's study of the *Cholas*, a Latina gang in the San Fernando Valley (in southern California), echoes this theme. She notes that, while the *Cholas* in many respects resemble male gangs, the gang did challenge the girls' traditional destiny within the barrio in two direct ways. First, the girls reject the traditional image of the Latino woman as wife and mother, supporting, instead, a more macho homegirl role. Second, the gang supports the girls in their estrangement from organized religion, substituting instead a form of familialism that "provides a strong substitute for weak family and conventional school ties" (Harris, 1988: 172).

Kitchen (1995: 43) notes that many female gang members "are rejecting the roles as mere extensions of male gangs, and working for males as drug runners and prostitutes. These females see the only way out of the ghetto life, while keeping their self-respect, is through the creation of their own crews, with their own rules and values."

Fighting protects female gang members from this victimization. The gang provides a "number of discrete functions" that serve as a "bulwark against a very hostile environment" (Davis, 1999: 256). The girls are most often from families that pay little, if any, attention to them and they are starved for familial relationships; they long for a close circle of people on which they can depend and trust.

Harris found that while girls try to maintain an independence from males, they often allow the males to dominate; in gangs, the males exhibit an attitude of territoriality toward the girls. Girls are more likely to interact frequently, "together, all the time, everywhere," than boys. Informally they "hang out" together and formally, they hold policy discussions and planning sessions (Harris, 1997: 157).

The girls in the Laidler and Hunt study described their boyfriends as "possessive, controlling, and often violent." This differed from the relationship with their other members with whom they kept a close and supportive relationship and did not fight, but rather, "talked out" their problems (Laidler and Hunt, 1997: 157). Although the males in these gangs were often protective of the females, they also victimized them, unlike the independent female gang members. This victimization took the form of verbal, physical, and, sometimes, sexual abuse. Their boyfriends used similar actions to control their girls; many of these males did not approve of the girls "hanging out" on the streets (Laidler and Hunt, 1997: 161). Laidler and Hunt concluded that any type of female gang affiliation presents girls with violence-prone situations and places them at high risk for abuse.

Most of the girls in Moore's study (1991) denied that the gang boys treated them like possessions. However, 41 percent of the older men and 56 percent of the younger men agreed that the girls were indeed treated as such. Three themes emerged from the male views. First, they believed that the gang was a male preserve and "any girl who joins is worthless and deserves whatever happens to her." A second theme centered on male dominance over women. As one young man said, "When you're young you want to be on top. You don't want no girls telling you what to do" (Moore, 1991: 54). The third theme had to do with sexuality, one of the developmental imperatives of adolescent males. One male gang member stated that 90 percent of the girls were "treated like a piece of ass. . . . We just used them as sexual need things, and companions . . ." In more recent cliques, sexual activity began at an earlier age—14.5 years was the median age of the first sexual experience of younger cliques, whereas it was 15.2 years for older cliques (Moore, 1991: 55).

Moore also notes that the practice of dating partners from other gangs (which the majority of both boys and girls do) often caused gang fights. One gang member said, "many wars started with other neighborhoods because of a love affair" (Moore, 1991: 56). On the other hand, there were times when the women helped prevent a fight with a rival gang.

In the earlier cliques it was not unusual for gang members to have friends outside of the gang; in fact, Moore found that 65 percent of the earlier gang members had such friends. However, in more recent cliques, this percentage dropped to only 34. Additionally, significant gender differences were found. Girls were more likely to date boys from gangs; in contrast, boys were more likely to date girls who were not in gangs, who were "squares." The boys reported that they enjoyed dating nongang girls and believed that these square girls "were their future," as they would be a stabilizing influence. One male gang member said, "you know that they were going to be good. You know they [were]going to take care of business and in the house, be a good housewife, you know what I mean" (Moore, 1991: 75). Another change noted by Moore was that the men from more recent cliques were more likely to report that their girlfriends disapproved of their gang membership.

Latino gang girls have had to negotiate within a Mexican American culture that is "particularly conservative with regard to female sexuality" (Moore, Vigil, & Levy, 1995: 29). In their neighborhoods and in their relations with the boys in the gang, the persistence of the double standard places the more assertive and sexually active girls in an anomalous position. Essentially, they must contend with a culture that venerates "pure girls" while also setting the groundwork for the sexual exploitation by gang boys of other girls. One of their respondents reports that the boys sometimes try to get girls high and "pull a train" [where a number of males have sex with one girl], something she clearly rejects for herself—even though she admits to having had sex with a boy she didn't like after the male gang members "got me drunk" (Ibid.: 32) (see also Portillos & Zatz, 1995).

In the San Francisco study (Lauderback et al., 1992) most of the girl gang members have children of their own, who are brought along to many of the picnics. The fathers of their children are not involved in their children's lives, nor are many other members of their families. Also, their experiences with the men in their lives have been mostly negative. The men in their lives "are generally abusive, verbally and physically, and controlling." One member commented on her child's father: "They just get you pregnant and they go on about their business with somebody else" (Lauderback, 1992: 69). However, they would like to have a man in their lives, one who would be working and would be a family man.

Miller's study of gangs in St. Louis and Columbus arrived at findings almost identical to those noted above. She found that being affiliated with a male gang or being part of a mixed-sex gang (the overwhelming majority of gangs in both cities were mostly male) provided "at least a semblance of protection from, and retaliation against, predatory men in the social environment" (Miller, 2001: 157). The dependency upon men is clearly stated by one girl gang member who said "You feel more secure when, you know, a guy's around protectin' you," adding that "not as many people mess with you" (Ibid.).

Ironically, notes Miller, although being a gang member offers some protection, at the same time it tends to open up possibilities of being victimized by rival gangs and the violence often associated with gang life in general. However, in contrast to family violence, gang violence is more "structured," as it is governed by various rules and regulations in that "they know which situations put them at risk, that there are known methods for response, and that they aren't in it alone." Thus, violence within the context of gangs is "perceived as more palatable for many young women" and it gives them some sense of empowerment that they did not have in their families (Miller, 2001: 158). Nevertheless, girls still get victimized, both by males in rival gangs and by some male members of their own gang. In fact, compared with nongang members, girl gang members are more than twice as likely to be sexually assaulted, twice as likely to be threatened with a weapon, and 15 times more likely to be stabbed (Ibid.: 152).

One of the most glaring examples of girls' victimization within mostly male gangs is the "sexing in" initiation practice. Although there was an unwritten rule prohibiting talking openly about this practice, Miller's respondents gave vague references to being "sexed in" to the gang. She discovered that getting sexed into the gang placed girls in a very vulnerable position that "increased their risk of ongoing mistreatment at the hands of their gang peers." Such mistreatment included both verbal and sexual abuse (Miller, 2001: 172).

Campbell suggests a close connection between gender relationships, violence, and victimization. She asks: If gangs represent the "zenith of untamed masculine hostility" (as so many male gangs do), then why should young girls be attracted to gang life? She notes that the typical male gang member's answer is that girls join gangs because they "want tough men and gravitate to gangs in pursuit of them." Campbell, however, responds by noting that many observers (including many researchers) assume that "violence equals masculinity" and ignore the distinction between instrumental and expressive violence (1993: 125–126). For the girls who join gangs, says Campbell, their fear and loneliness drive them toward an instrumental view of violence. Further, their use of violence is mostly for the sake of their reputation. Campbell writes that these girls

> know what it is to be victims, and they know that, to survive, force must be met with more than unspoken anger or frustrated tears. Less physically strong and more sexually vulnerable than boys, they find that the best line of defense is not attack but the threat of attack. The key to this is the development of a reputation for violence, which will ward off opponents. There is nothing so effective as being in a street gang to keep the message blaring out: "Don't mess with me—I'm a crazy woman" (Ibid.: 133).

For most gang girls, and indeed most girl delinquents in general, being a victim and/or witnessing victimization within their own home is something they have grown used to (Ibid.: 133–135). Much like their male counterparts, they experience a great deal of indirect violence in the sense that they see so much around them in their neighborhoods. As Campbell notes:

> The neighborhoods in which gangs thrive are among the poorest and most crime-ridden in the city. Burglaries and robberies are commonplace. Assaults in bars and on the streets are frequent. Drug dealers and pimps own the sidewalks. No one is safe there, not even a gang girl when she is walking alone. . . . (Campbell, 1993: 135–136).

Thus, within such a context, it is easy to understand how girls can be attracted to a gang.

Family-Related Issues

Females most at risk for gang involvement come from homes in crisis. Easton (1991) finds that these homes most often are those which have marital discord, are headed by a single parent, display prevalent alcohol and drug abuse, have physical and/or sexual abuse occuring, and have sibling or parental gang involvement.

Girls usually become active in gangs in early adolescence. Many have children and some are married. Girls are most commonly identified as either "good girl" with "typically middle class values (love, marriage, better social and life situation)" or "bad girl" with no "illusions about her socioeconomic status and the lack of opportunities it affords . . . likely to have performed poorly in school . . . struggle for money is relentless" (Davis, 1999: 254).

Moore has noted that "neighbors, family and—for the men—girlfriends all tended to have been more actively opposed to gang membership in recent cliques as compared with older cliques. The gangs of the 1970s, then, were operating both with less involvement with square friends and in a climate of disapproval: They were defined as deviant groups, and conventional neighbors, parents, and girl/boyfriends tried to discourage membership" (Moore, 1991: 76). Not surprisingly, girls had more restrictions placed upon them. Whereas all of the respondents reported that their parents were strict, the female gang members were more likely to report this, especially those from earlier cliques.

Moore reports that 29 percent of the women said that someone in the family had molested them. Incest was more common among the earlier cliques than in more recent ones. Not surprisingly, incest was associated with the patriarchal family system. Fathers who molested their daughters were also more likely to assault their wives, who were more likely to be strict with, and to devalue, their daughters. The victims of incest were more likely to report that their fathers were alcoholics (Ibid.: 96). Another finding, not unexpected, was that most of the girls never told anyone about the incest and received no help (Moore, 1991: 98).

Moore also reports that girls were more likely to run away from home than boys, which is not surprising given the fact that they were more likely to be the victims of incest. Boys from more recent cliques were more likely to run away than those from earlier cliques. For the girls no difference was found between the two generations.

There was a lot of stress in the families of these gang girls, which caused many problems in childhood (as noted by Werner and Smith, 1982). Alcohol was one of several concerns. In one-fourth of the men's homes and in almost half of the women's homes someone was either physically handicapped or chronically ill. In most homes some member of the family died when the gang member was growing up, usually a grandparent, but in 30 percent of the homes it was the father (Moore, 1991: 100–101).

Moore also discovered that there was the additional problem of deviance of other family members. A heroin addict (usually a brother) lived in the home of 20 percent of the men and 45 percent of the women. Also, the majority of the respondents (57 percent of the men and 82 percent of the women) reported that they witnessed a member of their family being arrested when they were growing up. In over half it was a brother, while in 28 percent of the homes it was the father (Moore, 1991: 101).

Moore concludes that, first, the problems in these families were varied, and there were few significant differences between earlier and more recent cliques. Second, it is clear that more of the women came from troubled families than the men. They were more likely than the men to come from families with an alcoholic, a chronically ill relative, someone who died, someone who was a heroin addict, or someone who had been arrested. For the girls, the gang may have been more of a refuge or escape than was the case for the boys (Moore, 1991: 101; Jankowski, 1990).

Some of these earlier family problems were repeated in the girls' own relationships with men. Almost all of the girls Moore studied (both addicts and nonaddicts) had been married at least once. But the marriages did not last very long, especially for men who had used heroin early in life. A term in prison usually ended the marriage (Moore, 1991: 111).

Heroin users began living with a mate at an earlier age than others. There were gender differences here, as the heroin-using women were twice as likely as the men (42 percent versus 21 percent) to live with someone at age 16 or younger, in contrast to only 7 percent of the nonusing men and 8 percent of the nonusing women (Ibid.: 112).

Even among nonusers, marriage (and relationships in general) was unstable. One main reason was that so many of the men continued to hang out with their gang after getting married. Hanging out with the gang led to problems for the family, because the gang remained of central importance to the man, even more than the marriage. Also, when there were problems in the marriage, the gang became a convenient escape. (Many men escape to their circle of friends—for example, drinking buddies at the bar, golfing partners, business partners, and so on—whenever their marriages are rocky or even when there's nothing wrong.) A third source of problems was that so many marriage partners were both gang members; hence there were two people, not one, unwilling to give up the gang (Ibid.: 112–113). (It may be like an addiction, in that the addicted person is unwilling to give up the addiction to save a relationship or his/her family.)

Most of them had children, with men having fewer than the women (an average of 2.9 for the men versus 3.4 for the women); heroin users had the fewest. Whereas the majority (85%) of the women raised their children, less than half of the men did (43%). Heroin users were even less likely to raise their children. Women were much more likely than the men to mention parenthood as a turning point in their lives (43 percent versus 19 percent) (Ibid.: 114).

Most of the women the men married were not in a gang; therefore, square mothers brought up most of their children. In contrast, the gang tradition (whatever this may be) was more likely to be found in the gang woman's household, because she was more likely to marry a gang member. Most of the respondents said they did not want their children in gangs (Ibid.: 114).

Similar findings were reported in the Hawaii study (Joe & Chesney-Lind, 1993). Here the majority of both girls and boys live with both parents. Also, most of them reported being physically abused (55 percent of the boys and 62 percent of the girls). A key difference is that 62 percent of the girls reported having been either sexually abused or sexually assaulted.

Jody Miller's study sheds additional light on this subject, while underscoring the above research findings. In comparing girls who joined gangs with those who did not, she discovered that those who joined gangs were more likely to: (1) witness physical violence between adults in the family, (2) be abused by a family member, (3) live in a home where drug use was common, (4) have "multiple family problems" (violence, abuse, alcohol or drug abuse, family member in jail or prison, etc.). Additionally, over half of the gang members reported being sexually assaulted, mostly at the hands of either family members or men to whom these girls were exposed through family members (Miller, 2001: 46). One girl gang member told Miller that "My family wasn't there for me. My mom smokin' crack and she act like she didn't want to be part of my life . . . " Another said she joined the gang at a time when she was "fighting with my mama 'cause she was on drugs" (Miller, 2001: 47). Miller also describes girls like Erica, who was raped by both her father and uncle and witnessed her own mother being raped. She said she joined the gang "just to be in somethin'" and so it would be "like a family to me since I don't really have one of my own" (Miller, 2001: 49).

As already noted, Miller found that girls who joined gangs were more likely to have a member of their family already in a gang. Specifically, half of the gang members, but only 17 percent of the nongang members Miller studied, had siblings already in gangs and 60 percent had more than one family member in a gang, compared with only 28 percent of the nongang members (Miller, 2001: 52).

One interesting finding from Miller's study is that the involvement of other family members in gangs was more salient in St. Louis than in Columbus. Recall that the social conditions were more severe in St. Louis (poverty, unemployment, etc.) than in Columbus. These differences led Miller to conclude that there was a much greater influence of extended family members on the lives of girls in St. Louis than was the case in Columbus. One of the reasons Miller cites is the fact that 72 percent of those living in gang members' neighborhoods in St. Louis were African American, compared with only 59 percent in Columbus. This led Miller to conclude (based on a great deal of research) that "African American families living in poverty often rely to a greater degree on extended family for economic, social, and emotional support." This may explain why girl gang members in St. Louis spend more time with relatives who are outside the immediate family, such as cousins, uncles, etc. (Miller, 2001: 53).

School and Work

It should not be too surprising that gang members have had problems in school. Indeed, numerous studies of delinquency in general have found school problems are strong predictors of chronic delinquency (for a good review see Bartollas, 2000: ch. 9). Researchers have noted that school problems are of critical importance for male gang members (Shelden, Tracy, & Brown, 2001). Thus, we have still another illustration of the common themes among both male and female gang members.

Kitchen's gang members had very negative attitudes toward the school system. Even though seven out of 10 graduated from high school, they all felt unprepared to compete in the legitimate economy. A typical response was as follows: "Mostly school is a waste. The teachers don't care nothing about us. . . . It has nothing to do with the real world." Another said, "School doesn't teach you about real life. All it prepares you for is a minimum wage job. . . ." (Ibid.: 119). Most believed that once one begins to sell drugs, one gets used to the money, and it becomes harder and harder to enter into the regular workforce. One respondent stated, "Most kids know that they don't need school to sell drugs" (Ibid.: 120).

Gang members, as a general rule, are highly likely to drop out of school. For instance, the study of San Francisco gangs by Lauderback et al. (1992) found that the median number of years of education was 10, and only about one-third were actually in school at the time of the interviews. Lauderback et al. conclude, in a statement that echoes Campbell, that "the prospects for these young women, unmarried, with children, less than a high school education, and few job skills, can only be considered bleak" (Ibid.: 70). Fishman's study of the Vice Queens in Chicago found that most attended school only sporadically because they experienced much conflict with school officials. Most eventually dropped out of school. Only two of the 19 hard-core members had jobs at the time the study ended. Most did not have any interest in working, as they generally expected "that their old man will take care of them" (Fishman, 1988: 10).

Many have noted that school is often deemed totally irrelevant to the lives of gang members and presents a motivation to drop out and become part of a gang. Davis, for instance, has concluded: "In lives filled with boredom, the gang interjects excitement and 'something happening.'" For most girl gang members, success is elusive: "School is a road that leads to nowhere, and emancipation and independence are out of reach, given their limited family and community networks . . . avenues of opportunity for urban underclass girls are blocked by several sobering realities" (Davis, 1999: 257). These include lack of education, training, access to meaningful employment, and few, if any, career possibilities.

Harris's study of the *Cholas* found that the bonds to both family and school were weak (see our discussion of the "social bond" theory in Chapter 7). None of the females in her study completed high school. The gang, therefore, became the source of status and identity; "the most prevalent peer group association in the barrio, the one most readily available, and [it] provides a strong substitute for weak family and lack of conventional school ties" (Harris, 1997: 156).

Closely related to school problems are, quite naturally, work-related problems. As a general rule, gang members of both sexes have not had good work records. However, contrary to popular myths, most gang members, especially girls, have had plenty of experience in the workforce, although mostly in the very low-wage service economy. Moore found that there were several differences between earlier and later gang cliques concerning employment. In the earlier cliques, before a severe economic downturn in California, 61 percent of the men and 44 percent of the women had jobs; in the more recent cliques, the figures were 48 percent and 61 percent, respectively. Those who used heroin were the least likely to have a job.

Of those working, about one-third (both men and women) worked in semiskilled factory jobs; about one-third of the women but a fraction of the men were unskilled workers. Neither the men nor the women earned much— the median was $1,200 per month, although some earned more than $1,800 per month. Most found jobs through personal connections, such as friends, relatives, and gang members. Most were reasonably happy with their jobs and,

interestingly, most recognized that they would need more educ
training to advance themselves (Harris, 1997: 116).

In most households at least one person was working. Roug
of the men had received some form of government assistance (
ployment compensation, and so on), whereas women were less likely to receive
it. Approximately one-fourth (no gender differences) got income from illegal
sources, mostly from small-scale drug sales and hustling (Harris, 1997: 117).

Some Concluding Thoughts

What emerges from a review of research on girl gangs is a portrait of young
women who, just like their male counterparts, find themselves trapped in hor-
rible social conditions characterized by widespread poverty and racism. Fishman's closing statement in her study of the Vice Queens places African
American girl gangs like them in a larger context, as she writes that:

> There has been little improvement in the economic situation of the
> black community since 1965. As black females growing up, the Vice
> Queens' situation was bleak. They lived in a black lower income commu-
> nity characterized by high chronic unemployment and intermittent em-
> ployment as well as high homicide, crime, drug addition and alcoholism
> rates. . . . The situation for teen-age black girls today is even bleaker than it
> was for the Vice Queens during the early sixties. The findings suggest that
> as black girls are increasingly exposed to the worsening conditions within
> their low income neighborhoods where legitimate opportunities become
> increasingly restricted, then they will increasingly turn to black female aux-
> iliary gangs which provide these girls with the opportunity to learn the
> skills to make adaptations to poverty, violence and racism. Thus black girls
> who join gangs today are no different than their sisters, the Vice Queens,
> but they have gone one step further. In response to the economic crisis
> within their communities, black female gangs today have become more
> entrenched, more violent and more oriented to "male" crime. These
> changes in the content of the black female gang appear not to be related
> to the women's liberation movement but to forced "emancipation" that
> stems from the economic crisis within the black community (Ibid.: 28–29).

Fishman's dismal speculation about the situation of girl gangs in contemporary
poverty-stricken neighborhoods can be easily transferred to the conditions in
the areas already cited: Campbell's Hispanic gangs in the New York area,
Moore's Chicana gangs in East Los Angeles, the gangs in Potrero Hill in San
Francisco, the gangs in Ft. Wayne, Indiana, the various ethnic girl gangs in
Hawaii, and Miller's girls in St. Louis and Columbus.

Moore makes a very interesting statement that should be carefully considered. She notes that the stereotypic gang is "quintessentially male, with no
place for women." This image is held by both gang and nongang males. It is
interesting to note that gang boys acknowledge the presence of the girls by

referring to the gang as a family. This idea is missing from the media stereotype. Moore makes a valid point when she says that if the image of a gang included girls, it would "humanize the gang too much, to force the audience to think of domestic relationships as well as pure male brute force. It might also challenge the simplified and comfortable notions about women" (Moore, 1991: 136–137).

The closing statement in Moore's study is instructive and reminiscent of what Thrasher said nearly 70 years ago (see Chapter 5): "Institutions develop when there are gaps in the existing institutional structure. Gangs as youth groups develop among the socially marginal adolescents for whom school and family do not work. Agencies of street socialization take on increased importance under changing economic circumstances, and have an increased impact on younger kids, whether they serve as beeper-driven flunkies for drug-dealing organizations or are simply recruited into an increasingly adult-influenced gang" (Moore, 1991: 137–138).

SUMMARY

Girls' involvement in gangs has never been as frequent as that of their male counterparts. When they have been involved, it has usually been as so-called auxiliaries to male gangs. However, the extent to which girls have been involved in gang life may be understated because of the vague definitions of gang, gang member, and even gang involvement. As has been stated in this chapter, most male gang members have relationships with females, and this, almost by definition, makes every such female at least an associate gang member.

Media images of girl gangs continue to reflect common stereotypes, typical of how the media work in general. The images are exaggerations of "violent women" who have reached levels of behavior similar to males in just about everything. Largely ignored is the larger social context of poverty, class inequality, and racism that pervades their lives.

There is a general consensus in the research literature that girls become involved in gang life for generally the same reasons as their male counterparts do—namely, to meet basic human needs, such as belonging, self-esteem, protection, and a feeling of being a member of a family. The backgrounds of these young women are about the same as those of male gang members: poverty, single-parent families, minority status, and so on.

The case studies of girl gang members in many different parts of the country reveal the common circumstances in their lives. The crimes that they commit are for the most part attempts to survive in an environment that has never given them much of a chance in life. Most face the hardships that correspond to three major barriers—being a member of the underclass, being a woman, and being a minority. The gang, though not a total solution, seems to them a reasonable solution to their collective problems.

NOTES

1. For exceptions see Brown, 1977; Bowker and Klein, 1983; Campbell, 1984 and 1990; Ostner, 1986; Fishman, 1988; Moore, 1991; Harris, 1988; Quicker, 1983; and Giordano, Cernkovich, and Pugh, 1978.

2. Moore's 1991 study was a follow-up to her original study completed in the 1970s (Moore, 1978). The more recent study compared an earlier generation of gangs (those growing up in the 1940s through the 1950s) with a more recent generation (1960s and beyond). This is what we mean when we refer in this chapter to "earlier" and "later" gang cliques.

3. In addition, similar studies, using comparison groups in Arizona (Zatz, 1985) with Hispanic gangs and in Las Vegas (Shelden, Snodgrass, & Snodgrass, 1993) with African American and Hispanic gangs, while not focusing on gender, found little to differentiate gang members from other "delinquent" or criminal youth.

4. In the first edition of this book we noted that there is another type of gang involvement on the part of girls and young women. We noted at that time that, as far as we could determine, this had not been noted in the literature. This remains true with the second edition. This involvement is in the everyday relationships of girls with males who happen to be in gangs, either as steady girlfriends, occasional dates, lovers, wives, or just friends. Should these girls also be called auxiliary gang members? Is this not similar to the situation of many young males who, because they happen to know regular gang members or are occasionally seen in the company of them, are therefore labeled as gang members (associates, wannabes, and so on) by the police? If we want to extend the often vague definition of a gang member to its logical conclusion (that is, to include everyone who knows a gang member or is seen with one), then there are probably just as many female gang members as there are males.

5. Status offenses, such as running away, truancy, and other offenses, are applicable to juveniles only.

5

Theories of Female
Crime and Delinquency

C riminology has long suffered from what Jessie Bernard has called the
"stag effect" (cited in Smith, 1992: 218). It has attracted male scholars
who wanted to study and understand outlaw men, hoping perhaps
that some of the romance and fascination of this role would rub off. As a result, what came to be known as the field of criminology was actually the study
of male crime and, largely, male victimization.

Feminist criminology challenged the overall masculinist nature of criminology by pointing to the repeated omission and misrepresentation of women
in criminological theory. As Maureen Cain (1990: 2) explains, "women and
girls exist as Other: that is to say, they exist only in their difference from the
male, the normal." Women's crime was overlooked almost completely, and female victimization was ignored, minimized, and trivialized.

Consistent with this, delinquency theory has ignored girls, and as a result, there is considerable question whether existing theories that were developed to explain boys' delinquency can explain girls' as well. As this
chapter demonstrates, the major sociological theories of juvenile delinquency focused almost exclusively on the explanation of male delinquency.
They were also formulated with little awareness of the importance of gender—the network of behaviors and identities associated with the terms *masculinity* and *femininity*—that is socially constructed from relations of
dominance and inequality between men and women (Daly & Chesney-

Lind, 1988). Accordingly, can these theories serve as comprehensive theories of delinquent behavior, as some (Smith, 1979; Simons, Miller, & Aigner, 1980) have argued? This chapter explores this question.

This chapter also examines the work of early researchers on female delinquency. Pioneers to varying degrees, they were greatly handicapped by intellectual isolation. Hence, there is little utility in restricting a discussion of theories about girls' delinquency to what was, until recently, the very lean literature on girls' offending. Instead, we suggest that what is needed is a rethinking of female delinquency in light of what is coming to be known about girls' lives and options. The discussion draws upon the best of the male-centered delinquency theories in addition to recent empirical work about girls' offending in an attempt to begin to sketch out a theory of female delinquency.

This chapter begins this process by reviewing the inherited legacy of "girls'" theories and considers the ability of major delinquency theories to explain female delinquency without revision. In the next chapter an attempt is made to place what we know about girls' delinquency within the broader context of the realities of girls' lives, especially the lives of poor and minority girls.

In these two chapters it will also be suggested that the extensive focus on male delinquency and the inattention to the role played by gender and patriarchal arrangements in the generation of adolescent delinquency and conformity have rendered most delinquency theories inadequate to the task of explaining female behavior—either conforming or rule violating. Inattention to gender has probably also hampered criminologists' ability to explain male delinquency fully—particularly because serious violent crime is such an exclusively male phenomenon (see Messerschmidt, 1986; Daly & Chesney-Lind, 1988).

This chapter argues the urgent need to rethink current models in light of girls' situations in a male-dominated society. That is the task that confronts those trying to understand girls' misbehavior and social responses to that misbehavior.

The proposed overhaul of delinquency theory is not, as some might think, solely an academic exercise. It is incorrect to assume that because girls are charged with less serious offenses, they actually have few problems and are treated gently when they are drawn into the juvenile justice system. Indeed, the extensive focus on disadvantaged males in public settings has meant that girls' victimization and the relationship between that experience and girls' crime have been systematically ignored. Also missed has been the central role played by the juvenile justice system in the sexualization of girls' delinquency and the criminalization of girls' attempts to escape sometimes impossible family situations. The official actions of the juvenile justice system should be understood as major forces in girls' oppression; these actions have historically served to reinforce the obedience of all young women to demands of patriarchal authority, no matter how abusive and arbitrary.

EARLY THEORIES OF
FEMALE DELINQUENCY

One of the first scholarly attempts to explain female criminal behavior was undertaken by Caesar Lombroso, whose *Female Offender* (1895), written with William Ferrero, is a classic in criminology. It set the stage for much of the work on the topic that followed over the next ninety-plus years (Klein, 1973). An enthusiastic proponent of social Darwinism, Lombroso drew on the concept of atavism to explain criminal behavior. He asserted that all criminal behavior could be explained as the behavior of "biological throwbacks"—the result of arrested evolutionary processes. Criminals were thought to be less highly evolved than normal, law-abiding citizens. Further, criminals could often be distinguished by certain "primitive" or "deviant" body traits, such as moles, excessive body hair, receding foreheads, tattoos, and bumps on the head. Lombroso's book is filled with figures on the weight of women's lower jaws and brains, and measurements of women's eyes, noses, craniums, and hands.

Lombroso found that women criminals were less identifiable than their male counterparts, and in attempting to explain this pattern, he gave considerable information about the lives of the women he was studying. For example, on several occasions he speculates, with some degree of frustration, that women offenders showed fewer atavistic signs because many of them, particularly the prostitutes, were very young:

> Very often, too, in women, the [degenerate] type is disguised by youth with its absence of wrinkles and the plumpness which conceals the size of the jaw and cheek-bones, thus softening the masculine and savage features. Then when the hair is black and plentiful . . . and the eyes are bright, a not unpleasing appearance is presented. In short, let a female delinquent be young and we can overlook her degenerate type, and even regard her as beautiful; the sexual instinct misleading us here as it does in making us attribute to women more of the sensitiveness and passion than they really possess. And in the same way, when she is being tried on a criminal charge, we are inclined to excuse, as noble impulses of passion, an act which arises from the most cynical calculations. (Lombroso & Ferrero, 1895: 97)

Lombroso maintained that females were congenitally less inclined toward crime than males because of their sedentary nature and their biological roles as caretakers of children. The female criminal was, in his view, a rare creature because women, although often childlike, jealous, and vengeful, were most often controlled by maternity, piety, weakness, and an underdeveloped intelligence. When a woman did deviate, however, she was believed to be the most vile criminal of all, excelling in cunning, spite, and deceitfulness because "her wickedness must have been enormous before it could triumph over so many obstacles" (Lombroso & Ferrero, 1895: 152). In essence, Lombroso contended that women criminals were particularly depraved in that they exhibited extremely masculine traits compounded by the worst qualities in women.

Lombroso's work on female crime, then, stressed women's presumed reliance on their biological nature. He also speculated that women's crimes were often caused by "a preoccupation with sexual matters" (Lombroso & Ferrero, 1895: 243). Lombroso's work, however flawed it appears now, actually set the tone for much of the later work on female delinquency and criminality. In essence, although most theories about male crime gradually began to consider a variety of causal factors, theories about female crime continued for many years to focus almost exclusively on women's anatomy and, particularly, sexuality. Further, although the female juvenile delinquent was occasionally viewed with more intense hostility than her male counterpart, she was also seen as more receptive to reform than her older sister.

Such a theme is found in W. I. Thomas's *The Unadjusted Girl* (1928). The book continued Lombroso's focus on women's sexuality but also typified a more benevolent orientation toward female offending. As such, it represents another major theme in the early work on female delinquency: through early intervention girls can be saved, particularly from their sexuality. Based upon Thomas's evaluation of case records drawn from the Girls' Protective Bureau and the Cook County Juvenile Court in Chicago, the book is one of the first scholarly attempts to explore the source of female delinquent behavior. Most of the cases involved young women taken into custody because of the "wholesale arrests of girls and women on the suspicion of venereal disease" (Thomas, 1928: v) during World War I, so it is not surprising that Thomas determined that nearly all female delinquency was an expression of sexual problems.

Initially, Thomas states that the definition of young women as sexual property is culturally determined:

> The role which a girl is expected to play in life is indicated to her by her family in a series of aesthetic–moral definitions of the situation. Civilized societies have endowed the young girl with a character of social sacredness. She is the subject of far-going idealization. "Virginity" and "purity" have an almost magical value (Thomas, 1928: 98).

This awareness of the arbitrary emphasis on young women's sexuality sets Thomas apart from his contemporaries. Still, in many ways his work echoes the themes that can be found in other writings on female delinquency during what was known as the Progressive Era (1890–1920)—a time when middle-class social reformers were keenly concerned about controlling the burgeoning immigrant classes. The authors tended to be professional and amateur "child savers" who, as supporters of the then-fledgling family court system, often stressed the need to control the "immorality" of working-class girls. Also, they often argued that extensive intervention and removal from corrupting influences were the only solutions to girls' offending (Schlossman & Wallach, 1978; Messerschmidt, 1987).

Thomas asserted, for example, that young women were not involved in sexual activity out of curiosity but, rather, were encouraged to use sex as "capital" to obtain other valued goods (clothing, money, and so on). He did not condemn this arrangement but instead deplored a social-class system that enabled upper-status women to sell themselves only once (for marriage) and forced poor women to settle for less ("entertainment, affection and perhaps gifts"). Thomas repeatedly debunked the notion that women were being punished for simple sexual experimentation: "The cases which I have examined . . . show that sexual passion does not play an important role, for the girls usually become 'wild' before the development of sexual desire, and their casual sexual relations do not usually awaken sex feeling" (Thomas, 1928: 109). Nor was he hesitant about the source of the problem ("bad family" and "demoralization") and its solution: the family court. As he wrote, "During the past decade some of these [family] courts have reached a high degree of elaboration and perfection. Their service has been very great in checking the beginnings of demoralization. The court is much wiser than the parents of children and incidentally does much to influence home life" (1928: 119).

Thomas hoped that the family court would remedy the problems he detailed in reformatories, and he placed great hope in sensitive and enlightened casework. Similar sorts of characterizations of the nature of female delinquency and enthusiasm for extensive intervention into the lives of girls and young women can also be found in Sheldon and Eleanor Glueck's *Five Hundred Delinquent Women* (1934). Covering roughly the same period, these authors discussed incarcerated women, rather than girls, but their work contains rich background information on youthful female offenders of that era (two-fifths of their population were under the age of twenty-one). They saw the women, half of whom had been prostitutes and four-fifths of whom had venereal infections, as "a sorry lot" (Glueck & Glueck, 1934: 300) and believed that extensive work with them, including lengthy sentences in reformatories and even voluntary sterilization, was a progressive step.

The Gluecks carefully documented the links between adolescent involvement with the criminal justice system and later involvement with the adult justice system. For example, they noted that nearly half their adult sample had been arrested as juveniles for either "immorality" or "stubbornness" (Glueck & Glueck, 1934: 301) and that the women "were born and bred in households in which poverty or near-poverty and its attendant evils and miseries were the common lot" (Glueck & Glueck, 1934: 299).

Otto Pollak's *The Criminality of Women* (1950) and his edited collection, *Family Dynamics and Female Sexual Delinquency* (Pollak & Friedman, 1969), represent at once a continuation of reliance on a biological model of female offending as a way of explaining women's deviance and a return to the distrust of female criminals found in Lombroso's work. With specific reference to girls' offending, Pollak speculated that "precocious biological maturity" played an important role in female sexual delinquency (Pollak, 1950: 124). In a fascinating and contorted manner, Pollak attempted to explain why this factor played a role in female but not male sexual delinquency (since, by his own admission, there were few male sexual delinquents):

The male has to be active while the female has to be passive. In the active attempt to find satisfaction for the sex urge, physiological precocity does not seem to help the boy very much but for the girl who has to wait until she is "propositioned," the appearance of sexual maturity furnishes the opportunity for sex delinquencies that do not come the way of her normally developed age mates (Pollak, 1950: 125).

Pollak noted that official statistics showed that women committed substantially fewer crimes than did men. Here, as well, he focused on the importance of biological and psychological factors to account for female crime and the low official arrest rates for women. He maintained that women offenders were more deceitful than men (hence, much of their crime went undetected). Pollak linked this female ability to the passive role taken during intercourse. Women were able to conceal or manufacture sexual arousal, but men were not so privileged; they had to achieve an erection. As he further comments, "It cannot be denied that this basic physiological difference may well have a great influence on the degree of confidence which the two sexes have in the possible concealment and thus on their character pattern in this respect" (Pollak, 1950: 10). According to Pollak, such concealment and deceit are learned during girlhood, when "natural aggressions are inhibited and forced into concealed channels" (Pollak, 1950: 11).

In a later work (Pollak & Friedman, 1969), Pollak appeared to place greater emphasis on a Freudian perspective on family dynamics, particularly the erosion of the "patriarchal family" and the presumed appearance of the "matriarchal family," in the causation of female delinquency. Patriarchy, in his view, "provided balance to the one-sided impact upon male personality formation of having to encounter adulthood first of all, and in essence for most of his life, in terms of femininity associated with maternal traits." Under this system, "both sexes can go through the full cycle of development. Boys can become men, and mothers are permitted to start out as girls and possibly remain girls in relation to their husbands" (Pollak & Friedman, 1969: 31). The problem with the egalitarian family (Pollak refers to this as a "matriarchal family") is that it "prematurely" forces girls into womanhood. His hope for the future is manifest when he states, "When women will permit boys to become men, and men will be able to help women to be girls, the power structure of the family of the future may become equitable on the spouse and parental level" (Pollak & Friedman, 1969: 32).

Several articles and two major books written during the 1950s and 1960s describe incarcerated girls (see Felice & Offord, 1971). These works establish the astonishing stability of girls' official delinquency as "sexual" delinquency during the first half of this century while also reflecting the uncritical stance taken by academics and practitioners about the court system's intervention in the lives of girls to enforce their conformity to sexual norms that are discriminatory because behavior that is condemned in girls is tacitly supported in boys.

Typical of work in this area is Cowie, Cowie, and Slater's *Delinquency in Girls* (1968), a "psychiatric" study that discussed the characteristics of 318 girls in a single juvenile institution in Great Britain during 1958. The authors said that "these girls had to be removed from society into the security of a residential school much more for their own sakes than to protect society" (Cowie, Cowie, & Slater, 1968: 166). Most were incarcerated for offenses that represented, in the authors' view, "sex delinquencies," including a variety of status offenses (needing "care and protection," "being refractory," and "beyond control") (Cowie, Cowie, & Slater, 1968: 67).

The authors explored the environmental causes of female delinquency but also emphasized the role played by anatomy in the production of differences in male and female delinquency. They considered "chromosomal and geodetical factors" and, concerning the preponderance of girls charged with sexual delinquency in court populations, declared the following:

> The fact that girls mature earlier than boys, but have their peak age for delinquency one year later, is not so paradoxical as it appears. The girls' delinquency is predominantly in the form of sexual behavior (e.g., promiscuity) requiring a more advanced degree of maturation than the (mainly non-sexual) delinquencies of the boys (Cowie, Cowie, & Slater, 1968: 169).

Elsewhere, however, Cowie, Cowie, and Slater wrote that social factors may also play a role in female behavior: "The female mode of personality, more timid, more lacking in enterprise, may guard her against delinquency" (1968: 167). They also noted, in passing, that "a disconcerting number of [the girls] say they ran away from home because of sexual advances made by near relatives" (Cowie, Cowie, & Slater, 1968: 112), although this fact is quickly dropped, and they discuss in the conclusion, in detail, the need for better mental health to counter disruptions in home life.

An American book, *The Delinquent Girl* (Vedder & Somerville, 1970), covers much the same territory, examining the backgrounds of girls in U.S. training schools. Although the authors were less interested in the biological source of girls' delinquency, like their British counterparts they mentioned that approximately 75 to 85 percent of the offenses leading to the commitment of delinquent girls were in essence sexual offenses. Yet this pattern was masked because "in most instances the most innocuous charges of 'running away,' 'incorrigibility,' and 'ungovernability' and the like are used on the official record" (Vedder & Somerville, 1970: 147).

In general, Vedder and Somerville described, in rather unself-conscious terms, the "types" of female delinquents of that period: the runaway, the incorrigible girl, and the sex-delinquent girl. They occasionally bemoaned the sexual double standard that, for example, resulted in the incarceration of pregnant girls, but were quick to explain it away as due to the "lack of other resources" (an excuse that surfaces repeatedly in discussions of the treatment of delinquent girls). More troubling is the authors' attempt to deal with incest by citing a theorist who suggests that girls often run away from home "because they fear the incestual consequences of [their] own impulses" (Vedder & Somerville, 1970: 154) and try to leave this disturbing situation.

However, the authors were troubled by the high number of black girls they found incarcerated in large metropolitan areas and urged greater reliance on community-based programs. They remained enthusiastic about court intervention and committed to traditional family norms, saying at one point, "While studying delinquent girls, we should keep this thought in mind: when you train a man, you train an individual; when you train a woman, you train a family" (Vedder & Somerville, 1970: viii).

Another enthusiastic supporter of enlightened intervention, but one whose perspective and methodology were more ambitious, was Gisela Konopka. Her early book, *The Adolescent Girl in Conflict* (1966), and her more recent *Young Girls: A Portrait of Adolescence* (1983) represent efforts to interview large numbers of adolescent women in order to gain a better understanding of their world. In the first book, Konopka focused on girls in trouble and noted that most of the behaviors that bring young women into the juvenile justice system were "accompanied by some disturbance or unfavorable behavior in the sexual area" (Konopka, 1966: 4). Although Konopka did not explore whether this characterization is accurate, she did touch on one important consequence: such sexual behavior "hits close to the personal feeling of most people, especially women" because of their own ambivalence about their sexuality. She went on to suggest that this "hidden fear of sex" may lay behind the "almost unbelievably neglectful—and sometimes cruel—treatment of girls in many institutions and communities" (Konopka, 1966: 4).

For this work, the only one to directly address delinquent girls, Konopka interviewed 181 girls. Most were adjudicated delinquents and unwed pregnant girls. Through a multitude of case studies Konopka identified some key concepts in female delinquency, including, in her view, the "unique dramatic biological onset of puberty"; the "complex identification processes" (particularly the mother–daughter conflict); the "changing cultural position of women" (by which Konopka meant the stereotyped and low-paying jobs available to working-class women, little legitimate outlet for aggressive drives, and increased resentment of the "double standard"); the "faceless adult authority"; and the resulting loneliness (Konopka, 1966: 119). She hoped that her work would both contribute to the understanding of the adolescent girl in conflict and demonstrate how treatment using the social group work method would be helpful.

Konopka's more sophisticated understanding of girls' reality still ultimately assumed that girls and women were largely controlled by their biology and their sexuality. Indeed, she, like most authors of the early works on female delinquency, assumed that most female delinquency is either "sexual" or "relational" rather than "criminal" in nature, and was convinced that social intervention administered by sensitive and informed individuals could help young women with their problems.

Based almost without exception on studies of officially labeled and/or incarcerated juvenile females (roughly three-quarters of whom were charged either directly or indirectly with sexual offenses), these authors rarely questioned the equity of the family courts' exclusive preoccupation with female sexuality. Most assumed that the courts' populations accurately reflected the nature of female delinquency. Therefore, the consistent theme in these works was how best to diagnose and treat members of those populations and return them to their "proper" roles, in that fashion protecting them from environments that might lure them back into sexual activity. Obviously, this approach tended to neglect the role played by class or ethnicity, for these were not viewed as relevant to female criminality (although both factors usually are relevant when it comes to explaining male crime). The approach also severely underestimated the role played by agents of the juvenile justice system (police, probation officers, and judges) in the shaping of the female delinquency problem.

Aside from these basic sources, it is accurate to say that until recently the remaining literature on female delinquency fell into one of two general categories—both of which made many of the assumptions of the works described above. The first category comprised many articles containing descriptions of officially labeled and/or incarcerated female youth, suggestions about treatment strategies for female delinquency, and literature on the social organization of female institutions (see Felice & Offord, 1971; Gelsthorpe, 1986). The second category included a few sociological attempts to develop a coherent theory of female delinquency. Because so few researchers have paid serious attention to female delinquents (most concentrated on adult females, if they paid any attention to women at all), this early literature was flawed by its intellectual isolation. In brief, those who have elected to study female delinquency or criminality have confronted an enormous task of theory building (because the bulk of the available theoretical literature was seen as inapplicable to women).

Before undertaking a review of the early theoretical literature, however, a more basic question must be addressed: Need such a review occur? Many would suggest that major delinquency theories, albeit developed to explain male delinquency, are adequate to the task of explaining female delinquency. To understand why this is not necessarily the case, it is important to explore the dimensions of the androcentric bias found in the dominant and influential delinquency theories. Most of the major sociological theories are reviewed in the following section. The next chapter reviews contemporary research efforts that use, in part, certain elements of these classic theories that show promise in explaining female delinquency. Then the beginnings of a feminist model of female delinquency are explored by blending promising contemporary theoretical and empirical work on girls' lives and problems.

SOCIOLOGICAL THEORIES OF (MALE) DELINQUENCY: DO THEY APPLY TO GIRLS?

A careful review of the major sociological theories of delinquency reveals that virtually all of them attempted to explain the phenomenon by using data on the delinquency of boys. From the start, the field of delinquency research focused almost exclusively on visible lower class, male delinquency, often justifying the neglect of female delinquency in the most cavalier of terms.

Social Disorganization/Social Ecology Theory

Social disorganization theory has been one of the most popular and enduring sociological theories of crime and delinquency. Variations of this theory have been called the *social ecology* perspective, since it has a lot to do with the *spacial or geographical distribution* of crime, delinquency, and gangs (Lanier & Henry, 1998: ch. 9; Stark, 1987). Modern versions of this perspective began with the work of several sociologists at the University of Chicago during the first three decades of the 20th century. The original idea behind the spatial distribution of crime can be traced back to the mid-19th century with the work of two rather obscure scientists, Adolphe Quetelet (1796–1874), a Belgian astronomer and mathematician, and a French lawyer and statistician named Michel Guerry (1802–1866). These two were actually the first scientists who collected and analyzed various crime data and examined the residences of offenders, matching them with various socioeconomic variables, such as poverty, infant mortality, unemployment, and other social indicators. This began what became known as the *Cartographic School* of criminology—in other words, "map-making," which involved merely plotting on a city map the location of criminals and various social indicators (with colored dots, for instance, as police departments still do today when, for example, they plot the locations of certain crimes, such as serial rapes, or the locations of a series of muggings, auto thefts, etc.).[1]

This idea of "map-making" and the more general notion that crime is *spatially* distributed within a geographical area became one of the hallmarks of what came to be known as the *Chicago School* of sociology (named after the many researchers in the sociology department at the University of Chicago during the early 20th century). Within the city of Chicago (and other major cities of the era) these researchers noticed that crime and delinquency rates varied by areas of the city (just as Guerry and Quetelet had done 50 years earlier). The researchers found that the highest rates of crime and delinquency were also found in the same areas exhibiting high rates of multiple other social problems, such as single-parent families, unemployment, multiple-family dwellings, welfare cases, and low levels of education.

One of the key ideas of the social ecology of crime is the fact that high rates of crime and other problems persist within the same neighborhoods over long periods of time, *regardless of who lives there*. As several gang researchers have noted, some gangs in certain neighborhoods have existed for as long as 50 or more years, often spanning three generations. This has been especially the case in East Los Angeles.[2] Thus, there must be something about the *places* themselves, perhaps something about the *neighborhoods*, rather than the people per se, that produces and perpetuates high crime rates (Stark, 1987).

The social ecology perspective borrows concepts from the field of plant biology, specifically studying human life and problems using notions derived from studies of the interdependence of plant and animal life. From this perspective, people are seen as being in a relationship to one another and to their physical environment. Further, just as plant and animal species tend to *colonize* their environment, humans colonize their "geographical space."[3] One of the most important ideas originating from these Chicago sociologists (specifically Robert Park and Ernest Burgess) was the *concentric zone* model of city life (Burgess, 1925). This perspective on city life and land use patterns identified specified zones emanating outward from the central part of the city. Five zones were identified:

Zone 1: Central Business District

Zone 2: Zone in Transition

Zone 3: Zone of Workingmen's Homes

Zone 4: Residential Zone

Zone 5: Commuter Zone

According to this theory, growth is generated (from mostly political and economic forces) outward from the central business district. Such expansion occurs in concentric waves, or circles. Such expansion and movement affects neighborhood development and patterns of social problems. Studies of the rates of crime and delinquency, especially by sociologists Henry Shaw and David McKay, demonstrated that over an extended period of time, the highest rates were found within the first three zones, *no matter who lived there.* These high rates were strongly correlated with such social problems as mental illness, unemployment, poverty, infant mortality, and many others (Shaw & McKay, 1972).

Such a distribution is caused by a breakdown of institutional, community-based controls, which in turn is caused by three general factors: industrialization, urbanization, and immigration. People living within these areas often lack a sense of community because the local institutions (for example, schools, families, churches) are not strong enough to provide nurturing and guidance for the area's children. It is important to note that there are important political and economic forces at work here. The concentration of human and social problems within these zones is not the inevitable "natural" result of some abstract laws of nature, but rather the actions of some of the most powerful groups in a city (urban planners, politicians, wealthy business leaders, etc.).

Unfortunately, Shaw and McKay focused almost exclusively on male delinquents in Chicago (more than 60,000) and repeatedly referred to the rates as "delinquency rates" (although they occasionally make parenthetical reference to data on female delinquency) (see Shaw & McKay, 1942: 356). Similarly, Shaw's case studies (1930, 1938) traced only male experiences with the law. In none of these works was there any justification given for the equation of male delinquency with delinquency.

Early fieldwork on delinquent gangs in Chicago set the stage for another important type of delinquency research. Yet here, too, researchers focused almost exclusively on male gangs. Thrasher (1927) studied over a thousand juvenile gangs in Chicago during roughly the same period that Shaw and McKay's more quantitative work was being done. He devoted approximately one page in a book of three hundred or so pages to a discussion of the five or six female gangs he encountered in his field observations. Thrasher did mention, in passing, two factors he believed accounted for the lower number of girl gangs: ". . . first, the social patterns for the behavior of girls, powerfully backed by the great weight of tradition and custom, are contrary to the gang and its activities; and secondly, girls, even in urban disorganized areas, are much more closely supervised and guarded than boys and are usually well incorporated into the family groups or some other social structure" (Thrasher, 1927: 228). An often-quoted passage from Thrasher's book presents his general theory of gang delinquency, which gives the reader the distinct impression that the problems the gang attempts to solve are problems facing boys only:

> . . . the spontaneous effort of *boys* to create a society for themselves where none adequate to their needs exists. What *boys* get out of such associations that they do not get otherwise under the conditions that adult society imposes is the thrill and zest of participation in common interests, more especially in corporate action, in hunting, capture, conflict, flight, and escape. Conflict with other gangs and the world about them furnishes the occasion for many of their exciting group activities. . . . (Thrasher, 1927: 32–33, emphasis added).

> The failure of the normally directing and controlling customs and institutions to function efficiently in the *boy's* experience is indicated by the disintegration of family life, inefficiency of schools, formalism and externality of religion, corruption and indifference in local politics, low wages and monotony in occupational activities, unemployment and lack of opportunity for wholesome recreation. All these factors enter into the picture of the moral and economic frontier, and, coupled with deterioration in the housing, sanitation, and other conditions of life in the slum, give the impression of general disorganization and decay. . . . The gang functions with reference to these conditions in two ways: It offers a substitute for what society fails to give; and it provides a relief from suppression and distasteful behavior. It fills a gap and affords an escape (Thrasher, 1927: 228–231, emphasis added).

The social disorganization/ecology approach to delinquency,[4] particularly its emphasis on the role played by social class in delinquency causation, deeply influenced several sociologists whose theories are generally characterized as "strain" theories of delinquency. It is to their work that we now turn.

STRAIN THEORY

Strain theory originated with Robert Merton, who borrowed the term *anomie* from the nineteenth-century French sociologist Émile Durkheim and applied it to the problem of crime in America.[5] The concept of *anomie* refers to inconsistencies between societal conditions and opportunities for growth, fulfillment, and productivity within a society (the term *anomia* has been used to refer to those who experience personal frustration and alienation as a result of anomie within a society). It also involves the *weakening of the normative order* of society—that is, norms (rules, laws, etc.) lose their impact on people. The existence of anomie within a culture can also produce a high level of flexibility in the pursuit of goals, even suggesting that it may at times be appropriate to deviate from the norms concerning the methods of achieving success.

Durkheim, writing during the late 19th century, suggested that under capitalism there is a more or less chronic state of "deregulation" and that industrialization had removed traditional social controls on aspirations. The capitalist culture produces in humans a constant dissatisfaction resulting in a never-ending longing for more and more. And there is never enough—whether of money, material things, or power. There is a morality under capitalism that dictates "anything goes," especially when it comes to making money (it certainly applies to the modern corporation).

What Durkheim was hinting at (but never coming right out and saying—this was said very forcefully by Karl Marx) was that a very strong social structure is needed to offset or place limits on this morality. In other words, strong institutions such as the family, religion, and education are needed to place some limits on us. But the failure of these institutions can be seen in our high crime rates and the fact that the economic institution is so powerful that it has sort of "invaded" and become dominant over other institutions. (More will be said about this shortly.)

Building on Durkheim's notion of anomie, Robert K. Merton developed one of the most enduring criminological theories (1938, 1957). The basic thesis of Merton's version of strain theory is this: Crime stems from the lack of articulation or "fit" between two of the most basic components of society: *culture* and *social structure*.[6] Here we refer to culture as consisting of (1) the main value and goal orientations or "ends" and (2) the institutionalized or *legitimate means for attaining these goals*. Social structure, as used here, consists of the basic *social institutions* of society, especially the economy, but also such institutions as the family, education, and politics, all of which are responsible for distributing *access* to the legitimate means for obtaining goals.

According to Merton, this "lack of fit" creates *strain* within individuals, who respond with various forms of deviance. Thus, people who find themselves at a disadvantage relative to legitimate economic activities are motivated to engage in illegitimate activities (perhaps because of unavailability of jobs, lack of job skills, education, and other factors). Within a capitalist society like that of America, the main emphasis is on the "success" goals, while less emphasis is on the legitimate *means* to achieve these goals. Moreover, these goals have become *institutionalized* in that they are deeply embedded into the psyches of everyone via a very powerful system of corporate propaganda.[7] At the same time, the legitimate means are not as well defined nor as strongly ingrained. In other words, there is a lot of discretion and a lot of tolerance for deviance from the means, but not the goals. In consequence, "strain" or pressure is placed "upon certain persons in the society to engage in nonconformist rather than conformist conduct" (Merton, 1938: 672). One result of such a system is high levels of crime.

Another important point made by strain theory is that our culture contributes to crime because the opportunities to achieve success goals are not equally distributed. We have a strong class structure and immense inequality within our society, which means that some have extreme advantages over others.[8] Another way of saying this is that *culture promises what the social structure cannot deliver*, that being equal access to opportunities to achieve success. People faced with this contradiction (one of many under capitalism) face pressures or "strains" to seek alternatives.

According to Merton, there are several possible alternatives, which he calls "modes of adaptation." In his now-famous typology of adaptations (reproduced in almost every criminology textbook), Merton suggested several alternatives, which include: (1) *conformity*—accepting both the legitimate means and the success goals; (2) *ritualism*—accepting the means but rejecting the goals (one just goes to work every day but has given up the goal of "success"); (3) *innovation*—where the person accepts the *goals* of success but rejects the legitimate *means* to obtain them; (4) *retreatism*—where one rejects both the goals *and* the means and more or less drops out of society (to become, for instance, part of a drug subculture); (5) *rebellion*—where one rejects both the goals and the means, but instead of retreating, begins to substitute *new* definitions of success and the means to obtain them. Obviously, the adaptation known as *innovation* directly relates to criminal activity, including gang activities.

Merton's theory does not adequately address crime and delinquency among girls and women. As Morris has argued (1987: 6–8), women seem to have the same aspirations as men (e.g., success goals such as jobs that pay well, higher education, and wealth, yet obviously do not have the same opportunities as men because of various forms of discrimination. By Merton's logic, women should experience more strain than men and hence should commit more crime than men. The fact that they do not seriously challenges Merton's theory.

One of the most popular offshoots of Merton's strain theory is known as *opportunity theory*, which was developed in the late 1950s by Richard Cloward and Lloyd Ohlin (1960). These authors argued that (1) blocked opportunity aspirations cause poor self-concepts and feelings of frustration and (2) these frustrations lead to delinquency, especially within a gang context. A key concept here is *differential opportunity structure*, which is an uneven distribution of legal and illegal means of achieving economic success, especially as they are unequally divided according to class and race. Cloward and Ohlin argued that while legitimate opportunities are blocked for significant numbers of lower class youths, the same cannot be said for illegitimate opportunities (for example, selling drugs and other crimes). Their major thesis was that

> The disparity between what lower class youth are led to want and what is actually available to them is the source of a major problem of adjustment. Adolescents who form delinquent subcultures, we suggest, have internalized an emphasis upon conventional goals. Faced with limitations on legitimate

avenues of access to these goals, and unable to revise their aspirations downward, they experience intense frustrations; the exploration of nonconformist alternatives may be the result (Cloward & Ohlin, 1960: 86).

Among the specific assumptions of this theory is that blocked opportunities (or aspirations) create feelings of frustration and low self-esteem, which in turn often lead to delinquency and frequently gang behavior. Cloward and Ohlin postulate that three different types of gangs emerge and that these types correspond with characteristics of the neighborhoods (which affect opportunities to commit different types of crimes) rather than of the individuals who live there. [The three types of gangs are (1) *criminal gangs*, which are organized mainly around the commission of property crimes and exist in areas where there is already in existence relatively organized forms of adult criminal activity (thus adult criminals are seen as successful role models by youths who live there); (2) *conflict gangs*, which engage mostly in violent behavior, such as gang fights over turf; these gangs exist in neighborhoods where living conditions are for the most part unstable and transient, resulting in the lack of any adult role models, whether conventional or criminal; and (3) *retreatist gangs*, engaging in mostly illegal drug use and existing in those neighborhoods dominated by a great deal of illegal drug activity. These youths are described as double failures by Cloward and Ohlin.]

It should come as no surprise that Cloward and Ohlin's work concentrated exclusively on male delinquent behavior. However, part of their explanation for this centered on the notion that under the conditions of modern society the adult male is typically away from the home working or (as in the case of many female-headed households) wholly absent. One result of this is that "boys have trouble forming a clear masculine self-image" (Cloward & Ohlin, 1960: 49). While they are growing up, the mother tends to become a central object of identification for these boys, but upon reaching adolescence, they "encounter strong cultural expectations that they behave as males" and consequently experience much strain. Continuing, Cloward and Ohlin wrote the following (1960: 49):

> Engulfed by a feminine world and uncertain of their own identification, they tend to "protest" against femininity. This protest may take the form of robust and aggressive behavior, and even of malicious, irresponsible, and destructive acts. Such acts evoke maternal disapproval and thus come to stand for independence and masculinity to rebellious adolescents. This is the process designated by such terms as "masculine protest" or "compulsive masculinity."

A persistent theme, then, in a number of "strain" or anomie theories is the notion that masculinity, of one sort or another, is at the core of delinquency. In carefully reading these influential works, one reaches the unavoidable conclusion that uncritical constructions of traditional gender roles found their way into the core of these theories. As we shall see, however, the idea that masculinity or masculine attributes increase delinquency has met with very little support. More to the point, it is unclear how such theories would address the situation of girls in poor neighborhoods.

Cultural Deviance Theories

One of the most common offshoots of Merton's strain theory has come to be called *cultural deviance theory* (often called "subcultural" approaches). This theory proposes that delinquency is a result of a desire to conform to cultural values that are to some extent in conflict with those of conventional society. In part, this perspective is a direct offshoot of social disorganization theory because part of that theory (as noted previously) suggests that criminal values and traditions emerge within communities most affected by social disorganization. The variant theories posit that a distinct subculture exists within the lower class that generates high rates of delinquency.

Cohen's "Culture of the Gang"

Cohen's theory of delinquent gangs, for example, was articulated in the now-classic *Delinquent Boys: The Culture of the Gang* (1955). Cohen's view incorporates the following assumptions: (1) a high proportion of lower class youth (especially males) do poorly in school; (2) poor school performance relates to delinquency; (3) poor school performance stems from a conflict between dominant middle-class values of the school system and values of lower class youth; and (4) most lower class male delinquency is committed in a gang context, partly as a means of meeting some basic human needs, such as self-esteem and belonging.

There are two key concepts in Cohen's theory: (1) *reaction formation,* meaning that one openly rejects what he or she wants, or aspires to, but cannot achieve or obtain, and (2) *middle-class measuring rod*—evaluation of school performance *and* behavior within the school is based upon norms and values thought to be associated with the middle class, such as punctuality, neatness, cleanliness, nonviolent behavior, drive and ambition, achievement and success (especially at school), and deferred gratification. Cohen argues that delinquents often develop a culture that is at odds with the norms and values of the middle class, which they turn upside down and rebel against. Much of the resulting behaviors are described by Cohen as "short-run hedonism" that is "malicious, negativistic, and non-utilitarian."

Cohen excluded girls from his analysis, and his justification is illuminating:

> My skin has nothing of the quality of down or silk, there is nothing limpid or flute-like about my voice, I am a total loss with needle and thread, my posture and carriage are wholly lacking in grace. These imperfections cause me no distress—if anything, they are gratifying—because I conceive myself to be a man and want people to recognize me as a full-fledged, unequivocal representative of my sex. My wife, on the other hand, is not greatly embarrassed by her inability to tinker with or talk about the internal organs of a car, by her modest attainments in arithmetic or by her

inability to lift heavy objects. Indeed, I am reliably informed that many women—I do not suggest that my wife is among them—often affect ignorance, frailty and emotional instability because to do otherwise would be out of keeping with a reputation for indubitable femininity. In short, people do not simply want to excel; they want to excel as a man or as a woman (From *Delinquent Boys* by Albert Cohen, Copyright © 1955 by The Free Press; Copyright renewed 1983 by Albert K. Cohen. Reprinted with permission of The Free Press, a division of Simon & Schuster.)

From this, Cohen concludes that the delinquent's response "however it may be condemned by others on moral grounds, has at least one virtue: it incontestably confirms, in the eyes of all concerned, his essential masculinity. The delinquent is the rogue male" (Cohen, 1955: 139–140). This, the author concludes, predisposes poor youths (particularly male youths) to criminal misconduct. However, Cohen's comments are notable in their candor and probably capture both the allure that male delinquency has had for at least some male theorists and the fact that sexism has rendered the female delinquent irrelevant to their work.

Miller's "Lower Class Culture"

Walter B. Miller, in a 1958 article, took a slightly different approach to "lower class culture." He argued that the culture developed its own standards of behavior and values, many of which run counter to those of mainstream society and ultimately result in delinquent or criminal behavior. The values are described by Miller as *focal concerns* about trouble, toughness, smartness, excitement, fate, and autonomy. These are "issues which command widespread and persistent attention" and "constitute a distinctive patterning of concerns which differ significantly, both in rank order and weighing, from that of American middle class culture" (Miller, 1958: 6).

Miller argued that lower class delinquency, especially gang delinquency, stemmed largely from the street corner male group. This "one-sex peer group," as Miller called it, is mostly the result of a "female-headed" household. Because the father is so often absent and the mother cannot provide models of male behavior, the young male is forced to learn the male role from his peers (which results in highly exaggerated forms of masculinity).

One of the problems of Miller's thesis is that he at least indirectly blamed the female householder for the delinquency of her sons (and there is no mention of how this may account for the delinquency of girls), with no reference to possible structural sources of this circumstance (that is, the patriarchal social system, economic discrimination, racism). Moreover, there is no evidence that these "focal concerns" are all exclusive to the lower class (a fact that Miller himself admitted); in fact, many of them may apply generally to common definitions of "masculinity" (being tough, smart, autonomous, and so on are often seen as stereotypically male traits). Finally, empirical evaluations of Miller's theory have been limited and have produced mixed results (Shoemaker, 1990: 138–141).

Differential Association

One body of theory attempting to explain human behavior is known as *learning theory*, which argues that behavior is the outcome of a learning process. One learns behavior, as one learns values, beliefs, and attitudes, through one's association with other human beings. One of the earliest versions of this theory as it applies to delinquency and crime was the theory of *differential association* theory originally developed by Edwin Sutherland in the second and third editions of his now-classic *Criminology*. Its basic premise is that criminal behavior, like other forms of human behavior, is learned in association with close, intimate friends. More specifically, the learning of criminal behavior includes learning its techniques and developing the motives, drives, rationalizations, and attitudes pertaining thereto. Also, the motives, drives, rationalizations, and attitudes are learned from definitions of legal codes as favorable or unfavorable toward violation of the law, depending upon the prevailing perspective within one's immediate environment. The key proposition of the differential association theory is that "a person becomes delinquent because of an excess of definitions favorable to violation of law over definitions unfavorable to violation of law" (Sutherland & Cressey, 1978: 75).

Sutherland's research (which included white-collar crime and professional theft), however, was also male-oriented. In describing his notion of how differential association works, for example, he wrote: "In an area where the delinquency rate is high a boy who is sociable, gregarious, active, and athletic is very likely to come in contact with the other boys in the neighborhood, learn delinquent behavior from them, and become a gangster" (Sutherland & Cressey, 1978: 77).

Control Theory

There have been several variants of what is commonly known as control theory or social control theory or social bond theory. Their basic assumption is that because all human beings are capable of deviant behavior, the central question is not why people commit crime, but rather, why they do not. Explanations have ranged from "personal controls," such as a positive self-concept (Reiss, 1951; Reckless, 1961), to the lack of effective family and other external controls (Nye, 1958; Toby, 1957), to the lack of an effective "social bond" (Hirschi, 1969).

The most popular variant has been Travis Hirschi's development of the concept of *social bond* (1969). According to this view, those with close bonds to social groups and institutions (e.g., family, school) are the least likely to become delinquent because the bonds help keep people "in check." Four major elements constitute the social bond: (1) *attachment* refers to one's connection (mostly of an emotional kind) to conventional groups, such as one's immediate family, peers, the school, and so on; (2) *commitment* refers to the sort of "investment" one makes in conventional society or, as Toby (1957) once stated, a "stake in conformity" because one stands to lose a great deal (respect from others, the time one has spent preparing for a career, and the like) if one violates the law; (3) *involvement* refers to one's participation in traditional activities, such as going to school, working, and participating in sports, because if one is busy with such activities presumably there is little time for deviant activities (this is related to the old saying "idleness is the devil's workshop"); and (4) *belief* refers to an acceptance of basic moral values and laws.

Hirschi tested this theory with a self-report survey of about four thousand junior and senior high school *boys*. What about girls? In a footnote, Hirschi explained that "in the analysis that follows, the 'non-Negro' becomes 'white,' and the girls disappear" (Hirschi, 1969: 35–36). Briefly, Hirschi found that, with some exceptions, the facts he collected tended to support his theory. Specifically, youths who had the strongest attachments were the most committed, had the strongest belief in conventional moral values and the law, and were the least delinquent. Concerning involvement, Hirschi came up with some mixed results. For instance, youths who worked and spent time reading books, dating, and so on were the most likely to be involved in delinquent activities. However, his self-report data focused mainly on rather trivial offenses, which might explain why he found no correlation between class and rate of delinquency. Furthermore, subsequent research has not demonstrated that control theory accounts for serious and repetitive crime (Vold & Bernard, 1986: 247–248).

A major effort to extend a form of control theory to the delinquency of girls was undertaken by Hagan and his associates in a number of important papers (see Hagan et al., 1985). Given the importance of this perspective, it is considered at length in the next chapter.

Labeling Theory

Labeling theory does not consider original causation in delinquency or criminal behavior. Instead of asking why a person committed a deviant act, the emphasis is on the response to the act. What is most important, from this perspective, is what is made of an act *socially* (Schur, 1971: 8).

The labeling perspective addresses three general problem areas concerning deviance (Schur, 1971: 37–39): (1) collective rule making (addresses why certain behaviors are considered "deviant" or "delinquent"); (2) organizational processing (addresses the processing of deviants through the criminal or juvenile justice system and examines the factors that determine decision making within the system); and (3) interpersonal relations (addresses how negative labeling affects one's self-concept and possibly perpetuates rather than deters deviant behavior). Each of these areas could relate to gender by, for instance, asking why people of one gender rather than another are labeled as "delinquent," by comparing how males and females are processed through the judicial system, and by examining how the self-concepts of males and females are differentially affected by such labeling (e.g., whether negative labeling affects girls more so than boys).

An important aspect of this perspective comes from the distinctions between primary and secondary deviance (Lemert, 1951). Primary deviance includes acts that the perpetrator and/or others consider alien (that is, not indicative, incidental) to one's true identity or character. In other words, an act is "out of character" (commonly expressed by others as "this is not like you"). These acts have only marginal implications for one's status and psychic structure. They remain primary deviance as long as one can rationalize or otherwise deal with the behavior and still maintain an acceptable self-image and an image acceptable to others. Secondary deviance, on the other hand, refers to a process whereby the deviance takes on self-identifying features; that is, deviant acts begin to be considered indicative of one's true self, the way one "really" is. Deviance becomes secondary "when a person begins to employ his deviant behavior or a role based upon it as a means of defense, attack, or adjustment to the overt and covert problems created by the consequent societal reaction to him . . ." (Lemert, 1951: 76).

One of the few attempts to apply this theory to female crime was made by Rosenblum in her study of prostitution (1980). Rosenblum (1980) suggested that entry into the sexual netherworld is a transition from "primary deviance" to "secondary deviance," to use Lemert's terms (1951, 1967). As we saw in Chapter 2, the same processes are likely to be at work in the lives of juvenile prostitutes who resort to "survival sex" while on the run from home.

Labeling theory has also provided those critical of "status offenses" and other attempts to label women as deviant with a powerful theoretical perspective. Schur himself, in an important extension of his theory, *Labeling Women Deviant* (1984), argued that women's powerlessness has resulted in an extensive array of labels used against women to characterize them as "deviant" and to devalue and objectify the "very condition of womanhood itself." Indeed, our book is deeply shaped by notions derived from labeling theory. We will be spending as much time discussing official reactions to girls' delinquency as on describing the behavior that brings girls into the juvenile justice system.

One of the most significant perspectives on crime and criminal behavior to emerge from the labeling tradition was Quinney's theory, espoused in *The Social Reality of Crime* (1970). In a truly landmark textbook on crime and criminal justice, Quinney organized his theory around six interrelated propositions, which are as follows (1970: 15–25):

1. Crime is a definition of human conduct that is created by authorized agents in a politically organized society.

2. Criminal definitions describe behaviors that conflict with the interests of the segments of society that have the power to shape public policy.

3. Criminal definitions are applied by the segments of society that have the power to shape the enforcement and administration of criminal law.

4. Behavior patterns are structured in segmentally organized society in relation to criminal definitions, and within this context persons engage in actions that have relative probabilities of being defined as criminal.

5. Conceptions of crime are constructed and diffused in the segments of society by various means of communication.

6. The social reality of crime is constructed by the formulation and application of criminal definitions, the development of behavior patterns related to criminal definitions, and the construction of criminal conceptions.

An important component of Quinney's theory is four interrelated concepts, which include (1) process, (2) conflict, (3) power, and (4) action (8–15). By "process," Quinney is referring to the fact that "all social phenomena . . . have duration and undergo change" (8). The "conflict" view of society and the law is that in any society "conflicts between persons, social units, or cultural elements are inevitable, the normal consequences of social life." Further, society "is held together by force and constraint and is characterized by ubiquitous conflicts that result in continuous change" (9–10). Power is an elementary force in our society. Power, says Quinney, "is the ability of persons and groups to determine the conduct of other persons and groups. It is utilized not for its own sake, but is the vehicle for the enforcement of scarce values in society, whether the values are material, moral, or otherwise" (11). Power is important if we are to understand public policy. Public policy, including crime control policies, is shaped by groups with special interests. In a class society, some groups have more power than others and are therefore able to have their interests represented in policy decisions, often at the expense of less powerful groups. Thus, for instance, white, upper class males have more power and their interests are more likely to be represented than those of working-class or lower class minorities and women. Finally, by "social action," Quinney is referring to the fact that human beings engage in voluntary behavior and are not completely determined by forces outside their control. From this perspective, human beings are "able to reason and choose courses of action" and are "changing and becoming, rather than merely being." It is true that humans are in fact shaped by their physical, social, and cultural experiences, but they also have the capacity to change and achieve maximum potential and fulfillment (13–14).

Quinney's perspective eventually led some scholars to begin to question not only the criminal justice system, but the very social structure and institutions of society as a whole. In particular, some research in the labeling tradition directed our attention to such factors as class, race, and sex in not only the formulation of criminal and delinquent definitions (including the definition of certain "status offenses") but also as major causes of crime and delinquency. This in turn led to a critical examination of existing institutions of American society (including the juvenile justice system) and to a critique of the capitalist system itself. A critical/Marxist criminology emerged from such efforts.

Critical/Marxist Perspectives

Quinney and Wildeman place the development of a critical/Marxist line of inquiry in the historical and social context of the late 1960s and early 1970s. They note that:

> It is not by chance that the 1970s saw the birth of critical thought in the ranks of American criminologists. Not only did critical criminology challenge old ideas, but it went on to introduce new and liberating ideas

and interpretations of America and of what America could become. If social justice is not for all in a democratic society—and it was clear that it was not—then there must be something radically wrong with the way our basic institutions are structured (Quinney & Wildeman, 1991: 72).

In *Class, State, and Crime,* Quinney outlined his own version of a critical or Marxist theory of crime. Quinney linked crime and the reaction to crime to the modern capitalist political and economic system. This viewpoint suggests that the capitalist system itself produces a number of problems that are linked to various attempts by the capitalist class to maintain the basic institutions of the capitalist order. These attempts lead to various forms of accommodation and resistance by people who are oppressed by the system, especially the working class, the poor, and racial and ethnic minorities. In attempting to maintain the existing order, the powerful commit various crimes, which Quinney classified as crimes of control, crimes of economic domination, and crimes of government. At the same time, oppressed people engage in various kinds of crimes related to accommodation and resistance, including predatory crimes, personal crimes, and crimes of resistance (Quinney, 1977: 33–62).

Much of the "delinquent" behavior that girls engage in can be understood as an attempt by oppressed people to accommodate and resist the problems created by capitalist institutions, especially the family (since so many girls begin their "careers" in delinquency by running away from an oppressive family situation). Many of these girls adapt to their disadvantaged positions by their involvement in "accommodative" and "predatory" criminal behavior (e.g., shoplifting, prostitution, drug use).

A critical/Marxist perspective goes even further by focusing on "those social structures and forces that produce both the greed of the inside trader as well as the brutality of the rapist or the murderer. And it places those structures in their proper context: the material conditions of class struggle under a capitalist mode of production" (Quinney & Wildeman, 1991: 77). The "material conditions" include the class, gender, and racial inequalities produced by the contradictions of capitalism (which produce economic changes that negatively affect the lives of so many people, especially the working class and the poor). For young minority women who live in poverty, the results can be multiplied fourfold in that they have to cope with the disadvantages of gender, age, race, and class.

According to Lanier and Henry, there are six central ideas common to critical/Marxist theories of crime and criminal justice. These are as follows (Lanier & Henry, 1998: 256–258):

1. *Capitalism shapes social institutions, social identities, and social action.* In other words, the actual "mode of production" in any given society tends to determine many other areas of social life, including divisions based on race, class and gender, plus the manner in which people behave and act toward one another.

2. *Capitalism creates class conflict and contradictions.* Because a relatively small group (a "ruling class" consisting of perhaps 1–2% of the population) owns and/or controls the "means of production," class divisions have resulted and [created]the inevitable class conflict over control of resources. The contradiction is that workers need to consume the products of the capitalist system but in order to do this they need to have enough income to do so and thus increase growth in the economy. However, too much growth may cut into profits. One result is the creation of a *surplus population*—a more or less steady supply of able workers who are permanently unemployed or underemployed (also called the "underclass").

3. *Crime is a response to capitalism and its contradictions.* This notion stems in part from the second theme in that the "surplus population" may commit crimes to survive. These can be described as crimes of *accommodation* (Quinney, 1980). Crimes among the more affluent can also result (see next point), in addition to crimes of *resistance* (e.g., sabotage and political violence).

4. *Capitalist law facilitates and conceals crimes of domination and repression.* The law and legal order can often be repressive toward certain groups and engage in the violation of human rights, which are referred to as *crimes of control and repression.* Crimes of *domination* also occur with great frequency as corporations and their representatives violate numerous laws (fraud, price-fixing, pollution, etc.) that cause widespread social harms, but are virtually ignored by the criminal justice system.

5. *Crime is functional to capitalism.* There is a viable and fast-growing *crime control industry* that provides a sort of "Keynesian stimulus" to the economy by creating jobs and profits for corporations (e.g., building prisons, providing various products and services to prisons, jails, police departments, courthouses) (Shelden & Brown, 1997, 2003; Shelden, 2001).

6. *Capitalism shapes society's response to crime by shaping law.* Those in power (especially legislators) define what is a "crime" and what constitutes a threat to "social order" and, perhaps more important, *who* constitutes such a threat—and this usually ends up being members of the underlcass. Various "problems" that threaten the dominant mode of production become "criminalized" (e.g., certain drugs used by minorities, rather than drugs produced by corporations, such as cigarettes, prescription drugs, and, of course, alcohol).

The importance of the capitalist system in producing inequality and hence crime is apparent when examining recent economic changes in American society and the effects of these changes. In recent years particularly, many scholars have begun to seek an explanation of gangs (and crime in general) by examining changes in the economic structure of society and how such changes have contributed to the emergence of what some have called an "underclass" that in many ways represents what Marx called the "surplus population" in addition to the "lumpenproletariat."[9] In many ways, this perspective is an extension of some of the basic assumptions and key concepts of the social disorganization/ecology, strain, and cultural deviance theories, in addition to critical/Marxist perspectives.

A Concluding Note

The persistent focus on social class found in traditional delinquency theory and the absence of interest in gender in delinquency are ironic for two reasons. As even the work of Hirschi demonstrated, and as later studies validated, a clear relationship between social-class position and delinquency is problematic, but it is clear that gender has a dramatic and consistent effect on delinquency causation (Hagan, Gillis, & Simpson, 1985; Hagan, 1989). The second irony, and one that consistently eludes even contemporary delinquency theorists, is that although academicians have had little interest in female delinquents, the same cannot be said about the juvenile justice system. Indeed, work on the early history of the separate justice system for youths reveals that concerns about girls' immoral conduct were really at the center of what some have called the "child-saving movement" (Platt, 1969; Schlossman & Wallach, 1978; Messerschmidt, 1987) that set up the juvenile justice system.

More to the point here, why has gender consistently been such a good predictor of conformity? That question was addressed by two early theorists, George Grosser and Ruth Morris, whose major contributions, their doctoral dissertations, remain unpublished. Their explanations represent the first attempts to link female delinquency with the phenomenon of gender roles and differential socialization.

GENDER ROLES AND DELINQUENCY IN GIRLS: THE BEGINNINGS OF A THEORY OF FEMALE DELINQUENCY

One of the earliest theorists to apply the concept of gender roles to the study of female delinquency was George Grosser (1952). His work, on which Cohen relied, contended that the differential gender-role socialization of males and females pushed women to achieve success through affiliation (marriage) and encouraged males to achieve success through accomplishment. Female delinquency, which was assumed to be primarily sexual or "relational," was both an extension and violation of the female subculture in the same way that aggressive and criminal behavior was a product of the male subculture.

Ruth Morris accepted the notion that female delinquency was deeply influenced by male and female socialization. She designed rigorous studies to explore differences between female and male delinquents as well as differences between these delinquents and nondelinquents. Morris attempted in her dissertation (1963) and two published papers (1964, 1965) to develop a comprehensive theory of female delinquency that would explain both its sexual character and, in comparison with male delinquency, its lesser frequency and prevalence.

She made a series of major discoveries about the dynamics of female delinquency and about the limitations of a sex-role theory of delinquency.

To explain the smaller number of female delinquents, she speculated that women experience both reduced access to illegitimate means to reach success goals (i.e., criminal opportunities) and greater social disapproval of delinquent acts than do their male counterparts. In addition, because girls were expected to abide by stricter moral standards, Morris also suspected that a stronger sense of guilt and disapproval would accompany deviant behavior among females. In other words, she believed there was an absence of subcultural and cultural support for girls' misbehavior. In a study of matched groups of fifty-six delinquent and nondelinquent youths (both males and females), Morris found that girls experienced a greater amount of shame than boys when questioned about their involvement with the police and tended to deny delinquent acts they had committed. She also found that there is less disapproval (by authority figures such as parents) of boys than of girls who commit the same offense (Morris, 1965: 254). Finally, she explored the dynamics of male and female delinquency by asking youths with whom they would commit delinquent offenses. Here she found that youths were much more likely to commit offenses with members of the same sex (Morris, 1965: 264).

To explain the predominance of status or what she called relational offenses among girls, Morris suggested that because "factors which interfere with reaching culturally defined success goals by legitimate means are most likely to lead to deviancy" (1964: 82) and because these goals are different for males and females, the sources and character of delinquent behavior would, of necessity, be different. She further suggested that obstacles to economic power and status would be most likely to lead to delinquency in males, and obstacles to maintaining positive effective relationships would most likely produce delinquency in females. In research testing her hypothesis, Morris found that female delinquents were more likely than a matched sample of nondelinquents to come from broken homes, or from families with many problems and tensions, and to be rated low in personal appearance and grooming skills.

Other theorists have also argued that female delinquents are more sensitive to family disruption than either female nondelinquents or males, but the research on this is, largely, unconvincing. As Shover et al. (1979) observe in their review of the evidence on this point, "usually this assertion has been supported by research on officially adjudicated delinquents." Because it is now known that young women are more often reported to the police by their parents, it might appear that family discord is a more important factor for females, even in the absence of any relationship between family problems and female delinquency.

A related hypothesis is that girls would report stronger family bonds and, therefore, significantly lower delinquency. Canter, using a national probability sample of 1,725 adolescents, tested this notion. While finding significantly higher rates of delinquency for males, "the expected sex differences in family bonds were not observed." The lack of family bonds was modestly correlated with delinquency in both sexes, but there was "evidence of their greater association among males in many cases" (Canter, 1981: 1). However, a study of self-reported adolescent marijuana use by Anderson (1977) did find a stronger relationship for girls between "attachment" to the family and the extent of the use of this drug, which the author attributed to the fact that girls are more closely supervised and given more restrictions by their parents.

Yet another study (Norland et al., 1979), based on a self-report sample of high school youths, examined family dynamics (in particular, family conflicts) and found them to be important predictors of both male and female delinquency. Although this study ascertained that "the total effect of family conflict on delinquency" was stronger for females than males, the relationship was largely "indirect" through reduced identification with parents, adoption of more relativistic beliefs about law, reduced parental supervision, and increased exposure to social support for delinquency. Examining the "direct" effects of family conflict on property and aggression offenses, the researchers found them to be greater for males than for females; only for the status offenses did the effects of family conflict appear to be slightly greater for females.

In a related exploration of this same notion, Block (1984) found in her longitudinal study of ego and cognitive development from the preschool period to late adolescence that family experiences affect male and female youth differently. Specifically, although family disruption (e.g., separation, divorce, death of a parent) "was significantly associated with a number of negative psychological characteristics in the sample of boys, family disruption was relatively independent of the quality of psychological functioning in the sample of girls" (Block, 1984: 138). More to the point, less extreme changes in the family (e.g., moving to a new neighborhood, changes of school not part of the regular sequence, changes in the employment status of mother and/or father) were, in girls, found to be associated with ego resiliency (the ability to cope with stress, tolerance of ambiguity, self-reliance) and with moderate ego undercontrol (curiosity, testing or stretching limits, lesser inhibition and constriction, and self-assertion). No such relationship was found in the boys she studied. These speak to the need to examine, in more detail, the ways in which boy and girls experience family life—something we pursue in the next chapter.

Another of Morris's notions—that female delinquents experience frustration in the legitimate realization of female goals (e.g., dating and marriage)—has also not been directly confirmed or disproved. For example, Sandhu and Allen (1969) concluded that "delinquent girls showed significantly less commitment to marital goals, expressed less desire to marry, and perceived fewer obstacles in the fulfillment of their marital goals as compared to nondelinquent girls." Morris (1963) also had problems with this portion of her argument, reporting that her data failed to provide conclusive support for the notion that male delinquency is caused by "status" frustration and that female delinquency is caused by "relational frustration," in part because delinquent females seemed to report low concern for both status and relational goals.

On the other hand, in another examination of differential opportunity theory, Datesman, Scarpitti, and Stephenson (1975) found some evidence that girls arrested for "public policy offenses" (such as status offenses) had the lowest perception of opportunities among both delinquent and nondelinquent women. However, they cautioned that causality is difficult to establish because sexual activity among young women, in an environment that condemns such behavior, may cause girls to experience less success in obtaining dates. Finally, both Morris and Datesman and her associates found strong evidence that the female delinquent enjoys significantly less subcultural support than her male counterpart, with both males and females being less tolerant of female delinquency.

These approaches to the study of female delinquency (particularly the early efforts) were hampered by stereotypical assumptions about the concept of gender and about the nature of youthful female misbehavior. They tended to assume that most female delinquency is sexual or interpersonal in nature, in contrast to male delinquency, which was presumed likely to be more aggressive and criminal (which may be equally erroneous because most male delinquent behavior is nonaggressive and petty in nature). Second, they assumed that differential socialization of male and female children plays a significant (though largely unspecified) role in the generation of basic personality characteristics that, in turn, makes it less likely for women to consider illegal behavior.

Because of the widespread acceptance of these two assumptions, it has also been assumed that young women who deviate from stereotypical "feminine" characteristics might become "more delinquent" because most delinquency was assumed to be expressive of "masculine" values and attributes. This assumption, which supplied the basis for the notion that the women's movement would increase female delinquency, was extensively accepted, although there were virtually no efforts to test it empirically. Recently, however, several studies have attempted to evaluate what might be called a "masculinity" hypothesis and have come up with decidedly mixed results. For instance, Cullen, Golden, and Cullen (1979), using a university student sample ($N = 182$) and a "masculinity scale" of six "stereotypically masculine traits" (aggression, independence, objectivity, dominance, competitiveness, and self-confidence), found that females who possessed male traits have a higher likelihood of involvement in delinquency. However, they also found that "while male traits seemingly increased the likelihood that members of both sexes will engage in delinquency, their effects are greater for males than females" (1979: 307).

Another series of studies offers less support for the masculinity hypothesis. Norland, Wessel, and Shover (1981) used a high-school-student sample of 1,002 and a questionnaire measuring "masculinity" (focusing on such variables as leadership, competitiveness, aggressiveness, successfulness, and ambition). They found that masculinity was directly related only to status offenses and not at all related to property and violent offenses. For females, those with more of these "masculine" characteristics (the variables listed above) were less involved in delinquency than those reporting fewer such traits. The authors attributed this to the fact that females exhibiting these traits are more likely to have attachments to conventional others (i.e., nondelinquents).

Using the same self-report data, Loy and Norland (1981) employed a far more sophisticated conceptualization of masculinity. Specifically, they developed two Likert-type measures (in which respondents indicate whether they "strongly agree," "agree," "disagree," or "strongly disagree" with a statement) of gender-role expectations—one for traditional masculinity and another for traditional femininity. People were called androgynous when they scored above the midpoint on both scales. Traditional males and females were those who scored significantly higher on their respective scales. Finally, the researchers developed an "undifferentiated" category for youths who scored below the midpoint on both scales.

Dividing the self-reported delinquency of both sexes into property, status, and aggressive behaviors, Loy and Norland found that undifferentiated females were far more delinquent in all areas than their traditional or androgynous counterparts. Moreover, the mean number of aggressive acts for undifferentiated females was roughly six times larger than that for either of the other two groups of girls. For males, a different pattern is found, with traditional males reporting the greatest amount of delinquency; the difference was particularly marked for aggressive behavior.

Thornton and James (1979) conducted a similar survey and found that sex "remains related to delinquency when masculine self-expectations are controlled." By controlling for sex, the authors found that the fourteen delinquent acts they examined were not related to masculine identification for either males or females. Unfortunately, they did not investigate different types of delinquency separately.

A study that looked into the relationship between gender identity and pathology (operationally defined as alcohol and drug problems in addition to delinquency) in a random sample of 1,308 youths in New Jersey also yielded very mixed results. The authors found, contrary to their expectations, that "masculinity" (measured by using such variables as assertiveness, goal orientation, and separation from others) was positively related to delinquency only in twenty-year-old males (not teenagers). Those of both sexes scoring high on the "masculinity" scale were the least likely to have alcohol and drug problems. With specific reference to females, girls with low scores reported more psychological distress but lower rates of delinquency (Horowitz & White, 1986).

In general, these studies reveal that popular notions about the relationship between "masculinity" or masculine characteristics (as conventionally defined) and delinquency must be explored more carefully. It is not so much that there is no relationship between gender and delinquency; rather, it is that the complexity of the relationship is only beginning to be understood. Such exploration is critical, given the presumed impact that the women's movement has had on girls' and women's crime. Indeed, one of the major debates in criminology during the past decade was whether the increase in female delinquency and crime seen during the 1960s and 1970s was at least partially attributable to this social movement.

THE WOMEN'S MOVEMENT
AND FEMALE CRIME

One of the most widely held beliefs concerning female delinquency and crime is that because of the women's movement during the 1960s and early 1970s, there was a dramatic increase in female criminal activity. Women's crime became "the shady side of liberation." The reasons for this belief should not be difficult to understand or to predict. Since the 1800s, criminologists have been issuing dire warnings to the effect that the emancipation of women would result in a dramatic change in the character and frequency of women's crime. Lombroso spoke of the dangers of educating women and said that "removing the constraints of domesticity and maternity" would bring out the "innocuous semi-criminal" within all women.

W. I. Thomas quoted approvingly the following 1921 passage from the *New York World* (Smart, 1976: 70–71):

> The modern age of girls and young men is intensely immoral, and immoral seemingly without the pressure of circumstances. At whose door we may lay fault, we cannot tell. Is it the result of what we call "the emancipation of woman," with its concomitant freedom from chaperonage, increased intimacy between the sexes in adolescence, and a more tolerant viewpoint towards all things unclean in life? This seems the only logical forbear of the present state.

The same theme appears over forty years later in a U.S. Commission on the Causes and Prevention of Violence statement: "It is also the case that the 'emancipation' of females in our society over recent decades has decreased the differences in delinquency and criminality between boys and girls, men and women, as cultural differences between them have narrowed" (Smart, 1976: 71).

When the number of girls and women arrested in the United States climbed dramatically between 1960 and 1975, it appeared to many that this was precisely what had happened. Two books by prominent female criminologists appeared in the mid-1970s to explore the linkages (Adler, 1975; Simon, 1975). The most widely publicized was Freda Adler's *Sisters in Crime,* in which she argued that the women's movement had changed traditional attitudes toward acceptable behavior for women and had also opened up opportunities previously unavailable to female criminals. The movement had allowed women to make gains in the financial arena and, Adler believed, also in the criminal sphere.

With specific reference to girls' delinquency, Adler argued that changes were occurring in young girls' behavior as well:

> Girls are involved in more drinking, stealing, gang activity, and fighting—behavior in keeping with their adoption of male roles. We also find increases in the total number of female deviances. The departure from the safety of traditional female roles and the testing of uncertain alternative roles coincide with the turmoil of adolescence creating criminogenic risk factors which are bound to increase. (Adler, 1975: 95)

As we saw in Chapter 2, official arrest statistics for the period appeared to support Adler's notion; between 1960 and 1975, for example, arrests of young girls increased by 254 percent, with an increase of 425 percent in index crimes. With this global figure came alarming jumps in arrests of girls for nontraditional offenses: murder up 275 percent, aggravated assault up 438 percent, and robbery up 647 percent. But, as we have already seen, there were many problems with these data. Notably, the increases were based on extremely small base numbers (e.g., in 1960 there were only 28 arrests of girls under eighteen for murder, [6 arrests for rape], 355 arrests for robbery, and 676 arrests for aggravated assault), and they occurred during a period when large numbers of young people entered the crime-generating years. Indeed, arrests of boys also showed remarkable increases: murder, 206 percent; aggravated assault, 217 percent; and robbery, 361 percent (FBI, 1976: 183). Added to this, self-report data covering the period did not show similar changes in girls' behavior, and the increases were not sustained into the late 1970s.

Adler's work can also be criticized for the misleading but common use of the term "serious crime." The term is usually substituted for the FBI's "index crimes," and the bulk of these crimes fall within the category of larceny–theft (mostly shoplifting). Over 80 percent of the increases in arrests for index crimes among girls was accounted for by larceny–theft. Moreover, those who made much of the numbers failed to consider that minor changes in police practices could have produced these changes in official rates (Smart, 1982); this is an important aspect of the increases observed and is dealt with in Chapter 6.

Another set of studies, though, directly addresses Adler's notion that as women begin to question the traditional female role or support other feminist ideals, they will become increasingly delinquent. James and Thornton (1980) questioned 287 young women about their attitudes toward feminism and the extensiveness of their delinquent behavior. They ascertained that attitudes toward feminism had little direct effect on the commission of status offenses, but did have slight direct effects on property and aggressive delinquency. However, in the latter case, the influence was found to be negative, which clearly does not support the notion that the women's movement is providing attitudinal support for female entry into the criminal world. Indeed, this negative relationship held even when the young women were encountering such delinquency-producing forces as "high degrees of delinquency opportunity," "social support for delinquency," and "low levels of parental control."

Cernkovich and Giordano (1979) examined the attitudes of girls in three high schools and two state institutions regarding the acceptability of nontraditional female behavior. They too found a lack of significant associations in addition to some negative associations, indicating, in the authors' words, that "the more delinquent girls were actually less liberated." Like earlier researchers, they also noted that delinquent girls were less attached to marriage and children (as goals), but quickly added that "it did not appear that they were reaching for male-dominated occupations as an alternative" (Cernkovich & Giordano, 1979: 479).

Figueria-McDonough (1984) surveyed a sample of male and female high school youths in the Midwest and looked specifically at the role of feminist orientations on delinquency. Regarding girls' support for public, private, and personal feminist principles, she found that feminist orientations were not important predictors of delinquency but were, instead, significantly associated with career orientations that, in turn, had a notable direct effect on grades. There was evidence in this research, as well, that feminist orientations were linked to class and race, with higher class and white women more likely to have a public and private feminist orientation.

In conclusion, serious research efforts to locate the "dark side of the women's movement" have almost without exception been unsuccessful. Careful analyses of existing data fail to support the notion that girls have been committing more nontraditional (i.e., "masculine") crimes. Some have even gone so far as to characterize the whole debate as an "intellectual dead end" (Miller, 1983: 59), but it was probably more than that. It seems peculiar, for example, that so many academics would be willing to consider a hypothesis that assumed improving girls' and women's economic conditions would lead to an increase in female crime when almost all the existing criminological literature stresses the role played by discrimination and poverty (and unemployment or underemployment) in the creation of crime. Because rectification of these social injustices has been forwarded as a major solution to crime, it is more than curious that in the case of women's crime, the reverse was argued with such ease and received such wide public acceptance. More tragically, the debate distracted long-overdue academic attention from the genuine causes of girls' delinquency and from the problems girls were experiencing with the juvenile justice system.

Feminist Criminology[10]

Generally, the first feminist scholarship has looked to document the androcentric biases within whatever fields it has touched, and to spur a long-overdue exploration of women and women's experiences. That this is occurring in sociology, criminology, and sociolegal studies is without doubt.

Feminists, though, suggest that the focus on gender goes beyond simply adding another variable to the empirical study of law and legal institutions (i.e., "add women and stir"). A focus on gender and gender difference is not simply a focus on what some scholars term "women's issues." It is a far more encompassing enterprise, raising questions about how gender organizes the discipline of criminology and sociolegal studies. The contemporary feminist research has contributed to our understanding of women's experiences in a way that is not simply in contrast to men's.

A number of feminist scholars have attempted to explain the cause of crime, gender differences in the crime rate, and the exploitation of female victims from a feminist perspective—to begin the project of crafting the many possible feminist criminologies.

Marxist feminists view gender inequality as stemming from the unequal power of men and women in a capitalist society. They trace the origins of gender differences to the development of private property and male domination over the laws of inheritance. In capitalism, men control women both economically and biologically, and this "double marginality" explains why females in a capitalist society commit fewer crimes than males. It is because they are isolated in the family and have fewer opportunities to engage in elite deviance (white-collar crimes); they are also denied access to male-dominated street crimes. Because capitalism renders women powerless, they are forced to commit less serious, nonviolent, self-destructive crimes such as drug possession and prostitution. Powerlessness also increases the likelihood that women will become the target of violent acts.

In contrast, *radical feminists* view the cause of female crime as originating with the onset of male supremacy, or patriarchy; the subsequent subordination of women; male aggression; and the efforts of males to control females sexually. They focus on the social forces that shape women's lives and experiences in order to explain female criminality. For example, they attempt to show that physical and/or sexual victimization of girls and women can be underlying causes of criminal behavior (Chesney-Lind, 1992; Owen & Bloom, 1995). Exploitation of women by men acts as a trigger for behavior by female victims, causing them to run away or begin abusing drugs at an early age. Beyond this, radical feminists have documented the enormous toll that male violence continues to take on the lives of adult women and to link both childhood and adult victimization experiences with behaviors like drug use that propel women into the criminal justice system.

Other scholars, notably Messerschmidt and Connell, have extended the feminist project into a consideration about the way in which gender and class work in the lives of men. Specifically, Connell has noted that gender becomes a source of oppression when the norms of the dominant class promote a certain form of what Connell calls "hegemonic masculinity" (1990: 521), whether it be the exercise of authority or a capacity for violence. To this insight, Messerschmidt has added the notion that from a socialist feminist perspective, power (in terms of gender and class) is central to an understanding of serious forms of criminality. According to Messerschmidt (1986), the notion of "gendered power" is central to understanding why men commit more crimes and more serious crimes than women do. The interaction of gender and class creates positions of power and powerlessness in the gender/class hierarchy, resulting in different types and degrees of criminality and various opportunities for engaging in them (Messerschmidt, 1993: 56).

Clearly, feminist criminology, particularly that informed by the radical feminist concern for sexual victimization, offers a great deal to the study of female delinquency. Unfortunately, until recently even feminist criminology has failed to fully explore the interaction of race and gender in girls' offending (Bloom, 1996). Nonetheless, the feminist emphasis on the gendered nature of girls' (and boys') crime offers the best hope for understanding girls' delinquency.

SUMMARY

This chapter reviewed the early efforts to explain female delinquency, as well as the major schools of thought in delinquency theory. We concluded that the theories that developed solely to explain female delinquency were seriously handicapped by their intellectual isolation and stereotypical constructions of gender.

Less widely appreciated has been the impact of gender and stereotypical thinking on the major theories of delinquency causation. For this reason, this chapter also sought to explore the roots of these theories, as well as to begin consideration of their applicability to girls' delinquency.

The early theories of female criminality, beginning with the work of Lombroso, emphasized the role of biology in women's and girls' offending. Much of what was to follow was deeply affected by the notion that girls' anatomy and particularly their sexuality played a major role in the causation of their delinquency. This theme was repeated in the works of Thomas, Pollak, the Gluecks, and many others. The research of Konopka, while still focusing on female sexuality, did suggest that the social and economic problems confronted by poor and minority girls needed to be discussed as well.

Key sociological theories of delinquency (ecological, strain, differential association, control, labeling, Marxist/critical) were also reviewed. These theories tended to ignore, for all practical purposes, the delinquency of girls, and a number suggested that delinquency itself was an extension of masculinity. Key works in delinquency theory were based on male samples or case studies of all-male groups. Often girls were dismissed in cavalier terms or relegated to footnotes, and not infrequently mothers were blamed for the delinquency of sons.

Early and current research on the connection among gender roles, gender role socialization, and female delinquency offers a more promising start for understanding female (and, to a degree, male) delinquency. These studies, although hampered by their own stereotypes about the lives of girls, did begin to explore such things as the levels of supervision of young people, greater disapproval of female delinquency, and the role of family conflicts in delinquency. Notions that "masculinity" might cause delinquency were specifically reviewed by a number of researchers, with decidedly mixed results.

This chapter considered the most popular of these theories, that the women's movement of the late 1960s and early 1970s caused an increase in girls' delinquency. Close examination of the available evidence (using both self-report and arrest data) found no such relationship. Instead, studies that asked delinquent and nondelinquent girls about their attitudes toward gender found that delinquent girls had more traditional attitudes regarding women's place.

In general, this chapter suggests that if a theory of female delinquency is to emerge, it must draw on the best of a flawed heritage. Theories of boys' delinquency cannot be completely rejected, but their uncritical grounding in male behavior must be recognized and corrected. Theories of female delinquency must get past commonsense constructions of femininity to a broader appreciation of the role of girls' situations and lives in their troubles with the juvenile justice system. This is the hope offered by feminist criminology, and it is the perspective of the next chapter, which considers girls' lives and their problems with the law.

NOTES

1. For a more detailed discussion of the work of Guerry and Quetelet, along with the "Chicago School," see Lanier and Henry (1998, pp. 183–192); see Quinney and Wildeman (1991, pp. 48–50).

2. See Moore (1978 and 1991) for documentation of this phenomenon.

3. Lanier and Henry (1998: 182). Lanier and Henry also note that the term "social" or "human" ecology comes from the Greek word *oikos* which translates roughly into "household" or "living space."

4. The importance of the ecological approach to delinquency is not confined to history. The upsurge in interest in youth gangs (Huff, 1990) has resulted in a renewed interest in this perspective. Although the ecological approach is doubtless of great relevance to an understanding of the emergence of youth gangs, it is troubling that current proponents also seem to be carrying forward the almost exclusive focus on male delinquency found in the earliest work in this area. Albert J. Reiss, in an essay that discusses, in part, the relationship between social status and delinquency, notes, for example, that "low-status male youths are more likely than those from middle or upper strata to be delinquent in each kind of status neighborhood, but a boy living in a high-crime-rate area was far more likely to be delinquent than the same status boy in a low-crime neighborhood" (Reiss, 1986: 11).

5. This is spelled out in Merton (1957).

6. The reader is encouraged to merely browse through any introductory sociology textbook to find numerous references to these two terms. In fact, one definition of *sociology* itself could easily be "the study of culture and social structure."

7. For an excellent discussion of the role of corporate propaganda, see the following: Herman and Chomsky (1988); Chomsky (1989); Fones-Wolf (1994); Carey (1995).

8. For a quick and easy-to-read look at inequality, see Folbre and the Center for Popular Economics (1995); see also Domhoff (1998) and Rothman (1999).

9. It is important to emphasize that Marx did distinguish between these two terms. The "lumpenproletariat" was seen by Marx as the bottom layer of society, the "social junk," "rotting scum," "rabble," etc. In short, they were described as the "criminal class." The "surplus population" referred to working-class men and women who, because of various fluctuations in the market (caused chiefly by contradictions within the capitalist system) were excluded, either temporarily or permanently, from the labor market.

10. This summary is drawn from a larger paper titled "Feminist Criminology: Thinking About Women and Crime" by Meda Chesney-Lind and Barbara Bloom, in Brian Maclean (ed.), *Thinking Critically About Crime* (Vancouver: Press Gang, 1999).

6

Girls' Lives and
Girls' Delinquency

The last two decades have seen a marked increase in public and academic discussions of girls' issues. Much of this attention is due to the publication in the early 1980s of Carol Gilligan's influential and controversial book, *In a Different Voice*. In this work, Gilligan (1982) argued powerfully for a different approach to girls' development. Initially her work was confined to a rather narrow discussion of the evidence that the "moral" reasoning of girls and boys differed when confronted with difficult "scenarios." She argued that in thinking about these moral dilemmas, girls were more likely to use "an ethic of care" and boys to use "an ethic of justice" (Gilligan et al., 1982: 174). More important, though, her work stressed the need to listen to girls' voices and to begin to study girls' and women's experiences "in women's own terms" (Gilligan et al., 1982: 173; see also Gilligan et al., 1988).

A decade later, the American Association of University Women undertook a landmark study of the treatment of girls in schoolrooms across the United States, "Shortchanging Girls, Shortchanging America" (1991). The study, which surveyed over three thousand children aged nine to fifteen in twelve locations across the country, found that boys and girls have equally high levels of self-esteem in elementary school. As children age, self-esteem tends to drop, but the researchers found that such a drop was far more dramatic in girls. By high school, only 29 percent of girls are "happy with themselves" compared with 46 percent of boys (AAUW, 1992: 24). Moreover, this important study, unlike the earlier Gilligan research, included girls of color and girls from a wide array of class backgrounds. The AAUW study itself set the stage for other more qualitative assessments of girls' lives, particularly girls' problems with depression and food (Pipher, 1994) and girls' experiences in school classrooms and playgrounds (Thorne, 1994; Orenstein, 1994).

Finally, within criminology the notion that the women's movement caused some change in girls' and women's behavior has had at least one positive effect: it shifted some much-needed attention to girls' lives. This interest was accelerated and refocused by the more recent interest in girls in gangs. As a result, explanations of the differences in male and female delinquency that relied solely on simplistic and mechanistic notions about the relationship between masculine or feminine attitudes and/or personality characteristics and delinquent behavior are gradually giving way to more complicated efforts to consider systematically the way gender works in the everyday lives of young women and young men in our society.

Some might suggest that gathering this information is unnecessary because existing delinquency theories can "explain" female deviance in that they tap the same variables that are important in the lives of both sexes: poverty, relationships with peers, family problems, racism, school experiences, and so on. Such formulations seem reasonable on the surface but ignore one fundamental problem. All the established theories of delinquency were developed with no awareness of and concern about gender and, more specifically, gender stratification. Clearly, though, gender has a dramatic effect on most aspects of girls' lives. Attempts to adapt male-oriented theory to explain female conformity and deviance must, then, start from the realization that all theories of delinquency were built around the lives and experiences of males, whose development, behavior, and options are radically different from those of females.

This is not simply an observation about the power of gender identity or even gender roles (although such power is undeniable). In a patriarchal society, gender stratification is as powerful as class. A complete idea of gender, then, must include its institutional manifestations in addition to its psychological and social–psychological dimensions. Patriarchy, for purposes of this discussion, should be understood as a multifaceted system that enforces masculine control of the sexuality and labor power of women (Lerner, 1986; Messerschmidt, 1987; Lorber, 1994).

A feminist approach to delinquency means construction of explanations of female behavior that are sensitive to its context in a male-dominated, or patriarchal, society. Clearly, the shape of female behavior and misbehavior is affected by gender stratification, as are the responses of a male-dominated system to female deviance. So a feminist analysis of delinquency would also examine ways in which agencies of social control—the police, the courts, and the prisons—act to reinforce a woman's place in male society (Harris, 1977; Chesney-Lind, 1977). We will turn to this consideration in the next few chapters.

More to the point here, a feminist model of delinquency would focus more extensively on the growing literature available about girls' actual lives and the role played by girls' problems, including those caused by racism and poverty, in their delinquency behavior. Fortunately, a small but growing literature is now developing on girls' lives, and much of it bears directly on girls' crime. It is out of this literature that a gender-sensitive theory of girls' delinquency will emerge.

GROWING UP FEMALE

All children are deeply affected by their gender. For example, some theorists suggest that by the age of two, rudimentary psychological gender identity has been formed and children are already perceiving the association of particular behaviors, traits, activities, and occupations with women or men (Money, Hampson, & Mapson, 1957; Kuhn, Nash, & Brucken, 1978; Cowan & Hoffman, 1986). By preschool or first grade, children are well aware of their gender, stereotype one another's gender activities, know which parents they are most like, have a thorough knowledge of gender stereotypes, and know the gender of family members and peers (Fagot, 1984; Lott, 1987). Obviously, there are developmental stages in the socialization process, and, by adolescence, the experience of gender in shaping girls' lives and options may be increasingly external. Katz, for example, has suggested three stages in gender development: learning what is appropriate behavior for a male or female child, acquiring concepts about what is appropriate as a potential male or female adult, and behaving in ways that are deemed appropriate for male and female adults through the life span (Katz, 1979: 9). Most delinquency research has failed to differentiate these stages and has focused on the consequences of the earliest gender socialization experiences—and particularly on the impact of "masculinity and femininity" on behavior—concepts one student in the area called among the "muddiest" in the psychological vocabulary (Constantinople, 1973: 390).

Distinct things happen in the lives of young people during early and late adolescence, periods that Katz (1979) suggests are preparing youths for adult roles. These concern, in early adolescence, adjusting to puberty and sexual feelings, and greater reliance on peers than on teachers or parents as sources of information about the world. By late adolescence, each sex has acquired an interest in the other, but the effect of the differential futures available to males and females is already being felt. Indeed, even by the end of grade school, girls begin to evaluate themselves more negatively than do boys (Loeb & Horst, 1978; Silvern, 1978; Katz, 1979).

Thorne's qualitative evaluation of gender in elementary school classrooms and playgrounds breaks new ground by exploring the ways in which gender is created and recreated with little direct input from teachers. Most important to Thorne were the informal playground interactions in which the boundaries between girls and boys are sorted out along with themes of aggression and sexuality. These settings revolve around exchanging insults ("girls are dumb"; "boys are stupid") between homosocial groups (Thorne, 1994: 5). Particularly salient were boys' displays of "masculine superiority" that also involved a "contempt for things feminine" while also setting the stage for "adult male privilege and sexism." Additionally, she notes that this behavior (often tolerated as "boys will be boys") can rather quickly permit harassment and verbal put-downs of girls inside and outside of the classroom, beginning to inhibit their active participation in classrooms.

While boys are being channeled into sports and away from intellectual activities and other, more "feminine," undertakings, girls are being pushed, according to Thorne, into a "heterosexualized" femininity that begins to stress, even in grade school, girls' "attractiveness" to boys. Tied up in this are girls' engaging in "goin' with rituals" (Thorne, 1994: 170) and active efforts to establish couples, behaviors that Thorne links to girls later lowering their ambitions in exchange for boys' approval—since ultimately, as Thorne correctly notes, "the culture of romance perpetuates male privilege" (170).

As Thorne's work indicates, the impact of gender on girls' lives is perhaps most clearly seen in studies that review girls' experiences in the higher grades. By the end of high school, girls are developing lower occupational aspirations than boys, even when they possess the same abilities and advantages (Marini, 1978). Girls are also dropping out of the math and science classes that would prepare them for the more remunerative jobs (Ehrhart & Sandler, 1987); one reason for this might be that girls studying science describe themselves as less feminine, less attractive, and less popular (Project on Equal Education Rights, 1984). Also, peer pressure may explain the absence of girls from science classes. Although girls do as well as boys in computer classes, for example, they do not join the boys' after-school computer clubs, in part because the boys admitted harassing the girls deliberately (Project on Equal Education Rights, 1984; Ehrhart & Sandler, 1987); girls may also feel pressure in such settings not to compete with boys (Weisfeld, 1986).

In essence, while pressure to succeed in academic environments still affects girls during adolescence, they are also being pressured to develop heterosexual relationships and have become much more peer oriented. Opinions of teachers and parents are less important than they once were, and attributes that are outside their control, notably physical attractiveness and success with males (Lerner, Orlos, & Knapp, 1976), mean greater disparity between childhood and adolescent sex roles for girls. Physical attractiveness, in particular, figures prominently in girls' popularity with boys and ultimately in their ability to marry well-to-do, successful men (Elder, 1969).

Thorne's important observations on the ways in which "goin' with" rituals in grade school set the stage for intermediate and high school dating add an important dimension to this discussion. Specifically, teenage girls are pushed by hegemonic, heterosexualized femininity into cultivating a "teen" femininity that, while often challenging adult and race-based authority in the classroom, ultimately involves a series of "double binds" and "traps" (1994: 156) for girls. As noted previously, this construction recreates and reinforces the sexual double standard, by labeling girls who are too overtly sexual as "sluts." But more ironically, the construction of young girls as the objects of male desire means that girls' self-esteem and prestige are far more tied to externals (and particularly male approval) than are boys' (Thorne, 1994: 156).

In fact, in studies of "popularity" among boys' and girls' elementary school cliques in Colorado, Adler, Kless, and Adler (1992) report that although single-sex cliques tend to have many of the same dynamics, boys' popularity and status tend to be tied to their accomplishments, whereas girls' status tends to be determined by externals. Specifically, they found that for this group of middle-class, largely white youth, boys achieved status on the basis of "athletic ability, coolness, toughness, social skills, and success in cross-gender relationships" (169); girls, on the other hand, gained popularity because of "their parents' socioeconomic status and their physical appearance, social skills, and academic success" (169). They also concluded, as did Thorne, that boys prosper to the degree that they internalize and express the "cult of masculinity" (183). Girls tend to become absorbed in a "culture of compliance and conformity" as well as a "culture of romance" in which they "fantasize about romantic involvements with boys." Finally, girls care about an "inner space," which reflects an "ideology of domesticity," by living indoor lives, focusing on intimacy and cooperation.

Such a constellation of findings is all the more troubling because adolescent girls rate popularity so highly. In a study of high school seniors, Rosenberg (1965) found that when asked if they would most like to be independent, successful, or well liked, 60 percent of adolescent girls and only 35 percent of boys chose being well liked. In contrast, boys were much more likely than girls to choose successful (46 percent and 29 percent). Apparently, even girls who are strongly committed to feminist ideals become "realistic" during late adolescence as they begin to fear that their attitudes might endanger their ability to attract more traditional males (Katz, 1979). Some have labeled this the "double bind" between femininity and achievement that confronts adolescent girls: "the adolescent girl [is] finding it difficult to combine, because of imposed cultural contingencies, being a worthwhile individual and a proper female" (Hyde, 1985: 162).

Class and ethnic differences in gender are also marked, and these become more important during the intermediate and high school years. Higher social classes tend to be less rigid in sex distinctions; in working- and lower class families, there is much more concern about sex segregation. Children from working-class backgrounds tend to differentiate sex roles at earlier ages and to have more traditional standards than do middle-class children (Rabban, 1950).

Adolescence takes on different meanings for girls from working-class backgrounds. Their last years in school represent "the terminal year"—the last chance to find a husband as a way of escaping from an often-oppressive family system (Rubin, 1976). For these girls, being grown up means being married and having children.

For many low-income girls, as this book shows, even this option is not viable. School life has begun to introduce problems—particularly during intermediate school—as the cost of being poor becomes more explicit. In addition, traditional popularity, with its emphasis on dress, white standards of beauty, academic achievement, and school activities, becomes increasingly elusive.

Important work on the role of race in girls' experiences with school, particularly in intermediate school, comes from Orenstein's qualitative study of two middle schools in California—one that serves a predominantly white community and another that serves a mixed African American and Latino community. Orenstein's discussion of girls' problems in a predominantly white school more or less parallels the conventional discussions of girls' falling self-esteem and girls' problems with body image. Particularly important in these schools are the pervasive problems of eating disorders as girls strive for an ever more waiflike standard of white beauty (see also Pipher, 1994). One young girl explains, while "taking bites," that she "always tries to be a little hungry" (Orenstein, 1994: 97).

Different and much more disturbing themes emerge in the lives and classrooms of girls of color across town. African American girls, while initially praised for their social "maturity," find that their academic needs are ignored (180), and, ultimately, their assertiveness is viewed either as a nuisance or even a menace (see also Fordham, 1993). Faced with peer views that define achieving academically as "you talk white, you a schoolgirl, you a nerd" (157), and teachers who ignore them in classrooms, many young African American women simply give up. Resisting pervasive educational neglect (see also Arnold, 1995), the girls disconnect from achievement and instead find themselves "attaining a sense of purpose and assuaging loneliness through too early motherhood" (183).

The AAUW study also explored ethnic differences in girls' experiences with education and found many of these same patterns. Specifically, the study found that while African American girls maintain higher levels of self-esteem during high school than do white girls, "the schools do not provide the same supports for academic self-esteem," so the girls maintain their positive outlook by becoming "dissociated from school" (AAUW, 1991: 27).

Hispanic girls are less confident than their African American counterparts, although they still feel only marginally better about themselves in high school than do white girls (30 percent compared to 29 percent agreeing that they are happy with themselves). Their problems arise in "confidence in family relationships, school, talents and importance" (AAUW, 1991: 27).

Another key difference in the lives of girls of color in marginalized neighborhoods and schools is their relationships with boys. Whereas the girls at predominantly white schools complain bitterly about sexual harassment and boys belittling them in classrooms (Orenstein, 1994: 129), Hispanic and African American girls must also negotiate the gangs that are omnipresent in their neighborhoods, the violence from other girls, and, finally, male violence. And, as noted above, both African American girls and Latinas also face early pregnancy and motherhood.

Latinas, though, unlike their African American counterparts, must face entrenched cultural attitudes that expect them to work at home and to remain sexually pure while deemphasizing academic success (203); language difficulties also make it extremely unlikely that Latinas will be recognized as leaders in school (200). Finally, the machismo that characterizes masculinity in their community, and particularly gang behavior, also has sinister meanings for young Latinas.

In a graphic example of the sort of male violence both African American and Latina girls must handle, Orenstein recounts the story that two of her Latina respondents (Marta and Alanna) tell, about when they were forced in a car with a group of boys they didn't know well. After the boys lock the door, they tell the two young women that they are "going to take you in the hills and fuck you" (208). The girls scream "let us out," and as they get closer to their home they are released. However, one of the boys grabs Marta's ankle while another lurches the car forward, and she trips and falls in the gutter as the boys speed off. Later the boys drive by again and block them, and one of the boys holds out a gun, aiming it at one of the girls, saying "You fucking *puta*," and pulls the trigger. The gun isn't loaded.

Although these young women agree that "men stink," they find what pleasure they can in even this sort of rough attention, "recast mistreatment as excitement," and turn to these sorts of men for protection from other, violent men in their neighborhoods: "because guys protect you from other guys" (209). Protection, as well as friendship, also comes from gang membership even though their parents disapprove.

Few low-income girls can achieve traditional marriage because the boys in their lives cannot support them. Adulthood and freedom come through motherhood that until recently was "state supported" (Presser, 1980; Campbell, 1984a). Lower class life also means exposure for girls and boys to the "underclass" ways of making money that exist in low-income communities. Miller, in her study of "street women" in Milwaukee, stresses the fact that many low-income females in the ghetto are recruited during adolescence by older males who organize them into pseudofamilies and involve them in a variety of criminal activities—chiefly prostitution (Miller, 1986).

Much the same sort of pattern was observed by Campbell in her research on Puerto Rican gang girls in New York City. Campbell's respondents, though, participated in underclass criminality through association with male gang members. These girls survive in the "jungle-like quality of city life" by engaging in a wide array of criminal acts, including drug selling, prostitution, burglary, shoplifting, and intergang violence (Campbell, 1984a: 459). It is important that despite their involvement in criminal activities, Campbell's girls did not define themselves as "criminals," reserving that label for crazy people (such as Charles Manson). While learning to survive on the streets of desperately poor neighborhoods, these girls are developing strengths that their middle-class sisters are less likely to develop.

So, for example, although African American and Hispanic girls are socialized, like their white counterparts, to seek major identity through the nurturance of others, they are also socialized to become self-sufficient and to be more independent than white women (Ladner, 1971). On the other hand, studies of girls in training schools, who are presumably drawn from these lower and working-class communities, find them to be more traditional in gender-role orientation than their more middle-class peers. Reconciling these findings seems difficult unless one recognizes that these girls are developing street survival skills that are devalued in a lower class culture, with its heavy emphasis on sex segregation and protest masculinity (Chesney-Lind & Rodriguez, 1983; Campbell, 1984a; Messerschmidt, 1986). Consequently, lower class and working-class girls may be streetwise, but they still fantasize about an "ideal" life where they would not need to use such skills. They tend to have fantasies about lives as glamorous models or movie stars, and they also may fantasize about a relationship with a male who will rescue them from having to scramble economically.

Additionally, it needs to be recalled that neither the underclass nor mainstream society offers much to minority girls. In a study of African American youth who participated in an experimental preschool program in Harlem in the early 1960s, it was found that black girls lose their earlier academic lead over boys. Young African American men who participated in the study, but not young women, were found to be more successful in school and in employment than those who did not (Lott, 1987: 77).

GIRLS, PARENTS, AND PEERS

Consideration of the impact of girls' structural position in a male-dominated, socially and racially stratified society on their development is an important, though neglected, aspect of gender-role research. Critics of the purely developmental approach to the acquisition of gender roles, for example, stress the "role as rule approach" (Constantinople, 1973). This perspective, with its emphasis on the normative aspect of roles, is manifestly central to considerations of girls' deviance and its evaluation. It also stresses the role played by other elements of society in the enforcement of particular aspects of gender.

Critics also argue that gender roles are contradictory and inconsistent and that the proportion of individuals who violate these roles is high (Pleck, 1981). In this regard, it would be important to study which aspects of male and female disobedience of traditional gender scripts attract the most attention and which are neglected. In total, these critics suggest that notions of identity deemphasize the larger societal role in the enforcement of rules that attempt not only to create two kinds of people but also to guarantee the power of one group over the other.

Concerning the enforcement of traditional gender roles, considerable research has been done on parental and teacher behavior. Much of this work, though, has been conducted with very young children in preschool or elementary school settings. Nonetheless, the studies are instructive and suggest that teacher behavior still tends to encourage passivity, verbal orientation, and dependency in girls while encouraging boys to be independent, to explore, and to learn how things work (see Weitzman, 1984, and Ehrhart and Sandler, 1987, for reviews of this literature).

These studies also suggest that despite expectations that the women's movement would have a major impact on these patterns, such does not appear to be the case. For example, school textbooks are still gender typed, television programming is still powerfully affected by gender norms, and many adolescent girls (particularly those who expect to marry earlier) are still being encouraged to see the housewife and mother role as more important than a career and to pick a traditionally female occupation (Ehrhart & Sandler, 1987).

Even those female students interested in academic performance appear to be getting the message that science and language skills are not complementary. The process, called "counter-role modeling," is one in which teachers, particularly those in nonscience fields, give girls the impression that the only important thing for them to master for college entry and success is writing and research in nonscientific fields (Ehrhart & Sandler, 1987). Also interesting is the fact that women who reported having been influenced by their high school teachers and counselors in making college plans were less likely to major in science (5).

What of girls and their families during adolescence? Perhaps not surprisingly, little is known about this area of girls' experience. Block (1984: 73) notes that "the differential socialization hypothesis has been examined primarily (and for some areas exclusively) in samples of parents whose children were six years old and under." In her review of socialization studies, only 23 percent examined the socialization patterns of parents with older children. She believes this to be a significant omission because parents are likely to be less extreme in their socialization practices in the early years, with their "offspring . . . treated more as children than as boys and girls" (Block, 1984: 72). Specifically, she thinks that certain areas (notably achievement emphasis and tolerance for sexuality) have not become salient for differential socialization, and the tolerances of other areas (dependency and aggression) have not become strained.

Block's studies, one of which was a longitudinal study initiated in 1968 of ego and cognitive development from the preschool period to late adolescence, were designed to rectify this oversight. For example, in a 1965 study she examined parental self-reports as well as young adults' perceptions of their parents' child-rearing practices (the seventeen independent samples included responses from 696 mothers, 548 fathers, and 1,227 young adults). In general, she found clear evidence of differential socialization of males and females, that the gender-related socialization emphases are appreciably consistent when viewed from differing perspectives, evidence of consistency of parent and sex-of-child effects, and, most important, some evidence that "sex differentiation in socialization emphases appears to increase with the age of the child, reaching a maximum during the high school years." Such a pattern was also suggested by Maccoby (1966), particularly as it touches on the greater restrictiveness imposed on girls.

Looking specifically at the parent–daughter relationship, Block (1984: 88) noted that it is characterized by "greater warmth and physical closeness." Both parents have more confidence in the "trustworthiness and truthfulness" of their daughters than of their sons, and there is a greater expectation by mothers and fathers alike of "ladylike" behavior on the part of daughters. Both parents expressed a reluctance to punish girls, and daughters more than sons were encouraged to "wonder and think about life." Interestingly, mothers' child-rearing practices are more sex differentiated with respect to restrictiveness and supervision of their daughters than their sons. Restrictive parental behavior, according to Block, was associated with "parental anxiety, worry, and concern about the misfortunes that can befall young women as they grow up" (Block, 1984: 89).

Sons, by contrast, were encouraged in achievement, competition, and independence. Both parents also encouraged boys to "control the expression of affect," and there was more of a punishment orientation in parents of males. Fathers tended to be more authoritarian with their sons than with their daughters; they reported they were more strict and firm, that they believed in physical punishment, and that they were less tolerant of sons' aggression when it was directed against them. Fathers more than mothers also encouraged the assumption of personal responsibility in their sons. Mothers encouraged sons, more than daughters, to conform to external standards (Block, 1984: 87).

Bursik, Merten, and Schwartz (1985) surveyed adults in a predominantly white-collar suburban community located near a large Midwestern city. The adults were asked about the age at which teenagers should be allowed to undertake certain activities (including staying out with friends until midnight, riding in a car with other youths, having same-gender friends as guests at one's home without an adult present, going on a date without a chaperon, being left alone in the afternoon, being left alone in the evening, and participating in organized activities). There was a tendency to trust boys with certain activities (notably the last four) at a significantly earlier age than girls; there was still consensus that the first two activities (staying out until midnight and riding in a car with other youths) should be done only by older adolescents, and in these there was not a significant gender difference. In one instance, being left home alone with a friend of the same sex, girls were trusted at an earlier age.

Upon further examination, Bursik and his colleagues did find that some of this mixed pattern was because males in their sample were likely to feel that boys could be trusted in these activities a year earlier than girls (Bursik et al., 1985: 124); it is important to note that this relationship held up even when one examined the gender of the parent. They concluded both that "girls are considered to be responsible at a much earlier age by female adults than by male adults" and that female adults generally consider girls able to accept this responsibility at the same age as boys; adult males report a very strong differential (126). Their conclusion was that girls receive inconsistent messages about their ability to take on responsibility. They also mentioned that none of the behaviors they surveyed was explicitly sexual, so they could not directly measure for the presence or absence of the sexual double standard in parental concern about girls.

Block's summary of existing work on socialization, as measured by a scale sensitive to dimensions of concern for others, noted that it has different effects on boys and girls, and these consequences show up in adult adjustment. For men, socialization moves them to "more androgynous sex role identities" because some traditionally feminine concerns (conscientiousness, conservatism, interdependency) are emphasized and there is pressure to renounce negative aspects of the masculine role (opportunism, restlessness, impulsivity). For women, socialization does not move them toward concerns or personal qualities conventionally defined as masculine.

So women with less restrictive childhoods occupied higher occupational status as adults and were better adjusted; this was particularly true of women with low feminine/high socialized roles.

In a review of her own longitudinal study, plus the work of others, Block found that "boys, more than girls, are reared in ways encouraging curiosity, independence, and exploration of the environment." In contrast, the more restrictive child-rearing practices used by parents of girls (emphasis on physical proximity, expectations of "ladylike behaviors," close supervision, and provision of help in problem-solving situations) lessen the opportunity for girls to engage in active experimentation with the environment, to encounter discrepancies, and to engage in solution efforts (Block, 1984: 275–276).

In one of the starkest examples of this circumstance, Block and her associates videotaped teaching behaviors of parents and found several things. First, fathers "exert greater pressure than mothers for sex-appropriate behaviors." Second, fathers in the teaching situation with sons "set higher standards, attended to the cognitive elements of the tasks and placed repeated emphasis on achievement." With their daughters, fathers focused more on the interpersonal aspects of the teaching situation—encouraging, joking, playing, protecting, and supporting. Mothers with girls, in contrast, provided help in the problem-solving situation even when it was not required, although with sons they tended to reject bids for help. They also provided girls with more immediate physical comfort after a frustrating experience (Block, 1984: 269–270).

Block found that parents "oversocialize" their daughters, with traditional socialization patterns producing girls who are encouraged to "(over)control impulses, to be tractable, obedient, cautious, and self-sacrificing." She notes that while these psychological constructs "may have been functional in yesterday's world of large families, a predominant[ly] male work force, and shorter life span[s], their functionalism in today's world is problematic" (Block, 1984: 140).

Others might argue with Block's "oversocialization" hypothesis by pointing to the mounting evidence that girls are given considerable latitude by their parents to be "tomboys." Indeed, one study found that 63 percent of junior high girls said they were tomboys, and 51 percent of an adult sample recalled being tomboys (Hyde, 1985: 159). In contrast, boys (particularly in the preteen years) are given less latitude to explore opposite-gender behavior because parents fear the label of "sissy."

Another important modification of the "oversocialization" hypothesis is gleaned from the work of Gilligan on moral development in girls. It is now arguable whether there are pronounced gender differences in the moral reasoning processes of young children; Gilligan's true contribution to the study of gender may lie elsewhere (see Walker, 1984, for a review of these studies). Gilligan notes that the inattention in the literature to girls' development has meant that the value of care, connection, and relationships in the moral reasoning process tended to be slighted in favor of approaches that draw upon more traditionally male domains such as justice, with its emphasis on fairness, rationality, individuality, abstractions, detachment, and impersonality. Gilligan also suggests that traditional adolescent intimacy with mothers may promote, particularly in girls who are encouraged to stay at home or in closer proximity to mothers, more of a care orientation in day-to-day behavior (Gilligan et al., 1988: xxix). She also speculates that this might, in some way, be related to girls' lower rates of violent and assaultive crime.

GIRLS AND THE SEXUAL DOUBLE STANDARD

The experience of freedom that many girls have in early adolescence seems to change during later adolescence. There are several possible sources of this change. First, girls become far more concerned about popularity during the high school years. Consequently, the influence of parents declines as the peer group becomes much more important. This poses special problems for girls, in that parents have traditionally been actively involved in controlling them during this particular period because of the sexual double standard. We know from what little research exists on daughters' relationships with parents at this age that, compared with sons, daughters have been allowed less freedom to play away from home, have not been assigned chores that take them out of the home, have been required to return home earlier, and have not been encouraged to choose their own activities (Komorosky, 1953; Block, 1984). This means that as girls approach puberty, parents begin to exhibit an interest in monitoring them more closely—this precisely when they are becoming less adult oriented. Clashes between daughters and parents may be more likely during late adolescence. Much of the family disharmony is an outgrowth of the long-standing sexual double standard that tacitly encourages male sexual exploration and punishes female sexuality.

Some might expect this traditional orientation to be less relevant today because of changes in the female role, but parental behavior is seemingly more ingrained than many believed it to be. Indeed, Katz (1979) says that there is "no evidence that parental socialization practices are changing drastically" (Katz, 1979: 23; for more recent documentation of Katz's claim, see Steinem, 1992). She goes on to summarize her own research that suggests that although many parents are concerned about sex-role equality, particularly for their daughters, "there are few who depart significantly from traditional socialization practices" largely because they fear that if they do, their children might become "misfits" (Katz, 1979: 24). Certainly, recent research has continued to document the role played by the culture of romance and the specter of the "slut" in girls' subculture (Adler, Kless, & Adler, 1992; Thorne, 1994).

Whatever the reason, it seems that adolescent girls are in a world that has not altered much despite major changes in the adult female role. Hence, modern girls, like girls in the past, are more closely watched than their brothers. Some parents, often working-class or lower class parents, turn to the family or juvenile court to enforce their authority. (For many parents, maintaining control over their children, especially girls, is extremely important.) It has long been understood that a major reason for the presence of girls in juvenile courts was because their parents insisted on their arrest. In past years, conflicts with parents were by far the most significant referral source; in Honolulu, 44 percent of the girls who appeared in court in 1929–1930 were referred by parents (Chesney-Lind, 1973). In less dramatic ways, this pattern continues; Pope and Feyerherm (1982: 6) found in a California study that girls were "substantially more likely to be referred by sources other than law enforcement." Their figures showed that 7 percent of all girls referred to court, but only 2 percent of the boys, were referred by parents. Other research, less specific, shows that in 1993 well over half (60%) of all status offense referrals to juvenile courts came from sources other than law enforcement personnel (Butts et al., 1996: 8).

AN OVERVIEW OF GIRLS' VICTIMIZATION

The main focus of this book has been on girls as offenders, but there are several reasons to think about the degree to which girls are victims of crimes. First, the extent of girls' victimization is much greater than many suppose, particularly when data on physical and sexual abuse are included. As an example, whereas girls are roughly a quarter of all the women in the United States, they may well be half of those raped (*Washington Post,* 1994: A10). Other estimates are that 34 percent of all girls suffer some sort of abuse before they reach adulthood (Benson, 1990). More important, as this chapter will demonstrate, evidence of a link between victimization and subsequent delinquent behavior is becoming manifest—particularly for girls.

Girls' victimization cannot be discussed without some consideration of child abuse and neglect (this topic and its relationship to girls' delinquency are covered more thoroughly later in this book). There is some evidence that girls are most likely to be victims within these two categories, but precise figures are elusive. According to the American Humane Association's Child Protection Division, in 1984 there were 1,727,000 cases of child abuse and neglect (U.S. Department of Health and Human Services, 1986: 3). In another report, which covered the period 1976–1982, 50.3 percent of the victims were female and the average age of the victim was 7.4 years of age. About two-thirds of the victims were white, and about 40 percent of the incidents occurred in households headed by a female (in contrast, 17 percent of all American families during this period were headed by a female). Almost half (47%) of the incidents occurred in families that were receiving public assistance (Russell & Trainor, 1984: 22–25). Between 1986 and 1993 the number of abused or neglected children almost doubled, with those sexually abused increasing by 125 percent (Snyder & Sickmund, 1999: 40).

The most recent figures come from the National Clearinghouse on Child Abuse and Neglect. According to an April 2002 report, about 879,000 children were found to be victims of child abuse and neglect in 2000 (National Clearinghouse, 2002). About two-thirds suffered from neglect, while 19 percent were physically abused and 10 percent were sexually abused. These are confirmed cases, out of about three million referrals. White children constituted a slight majority (51%), while African Americans were 25 percent of the total and Hispanics represented 15 percent. Not surprisingly, the vast majority of the perpetrators are parents. As for sexual abuse, nonrelatives constituted 29 percent of the offenders, while 22 percent were fathers acting alone and 19 percent were other relatives.

The latest report also shows that, although rates of abuse and neglect had been declining in recent years (from 15.3 per 1,000 children in 1993 to 11.8 per 1,000 in 1999), there was a slight increase to a rate of 12.2 in 2000.

The gender difference in child sexual abuse is pronounced. National Clearinghouse data reveal that the rate of sexual abuse was significantly higher for girls (1.7 per 1,000) than for boys (0.4 per 1,000). This translates to around 42,500 girls who were sexually abused during the year 2000. It should be noted that these are only the reported cases. Other estimates suggest that there may be between 100,000 and 200,000 children sexually abused each year. Girls are much more likely than boys to be the victims of sexual abuse, particularly of family-related sexual abuse (the majority of sexual abuse cases). Finkelhor and Baron (1986: 96) estimate that the most meticulous studies reveal that roughly 71 percent of the victims of child sexual abuse are females. A *Los Angeles Times* survey in 1981 reported that 25 percent of American girls have been sexually abused by the age of sixteen (Trounson, 1981). Russell estimated that two out of every five females (38 percent) are sexually abused before their eighteenth birthday (Russell, 1984).

Finkelhor (1982: 96), in another study, noted that between 15 percent and 34 percent of adult women, but only 3 percent to 9 percent of adult men, report having experienced sexual abuse as children. A survey of college students found that 19 percent of the females, but only 9 percent of the males, reported that they had been sexually abused as children (Finkelhor, 1978).

These studies, all of somewhat recent vintage, are contributing to a growing awareness of the dimensions of girls' victimization. Later chapters show how that victimization is shaped by girls' gender, race, and class background. The relationship between girls' victimization and female delinquency will also be explored.

GIRLS' VICTIMIZATION
AND FEMALE DELINQUENCY

Parental commitment to two standards of adolescent behavior is one explanation for disparity in parental treatment of sons and daughters, but another possible and far more disturbing explanation for girls' problems with their parents deserves attention: physical and sexual abuse. Very high rates of physical and sexual abuse have been reported by those working with delinquent girls, ranging from a low of 40 percent to a high of 73 percent. Abuse is a particularly prevalent reason given by female runaways for their behavior; male runaways do not attribute their behavior to abuse in anywhere near the same degree (McCormack, Janus, & Burgess, 1986).

In-depth research (Koroki and Chesney-Lind, 1985) into the backgrounds of female offenders suggests that the victimization (both sexual and physical) of young women who find themselves in the juvenile justice system is extensive, and that such victimization is not confined to those in institutional settings. The research also highlighted how poverty and racism express themselves in the lives of young women, and probed how the young women, themselves, felt about their victimization and subsequent relations with the juvenile justice system. Four of the ten girls interviewed had been sexually abused, and seven had been physically abused, at home. All linked the status offenses that brought them to the attention of the court to their home situations and were angry that they were being labeled as criminals. Said one girl about her court hearing, "I felt like a criminal. Like a damn fool. I was pissed off because I didn't belong there. That wasn't the place for me" (Koroki & Chesney-Lind, 1985: 22).

These young women ran away from homes that bear little resemblance to those of stereotypical "intact" families, and, once on the streets, they were forced into crime in order to survive. The interviews show very clearly that they did not have much attachment to their delinquent activities. Likewise, the Wisconsin study found that over half of the girls who ran away had stolen money, food, and clothing. A few exchanged sexual contact for necessities (Phelps et al., 1982: 67). In their study of runaway youths, McCormack, Janus, and Burgess (1986: 392–393) found that sexually abused female runaways were significantly more likely than their nonabused counterparts to engage in delinquent or criminal activities, such as substance abuse, petty theft, and prostitution; no such pattern was found among male runaways.

Recently, the National Council on Crime and Delinquency (NCCD) conducted a detailed study of girls in trouble in the state of California (Acoca & Dedel, 1998; Acoca, 1999). In a careful review of about 1,000 case files plus detailed interviews with about 200 girls in county juvenile detention centers, the researchers confirmed—once again—what the authors of this book and many others have been saying for years: victimization in its various forms is typically the first step along a pathway girls take into the juvenile justice system (Widom, 2000).

In the NCCD study, 92 percent of the girls interviewed said that they had been subjected to emotional, physical, and/or sexual abuse. Alarmingly, one-fourth said that they had been shot or stabbed one or more times! And such violence tended to occur when they were between 13 and 14 years of age. Moreover, at about the same age, they began abusing drugs and alcohol. The correlation seems obvious and the researchers concluded that "both the experience of victimization and substance abuse correlated with multiple risky behaviors including truancy, unsafe sexual activity, and gang involvement" (Acoca, 1999: 6).

It is bad enough that they experience abuse in the home and within their communities, but worse still is that such abuse tends to continue after they enter into the juvenile justice system. Girls interviewed for the NCCD study reported consistent abuse on the part of staff members, such as the use of foul and demeaning language, "inappropriate touching, pushing, and hitting, isolation and deprivation of clean clothing," and strip searches with males present. Further, these acts were rather routine and pervasive throughout not only the juvenile justice system but also within other community agencies. The report noted that 11 percent had experienced or witnessed a death of one or both parents or a sibling (Acoca, 1999: 6). Clearly, the abuse which characterized their lives before entering the juvenile justice system continued rather than abated, which is ironic since many officials justify system intervention as necessary to protect the girls.

More recent years' data further confirm the connection between early abuse and later delinquency and also suggest that the pattern is found in countries other than the U.S. For instance, researchers studying the backgrounds of girls in custody in Canada have found a pattern of criminalizing girls' survival strategies, just as is done in the United States. In their examination of the lives of girls before coming into custody, Artz, Blais, and Nicholson (2000) found that only one of the seven girls they interviewed had lived at home consistently throughout her childhood. All of the other girls' lives had been characterized by multiple moves and multiple caregivers. Of the seven girls, files of three girls provided evidence of prior sexual abuse and all seven reported exposure to family violence. Although five of the seven girls were currently in custody for violent crimes, their original offenses were less serious in nature, ranging from shoplifting and theft to fire setting and drug charges. Six of the seven girls committed their first offense in the company of friends, with four of the six having been initiated into lawbreaking by older boyfriends.

Reitsma-Street (1999: 345) comments on policing practices that serve to enforce expectations of "good girls." Shunning and slandering are everyday means used to punish differences in and police the reputations of delinquent or nondelinquent girls. More public forms of policing girls include the youth justice system, which has steadily decreased its use of the least intrusive types of sentencing for girls.

DeKeseredy (2000: 25) comments on prostitution as another survival strategy for some adolescent females in Canada. He suggests that prostitution is often just a way for adolescent females to make a living, "a means of survival in a gender-stratified society." He notes that adolescent females are in higher demand as prostitutes than adult females and that the street culture that accompanies prostitution also serves to provide a sense of belonging and a sense of autonomy through financial independence for girls who have often not experienced security or safety within their family homes.

Corrado, Odgers, and Cohen (2000) are other Canadian researchers who have provided valuable insights into the experiences of young female offenders. Recently, they completed an extensive study of incarcerated female young offenders and concluded that young women are usually more of a risk to themselves than they are to others. They suggest that the youth justice system in British Columbia demonstrates a clear desire to protect female youth from drugs, street life, and forms of abuse. The girls in the study reported recognizing that incarceration was meant as an opportunity for them to "get off and stay off drugs, reduce the control and authority that 'pimps' may have on them, and/or remove them temporarily from abusive environments" (17). Whereas 27 percent of the girls in their study were incarcerated for a violent offense, the majority (68.8%) were incarcerated for relatively minor offenses: 44.8 percent for breaches of court orders and 23.8 percent for property offenses. Like Artz, Blais, and Nicholson (2000), they found that the majority of girls in their study had also experienced very little residential stability in their lives.

Review of the girls' criminal histories revealed that the majority of prior offenses were status offenses—only 6 percent of previous charges held by the girls in their sample were violent in nature. Further, Corrado, Odgers, and Cohen (2000) reported that after release from custody, 80.4 percent of the girls in their sample who recidivated during the one-year follow-up period committed nonviolent crimes, most commonly a breach of probation orders. Of the 13.4 percent of girls who reoffended violently, 13 had charges of Level 1 assault, and 2 had been charged with robbery.

Finally, these authors looked at drug use and responses to addiction and found no relationship between the use of marijuana, heroin, cocaine, acid, or downers and reoffending. They did, however, find that girls who were frequent crack cocaine users were more likely to be charged with an administrative breach offense. Further, they contend that most youth custody institutions are not adequately equipped to deal with the special needs of female youth with severe drug addictions.

Corrado, Odgers, and Cohen (2000) conclude that though the criminal justice system is proving to provide effective "short[-]term" protection for these girls, the "non-moralistic, paternalistic decision-making practices...under the justice-based Young Offenders Act" continue to result in incarceration of young women at high levels without long-term positive outcomes. These authors point to the need for innovative community programs in the form of noncustodial treatment and protection options to deal with the "multi-problem realities of young women's lifestyles and immediate priorities" (19).

In light of the foregoing information, a feminist perspective might add to traditional delinquency theories an explicit concern about the role of sexual abuse in girls' delinquency. Like young men, young women are frequently the objects of violence and abuse, but unlike young men's victimization, young women's victimization and their response to it are shaped by their status as young women. Hence, young women are much more likely than their opposites to be the victim of sexual abuse (an estimated three-quarters of sexual abuse victims are females), more likely to be victimized by a relative, and more likely to be abused over a long period (Browne & Finkelhor, 1986). In addition, their vulnerability is heightened by norms that require that they stay at home, where their victimizers have greater access to them.

Moreover, as we will see in the next chapter, females' victimizers (usually males) can invoke official agencies of social control in their efforts to keep young women at home and vulnerable. That is to say, abusers have traditionally been able to use the uncritical commitment of the juvenile justice system to parental authority to force girls to obey them. Until recently, girls' complaints about abuse were routinely ignored by the system. For this reason, statutes written to protect young people have, in the case of girls' delinquency, criminalized their survival strategies. If girls persist in their refusal to stay in abusive homes, they become embedded in the juvenile justice system, which has few alternatives other than incarceration.

Many young women on the run from homes characterized by sexual abuse and parental neglect are pushed, by the very statutes designed to protect them, into life on the streets. They cannot return to school or take a job to support themselves lest they be detected. Panhandling, petty theft, and occasional prostitution are their recourse. Also, young girls (but not necessarily young boys) are seen as sexually desirable—in fact, more desirable than their older sisters because of the double standard in aging (Bell, 1984). This means that life on the streets and survival strategies are shaped by patriarchal values. It is no accident that girls on the run from abusive homes or on the streets because of profound poverty get involved in criminal activities that exploit their sexual-object status. American society has defined as desirable young, physically perfect women, and girls on the streets, who have little else of value to trade, are encouraged to use this "resource." Certainly the criminal subculture views them from this perspective (see Miller, 1986).

Additionally, both in the past and the present, most female delinquency is placed within a context relative to girls' sexual behavior precisely because of women's defiance of patriarchal control over their sexual "capital"—control that historically has been central to the maintenance of patriarchy (Lerner, 1986). That young women have more of this capital has been one reason for the excessive concern that both families and official agencies of social control have expressed about youthful female defiance.

CONTEMPORARY DELINQUENCY
RESEARCH AND GENDER

Does contemporary delinquency research, which is increasingly likely to center on the female delinquent, offer any information on girls' lives and their delinquency? Clearly, this would be important to the construction of a theory of delinquency that would explain the misbehavior of both girls and boys. It would help as well to explain the gender gap in serious delinquency.

Studies that explore differences in the routine activities of male and female youths and differences in male and female perceptions of conformity and deviance, although few, have produced some interesting findings that begin to establish a link between the place adolescent girls occupy in society and their delinquent behavior. Jensen and Eve (1976) examined the effects of "relationship with parents," "attachment to law," "academic performance," and "participation in youth culture" and concluded that, even controlling for all of these factors, the "direct" contribution of gender to delinquency was significant.

Looking at both attitudes toward education and educational performance, Rankin (1980) found gender differences in the relationship of these variables to delinquency. Rankin did expect that they would have a greater effect on male than female delinquent behavior because males have traditionally been seen as more directly affected by occupational achievement. He ascertained, instead, that although negative attitudes toward school and poor school performance were significant in predicting delinquency in both sexes, the relationship was stronger for girls than for boys.

Farnworth (1984) found in her study of African American delinquency that girls who experience a low degree of satisfaction with school achievement report greater involvement in petty delinquency and status offenses; indeed, school problems were more important than family problems in the prediction of these forms of delinquency for girls. In contrast, boys did not show this pattern; "poor family relationships" were a better predictor of male delinquency, particularly property offenses. However, Farnworth did discover that there was a gender effect for violent delinquency that could not be explained by social ties to either family or school.

Poor school performance was strongly related to girls' delinquency in Figueria-McDonough's (1984) research as well. She also reported that school setting had a differential effect on male and female self-reported delinquency. Specifically, assertive girls in a school with a "single-mindedly academic, competitive environment" were more likely to be delinquent because, in her view, such a school tends to mimic patterns of adult success linked to gender inequality—bright girls in these schools apparently sought out illegitimate opportunities. In more "differentiated" school environments, assertive girls were able to find legitimate paths to success. Boys, too, had difficulty with the more competitive environment (but the relationship was less direct for them); male delinquency was higher here as well, suggesting that neither sex thrives in such an environment. This finding seems consistent with that of another study that examined tutors' interactions with high- and moderate-achieving fifth-grade girls and boys; tutors gave high-achieving girls the lowest levels of supportive, ego-enhancing feedback (Frey, 1979).

Shover and his colleagues (1979) compared the masculinity hypothesis (discussed earlier) and the "opportunity" and "attachment to conventional others" theories, using a self-report sample, and concluded that "the criminogenic importance of the traditional masculine role, itself, proved to be much less important than the traditional feminine role as a predictor of the extent of involvement in both types of delinquency (property and aggressive offenses)." For the female role, it appears that the observed effects are largely "indirect"; young women perceive less access to delinquent opportunities and express more attachment to conventional others than do males. This observation held particularly true for property offenses; for aggressive behavior, there was evidence for both males and females that opportunity does not appear to play as strong a role, and that even with increased opportunity there has been no increase in aggressive female criminality.

Two major studies of girls' friendship patterns explain why this might be the case. Morash (1986) interviewed 588 youths in the Boston area, all of whom had had contact with the juvenile justice system. First, she noted that girls were more likely than boys to refuse to participate in the study, again supporting Morris's notion that girls feel more embarrassment about such contacts (Morash, 1986: 50). Concerning girls' and boys' groups, she found that the latter were more involved in delinquent and sports activities, that girls were older when they joined groups, that girls were less likely than boys to have a regular meeting place outside their homes, and that girls' groups were less likely to be limited to one sex. Most important, despite much criminological speculation that as contact within groups increased, so would delinquency—a common notion in male delinquency theory—Morash found that this was not so for either girls' or boys' groups. Instead, the variable most consistently related to delinquency was delinquent orientation of peers, not group solidarity or attachment to peers (55). In essence, Morash concluded, girls had lower delinquency rates not because they were not in groups but because they tend to be in less delinquent groups. Her research could not ascribe a reason to the phenomenon.

Giordano and her associates' interviews with 942 youths (Giordano, Cernkovich, & Pugh, 1986) may help to supply an answer. From this more representative sample of young people they learned that females, no matter their level of involvement in delinquency, are more likely than males to have intimate relationships. That is to say, girls spend as much if not more time (if telephone calls are counted), in groups. However, girls' groups do not appear to exert the same influence on them as boys' groups do on boys. Boys, for example, tend to report that their groups exerted a variety of pressures on them, including pressure to engage in risk-taking behavior and delinquency. Norms in girls' friendship groups promote a friendship style (intimacy, self-disclosure, and so on) that may serve to inhibit delinquency even in the presence of factors that might promote it (Giordano, Cernkovich, & Pugh, 1986: 1194).

The role of groups in delinquency causation was also explored by Deschenes, Rosenbaum, and Fagan (1990). In their self-report study of drug use and its relationship to serious delinquency in six inner-city neighborhoods during the mid-1980s, they confirmed the gender difference in serious crime but found no such difference in minor offenses or property offenses (Deschenes, Rosenbaum, & Fagan: 1990: 10). Indeed, among this predominantly African American and Hispanic sample, girls committed property crimes at a greater rate than boys. Drug use was also gendered, with a greater proportion of males using hard drugs. However, the most interesting part of this study was its exploration of the dynamics of male and female delinquency and drug use. Here the researchers ascertained that the determinants of delinquency and drug use differed by gender. Specifically, peer delinquency was important in the delinquency of both girls and boys, but was more important for boys. For girls, two factors, victimization history and attachment to conventional values, played a far larger role in the causation and/or suppression of their delinquency than in that of their male counterparts. Likewise, the predictors of drug use differed by sex, with the degree of neighborhood violence being more important in predicting girls' drug use than boys', although peer drug use had great bearing on the drug use of cohorts.

Figueria-McDonough (1984) also found class to be important in her study of self-reported delinquency in a Midwestern high school sample. As noted earlier, she found little support for the notion that feminist orientations promote female delinquent activity. Instead, the model that best predicted female delinquency was one that she called a "subcultural deprivation model." That is, girls of low social class with low conventional aspirations, low school success, and high social activity are the most delinquent. Figueria-McDonough interpreted this to mean that "lower class position depresses aspirations[,] leading to lower school performance and high social activity[,] which strongly predicts delinquency" (Figueria-McDonough, 1984: 339).

Alder's research on female youth unemployment in Australia raises another aspect of the role of class in girls' troubles. Although not studying delinquent behavior directly, Alder, in her interviews with fifty unemployed young women in Melbourne, points to the plight of younger women who are being progressively squeezed out of the labor market by greater numbers of older, more experienced women. Alder's work also challenges the notion that unemployment is an "adult" problem; most of the women she interviewed were between sixteen and nineteen years of age and had been unemployed for eighteen months. Most had had problems coping with schoolwork or had had conflicts with teachers and had left school in the ninth grade. Despite a deep desire to work, unemployment was their normal condition, interspersed with infrequent short periods of unsatisfactory employment. Alder found that unlike unemployed males, unemployed females were more "home bound" (i.e., engaged in dependent domesticity). They also felt that unemployment caused a questioning of their femininity and, particularly, their sexual status. The chronic unemployment led to drug and alcohol abuse, and petty criminal activity, especially the shoplifting of clothes and cosmetics (Alder, 1986).

A British self-report study (Mawby, 1980) adds yet another dimension to the restriction of girls to a certain setting, particularly the home. In looking for the sources of the gender gap in delinquency, Mawby learned that girls' attitudes toward the police were more positive than boys', and they were less likely to report criminal victimization. Most interesting, however, were the findings regarding differences in male and female behavior that would have an indirect effect on both the visibility of female deviance and the likelihood that the setting provides criminal opportunities. Thus, the data indicated that girls' movements were more "controlled." Young women were more likely to "play or muck about" the home, and boys to "play or muck about" on deserted land (540). Girls, when they stole, stole from homes or schools; boys stole from building sites or by breaking into empty buildings. These findings are consistent with other research that suggests that girls are allowed fewer excursions from home, are more closely supervised in their activities, and are assigned chores that keep them homebound—in contrast to boys, who are assigned chores out of the home and/or farther from home (Block, 1984: 231).

Norms such as these may play another role in the generation of the gender gap in delinquency. They could contribute to a sex differential in vulnerability to arrest. For example, it is known that young women are now using drugs, particularly marijuana, in large amounts, but they are less vulnerable than young men to arrest for this activity. Studies of illegal drug use among college students showed that males tended to buy drugs (from other males) and that females were far more likely to have been given the drugs they used (usually by males) (Bowker, 1976).

Another study (Johnson et al., 1977) revealed that differences in male and female drug use were exaggerated by official statistics, and the researchers concluded that this pattern was explained almost entirely by the fact that males are far more likely than females to be arrested. Their data on the circumstances of arrest suggest that men tended to use marijuana in settings that made them more prone to attention from the police: "on the streets," they were more likely than women to be arrested by general patrol officers, to be arrested more often in vehicles, and to be arrested more often alone.

In contrast, women were more likely to be arrested in raids on private residences. But because use of marijuana in such locations is usually less visible than public use or transport, and because police raids of homes are strictly regulated by statute, fewer women are arrested. In essence, it appears that restrictions on female mobility (Mawby, 1980), in addition to social norms that encourage women to rely on men to obtain marijuana for them (Bowker, 1976), may cushion females from drug arrests. Put another way, young women may enjoy lesser vulnerability to arrest because of the settings within which they commit their offenses (Hindelang, 1979).

Interest in the control of girls' behavior also found its way into recent work on the "power-control" model of delinquency (Hagan, Simpson, & Gillis, 1985; Hagan, 1989). The authors speculated that girls commit less delinquency in part because their behavior is more closely controlled by the patriarchal family. They also sought to examine the dynamics of power within the parental relationship as these relate to the supervision of girls and the quality of girls' relationships with their mothers. The authors used a self-report study of 436 youths in the Toronto area; follow-up telephone interviews with the youths' parents were also included in a series of studies published with these data.

The promising conceptualization of Hagan and his associates is hampered by a limited definition of patriarchal control. Among other things, it results in their arguing that a mother's working outside the home leads to increases in a daughter's delinquency because the daughter finds herself in a more "egalitarian family"—a family less likely to supervise the female children. Although it is intriguing, this is essentially a not-too-subtle variation on the "liberation" hypothesis. Now, mother's liberation or employment causes daughter's crime. Besides the many methodological problems with the work of Hagan and his associates (the authors assume that most adolescents live in two-parent families, argue that female-headed households are equivalent to upper status "egalitarian" families in which both parents work, and merge "direct control" of youthful behavior with "indirect control" through attachment to parents), there is a more fundamental problem with the hypothesis: no evidence suggests that as women's labor force participation has increased, girls' delinquency has increased. Indeed, during the past decade, when both women's labor force participation and the number of female-headed households soared, aggregate female delinquency measured both by self-report and official statistics either declined or remained stable (Ageton, 1983; Federal Bureau of Investigation, 1986; Chilton & Datesman, 1987).

More to the point, the argument suggests that girls are unaffected by class, that somehow girls from upper status families whose mothers work are equivalent to girls who are growing up in poverty with a single mother. Such an argument is simply too one-dimensional and neglects other forms of control and supervision that girls experience. It also neglects the role of victimization in girls' delinquent behavior.

A test of this model on a national sample (Morash & Chesney-Lind, 1991) found, for example, that gender differences in delinquency appeared regardless of patriarchal or egalitarian family structure. Family social class, rather than socialization for risk taking, which is thought to fuel male delinquency, played a strong role in the causation of youthful delinquency. The quality of the relationship with the mother ("relational control") was very important in explaining low levels of delinquency, particularly for boys. Finally, for both boys and girls, the experience of negative sanctions (a form of control not considered by Hagan and his associates) was found to explain delinquency.

Other tests of the model have also failed to confirm critical elements of the Hagan theory (see Hill & Atkinson, 1988; Singer & Levine, 1988; Jensen & Thompson, 1990). However, Hagan and his associates are to be commended insofar as they focused on the importance of gender and patriarchy in the shaping of both male and female behavior.

Further explorations of the varieties of social control that girls experience and the relationship of such control to their delinquency are clearly needed. For example, one result of seeing the effects of identification with the mother as a negative influence on delinquency is to correct the stereotypical assumption that in all arenas of life women act out of weakness and men out of power. This is a central theme of Naffine's book (1987), in which she specifically argued that criminological theories frequently portray girls' conformity in a negative light. Then these theories simultaneously make a connection between delinquency and such positively valued traits as assertiveness and occupational success, which are assumed to characterize boys.

In power-control theory, weak mothers set limits on conformist daughters. To illustrate, Hagan and associates (1985) wrote that "[w]omen are oversocialized; more specifically, overcontrolled." Why is it preferable to be socialized to take the kinds of risks and to have the perceptions of fun that predispose one to commit minor delinquency? There is no evidence that such socialization better prepares boys to succeed in the work environment. An alternative view suggested by both feminist theory and present research is that women are pre-disposed to nurturing relationships with their children, and the resulting strength of the mother–child identification produces prosocial behavior in both girls and boys (Morash & Chesney-Lind, 1991). As Naffine (1987: 75) suggested, women are not the passive, dependent, and compliant people that power-control theory assumes.

Another form of social control was measured indirectly by researchers ex-amining perceived chances of arrest. In a national sample of persons aged fifteen and over, Richards and Tittle (1981) found that women consistently give higher estimates of arrest probability than males. This difference arises largely because women feel more visible than men and have greater stakes in conformity (mean-ing that they anticipate more negative consequences if they deviate). The authors suggested that women "may think that legal sanction is somewhat certain be-cause they are more likely to think of themselves as subject to surveillance and general social reaction than men" (Richards & Tittle, 1981: 1196). Like Morris (1965), they suspected that women's greater relative stake in conformity may make deviance more threatening for them, and this in turn may lead to their high sanction–risk estimates. These variables, which the authors attached to women's "structural position" in society, were found to be more important than those that were more related to personality characteristics.

Perhaps the most intriguing exploration of another aspect of Hagen's power-control theory (that of an orientation toward risk taking) is provided by Heimer's symbolic interactionist approach to gender and race differences in delinquency. Using data drawn from a national sample of values and lifestyles among high school youth conducted annually since 1975, Heimer added data collected in 1988 to examine motivational pathways leading to delinquency. One of her key findings was that a gender difference exists in the pathways that *create* the attitudes favorable to delinquent behavior. Specif-ically, she found that in boys, high grades bolstered self-esteem, which in turn led to "definitions favorable to risk taking." An orientation favorable to risk taking was, in turn, found to be directly related to higher delinquency. For girls, however, high grades and positive self-esteem *discouraged* definitions fa-vorable toward risk taking and hence to committing delinquent behavior (159). Thus, Heimer concludes that whereas "positive self-esteem indirectly *decreases* delinquency among females, it indirectly *increases* delinquency among males" (1995: 159–162).

Beyond this, Heimer found that race effects differed for boys and girls as well. Specifically, she found that African American males (but not females) "engage in more violence than their white counterparts" (165). To explain this, Heimer observes that the constraints placed on African American males may encourage them to engage in "male posturing, including fighting and other forms of violent delinquency" (165). She also found that both African American girls and boys are *less likely* than their white counterparts to steal and use drugs (165).

Heimer's research shows how gender mediates and changes a youth's rela-tive orientation toward risk taking, which in turn begins to explain differences in delinquency—unrelated to girls' being "overcontrolled." More broadly, Heimer's findings suggest that boys and girls have different pathways to delinquent behavior, and she also signals the importance of considering *both* race and gender simultaneously when talking about the causes of delinquency.

SUMMARY

To explain delinquency among girls, it is necessary to begin considering the importance of gender stratification in a patriarchal society, especially because it is so important in shaping the daily lives of boys and girls. Studies of the socialization process indicate that the learning of gender roles is of central importance to both girls and boys. Part of this process is learning what is or is not "appropriate" for one's sex. Socialization, particularly during childhood, begins to develop in girls attributes that, although appropriate to their sex, are not highly valued in the dominant society. During adolescence, the enforcement of gender by parents, school personnel, and others in a young girl's life further underscores many traditional elements of a woman's place, particularly that she must be controlled so as not to jeopardize her reputation (the sexual double standard).

Research suggests that norms and expectations about gender, particularly for girls, have remained largely unaltered despite the women's movement. Girls' plummeting self-esteem is likely tied, particularly among white girls, to the overemphasis on physical attractiveness and unhealthy eating habits. For girls of color, invisibility within a school system that ignores or belittles you, as well as violence in your neighborhood, produce different problems. Finally, despite notions that *if* girls were treated like boys, they would be just as delinquent, research suggests that raising girls' self-esteem would actually lower their delinquency.

The evidence also seems to point to the fact that parents, school officials, and others often supervise and restrict girls' behavior to prevent sexual experimentation. Supervision may result in lower delinquency in some girls, but it may also fuel delinquency of another sort as girls rebel against traditional restraints. Such "control," when it takes the form of physical or sexual abuse, is clearly a force that causes girls' delinquency.

For working-class and lower class girls, the pressures of gender scripts are particularly acute. Unable to compete in a popularity contest built around white, middle-class standards of beauty, they are not necessarily free from these images of femininity. They also negotiate a more hostile educational terrain and experience more violence. They must carve out their own solutions to their situations, solutions that may involve them in illegal activity, but they often feel embarrassed about these choices and blame themselves for not being able to fulfill traditional female roles successfully.

Contemporary research on female delinquency suggests that girls' delinquency, like boys', is fueled by such elements as problems in school, poor school performance, perceived lack of access to legitimate opportunities, subcultural deprivation, attitudes toward conventional authority, and perceived chances of arrest. Added to this list are some experiences to which girls are uniquely vulnerable, such as sexual victimization. To say that these variables are important in girls' delinquency, though, is not to say that theories developed to describe the variables' importance in boys' lives can be used to explain girls' delinquency without modification. The challenge is to generate delinquency theories that are sensitive to the patriarchal context of all behavior—both conforming and law violating.

One such theory has appeared: the power-control model of delinquency. It is promising but in need of revision. In general, although the power-control theory points researchers to the importance of control in girls' lives, it neglects other critical variables—notably, social class, negative parental sanctions, and victimization. Moreover, it suggests that the employment of mothers may, in fact, be the primary cause of some female delinquency, a notion that other research has failed to confirm. Some researchers have gone so far as to say that girls' lower delinquency, particularly serious and violent delinquency, may be the result of positive attributes that girls accumulate as a consequence of growing up female and identifying with the positive aspects of their gender. In this sense, a feminist theory of delinquency, which has yet to be fully developed, would also force those who have long taken the male rate of delinquency as "normal" to think again about both adolescent conformity and deviance.

7

Girls and the Juvenile Justice System: A Historical Overview

From 1974 to 1993, the number of status offenders held in delinquency institutions dropped from roughly 172,000 to 3,200. Without merit, H.R. 3876 would allow States to hold juvenile status offenders in secure confinement for the purpose of reuniting such status offenders with their parents or legal guardians. This misguided movement back to an institution-based approach is inconsistent with studies showing that nearly all runaways leave home for understandable reasons such as flight from physical and sexual abuse and neglect.

MINORITY VIEWS, U.S. HOUSE OF REPRESENTATIVES,
REAUTHORIZATION OF THE JJDP, 1996[1]

G irls' experiences in the juvenile justice system are best understood if they are placed within the history of this unique set of institutions. The ways in which societies have dealt with youths' problems have varied tremendously over the past few centuries, and these have had a distinct impact on the lives of girls.

Juvenile justice reforms in the United States that indirectly benefited girls (particularly the efforts to deinstitutionalize status offenders) were, in the nineties, directly challenged by congressional initiatives that seek to refocus national attention on "youth violence" (Howard, 1996: 22). Republican lawmakers in both the House and the Senate introduced bills that, while ostensibly refocusing national attention on youthful violence, will also reinstitutionalize girls, dramatically cut back on state and federal oversight of juvenile institutionalization, and eliminate the small amount of money set aside for girls' programs (Howard, 1996) Happily, when the Juvenile Justice and Delinquency Prevention Act was finally reauthorized in October of 2002, girls were not completely forgotten and most of the draconian suggestions that surfaced at the end of the last century were shelved (Doi, 2002: 1). However, the Bush Administration has assigned juvenile justice a very low priority, permitted Congress to raid monies set aside to fund core aspects of this visionary legislation, and cancelled plans to establish a Girl's Institute in the Office of Juvenile Justice and Delinquency Prevention (Treanor, 2003).

As this chapter will show, these policy debates are part of a long history of the juvenile justice system's checkered past when it comes to girls. The history of the juvenile justice system (the police, the courts, and the correctional systems designed to handle youthful offenders) is very much a chronicle of the creation of organizations to monitor the social and moral behavior of youths. These institutions have also been shaped by politics that reflect each era's attitudes about gender, race, and class. Throughout all of these periods, official interest in youthful morality and criminality, lodged as it is in patriarchal society, clearly has special meaning for girls in the juvenile justice system.

THE DOCTRINE OF *PARENS PATRIAE*, STUBBORN CHILDREN, AND HOUSES OF REFUGE: ROOTS OF A DOUBLE STANDARD OF JUVENILE JUSTICE

In a long view of history, even the concept of childhood is of relatively recent vintage. According to Ariès (1962), art in the Middle Ages (A.D. 500 to 1400) did not even attempt to portray childhood, instead depicting children as little men and women. Adolescence as a separate social category did not appear until the nineteenth century; during earlier periods (when life expectancies often went little beyond the age of forty), young adults constituted the backbone of society. Children had relatively close ties to their families and communities until around the age of puberty; then, for all practical purposes, they became adults and began to live independently of parents. Autobiographies and biographies written during the early 1800s are replete with instances of young people beginning to work at ages as young as six or seven. Kett has noted that "children provided parents in preindustrial society with a form of social security, unemployment insurance, and yearly support" (Kett, 1977: 11–37).

Before the nineteenth century, then, the deviant behavior of young people was handled largely on an informal basis. This does not imply that all was well with the treatment of youths in previous centuries. For example, children were subjected to some extreme forms of physical and sexual abuse (de Mause, 1974; Empey, 1982). Strict laws governed the behavior of children (Sutton, 1988); however, in the United States, these laws were used only infrequently (Hawes, 1971; Rothman, 1971). Rothman (1971) noted, for example, that almshouses (a word used synonymously for workhouses and jails up until the nineteenth century) and other forms of incarceration were rarely used to handle the misbehavior of members of one's own community, and incarceration for long periods of time was almost nonexistent. In cases where children's misbehavior was especially troublesome, apprenticeship (usually involving sending a youth away from home to live with someone who could teach him or her a trade) was often used as a form of punishment (Bremner, 1970; Rendleman, 1979). For the most part, the control and discipline of children were left up to the family unit (Krisberg & Austin, 1993: 9).

The appearance of adolescence as a social category coincided with an increasing concern for the regulation of the moral behavior of young people (Platt, 1969; Empey, 1982). Although entirely separate systems to monitor and control the behavior of young people began to appear during the early part of the nineteenth century, differential treatment based upon age did not come about overnight. The roots of the juvenile justice system can be traced to much earlier legal and social perspectives on childhood and youth. One of the most important of these, for girls, was a legal doctrine known as *parens patriae*.

Parens patriae has its origins in medieval England's chancery courts. At that point it had more to do with property law than children; it was, essentially, a means for the crown to administer landed orphans' estates (Sutton, 1988). *Parens patriae* established that the king, in his presumed role as the "father" of his country, had the legal authority to take care of "his" people, especially those who were unable, for various reasons (including age), to take care of themselves. For children, the king or his authorized agents could assume the role of guardian to be able to administer their property. In time this legal doctrine evolved into the practice of the state's assuming wardship over a minor child and, in effect, playing the role of parent if the child had no parents or if the existing parents were declared unfit.

Rendleman (1979: 63) tells us that in England's American colonies, for example, officials could "bind out" as apprentices "children of parents who were poor, not providing good breeding, neglecting their formal education, not teaching a trade, or were idle, dissolute, unchristian or incapable." Later, during the nineteenth century, *parens patriae* supplied (as it still does to some extent) the legal basis for court intervention into the relationship between children and their families (Teitelbaum & Harris, 1977; see also Krisberg & Austin, 1993: ch. 2).

Another legal legacy of the colonial era that relates to the state's involvement in the lives of youth is the stubborn child law. Passed in Massachusetts in 1646, it established a clear legal relationship between children and parents and, among other things, made it a capital offense for a child to disobey his or her parents. This statute stated in part:

> If a man have a stubborn or rebellious son, of sufficient years and un-
> derstanding (viz) sixteen years of age, which will not obey the voice of his
> Father, or the voice of his Mother, and that when they have chastened
> him will not harken unto them: then shall his Father and Mother being
> his natural parents, lay hold on him, and bring him to the Magistrates as-
> sembled in court and testify unto them, that their son is stubborn and re-
> bellious and will not obey their voice and chastisement, but lives in sundry
> notorious crimes, such a son shall be put to death. (Sutton, 1988: 11)

This law was grounded in the distinctly Puritan belief in the innate wickedness of humankind, wickedness that required, for one thing, that children be sub-jected to strong discipline. Legal scholars suggest the law is unique in several other respects: it specifies a particular legal obligation of children; it defines par-ents as the focus of that obligation; and it establishes rules for governmental in-tervention should parental control over children break down (Sutton, 1988: 11).

It is important to consider the full implications of the notion of the state as parent and, more especially, father—a concept that is implied in both the *parens patriae* doctrine and, to some extent, in the stubborn child law. The objects of a patriarch's authority have traditionally included women in addition to chil-dren. The idea of patriarchy has also reinforced the sanctity and privacy of the home, and the power (in early years, almost absolute) of the patriarch to disci-pline wife and children (Dobash & Dobash, 1979: ch. 1). Further, the notion of *parens patriae* assumes that the father (or, in this case, the state or king) can legally act as a parent, with many of the implicit parental powers possessed by fathers. Therefore, as we shall see, governmental leaders would eventually use *parens patriae,* once a rather narrowly construed legal doctrine, to justify ex-treme governmental intervention in the lives of young people. Arguing that such intervention was "for their own good," "for their own protection," or "in the best interests of the child," the state during the eighteenth century became increasingly involved in the regulation of adolescent behavior.

In the United States, interest in the state regulation of youth was directly tied to explosive immigration and population growth. Empey (1982: 59) notes that between 1750 and 1850 the population of the United States went from 1.25 million to 23 million. The population of some states, such as Massachu-setts, doubled, and New York's population increased fivefold between 1790 and 1830. Many of those coming into the United States during the middle of the nineteenth century were of Irish or German background; the fourfold increase in immigrants between 1830 and 1840 was largely a product of the economic hardships faced by the Irish during the potato famine (Brenzel, 1983: 11). The social controls of small communities were simply overwhelmed by the influx of newcomers, many of whom were either foreign born or of foreign parentage.

In many eastern cities (especially New York), there were large numbers of what seemed to established residents to be "unsupervised" children. Desper-ately poor, most of them were recent immigrants, and many had ethnic back-grounds different from those of the American elite. In 1853 a leader of the

Boston establishment, Charles Eliot Norton, reflected the attitudes of much of the elite when he described immigration as a "sea of ignorance . . . swollen by waves of misery and vice . . . pouring from revolutionary Europe upon our shores" (Brenzel, 1983: 11). Several philanthropic associations emerged in response to the perceived problem. One of the most notable was the Society for the Reformation of Juvenile Delinquents (SRJD), founded in 1823 in New York City (Sutton, 1988: 69).

Composed primarily of wealthy businessmen and professionals, the SRJD persuaded the New York Legislature to pass a bill in 1824 that established the New York House of Refuge, the first correctional institution for children in the United States. The bill included the first statutory definition of "juvenile delinquency" and contained some vague descriptions of those subject to official intervention and commitment to the New York House of Refuge. Being "homeless," coming from an "unfit" home, and lacking a "good home and family" were examples (Hawes, 1971: 33). Important here is the fact that children committed to the House of Refuge (and others to follow) never committed an actual crime; they were deemed "incorrigible" or "beyond control." Most were living under conditions that those in authority deemed "unwholesome" or likely to lead to delinquency and criminality. The goal of the SRJD and like-minded groups was to identify potential delinquents, isolate them, and then "reform" them.

Also significant in these statutes regarding children was the first legal codification of the state's right to incarcerate juveniles after only "summary and informal hearings" (Sutton, 1988: 94). According to historical accounts, in many jurisdictions children were treated summarily; the laws "transformed routine discretion into formal policy" and in the process laid the foundation for separate standards of justice for adults and children.

Three other houses of refuge were soon opened: Boston in 1826, Philadelphia in 1828, and Baltimore in 1830 (Bremner, 1970: 679–682). They were ostensibly designed to provide education, religious instruction, training for future employment, and parental discipline. In other words, they were to be schools with a "homelike" atmosphere rather than prisons. The rhetoric of the founders and managers of houses of refuge fell far short of the reality experienced by the youth held in these facilities. A look at one of the most significant court challenges to the refuge movement and one that, perhaps not surprisingly, involved an adolescent female provides additional insight into the origins of the juvenile justice system.

EX PARTE CROUSE

Filed in 1838, *Ex Parte Crouse* arose from a petition of habeas corpus filed by the father of a minor, Mary Ann Crouse. Without her father's knowledge, Crouse had been committed to the Philadelphia House of Refuge by her mother on the grounds that she was "incorrigible." Her father argued that the incarceration was illegal because she had not been given a jury trial. The justices of the Supreme Court of Pennsylvania rejected the appeal, saying that the Bill of Rights did not apply to juveniles. Based upon the *parens patriae* doctrine, the ruling asked, "May not the natural parents, when unequal to the task of education, or unworthy of it, be superseded by the *parens patriae* or common guardian of the community?" (Pisciotta, 1982: 411). Note here that the logic was accepted, even though one of Crouse's parents felt able to care for her.

The ruling assumed that the Philadelphia House of Refuge (and presumably all other houses of refuge) had a beneficial effect on its residents. It "is not a prison, but a school," and because of this, not subject to procedural constraints (Sutton, 1988: 11). Further, the aims of such an institution were to reform the youngsters within them "by training . . . [them] to industry; by imbuing their minds with the principles of morality and religion; by furnishing them with means to earn a living; and above all, by separating them from the corrupting influences of improper associates" (Pisciotta, 1982: 411).

What evidence did the justices consult to support their conclusion that the House of Refuge was not a prison but a school? Sadly, only testimony by those who managed the institution had been solicited. However, a more objective review of the treatment of youths housed in these places might have led the justices to a very different conclusion. For instance, Pisciotta (1982) found that there was an enormous amount of abuse within these institutions. They were run according to a strict military regimen in which corporal punishment (girls in one institution were "ducked" under water and boys were hung by their thumbs), solitary confinement, and a "silent system" were part of the routine. Similar accounts of conditions in these facilities have been written by other researchers (Mennel, 1973; Hawes, 1971: 47–48; Bremner, 1970: 689–691). Work training was practically nonexistent, and outside companies contracted for cheap inmate labor. Religious instruction was often little more than Protestant indoctrination (many of the youngsters were Catholic). Education, in the conventional meaning of the word, was almost nonexistent.

Significantly, though, judges in the nineteenth century, when asked to review the care of juveniles, were reluctant to examine too closely state intervention into minors' lives if it was justified in familial terms. Ironically, such reviews were not undertaken even if a parent so requested (as in the Crouse case). The remainder of the nineteenth century witnessed intensification of the notion of the state as parent, and even greater threats to girls' rights.

THE CHILD-SAVING MOVEMENT
AND THE JUVENILE COURT

The *Progressive Era* (1890–1920) ushered in another shift and codification of attitudes toward youths in American society. Although social activists of that era used some of the language of the stubborn child law, their initiatives ushered in unprecedented government involvement in family life and more specifically into the lives of adolescents (Teitelbaum & Harris, 1977). The shift culminated in the creation of an entirely separate system of justice: the juvenile court. The child-saving movement, as it has been called, had a special meaning for girls.

Platt (1969: 3) described the child savers as a group of largely upper- and middle-class reformers "who regarded their cause as a matter of conscience and morality" and who "viewed themselves as altruists and humanitarians dedicated to rescuing those who were less fortunately placed in the social order."

The child-saving movement made much rhetorical use of the value of such traditional institutions as the family and education: "The child savers elevated the nuclear family, especially women as stalwarts of the family, and defended the family's right to supervise the socialization of youth" (Platt, 1969: 98). But while the child savers were exalting the family, they were also crafting a governmental system that would have authority to intervene in familial areas and, more specifically, in the lives of young people in ways that were unprecedented.

The culmination of the child savers' efforts, in the view of many, was the juvenile court. The first juvenile court was established in Chicago in 1899, and its enabling act was considered a prototype for legislation in other states. Similar courts soon appeared in Colorado (1900), Wisconsin (1901), New York (1901), Ohio (1902), and Maryland (1902). By 1928, all but two states had a juvenile court system (Platt, 1969: 139; Bremner, 1970: 515).

Based on an assumption of the natural dependence of youth, the juvenile court was charged with determining the guilt or innocence of accused underage persons and with acting for or in place of defendants' parents. The concern of the child savers went far beyond removing the adolescent criminal from the adult justice system. Many of their reforms were actually aimed at "imposing sanctions on conduct unbecoming youth and disqualifying youth from the benefit of adult privileges" (Platt, 1969: 199). Other students of the court's history have expanded on this point. They assert that the pervasive state intervention into the life of the family was grounded in colonial laws regarding "stubborn" and "neglected" children. Those laws incorporated the thinking of that time, that "parents were godly and children wicked" (Teitelbaum & Harris, 1977: 34), yet most child savers actually held an opposite opinion, that children were innocent and either the parents or the environment was morally suspect. Although the two views are incompatible, they have nevertheless coexisted in the juvenile court system since its inception. At various times one view or the other has predominated, but both bode ill for young women.

Legislation defining the scope of the first juvenile courts generally gave them charge over three broad aspects of the lives of children under the age of eighteen, the upper limit in most states: (1) children's violation of laws applicable to adults (e.g., crimes such as burglary, robbery, and larceny); (2) children's committing of status offenses (including such vague categories as "vicious or immoral conduct," "incorrigibility," "profane or indecent behavior," and "growing up in idleness") and being "beyond the control" of a parent or guardian; and (3) children's being neglected, abused, or abandoned by their parents or living with parents deemed "unfit" by authorities.

One of the unique features of the new juvenile, or family, courts was that they focused to a great extent on monitoring and responding to youthful behaviors that were "indicative" of future problems in addition to being violations of the law. For instance, part of the Tennessee juvenile code included the phrase "who are in danger of being brought up to lead an idle or immoral life" (Shelden, 1982: 432). Thus, girls and their moral behavior were of specific concern to the child savers. Scientific and popular literature on female delinquency expanded enormously during this period, as did institutions specifically devoted to the reformation of girls (Schlossman & Wallach, 1978; Messerschmidt, 1987; Odem, 1995).

The child-saving movement was keenly concerned about prostitution and other "social evils" such as white slavery (Schlossman & Wallach, 1978; Rafter, 1990: 54; Odem, 1995). Ironically, while child saving was a celebration of women's domesticity, the movement was not without female leaders (Platt, 1969; Rafter, 1990; Odem, 1995). In a sense, privileged women found in the moral purity crusades and the establishment of family courts a safe outlet for their energies. As the legitimate guardians of the moral sphere, middle-class women were seen as uniquely suited to patrol the normative boundaries of the social order. Embracing rather than challenging these stereotypes, women managed to carve out for themselves a role in the policing of women and girls (Feinman, 1980; Freedman, 1981; Messerschmidt, 1987; Gordon, 1988; Odem, 1995). Many early activities of the child savers revolved around monitoring young girls', particularly immigrant girls', behavior to prevent their straying from the path.

Just exactly how women, many of them highly educated, became involved in patrolling the boundaries of working-class girls' sexuality is a depressing but important story. Initially, as Odem's (1995) history of the period documents, middle-class women reformers were focused on regulating and controlling male, not female, sexuality. Involved in the social purity movement, these reformers had a Victorian view of women's sexuality and saw girls as inherently chaste and sexually passive. If a girl lost "the most precious jewel in the crown of her womanhood" (25), to their way of thinking, it was men who had forced them into sexual activity. The protection and saving of girls, then, led these women to wage an aggressive social movement aimed at raising the age of consent (which in many parts of the country hovered at ten or twelve years of age) to sixteen or above. The pursuit of claims of statutory rape against men was another component of this effort, and such charges were brought in a number of cases despite evidence that in about three-quarters of the cases Odem reviewed in Los Angeles, the girls entered into sexual relationships with young men willingly. Led largely by upper class and upper middle-class women volunteers, many of whom were prominent in the temperance movement (like Frances Willard), this campaign, not unlike the Mothers Against Drunk Driving campaign of later decades, drew an impressive and enthusiastic following, particularly among white citizens.

African American women participated in other aspects of progressive reform, but Odem notes they were less than aggressive on the pursuit of statutory rape complaints. She speculates that they rightly suspected that any aggressive enforcement of these statutes was likely to fall most heavily upon young African American men (while doing little to protect girls of color), and Odem notes that this is precisely what occurred. Of the very small number of cases where stiff penalties were imposed, Odem found evidence that African American men were not infrequently sent to prison to reform their "supposedly lax and immoral habits" while white men were either not prosecuted or were given probation.

Efforts to vigorously pursue statutory rape complaints, though, ran head-long into predictably staunch judicial resistance, particularly when many (but not all) cases involved young working-class women who had chosen to be sexually active. Eventually, as Odem's work documents, reformers (many of them now professional social workers) began to shift the focus of their activities. Now it was the "delinquent girl" herself who was the focus of reform, and "moral campaigns to control teenage female sexuality" began to appear. Reformers during this later period (1910–1925) assumed that they had the authority to define what was "appropriate" conduct for young working-class women and girls, which of course was based upon middle-class ideals of female sexual propriety. Girls who did not conform to these ideals were labeled as "wayward" and thus "in need of control" by the state in the form of juvenile courts and reformatories and training schools (Odem, 1995: 4–5).

Perhaps the clearest example of the ironies of this sort of child saving is Alice Stebbins Wells, a social worker who became the first policewoman in the United States. In 1910 she was hired by [the city of]Los Angeles because she argued that she could not serve her clients (young women) without police powers. Her work, and the work of five other female police officers hired during the next five years, was chiefly "to monitor 'dance halls, cafes, picture shows and other public amusement places' and to escort girls who were 'in danger of becoming delinquent to their homes and to make reports to their parents with a proper warning'" (Odem & Schlossman, 1991: 190; see also Odem, 1995).

Women reformers played a key role in the founding of the first juvenile court in Los Angeles in 1903 and vigorously advocated the appointment of women court workers to deal with the "special" problems of girls. This court was the first in the country to appoint women "referees," who were invested with nearly all the powers of judges in girls' cases. Women were also hired to run the juvenile detention facility in 1911. The logic for this was quite clear: "in view of the number of girls and the type of girls detained there . . . it is utterly unfeasible to have a man at the head of the institution," declared Cora Lewis, chairman of the Probation Committee, which established Juvenile Hall (Odem & Schlossman, 1991: 192). The civic leaders and newly hired female court workers "advocated special measures to contain sexual behavior among working-class girls, to bring them to safety by placing them in custody, and to attend to their distinctive needs as young, vulnerable females" (Odem & Schlossman, 1991: 190).

The evolution of what might be called the "girl-saving" effort was then the direct consequence of a disturbing coalition between some feminists and other

Progressive Era movements (Messerschmidt, 1987). Concerned about female victimization and distrustful of male (and to some degree female) sexuality, prominent women leaders, including Susan B. Anthony, found common cause with the more conservative social purity movement around such issues as the regulation of prostitution and raising the age of consent. Eventually, in the face of stiff judicial and political resistance, the concern about male sexuality more or less disappeared from sight, and the delinquent girl herself became the problem. The solution: a harsh "maternal justice" meted out by professional women (Odem, 1995: 128).

Girls were the losers in this reform effort. Studies of early family court activity reveal that almost all of the girls who appeared in these courts were charged with immorality or waywardness (Chesney-Lind, 1971; Schlossman & Wallach, 1978; Shelden, 1981). The sanctions for such misbehavior were extremely severe. For example, the Chicago family court sent half the girl delinquents but only one fifth of the boy delinquents to reformatories between 1899 and 1909. In Milwaukee, twice as many girls as boys were committed to training schools (Schlossman & Wallach, 1978: 72). In Memphis, females were twice as likely as males to be committed to training schools (Shelden, 1981: 70).

In Honolulu during 1929–1930, over half the girls referred to juvenile court were charged with "immorality," which meant there was evidence of sexual intercourse; 30 percent were charged with "waywardness." Evidence of immorality was vigorously pursued by both arresting officers and social workers through lengthy questioning of the girls and, if possible, males with whom they were suspected of having sex. Other evidence of "exposure" was provided by gynecological examinations that were routinely ordered in most girls' cases. Doctors, who understood the purpose of such examinations, would routinely note the condition of the hymen (Chesney-Lind, 1971; see also Gordon, 1988, and Odem, 1995). Girls were twice as likely as boys to be detained for their offenses and, on average, spent five times as long in detention as their male counterparts. They were also nearly three times more likely to be sentenced to the training school (Chesney-Lind, 1971). Indeed, half of those committed to training schools in Honolulu well into the 1950s were girls (Chesney-Lind, 1973).

Not surprisingly, large numbers of girls' reformatories and training schools were established during the Progressive Era, in addition to places of "rescue and reform." For example, Schlossman and Wallach (1978: 70) note that twenty-three facilities for girls were opened during the 1910–1920 decade (in contrast to the 1850–1910 period, when the average was five reformatories a decade), and these facilities did much to set the tone of official response to female delinquency. These institutions were obsessed with precocious female sexuality and were determined to instruct girls in their proper place.

According to Pisciotta (1983: 264–268), there was a slight modification of the *parens patriae* doctrine during this period. The "training" of girls was shaped by the image of the ideal woman that had evolved during the early part of the nineteenth century. According to this ideal (which was informed by what some have called the "separate-spheres" notion), a woman belonged in the private sphere, performing such tasks as rearing children, keeping house, caring for a husband, and serving as the moral guardian of the home. In this capacity, she was to exhibit such qualities as obedience, modesty, and dependence. Her husband's domain was the public sphere: the workplace, politics, and the law. He was also, by virtue of his public power, the final arbiter of public morality and culture (see Daly and Chesney-Lind, 1988). This white, middle-class "cult of domesticity" was, of course, very distant from the lives of many working- and lower class women who by necessity were in the labor force. Borrowing from Sheila Rothman (1978), Pisciotta (1983: 265) notes that the ideal woman was like a "Protestant nun." A statement by the Ladies Committee of the New York House of Refuge summed up the attributes that early court advocates sought to instill:

> The Ladies wish to call attention to the great change which takes place in every girl who has spent one year in the Refuge; she enters a rude, careless, untrained child, caring nothing for cleanliness and order; when she leaves the House, she can sew, mend, darn, wash, iron, arrange a table neatly and cook a healthy meal (Ibid.)

The institutions established for girls set about to isolate them from all contact with boys while training them in feminine skills and housing them in bucolic settings. The intention was to hold the girls until marriageable age and to occupy them in domestic pursuits during their sometimes lengthy incarceration. The child savers had little hesitation about such extreme intervention in girls' lives. They believed "delinquency" to be the result of a variety of social, psychological, and biological factors, and they were optimistic about the juvenile court's ability to remove girls from influences that were producing delinquent behavior. For this reason, the juvenile court was established to function in a way totally unlike other courts. For example, the juvenile court judge was to serve as a benevolent yet stern father. The proceedings were to be informal, without the traditional judicial trappings: initially, no lawyers were required, constitutional safeguards were not in place, no provisions existed for jury trials, and so on. Consistent with the *parens patriae* doctrine, the courts were freed from many of the usual constraints because it was thought they were acting in the best interests of the child.

Even the terminology of the juvenile justice system was, and to some extent still is, different. Children in many parts of the United States are "referred" to the court rather than being arrested; instead of being held in jail pending court action, they are "detained" in a "detention center" or "adjustment center"; rather than being indicted, children are "petitioned" to court; in place of a determination of guilt, there is an "adjudication"; and those found guilty (i.e., adjudicated) are often "committed" to a "training school" or "reform school" rather than being sentenced to a prison.

The juvenile court system also extended the role of probation officer, a position introduced in mid-nineteenth-century Boston.[2] The new role involved more than rudimentary supervision: "Nothing in the child's home, school, occupation, or peer-group relations was, at least in theory, beyond" the purview of the officer, who was "expected to instruct children and parents in reciprocal obligations, preach moral and religious verities, [and]teach techniques of child care and household management" (Schlossman, 1977: 99).

Envisioned as a "benevolent" institution that would emphasize treatment rather than punishment, the juvenile court turned out to be a mixture of the two orientations. The confusion can be traced to the court's mixed heritage, which combined a puritanical approach to stubborn children and parental authority with the Progressive Era's belief that children's essential goodness can be corrupted by undesirable elements in their environments. Finckenauer (1984: 116) termed the mixture "ambivalent" or "even schizophrenic."

Nowhere has the confusion and irony of the juvenile court been more clearly demonstrated than in its treatment of girls labeled as delinquent. Many of these girls were incarcerated for noncriminal behavior during the early years of the court.

"THE BEST PLACE TO CONQUER GIRLS"

Brenzel's (1975, 1983) history of the first reform school for girls—the State Industrial School for Girls in Lancaster, Massachusetts, established in 1856—and other studies of early training schools are vivid accounts of the girls and the institutions. The Lancaster school was intended "to be a school for girls—for the gentler sex . . . with all the details relating to employment, instruction, and amusement, and, indeed, to every branch of domestic economy" (Brenzel, 1975: 41). Such rhetoric would eventually find its way into the other girls' training schools. The Home of the Good Shepherd, established in 1875 in Memphis, Tennessee, was designed for the "reformation of fallen . . . women and a home or house of refuge for abandoned and vicious girls." Moreover, because the girls had "fallen from grace," they needed to be saved for the "preservation of the State's young manhood . . . " (Shelden, 1981: 58). Lancaster's first superintendent, Bradford K. Peirce, echoed this sentiment: "It is sublime to work to save a woman, for in her bosom generations are embodied, and in her hands, if perverted, the fate of innumerable men is held" (Brenzel, 1983: 4).

Lancaster, a model for all juvenile training schools, was to save children from "perversion through conversion," according to Brenzel. "Loving care" and confinement in an atmosphere free from the "sins and temptations" of city life would redirect girls' lives. What sorts of crimes had the girls committed? Over two-thirds had been accused of moral rather than criminal offenses: vagrancy, beggary, stubbornness, deceitfulness, idle and vicious behavior, wanton and lewd conduct, and running away (Brenzel, 1983: 81). Of the first ninety-nine inmates at Lancaster, only slightly over half (53%) were American born. Of the immigrant group, most spoke English and many were Irish. Significantly, at least half of the girls had been brought to Lancaster because of the actions of parents and relatives.[3]

Clearly, early training schools were deeply concerned with female respectability and hence worked to control the sexuality of lower and working-class adolescent girls. As Rafter (1990: 159) noted, such control within the institutional regime was supposed to train so-called loose young women "to accept a standard of propriety that dictated chastity until marriage and fidelity thereafter."

These institutions for girls strove for a familylike atmosphere, from which, after having been taught domestic skills, girls would be released to the care of other families as domestic workers. Gradually, however, vocational training in appropriate manual skills (sewing and the cutting of garments), age-group classification, and punishment characterized the institutional regime. By the late 1880s, Lancaster had devolved into a "middle place between the care of that Board [Health, Lunacy and Charity] and a Reformatory Prison" (Brenzel, 1983: 153). Lancaster's original goal of establishing a "loving family circle" had been supplanted by "harsh judgement, rudimentary job training and punitive custody" (Brenzel, 1983: 160).

THE JUVENILE COURT AND THE DOUBLE STANDARD OF JUVENILE JUSTICE

The offenses that bring girls into the juvenile justice system reflect the system's dual concerns: adolescent criminality and moral conduct. Historically, they have also reflected a unique and intense preoccupation with girls' sexuality and their obedience to parental authority. What happened to the girls once they arrived in the system?

Relatively early in the juvenile justice system's history, a few astute observers became concerned about the abandonment of minors' rights in the name of treatment, saving, and protection. One of the most insightful of these critical works, and one that has been unduly neglected, is Paul Tappan's *Delinquent Girls in Court* (1947). Tappan evaluated several hundred cases in the Wayward Minor Court in New York City during the late 1930s and early 1940s, and concluded that there were serious problems with a statute that brought young women into court simply for disobedience of parental commands or because they were in "danger of becoming morally depraved." He was particularly concerned that "the need to interpret the 'danger of becoming morally depraved' imposes upon the court a legislative function of a moralizing character." Noting that many young women were being charged simply with sexual activity, he asked, "What is sexual misbehavior—in a legal sense—of the nonprostitute of 16, or 18, or of 20 when fornication is no offense under criminal law?" (Tappan, 1947: 33).

Tappan believed that the structure of the Wayward Minor Court "entrusted unlimited discretion to the judge, reformer or clinician and his personal views of expedience" and cautioned that, consequently, "the fate of the defendant, the interest of society, the social objectives themselves, must hang by the tenuous thread of the wisdom and personality of the particular administrator." The arrangement was deeply disturbing to Tappan: "The implications of judicial totalitarianism are written in history" (Tappan, 1947: 33).

A more recent study, of the Los Angeles Juvenile Court during the first half of the twentieth century (Odem & Schlossman, 1991), supplies additional evidence of the juvenile justice system's historical preoccupation with girls' sexual morality, a preoccupation that clearly colored the Los Angeles court's activity into the 1950s.

Odem and Schlossman reviewed the characteristics of the girls who entered the court in 1920 and in 1950. In 1920, 93 percent of the girls accused of delinquency were charged with status offenses; of these, 65 percent were charged with immoral sexual activity (although the vast majority—56 percent—had engaged in sex with only one partner, usually a boyfriend). The researchers found that 51 percent of the referrals had come from the girls' parents, a situation they explained as working-class parents' fears about their daughters' vulnerability to the "omnipresent temptations to which working-class daughters in particular were exposed in the modern ecology of urban work and leisure." The working-class girls had been encouraged by their families to work (in fact, 52 percent were working or had been working within the past year), but their parents were extremely ambivalent about changing community morals, and some were not hesitant about involving the court in their arguments with problem daughters (1991: 196).

Odem and Schlossman also found that the Los Angeles Juvenile Court did not shirk from its perceived duty. Seventy-seven percent of the girls were detained before their hearings. Both prehearing detention and posthearing detention were common and "clearly linked" to the presence of venereal disease. Thirty-five percent of all delinquent girls and over half being held for sex offenses had gonorrhea, syphilis, or other venereal infections. The researchers noted that the presence of venereal disease and the desire to impose treatment (which in those times was lengthy and painful) accounted for the large numbers of girls in detention centers. Analysis of court actions revealed that although probation was the most common court response (61 percent were accorded probation), only 27 percent were released on probation immediately following the hearing. Many girls, it appears, were held for weeks or months after initial hearings. Girls not given probation were often placed in private homes as domestics or were placed in a wide range of private institutions, such as the Convent of the Good Shepherd or homes for unmarried mothers. Ultimately, according to Odem and Schlossman (1991: 198–199), about 33 percent of the "problem girls" during this period were sentenced to institutional confinement.

In a more detailed analysis, Odem (1995) has demonstrated that in the Los Angeles Juvenile Court women court officials acted as "maternal guardians" as they attempted to instill in these working-class girls a middle-class standard of "respectability" by "dispensing the maternal guidance and discipline supposedly lacking in the girls' own homes. Referees and probation officers scolded their charges for wearing too much makeup and dressing in a provocative manner." Odem quotes one juvenile court referee: "Any girl who will go before the public with her hair and eyelashes beaded and paint on her face is going to attract attention . . . [and] is surely inviting trouble" (Odem, 1995: 142). Girls were also chastised for visiting "amusement resorts" that the court thought "inappropriate and dangerous for adolescents" and were informed that sex before marriage was simply wrong.

It is obvious that such court officials were quite obsessed with the sexuality of these young women. Odem notes that after a girl was arrested, "probation officers questioned her relatives, neighbors, employers, and school officials to gather details about her sexual misconduct and, in the process, alerted them that she was a delinquent in trouble with the law." Following this, a girl was usually detained in juvenile hall and further questioned about her sexual behavior, starting with her first act of intercourse, while pressuring her to reveal the names of all her partners, the exact times and locations of sexual activities, as well as the number of times she had had sex. Further court discipline was leveled at those who did not give complete information (Odem, 1995: 143–144).

Between 1920 and 1950, the makeup of the court's female clientele changed very little: "the group was still predominantly white" (69 percent and 73.5 percent)—though the number of black girls rose from 5 percent to 9 percent—working class, and from disrupted families. However, girls were more likely to be in school and less likely to be working in 1950.

Girls referred to the Los Angeles court in 1950 were overwhelmingly referred for status offenses (78%), although the charges had changed slightly from 1920 charges. Thirty-one percent of the girls were charged with running away from home, truancy, curfew violation, or "general unruliness at home." Nearly half of the status offenders were charged with sexual misconduct, though again this was "usually with a single partner; few had engaged in prostitution" (Odem & Schlossman, 1991: 200). The rate of venereal disease had plummeted; only 4.5 percent of all girls tested positive. Despite this, the concern for female sexual conduct "remained determinative in shaping social policy" in the 1950s, according to these researchers (Odem & Schlossman, 1991: 200).

Referral sources changed within the intervening decades, as did sanctions. Parents referred 26 percent of the girls at mid-century, school officials referred about the same percentage in 1950 as in 1920 (21 percent and 27 percent), and police officers referred a greater number (54 percent compared with 29 percent in 1920). Sanctions shifted somewhat, with fewer girls detained before their hearings in 1950 (56 percent compared with 77 percent in 1920), but the Los Angeles court placed about the same proportion of girls in custodial institutions (26 percent in 1950, 33 percent in 1920).

Studies continue to pick up on problems with the vagueness of contemporary status offense categories, which are essentially "buffer charges" for suspected sexuality. Consider Vedder and Somerville's (1970: 147) observation in the 1960s that although girls in their study were incarcerated in training schools for the "big five" (running away from home, incorrigibility, sexual offenses, probation violation, and truancy), "the underlying vein in many of these cases is sexual misconduct by the girl delinquent." Such attitudes were also present in other parts of the world. Naffine (1987: 13) wrote that in Australia official reports noted that "most of those charged [with status offenses] were girls who had acquired habits of immorality and freely admitted sexual intercourse with a number of boys."

Another study, conducted in the early 1970s in a New Jersey training school, revealed large numbers of girls incarcerated "for their own protection." When asked about this pattern, one judge explained, "Why, most of the girls I commit are for status offenses. I figure if a girl is about to get pregnant, we'll keep her until she's sixteen and then ADC (Aid to Dependent Children) will pick her up" (Rogers, 1972).

Andrews and Cohn (1974) reviewed the handling of cases of ungovernability in New York in 1972 and concluded that judges were acting "upon personal feelings and predilections in making decisions." Included among their evidence were statements made by judges. For example: "She thinks she's a pretty hot number; I'd be worried about leaving my kid with her in a room alone. She needs to get her mind off boys" (Andrews and Cohn, 1974: 1388).

Similar concern about premature female sexuality and the proper parental response is evident throughout the comments. One judge remarked that at the age of fourteen some girls "get some crazy ideas. They want to fool around with men, and that's sure as hell trouble." Another admonished a girl, "I want you to promise me to obey your mother, to have perfect school attendance and not miss a day of school, to give up these people who are trying to lead you to do wrong, not to hang out in candy stores or tobacco shops or street corners where these people are, and to be in when your mother says" (Ibid.: 1404).

Empirical studies of the processing of girls' and boys' cases between 1950 and the early 1970s documented the impact of these sorts of judicial attitudes. That is, girls charged with status offenses were often more harshly treated than their male or female counterparts charged with crimes (Gibbons & Griswold, 1957; Cohn, 1970; Chesney-Lind, 1973; Datesman & Scarpitti, 1977; Kratcoski, 1974; Pope & Feyerherm, 1982; Schlossman & Wallach, 1978; Shelden, 1981; Odem, 1995). For example, Gibbons and Griswold (1957: 109) found in a study of court dispositions in Washington State between 1953 and 1955 that girls were far less likely than boys to be charged with criminal offenses, but more than twice as likely to be committed to institutions. Some years later a study of a juvenile court in Delaware discovered that first-time female status offenders were more harshly sanctioned (as measured by institutionalization) than males charged with felonies (Datesman & Scarpitti, 1977: 70). For repeat status offenders, the pattern was even starker: females status offenders were six times more likely than male status offenders to be institutionalized.

The double standard of juvenile justice also appeared in countries other than the United States. Linda Hancock found in Australia that females (most of whom were appearing in court for uncontrollability and other status offenses) were more likely than males to receive probation or institutional supervision. In addition, females charged with criminal offenses received lesser penalties than males and females brought to court under "protection applications" (Hancock, 1981: 8). May (1977) found that females in England were less often fined than males and more often placed on supervision or sent to an institution. In another English study, Smart (1976: 134) reported that 64 percent of females and 5 percent of males were institutionalized for noncriminal offenses. In Portugal in 1984, 41 percent of the girls were charged with status offenses, but only 16.8 percent of the boys were placed in institutions (Cain, 1989: 222). Likewise, a study of a juvenile court in Madrid revealed that of youths found guilty of status offenses, 22.2 percent of the girls but only 6.4 percent of the boys were incarcerated (225).

In short, studies of the juvenile courts during the past few decades suggest that court personnel participated directly in the judicial enforcement of the sexual double standard. Such activity was most pronounced in the system's early years, but there is evidence that the pattern continues, in part because status offenses can still serve as buffer charges for sexual misconduct. Some of the problem with status offenses, although they are discriminatory, is understandable. They are not like criminal cases, for which judges have relatively clear guidelines. Standards of evidence are delineated, elements of the crime are laid out in the statutes, and civil rights are, at least to some extent, protected by law.

In status offense cases, judges have few legal guidelines. Many judges apparently fall back on one of the orientations built into the juvenile justice system: the Puritan stance supportive of parental demands, more or less without question; or the progressive stance, whereby they take on the parental roles. These orientations were severely tested during the 1970s, when critics mounted a major drive to deinstitutionalize status offenders and divert them from formal court jurisdiction.

DEINSTITUTIONALIZATION AND JUDICIAL PATERNALISM: CHALLENGES TO THE DOUBLE STANDARD OF JUVENILE JUSTICE

By the mid-1970s, correctional reformers had become concerned about juvenile courts' abuse of the status offense category—though significantly little of this concern related to the history of gender bias that characterized some, but not all, of these categories. Instead, the argument was that "noncriminal youth" should be treated and helped, not inserted into a system that often detained and institutionalized them.

The movement to reform the treatment of status offenders was worldwide. In Victoria, Australia, for example, the 1978 Community Welfare Services Act attempted to remove the more explicitly sexual grounds of some status offenses (notably, "exposed to moral danger") and emphasized youths' inadequate care, neglect, and abandonment. Limitations were also placed on the court's authority to find a child "beyond control" of parents (Hancock & Chesney-Lind, 1982: 182). South Australia went even further and in 1979 passed the Children's Protection and Young Offender's Act, which essentially abolished status offenses (Naffine, 1989: 10). Canada's British Columbia repealed the act permitting incarceration of any youth in training schools in 1969 and actively encouraged the "disuse" of the portion of the Federal Juvenile Delinquents Act that dealt with youth found to be "beyond the control of their parents" (Province of

British Columbia, 1978: 16–19). Canada replaced the Federal Juvenile Delinquents Act with the Young Offender's Act in 1982, which had the effect of removing status offenders from federal legislation entirely.

In the United States the Juvenile Justice and Delinquency Prevention Act of 1974 (JJDPA) required that states receiving federal delinquency prevention money begin to divert and deinstitutionalize status offenders. Despite erratic enforcement of the provision and considerable resistance from juvenile court judges (discussed later in this chapter), girls were the beneficiaries of the reform effort. Incarceration of young women in training schools and detention centers across the country fell dramatically. Encouraging, too, is that studies of court decision making found less clear evidence of discrimination against girls in parts of the country where serious diversion efforts were occurring (Teilmann & Landry, 1981).

Despite the intentions of the Juvenile Justice and Delinquency Prevention Act of 1974, there is considerable evidence that status offenders are still being harshly sanctioned. Even more disturbing are recent efforts to roll back the modest gains made in more equitable and appropriate treatment of status offenders or—even worse—to repeal the whole initiative.

UNPOPULAR REFORM?

Court officials have always been extremely critical of deinstitutionalization (see Schwartz, 1989), and after the passage of the JJDPA, challenges were not long in coming. Hunter Hurst, director of the National Center of Juvenile Justice, said in 1975, as the Juvenile Justice and Delinquency Prevention Act was first being implemented, "Status offenses are offenses against our values." Girls are "seemingly overrepresented as status offenders because we have had a strong heritage of being protective toward females in this country." It offends "our sensibility and values to have a fourteen-year-old girl engage in sexually promiscuous activity"; "it's not the way we like to think about females in this country." Because these values are widely held, "be sure that the police, the church or vigilante groups" would do something about this behavior. "I would rather that something occur in the court where the rights of the parties can be protected" (Hurst, 1975: 7).

It is not surprising, then, that although great hopes rode on the Juvenile Justice and Delinquency Prevention Act, a 1978 General Accounting Office (GAO, 1978: 10) report concluded that the Law Enforcement Assistance Administration (LEAA), the agency implementing the legislation, was less than enthusiastic about the deinstitutionalization provisions. LEAA had actually "downplayed its [the act's] importance and to some extent discouraged states from carrying out the Federal requirement."

The GAO declared that monitoring of states' compliance with the law was lax or nonexistent (only nine states had what the GAO deemed complete data); definitions of what constituted detention and correctional facilities were confusing (for example, children in jail were frequently not counted); and LEAA was apparently reluctant to take action against states in noncompliance.

Just how deep the anti-deinstitutionalization sentiment among juvenile justice officials was became manifest during House hearings on the extension of the act in March 1980. Judge John R. Milligan, representing the National Council of Juvenile and Family Court Judges, testified as follows:

> The effect of the Juvenile Justice Act as it now exists is to allow a child ultimately to decide for himself whether he will go to school, whether he will live at home, whether he will continue to run, run, run, away from home, or whether he will even obey orders of your court. (United States House of Representatives, 1980: 136)

The juvenile justice officials were successful in narrowing the definition of status offender in the amended act so that any child who had violated a "valid court order" would not be covered under the deinstitutionalization provisions (United States Statutes, 1980). The change, never publicly debated in either house, effectively gutted the act by permitting judges to reclassify a status offender who violated a court order as a delinquent. This meant that a young woman who ran away from a court-ordered placement (a halfway house, foster home, or the like) could be relabeled a delinquent and locked up.

Before the enacted change, judges apparently engaged in other, less public efforts to circumvent deinstitutionalization. These included "bootstrapping" status offenders into delinquents by issuing criminal contempt citations, referring or committing status offenders to secure mental health facilities, and referring them to "semi-secure" facilities (Costello & Worthington, 1981–1982: 42).

One study of the impact of these contempt proceedings in Florida (Frazier & Bishop, 1990) described them as disadvantageous to female status offenders. The researchers reviewed 162,012 cases referred to juvenile justice intake units during 1985–1987 and found only a weak pattern of discrimination against female status offenders compared with male status offenders. In regard to contempt citations, the pattern did not hold: females referred for contempt were more likely than females referred for other criminal offenses to be petitioned to court, substantially more likely to be petitioned to court than males referred for contempt, and far more likely than males to be sentenced to detention. The typical female offender in the study had a probability of incarceration of 4.3 percent, which increased to 29.9 percent if she was held in contempt, a circumstance that was not observed among the males. The researchers concluded that "the traditional double standard is still operative. Clearly neither the cultural changes associated with the feminist movement nor the legal changes illustrated in the JJDP Act's mandate to deinstitutionalize status offenders have brought about equality under the law for young men and women" (22).

Frazier and Bishop's findings are all the more disturbing when we consider statistics on the number of states currently using the "valid-court-order" exclusion. According to Blume (1990), statistics published in December 1988 by the Office of Juvenile Justice and Delinquency Prevention (OJJDP) show thirty-seven states using these exclusions "at least once." In 1988 alone, twenty-four states reported using 4,990 of these exclusions, with 4,280 of them "accepted" by the OJJDP.

Other attacks on deinstitutionalization have come from several national committees convened to deal with youth problems. The National Advisory Committee (NAC), formed to advise the Office of Juvenile Justice and Delinquency Prevention and one of whose members was Judge Milligan, issued a report titled *Serious Juvenile Crime: A Redirected Federal Effort* (National Advisory Committee, 1984), in which it is argued that the federal government should not have become involved in the status offender issue. Seeking to "transform the federal effort against delinquency," the report urged that federal attention be shifted to "crime committed by the serious, violent or chronic offender" (15). Ironically, the report also criticized the extensive focus on status offenders as discriminating against minority and poor youth—a position developed by Robert Woodson while a fellow with the American Enterprise Institute (United States Senate, 1981: 410)—but did not mention the significant role played by deinstitutionalization in reducing sexism in juvenile justice.

Another attack on deinstitutionalization has emerged from the national concern for "missing and exploited" children. A report of the U.S. Attorney General's Advisory Board on Missing Children included the observation that many shelters, in order to "qualify for federal support," have "no authority to force a child to stay" while awaiting "reunion with parents or other placement" (Office of Juvenile Justice and Delinquency Prevention, 1986). The group recommended that Congress "amend the Juvenile Justice and Delinquency Prevention Act to ensure that each State juvenile justice system has the legal authority, where necessary and appropriate, to take into custody and safely control runaway and homeless children" (19). Even more recently, the OJJDP inaugurated research into "the effects of the deinstitutionalization of status offenders." A former administrator of the office characterized the effort as "incredible," noting that "the feds would now have us believe that after [Alfred] Regnery spent several years trying to reverse federal policies on status offenders, and after Attorney General Meese's Task Force on Missing and Exploited Children declared that these policies were counterproductive, they are interested in an honest assessment of the impact that federal mandates have had in this area" (Schwartz, 1989: 124). It should be noted in passing that the vast majority of so-called "missing and abducted children" have in fact either run away from home or were taken by a parent during a custody dispute and that the odds of being abducted by a complete stranger are about 1 in 25,200 (Kappler, Blumberg, & Potter, 1996: 57–59).

Strong criticism of deinstitutionalization also came from the Office of Juvenile Justice and Delinquency Prevention itself during the Reagan years. In its *Runaway Children and the Juvenile Justice and Delinquency [Prevention] Act: What Is the Impact?* (1985), case studies involving young girls and purporting to illustrate problems with deinstitutionalization are presented in detail, as are interviews with police officers and a few youth workers expressing frustration with the law. "The job of getting runaways off the street has been made 'almost impossible' by current law" is the report's summary of an interview with a New

York detective. "Some of the runaways with whom he maintained regular contact have been at large for several years. Even though he may know where they are and the dangers they face, he is virtually powerless. He may be able to take them off the street for a few hours, but he is unable to stop them when they decide to return" (7).

In the report's introduction, Alfred Regnery, then administrator of the OJJDP, suggested that blanket application of the deinstitutionalization provision has had "darker consequences." Specifically, "running away is legal. The question which needs to be asked is whether or not it is in the best interest of children to afford them such a right" (Office of Juvenile Justice and Delinquency Prevention, 1985: 2).

It does not require great discernment to conclude that opponents of deinstitutionalization are working diligently to divert federal attention from status offenders and simultaneously suggesting that perhaps deinstitutionalization has gone too far. And, although girls' victimization is often used to support such a view, a look at the juvenile justice system's treatment of young women in trouble makes it clear that, for girls, a retreat would be a disaster. Judicial sexism has haunted the juvenile justice system since its inception and has survived despite the substantial, although indirect, attempts at reform embodied by the Juvenile Justice and Delinquency Prevention Act of 1974. Just how serious a problem is developing is best appreciated by a review of trends in the institutionalization of girls, the subject of Chapter 8.

RECENT TRENDS: FINALLY A FOCUS ON GIRLS, AND THE REPUBLICAN BACKLASH

Hearings held in conjunction with the 1992 reauthorization of the Juvenile Justice and Delinquency Prevention Act addressed for the first time the "provision of services to girls within the juvenile justice system" (United States House of Representatives, 1992). At this hearing, the double standard of juvenile justice was discussed, as well as the paucity of services for girls. Representative Matthew Martinez opened the hearing with the following statements:

> In today's hearing we are going to address female delinquency and the provisions of services to girls under this Act. There are many of us that believe that we have not committed enough resources to that particular issue. There are many of us who realize that the problems for young ladies are increasing, ever increasing, in our society and they are becoming more prone to end up in gangs, in crime, and with other problems they have always suffered. (United States House of Representatives, 1992: 2)

Martinez went on to comment about the high number of girls arrested for status offenses, the high percentage of girls in detention as a result of violation of court orders, and the failure of the system to address girls' needs. He ended with this question: "I wonder why, why are there no other alternatives than youth jail for her?" (United States House of Representatives, 1992: 2). Testifying at this hearing were also representatives from organizations serving girls, such as Children of the Night, Pace Center for Girls, and Girls, Incorporated, as well as girls active in these programs.

Perhaps as a result of this landmark hearing, the 1992 reauthorization included specific provisions requiring plans from each state receiving federal funds to include "an analysis of gender-specific services for the prevention and treatment of juvenile delinquency, including the types of such services available and the need for such services for females and a plan for providing needed gender-specific services for the prevention and treatment of juvenile delinquency" (Public Law 102-586, November 1992). Additional monies were set aside as part of the JJDP Act's challenge grant program for states wishing to develop policies to prohibit gender bias in placement and treatment and to develop programs that ensure girls equal access to services. As a result, twenty-three states embarked on such programs—by far the most popular of the ten possible challenge grant activity areas (Girls, Incorporated, 1996: 26).

The 1992 act also called for the GAO to conduct a study of gender bias within state juvenile justice systems, with specific attention to "the frequency with which females have been detained for status offenses . . . as compared to the frequency with which males have been detained for such offenses during the 5 year period ending December, 1992; and the appropriateness of the placement and conditions of confinement" (United States House of Representatives, 1992: 4998).

This mandate will not necessarily produce a clear measure of the presence or absence of sexism in the juvenile justice system, since it controls for elements of the system that are, themselves, gendered. Specifically, because girls are overrepresented among those charged with status offenses, "controlling" for status offenses (or, more specifically, for the type of status offense) permits discrimination to remain undetected. The mandate does, though, recognize the central role played by status offenses in girls' delinquency.

Finally, although not specifically related to gender, the reauthorization moved to make more difficult the "bootstrapping" of status offenders into delinquents so that they can be detained. It specified that youth who were being detained due to a violation of a "valid court order" had to have appeared before a judge and been made subject to the order and had to have received, before issuance of the order, "the full due process rights guaranteed to such juvenile[s] by the Constitution of the United States." The 1992 act also required that before issuance of the order, "both the behavior of the juvenile being referred and the reasons why the juvenile might have committed the behavior must be assessed." In addition, it must be determined that all dispositions (including treatment), other than placement in a secure detention facility or secure correctional facility, have been exhausted or are clearly inappropriate. Finally, the court has to receive a "written report" stating the results of the review (United States House of Representatives, 1992: 4983).

Sadly, these changes, while extremely hopeful, were short-lived. Several recent sessions of congress sought major overhauls of the Juvenile Justice and

Delinquency Prevention Act, and virtually all of the initiatives they considered were ominous for girls. The bills generally attempted to refocus national attention on the "violent and repeat juvenile offender" (read boys) while also granting states "flexibility" in implementing some if not all of four core mandates of the original JD Act. Key among these mandates, of course, is the deinstitutionalization of status offenders, though conservative lawmakers are also taking aim at efforts to separate youth from adults in correctional facilities, efforts to reduce minority over-representation in juvenile detention and training schools, and efforts to remove juveniles from adult jails (Shiraldi & Soler, 1998).

In a debate that featured "guns, the Ten Commandments, the Internet, video games and the movies" (Boyle, 1999), there was considerable emphasis on punishment (such as allowing the prosecution of 13 year olds as adults). Most ominous for girls are efforts to loosen restrictions on the detention of status offenders. Here, conservative legislators were clearly influenced by juvenile court judges, who pushed for a recriminalization of status offenses. Judge David Grossman, who testified before Congress representing the National Council of Juvenile and Family Court Judges, contended that the deinstitutionalization was a "movement" whose time had passed: "All too often, it left the intended young beneficiaries of its advocacy adrift on the streets, fallen between the cracks" (Alexander, 1998, p. 46). He advocated, instead, that status offenders be returned to the court's jurisdiction.

Perhaps as a result of testimony of this sort, Senate Bill 254 calls for the National Institute of Justice to conduct a study "on the effect of on status offenders compared to similarly situated individuals who are not placed in secure detention in terms of continuation of their inappropriate or illegal conduct, delinquency or future criminal behavior, and evaluation of the safety of status offenders placed in secure detention." Even more worrisome, both current bills make it easier to hold youth in adult jails. The later provision is most disturbing, since girls were not infrequently held in such situations in the past (as de facto detention centers in rural America). Sadly, abuse is not uncommon in such settings. In Ohio, for example, a 15-year-old girl was sexually assaulted by a deputy jailer after having been placed in an adult jail for a minor infraction (Ziedenberg & Schiraldi, 1997). Due to the isolation and abuse in these settings, girls are also at great risk for suicide (see Chesney-Lind, 1988).

After seven years of wrangling, Congress re-authorized the legislation without many of the most draconian of these proposals. With minor exceptions, H.R. 2215 maintains the core requirements of the act and actually expands the concerns about racism in the juvenile justice system first embodied in the disproportionate minority confinement mandate to cover all elements of the juvenile justice system (Doi, 2002: 2). The Act also permits states to spend money on "programs to provide services to girls in the juvenile justice system" and retains the earlier Act's concern about the abuse of "violation of a valid court order."

However, this Congressional victory cannot wholly undo the Bush Administration's lack of interest in juvenile justice and particularly in girls. Ambitious plans to establish a Girl's Institute and a Girl's Study Group, proposed in the waning days of the Clinton Administration, were shelved by the Bush administration shortly after the attacks of September 11, 2001, Those who had sought the funds were told that the office would "continue to review gender issues and program needs of girls that could be addressed by Federal intervention in the future" (Ray, 2002). No one close to the scene, though, has particularly high expectations, particularly since the Bush administration has dramatically cut back on funds to OJJDP, allowed Congressional earmarks of funds that should be expended to maintain the core mandates of the original Act, and permitted the staff of OJJDP to shrink by nearly half its former size (Treanor, 2003: 24)

SUMMARY

The history of the juvenile justice system in the United States demonstrates that sexism has pervaded the institution since its inception. The roots of this pattern can be traced to colonial embellishments of the *parens patriae* doctrine, and it is probably no accident that the first and most significant legal challenge to this doctrine, *Ex Parte Crouse*, involved the incarceration of a girl on the grounds that she was "incorrigible." The Crouse case also illustrates that the evolution of the contemporary juvenile justice system was accelerated by the growth of institutions for delinquent and wayward youths, starting with houses of refuge and concluding with the establishment of large numbers of training and reform schools. These schools were set up largely to save young people from the temptations of city life and precocious sexuality, and there they were taught domestic skills and moral precepts.

Establishment of the first juvenile court in 1899 capped years of efforts by people described as child savers to extend state control over the lives of youth. Girls were the losers in the reform movement as vast numbers were referred to juvenile courts for immorality and waywardness in the early years. Enormous numbers of girls who appeared before the courts in the first few decades were detained, tried, and ultimately institutionalized for their offenses.

By mid-century, juvenile courts were still involved in controlling girls' sexuality, but the pattern was a little less distinct. Instead of being charged with "immorality," girls in the juvenile courts of the 1950s and 1960s were being charged with status offenses such as running away, which court observers called buffer charges for sexual misconduct. Girls continue to be arrested for this and other noncriminal status offenses, a pattern that also appears in other countries.

The double standard of juvenile justice was indirectly challenged in the 1970s by passage of the Juvenile Justice and Delinquency Prevention Act, which encouraged states to divert and deinstitutionalize status offenders. Despite some gains in the early years of this movement (such as a decline in the number of girls in detention centers and training schools), studies of courts in the later 1980s and early 1990s show that juvenile justice is far from gender blind. Moreover, challenges to deinstitutionalization during the 1980s and

1990s indicate that the gains made in eradicating gender bias continue to be in jeopardy—and could even be reversed. As juvenile courts enter a new millenium, it is unfortunately still all too easy to find evidence that girls coming into the system—and not just in the United States—are receiving a special, discriminatory form of justice.

NOTES

1. "Minority Views: The Act's Core Mandates Should Be Maintained." Appended to the Juvenile Justice and Delinquency Prevention Act Reauthorization (H.R. 3876), House Economic and Educational Opportunities Committee, conveyed in letter by signatory Patsy T. Mink, September 16, 1996.

2. The origins of probation can be traced to the efforts of a man named John Augustus, a Boston shoemaker who, during the 1840s, volunteered to take on the responsibility of supervising offenders in the community as a substitute to sending them to prison or jail. Since then, this rather unique idea has become highly bureaucratized, with the average probation officer supervising between fifty and one hundred offenders. The spirit of volunteerism and the offering of a helping hand in the name of true benevolence toward one's fellow human beings have turned into a job as a career bureaucrat. Many who engage in this line of work are overwhelmed by the responsibilities and often care little about the persons they supervise. In fact, the "supervision" is often little more than surveillance usually consisting of a few phone calls.

3. Similarly, many girls in the Home of the Good Shepherd in Memphis had been brought into the juvenile court because of running away, incorrigibility, or various charges labeled by the court as "immorality," including "sexual relations" that ranged from sexual intercourse to "kissing and holding hands in the park" (Shelden, 1981: 63). Schlossman and Wallach (1978), in a study of juvenile court records in four cities around the turn of the century, arrived at the same conclusion: "immorality" seems to have been the most common charge against females. Included under the rubric were "coming home late at night," "masturbating," "using obscene language," "riding at night in automobiles without a chaperon," and "strutting about in a lascivious manner" (Schlossman & Wallach, 1978: 72).

8

The Contemporary
Juvenile Justice System
and Girls, Part I:
Police and Juvenile
Court Processing

AN OVERVIEW OF THE
SYSTEM AND PROCESS

Previous chapters have established that girls entering the juvenile justice system have historically experienced a set of interactions that were not necessarily evenhanded, just, or fair. Is that still the case today? Current policy debates, particularly the question of whether the United States should continue to emphasize the diversion and deinstitutionalization of status offenders, establish an additional reason to examine girls' experiences with the modern juvenile justice system.

The juvenile court and juvenile correctional institutions are at the center of the modern juvenile justice system. The system also includes an array of social and legal agencies. Schools, the police, welfare agencies, and various other private community bodies refer youths to the juvenile courts, and the courts, in turn, often place youths in facilities run by nonjudicial agencies.

Juvenile courts vary a great deal in size and function. Some jurisdictions do not have a juvenile court per se; juvenile cases are heard in adult courts on special days. Juvenile courts may function in anything from a small courthouse with a skeleton staff to a large, bureaucratic complex with many separate divisions. Some juvenile courts are called "family courts" and handle a variety of family-related problems besides delinquency cases (for example, child custody, child support). Because many courts handle abuse and neglect (or dependency) cases, separate divisions within these courts have been established. In general, then, most juvenile courts in large urban areas have at least the following divisions: (1) intake and screening, (2) detention, (3) probation, (4) records (sometimes including a research division), (5) psychological services (testing, counseling, and so on), (6) protective services, (7) medical services, (8) volunteer services, (9) court services (judges, district attorneys, public defenders, and so on), and (10) parole or after-care.

Besides the court itself, the juvenile justice system generally includes a vast correctional apparatus that contains several types of treatment and punishment facilities: (1) short-term facilities, such as detention centers, shelters, and reception or diagnostic centers; (2) long-term facilities, such as training schools, ranches, forestry camps, farms, and halfway houses and group homes (Champion, 2001: 500–515; Bartollas & Miller, 2001: ch. 10). As of October 1997, there were over 1,121 public and 2,310 private facilities in the United States, housing about 106,000 juveniles (Snyder & Sickmund, 1999: 186).

As discussed in Chapter 7, youths who enter the juvenile justice system experience a form of justice and control quite different from that encountered by adults accused of crimes. Most notably, they are not accorded the constitutional rights given to adult members of society, although, because of landmark court cases in the 1960s and 1970s, youths charged with criminal offenses have some limited legal rights: advance notice of charges, a fair and impartial hearing, assistance of counsel (including the right to confront and cross-examine witnesses), and protections against self-incrimination. Also, charges of delinquency against them must be proved beyond reasonable doubt, and they are protected against double jeopardy (see Feld, 1988, 1998). Youths do not have other rights given to adults (for example, the right to bail and the right to trial by jury). Let us look at some important cases in the area of juvenile rights.

THE RIGHTS OF JUVENILES:
A REVIEW OF KEY CASES

As we saw in Chapter 7, a diminution in youths' rights accompanied the evolution of the juvenile justice system, largely because of the incorporation of *parens patriae* into the laws regarding juvenile offenses. The laws gave juvenile courts great latitude in defining delinquent behaviors and allowed them to operate without the formality and structure of adult courts. Between 1966 and 1971, however, four major Supreme Court decisions dealing with the rights of juveniles were handed down.[1]

In *Kent v. United States* (383 U.S. 541, 1966), a minor's waiver from the jurisdiction of a juvenile court to that of an adult court was reviewed. The procedure stems in part from an attempt to deal more severely with juveniles who are charged with serious crimes, such as rape and murder. In effect, a youth is waived to an adult court in which, from a legal standpoint, he or she is considered an adult and is treated as such.

This case involved sixteen-year-old Morris Kent, who in September 1961 raped a woman and stole her wallet. The juvenile court judge waived Kent to the jurisdiction of an adult court, but without a hearing, without having talked with Kent's lawyer, and without having released a copy of the information contained in Kent's social service file, upon which the waiver decision was partly based. Kent was convicted and sentenced in adult court to a term of thirty to ninety years in prison.

On appeal, the case came in 1966 before the Supreme Court, which reversed the conviction, holding that the District of Columbia Juvenile Court Act's waiver provisions were invalid. The ruling specified that prior to being waived to an adult court, a juvenile had a right to (1) a hearing on the move, (2) access to social service reports, and (3) a statement of reasons for the waiver.

Perhaps the most significant case regarding juvenile court procedures was *In re Gault* (387 U.S. 1, 1967). Gerald Gault, aged fifteen, was taken into custody, without notification of his parents, by the sheriff and brought to the juvenile court of Gila County, Arizona, on the complaint of a neighbor about a telephone call she believed had been made by him that included lewd remarks. At the time, Gault was on six months' probation after having been found delinquent for stealing a wallet. He was not given adequate notification of the charges and not advised that he could be represented by counsel, nor did his accuser appear in court. He was convicted of this offense and sentenced to the State Industrial School until the age of twenty-one. Had Gault been an adult, the longest sentence he could have received would have been six months in a local jail. Gault's attorneys filed a writ of habeas corpus in the Superior Court of Arizona, and its denial was subsequently affirmed by the Arizona Supreme Court.

On appeal to the U.S. Supreme Court, Gault's attorneys argued that the juvenile code of Arizona was unconstitutional. Reversing the decision, Justice Abe Fortas flatly declared that "the condition of being a boy does not justify a kangaroo court" (Faust & Brantingham, 1979: 299). The Court held that at the adjudicatory hearing stage, juvenile court procedures must include (1) adequate written notice of charges, (2) the right to counsel, (3) privilege against self-incrimination, (4) the right to cross-examine accusers, (5) a transcript of the proceedings, and (6) the right to appellate review. The *Gault* decision began what many have referred to as a "revolution in juvenile court practices." (Unfortunately, neither *Gault* nor subsequent court cases have considered a juvenile's rights prior to the adjudicatory hearing, such as intake and detention decisions.)

Another significant case was *In re Winship* (397 U.S. 358, 1970), which addressed how much proof is necessary to support a finding of delinquency. At the time, the standard was "a preponderance of the evidence." Rejecting the idea that the juvenile justice system was a civil system, the Supreme Court held that the due process clause of the Fourteenth Amendment required that delinquency charges in the juvenile system have to be proved "beyond a reasonable doubt," just as do charges in the adult system.

In *McKeiver v. Pennsylvania* (403 U.S. 528, 1971) the court dealt with the right of trial by jury, normally guaranteed to adults but traditionally denied to juveniles. Indeed, this issue was part of *Ex Parte Crouse*. However, in *McKeiver*, the court did not deviate from the traditional view with regard to juveniles, as it had in previous cases. It ruled that jury trials were admissible but not mandatory within the juvenile court. (Ten states currently allow jury trials for juveniles.) In this decision the court reasoned that a number of problems might arise if jury trials were mandatory, among them publicity, which would be contrary to the confidentiality characteristic of juvenile justice.

IMPLICATIONS OF SUPREME COURT RULINGS FOR GIRLS

Although the Supreme Court rulings just discussed were significant for juveniles' due process rights, several important issues remain unaddressed by the high tribunal. For instance, decision making at the intake stage, which often has to do with detention, and other early stages was not covered by these rulings. This is an especially salient issue for girls because of the widespread double standard, particularly with regard to detention.

More to the point, the rights accorded juveniles in key Supreme Court opinions are clearer in connection with criminal offenses than with status offenses. *Gault* applies only to youths charged with crimes (Horowitz, 1977; Feld, 1988; Federle, 1990). Indeed, some students of juvenile courts speculate that the shift during the late 1960s and early 1970s in most states to initiate separate proceedings for delinquency and status offense, or PINS, cases was a direct product of the desire to limit the impact of *Gault* and to preserve the juvenile courts' jurisdiction over status offenders. According to Horowitz (1977: 208), to the accepted policy reasons for separating PINS from delinquents, *Gault* added some reasons grounded in the desire of state officials to sustain the validity of their juvenile codes (in particular, to preserve their jurisdiction over status offenders) and to conduct as many proceedings as possible without the full panoply of constitutional safeguards made applicable by *Gault* and by later cases to delinquency hearings.

Horowitz notes that juvenile court officials were aware that the Supreme Court was beginning to scrutinize other status offenses for which youths were being tried on the adult level (such as being addicted to drugs) and hold them unconstitutional. The officials were also aware that the Supreme Court, in *Gault*, had mandated certain constitutional safeguards only when youths were accused of criminal offenses and when penal commitment was a possibility. By separating the proceedings for status offenders and delinquents, and by legally prohibiting confinement in a penal institution on a purely status offense charge, the officials could preserve the lower standard of proof that generally holds in status-offense proceedings. PINS adjudications generally require evidence of guilt based on a "preponderance of the evidence" rather than beyond reasonable doubt (Horowitz, 1977: 208). Juvenile courts have found ways around the prohibition of institutionalization of status offenders; the strategy, coupled with the Supreme Court's recent more conservative stance toward the rights of children (Federle, 1990), has meant that status offenders do not yet have the rights that offenders charged with crimes are guaranteed.

Additional evidence of the imbalance comes from a study of 17,195 referrals to Minnesota juvenile courts in 1986. Feld (1990: 34) found that although youths charged with felonies generally had attorneys present at adjudicatory proceedings (66.1%), as did many youths charged with misdemeanors (46.4%), only 28.9 percent of youths charged with status offenses had legal representation. Also, the pattern was more likely in urban and suburban courts than in rural courts; in the latter, for example, only 14.3 percent of the youths being adjudicated for status offenses were represented by counsel; in urban courts the number was 45.6 percent.

Something is being done, however, to remedy the abuses in the current application of the status offender category. Although efforts to extend due process rights to young people charged with status offenses have been disappointing (Ribach, 1971), challenges concerned with the constitutional imprecision of status offenses have been more successful. Although the conviction of a young woman for "walking with a lascivious carriage" was upheld in *State v. Mattiello* (4 Conn. 55, 225 A. 2d 507, App. Div. 1966), two more recent federal court decisions turned out differently. Statutes that permitted officials to take young people into custody because they were "in danger of leading an idle, dissolute, lewd or immoral life" (*Gonzales v. Maillard,* Civil No. 50424, N.D. Cal. 1972) or because they were "in danger of becoming morally depraved" (*Gesicki v. Oswald,* 336 F. Supp. 371, S.D.N.Y., 1971) were judicially deemed impermissibly vague. According to an amendment of the OJJDP Act in 1987, judges can still place status offenders in detention in cases where they are found to be in "contempt of court." For girls this may mean she may have done nothing other than violate a judge's order not to run away. There was also a Florida case in which a pregnant girl was locked up for failure to keep a doctor's appointment! A Florida State Supreme Court decision (*A.A. v. Rolle,* 604 So. 2d 813, 1992) forbade such a practice (Siegel & Senna, 2000: 25).

Efforts to extend these findings to other inexplicit sexual status offense categories have been discouraging. The constitutionality of the PINS category in New York State was upheld in *Mercado v. Rockefeller* (502 F. 2d 666, 2d Cir. 1974), and Washington State's incorrigibility statute was upheld in *Blondheim v. State* (84 Wash. 2d 874, 529 P. 2d 1096, 1975). In *Blondheim* the court was also asked to determine whether punishment for incorrigibility was "cruel and unusual punishment" because the law punished the "status" of incorrigibility; the argument was rejected (see also Sarri, 1978).

In the main, early legal attempts to curb or limit the juvenile or family court's authority over status offenders met with mixed success (Sarri, 1978). More recently, the legal signals are even less encouraging. Indeed, the current Supreme Court in some of its decisions, notably *Hazelwood School District v. Kuhlmeier* (108, S. Ct. 562, 1988), has been signaling a retreat from earlier decisions according juveniles certain rights—asserting in this case that a juvenile's speech can be censored when it is "unsuitable, ungrammatical or simply poorly written" (Federle, 1990: 25). Ironically, the same court appears to be making it easier to hold youths to adult standards by not specifically finding that the execution of youngsters who were between the ages of sixteen and eighteen at the time of their crimes constitutes cruel and unusual punishment (*Stanford v. Kentucky*, 57 U.S.L.W. 4973, 1989).

Finally, a Supreme Court case that has not received the attention given to the above cases may have more important implications for girls. *Parham v. J.R.* (442 U.S. 584, 1979) dealt with the rights of youths committed to mental hospitals—particularly the issue of whether a minor's guardians or parents can "voluntarily" institutionalize a youth in a private institution. Because this case is more immediately relevant to the discussion of the deinstitutionalization of status offenders housed in youth training schools, we will examine this case more fully in the next chapter.

GETTING INTO THE SYSTEM

Another way that the juvenile justice system differs from its adult counterpart concerns point of entry. Many youths come to the attention of the juvenile court because of a complaint or referral from sources other than law enforcement agencies (for example, parents or school officials). Predictably, there is a substantial variation, depending upon the offense. In 1997, 85 percent of the delinquency referrals but only 47 percent of status offense referrals came from law enforcement personnel (Sickmund, 2000). And within the status offense category there are important gender differences. Referrals having to do with liquor-law violators (68 percent of whom are male) are far more likely to originate with the police (94 percent). In contrast, only 40 percent of runaways (who overall are 60 percent female) were referred by law enforcement personnel. So one might logically believe that the juvenile justice system begins with apprehension by the police, but youths can also be brought into the system by parents or community agencies. Obviously, avenue of entry is extremely important in girls' delinquency.

In most jurisdictions the police have several options when contact with a juvenile is made (either because of a citizen complaint or an on-site observation of an alleged offense). First, they can, and often do, simply warn and release (for instance, telling a group of young people hanging around a street corner to "move along" or "go home"). Second, they can release after filling out an interview card ("field investigation card" or "field contact card"). Third, they can make a "station adjustment"; a youth is brought to the police station and then either (1) released to a parent or guardian, or (2) released with a referral to some community agency. Fourth, they can issue a misdemeanor citation, which will require the youth and a parent or guardian to appear in juvenile court at some future date (not unlike a traffic ticket). Fifth, they can transport a youth to the juvenile court after making a formal arrest.

Girls on the Streets

As we know, girls are more likely than boys to be arrested for minor property offenses and status offenses. This circumstance is stable despite efforts to deemphasize the official processing of youths arrested for noncriminal status offenses—which still account for more than one-fifth of girls' arrests and about ten percent of boys' arrests (see Chapter 2). Still, official arrest statistics do not tell the whole story. Studies of police interactions with juveniles, only some of which result in arrest, provide an important and often neglected perspective on official statistics and remind us that police have considerable discretion in carrying out their tasks. One indication of the volume of these interactions is provided by a study of all persons born in Philadelphia in 1958. The researchers found that 14 percent of girls and 33 percent of boys had one "police contact" before the age of eighteen (Tracy, Wolfgang, & Figlio, 1985: 5–6). Another study tells us that perhaps 60 to 70 percent of police contacts with juveniles on the street are handled informally and do not result in arrest (Monahan, 1970: 134). More recent studies confirm that for a good number of youths, some kind of contact with the police is a normal part of growing up (Tracy & Kempf-Leonard, 1996).

Changes in official arrest statistics could be the result of changes in the behavior of young people or changes in the behavior of those with the power to label behavior delinquent—in this case, the police. And, as we shall see, police are given considerable latitude in defining what is or is not delinquent—particularly for youths suspected of committing minor offenses.

Police officers make two independent decisions about the disposition of juvenile suspects: (1) the decision to make an arrest and (2) the decision to refer an arrested juvenile to family court. Generally, the harsher response is seen as the one that further inserts arrested youths into the juvenile justice system.

Early sociological studies of police behavior in the field rarely examined the effect of gender on the decision to make an arrest. One exception is Monahan's investigation of police dispositions of juvenile offenders in Philadelphia. In this study it was discovered that police were more likely to release a girl than a boy they suspected of committing a crime, equally likely to apprehend males and females they suspected of running away, and more likely to arrest girls they suspected of sex offenses (Monahan, 1970: 139).

A similar pattern emerged in a longitudinal study of delinquency in California in the late 1960s. Elliott and Voss conducted a self-report survey among high school students and then checked official records for evidence of police contact (not necessarily official arrests). They found sizable gender differentials in the frequency of such contacts. In their comparisons of rates of unofficial and official delinquency, boys were four times more likely than girls to experience police contact for a serious offense. The data showed that police contacts occurred in only 1 percent of the serious offenses admitted by females (in contrast to 4 percent of boys' serious offenses). Elliott and Voss said this was "not simply a reflection of differential involvement in delinquency behavior on the part of males and females" but that "official records are biased in favor of girls" when it comes to these sorts of offenses (Elliott & Voss, 1974: 84–87). To support their assertion, they referred to data they had gathered on auto theft that showed a male/female self-report ratio of 2:1 and a ratio of police contacts of 26:1. According to their study, "although females perceive themselves as partners in the theft of automobiles, apparently police officers apprehended only their male companions." They concluded that "there is a serious sex bias in official police contact reports" (87). Unfortunately, Elliott and Voss were not able to compare self-reported and official arrests for sexual offenses; hence, their data could not address the treatment of girls suspected of such offenses. However, they did find evidence that young women who admitted to serious criminal offenses were not being apprehended by official agencies in the same numbers as were their male counterparts.

Other studies linking self-reported delinquency to police contacts have also suggested that girls may be overrepresented in connection with nonserious status offenses—which are often buffer charges for suspected sexuality. Teilmann and Landry (1981: 74–75), for example, compared girls' arrests for running away and incorrigibility with girls' self-reports and found a 10.4 percent overrepresentation of females in the former and a 30.9 percent overrepresentation in the latter.

A study of 391 seriously criminal youths in Miami (Horowitz & Pottieger, 1991), conducted between 1985 and 1987, also found evidence of gender and race effects on arrest. The examination uncovered very complex and intriguing interactions between offense type and gender and race in self-reported delinquency and arrest records. Specifically, black male drug offenders were more likely to be arrested than their offense levels would suggest. In the area of property offenses, females and black males were more likely to be arrested than white males, and females who had committed major felonies were far less likely than their male counterparts to be arrested. Prostitution, an offense that was insignificant for boys, played a major role in girls' arrests, but girls are also more likely than boys to commit this offense, according to these researchers.

Only one study, that of Seattle youth by Sampson (1985), has suggested that self-report measures are fairly accurate measures of official delinquency. However, Sampson collapsed family and school delinquency into one variable. Moreover, in the analysis, measures of incidence of drug use and family offenses among females showed lower reliabilities than those found among males. In sum, research that compares or links self-report data to arrest data suggests that girls may be overrepresented among those charged with minor or status offenses when arrests are compared to actual behavior. There is also some indication that girls may be committing some serious offenses for which they are not being arrested.

An important complement to the objective, quantitative approach to police decision making is studies that examine police work in the field. Again, only a few have specifically looked into the role of the subject's gender in the decision to arrest, but those few provide interesting information.

DeFleur, in her study of the informal disposition of males and females suspected of drug offenses, discerned a tendency on the part of police to avoid arresting females as often as males if they behaved in stereotypic ways. If female suspects cried during drug raids, said they had been led astray by men, or expressed concern for their children, they appeared to have a direct influence on the officers' decision not to arrest. If, however, female suspects were aggressive or hostile, they were more likely to be arrested and processed (DeFleur, 1975: 101).

DeFleur was interested in arrests of both juvenile and adult women for only one type of offense; other researchers have clarified and amplified her findings. Visher (1983) examined 785 police-suspect encounters during 1977 in twenty-four police departments in three geographically separate American communities. She excluded morals offenses (prostitution and drug-related offenses), confining her study to routine criminal and public-order offenses. Scrutinizing many aspects of the arrest situation, Visher concluded that age was irrelevant in police interactions with males but relevant in interactions with females, with younger females receiving harsher treatment.

Visher also noted that "police officers adopt a more paternalistic and harsher attitude toward young females to deter any further violation of appropriate sex-role behavior" (Visher, 1983: 15). In addition, demeanor was an extremely important factor in the arrest decision: "female suspects who violated typical middle-class standards of traditional female characteristics and behaviors (i.e., white, older, and submissive) are not afforded any chivalrous treatment during arrest decisions" (Ibid.: 22–23). Women suspected of property offenses were actually more harshly treated than their male counterparts, many of whom were suspected of "minor" crimes of violence.

The initial encounter with the police is just the first stage in the processing of offenders. The second stage comes when the alleged offender is taken to the police station.

Girls at the Station House

What happens to a girl after her arrest? Does she fare better than an arrested boy once in the police station? It is there where police make decisions about which cases to handle informally, which youths to hold, and which to refer to the family or juvenile court. One hypothesis advanced over the years is that females (both adults and juveniles) are handled more leniently than males; in other words, they are treated in a chivalrous manner.[2] Evidence on this issue is somewhat mixed, and the pattern is more complicated than the early proponents of the chivalry hypothesis would have us believe.

Initial studies of police dispositions after arrest (Goldman, 1969; Terry, 1970; McEachern & Bauzer, 1967) spoke of a tendency to refer more girls than boys to formal court processing rather than releasing them, or to refer them to social service agencies, particularly when they were charged with status offenses.

An early 1980s study by Teilmann and Landry (1981) found a less consistent pattern of bias against girls; they found instead a generally harsh response to all youths charged with status offenses. Examining status-offender referral patterns in five counties across the United States that were starting deinstitutionalization programs in 1976, the two researchers reported a clear bias against youths charged with incorrigibility and running away from home. Girls charged with these offenses were not significantly more likely to be referred to court than boys (although in six of the ten comparisons, girls were slightly more likely to be referred to court) (Teilmann & Landry, 1981:59). Teilmann and Landry's work also demonstrated the enormous variability of police referral patterns. In one state, for example, nearly three-quarters of the males and females who were arrested were referred to court; in another state, less than one fifth were.

Other research on police handling of male and female status offenders does not produce consistent evidence of evenhandedness. Krohn, Curry, and Nelson-Kilger (1983) analyzed over ten thousand police contacts in a Midwestern city over a twenty-nine-year span (1948–1976). From their examination of police records, the authors concluded that girls suspected of status offenses were more likely than their male counterparts to be referred to juvenile court during all three decades. And contrary to the authors' predictions, court referrals for status offenses increased over time.

Criminal offenses exhibited a slightly different pattern. Girls suspected of misdemeanors were less likely than boys to be referred to court in the earlier years, but this pattern eroded considerably in the later years. The pattern was more mixed for felonies (Krohn et al., 1983: 426). Indeed, by the 1970s, the increase in female referrals for misdemeanors was slightly greater than for males. The authors wrote that "part of the apparent increase in female crime may be due to changes in official reactions to female offenders" (417). More recently, Bishop and Frazier found considerable gender and racial bias (1992), while Sampson found that socioeconomic status was even more significant (1986). All of this suggests that gender bias is aimed more often at poor girls of color.

Findings such as these suggest that a substantial amount of the increase in the arrests of juvenile women for criminal offenses in the late 1960s and early 1970s can be explained by changes in law enforcement patterns. Additional support for this notion comes from reviews of self-report studies, which over time show no apparent increase in traditionally masculine offenses committed by girls (Steffensmeier & Steffensmeier, 1980). Concerning the historic overrepresentation of females in the number of juveniles charged with status offenses, the data seem to indicate that the police, like parents, have traditionally participated in the double standard of juvenile justice by harshly responding to status-offense misbehavior by girls that they would ignore if it were done by boys.

For more evidence on the latter point, consider Linda Hancock's (1981) content analysis of police referrals in Australia: 40 percent of the referrals of girls to court mentioned sexual and moral conduct, but only 5 percent of the referrals of boys did so. Gelsthorpe's (1986) field research on an English police station also reveals how everyday police decision making resulted in disregard of complaints about male problem behavior in contrast to active concern about girls' problem behavior. Noteworthy here was the concern about the girls' sexual behavior. Gelsthorpe describes police persistence in pursuing a "moral-danger" order for a fourteen-year-old picked up during a truancy run. Over the objections of the girl's parents and the social services department, and in the face of written confirmation from a surgeon that the girl was still pre-menstrual, officers pursued the application because, in one officer's words, "I know her sort . . . free and easy. I'm still suspicious that she might be pregnant. Anyway, if the doctor can't provide evidence we'll do her for being beyond the care and control of her parents, no one can dispute that. Running away is proof" (1986: 136). This sexualization of female deviance is highly significant and explains why criminal activities by girls (particularly in past years) were overlooked or excused.

A similar pattern was also observed by another British study that found that girls' "non-sexual offenses were overlooked in favor of sexual misbehavior" by police officers (Smith, 1978: 83). Here is how one girl described what happened:

> It's funny because once when I was down at the cop shop for fighting, this woman saw the swastika on my arm and forgot all about what she was looking for. They never did nothing—just told me to stop fighting. But the woman cop, she kept on about the swastika and Hell's Angels. What a bad lot they were for a girl to go around with and how I had better stop going around with Angels or else I'd get a really bad name for myself. Then she kept asking me if I'd had sex with any of 'em or taken drugs (Ibid.).

Police concern about and harsh response to the moral behavior of girls are less anomalous when placed within the history of the juvenile justice system and the policing of girls' sexuality in earlier decades (Odem & Schlossman, 1991). Field studies of adult prostitution (LaFave, 1969; Carmen & Moody, 1985) have also consistently indicated that women are routinely harassed by police, that they are often swept up simply because they are "known" as prostitutes, and that they are occasionally brutalized by law enforcement officers. Other research (Miller & Graczkowski, 1985) documents the fact that male prostitutes are not treated similarly by police officers.

The situation is so bad that even when girls experience terrible victimization on the streets, they tend to avoid reporting it to the police. Cases of girls who report rapes or physical abuse at the hands of male intimates only to be locked up themselves as runaways or incorrigibles are, unfortunately, all too common. Take this instance reported by a journalist as she talked with young female runaways in the early 1970s:

Last year Mia, a 17-year-old girl who lived with her boyfriend with parental consent, was kidnapped and raped by another man. When she reported it to the police, they arrested her as a runaway and shipped her off to juvenile hall instead of going after the rapist. Wilma had a similar experience on the East Coast, when she went back for a visit. Raped and dumped by a man who gave her a ride, she made her way to the nearest police station, where she was promptly arrested. The judge, seeing her past record, said he would sentence her to a state reformatory until she was 21—unless the social worker put her on a plane to California within 24 hours (Macleod, 1974: 486).

Police also play a pivotal role in deciding if a youth will be held in a detention center or, when such a facility is not available, an adult lockup or jail. Because girls have long tended to be overrepresented among juveniles detained, the condition of these facilities is cause for great concern.

Essentially, research on police behavior in the field suggests that police attitudes toward girls have changed in some ways and not in others. Concerning increases in the arrests of girls for criminal behavior, what may be occurring is not so much a change in actual female behavior as an erosion of police chivalry—particularly when the girl's behavior in the arrest situation does not conform to traditional gender-role expectations.

There is also some indication that in at least some departments the erosion of chivalry in the treatment of girls and women suspected of crimes was a direct response to the women's movement. Police officials such as Ed Davis, chief of the Los Angeles Police Department in the early 1970s, blamed the women's movement for "a crime wave like the world has never seen before" (Weis, 1976: 17). More restrained commentators believed that the steep increase in female arrests in the early 1970s was partially a product of changed police attitudes. One officer said to a reporter, "They are being apprehended more frequently and not as sheltered as in the past, when we tended to overlook women" (Roberts, 1972: 72).

More generally, these data suggest that police have considerable latitude in not only the decision to arrest but also the decision about what to label the delinquent behavior they observe. As an example, in earlier decades (and arguably into the present), there was considerable concern about girls' sexuality. As a result, girls' violence tended to be ignored or minimized. Currently, there is far more public concern about girls' violence, and we have seen a considerable increase in girls arrested for these offenses. Whether these increases signal radical changes in girls' behavior or changes in enforcement practices is a key question in understanding girls' delinquency presently.

DELINQUENTS IN COURT

As we have seen, girls and boys formally enter the juvenile court after having been referred to it by a law enforcement agency or a parent or guardian. Sometimes a young person may receive a misdemeanor citation (not unlike a traffic citation) that informs the individual that he or she must appear in court on or before a certain date. Upon arrival, the boy or girl is subjected to intake screening, another unique feature of the juvenile court, during which two critical decisions are made, generally by a social worker or probation officer: first, whether the youth will be detained before the hearing, and second, whether a petition requiring a formal court appearance before a judge will be filed. Customarily, the youth and a parent or guardian are interviewed at intake.

The options available to the court representative at this stage vary somewhat among jurisdictions but fall into four categories: (1) dismissal; (2) informal supervision, or "informal probation"; (3) referral to another agency; and (4) formal petition to the court.

In most juvenile courts, the decision to detain is usually based upon written court policies. The three typical reasons for detention are (1) that the youth may harm others or himself or herself or be subject to injury by others if not detained; (2) the youth has no parent, guardian, or other person able to provide adequate care and supervision, is homeless, or is a runaway; and (3) it is believed that if not detained the youth will leave the jurisdiction and not appear for court proceedings. Several factors are usually spelled out for intake staff to take into consideration, and these include the nature and severity of the current offense and previous offenses (if any), the youth's age, the youth's conduct within the home and at school, ability of the parents or guardians to supervise the youth, whether the current offense is a continuation of a pattern of delinquent behavior, and the willingness of the parents or guardians to cooperate with the court.

It can be seen that youths who are experiencing problems at home or who are in arguments with their parents are at a distinct disadvantage in the intake stage. When the court processing of youths charged with status offenses is discussed, these facts should be kept in mind.

If youths are not diverted from further processing, they move to the adjudication stage of the juvenile court process. Adjudication is essentially the juvenile equivalent of an adult trial. It follows a petition ordering a youth to appear before the juvenile court judge for one of three basic types of hearings: (1) a plea hearing, wherein the youth simply enters a plea of guilty or not guilty (roughly like an arraignment in adult court); (2) a contested hearing, which ensues from a plea of not guilty (roughly like a trial in the adult system); and (3) a dispositional hearing, wherein the youth adjudicated as a delinquent (either upon pleading guilty or being found so in a contested hearing) is given a "sentence." The final disposition typically consists of one of the following: (1) a period of formal supervision by the court, after which the case is dismissed if the youth's behavior has been satisfactory; (2) formal probation, whereby the youth is placed under the direct control of the court probation department for a period of three to six months; (3) fine or restitution; or (4) commitment to one of several types of institutions, ranging from a community-based facility to tight-security training schools.

Institutional commitment is the most severe and perhaps the most controversial disposition, particularly in regard to offenses charged according to gender. This topic is explored in Chapter 9, but it should be noted here that females are far more likely than males to be committed to a juvenile correctional facility for a status offense. The most recent figures show that in 1999, 3 percent of the committed males and 13 percent of the females were status offenders (Sickmund & Wan, 2001). Disposition is essentially the end of the formal juvenile court processing. However, another stage follows institutional commitment: parole, or after-care—the period when the youth is supervised by the court parole officer, usually under the auspices of the state division of youth parole or after-care.

GENDER AND DELINQUENCY REFERRALS

What kinds of behavior result in referral to juvenile court? Are there significant differences between girls and boys in referrals? Juvenile court referrals include youths charged with both criminal violations and status offenses, such as incorrigibility (in some jurisdictions this condition is called "unmanageable" or "ungovernable," and in others the child is labeled "in need of supervision") and truancy. In some parts of the country, youths who are abused or neglected are also handled in juvenile courts.

According to OJJDP, in 1999 males constituted 76 percent of all delinquency referrals to juvenile courts. Males comprised 73 percent of all the "person" crimes during that year, the majority of which were "simple assaults" (representing two-thirds of all personal crimes). As for status offenses, 1997 data (1999 figures were unavailable) reveal that males constituted 58 percent of the total, but females were the majority of runaway cases (60 percent of the total). It should be noted that the status offense figures are for "petitioned" cases only, since many juvenile courts do not handle most status offense cases. Many of these cases are handled informally by local social service departments, so comparisons are difficult. We have learned that in subsequent reports, OJJDP will only report on a sample of petitioned status offense cases (Sickmund, 2003). Table 8-1 shows these data.

The foregoing data do seem to signal a drop in status offense referrals, although not as dramatic a decline as some expected in the wake of legal efforts to divert and deinstitutionalize status offenders. Because national data on status offense cases in juvenile courts are not as available as previously (as noted above), data from some individual states still show that a sizable number of juvenile court cases are status offenses. For instance, in Missouri's juvenile courts during the year 2000, status offenses constituted almost one-third (32%) of all cases (excluding abuse and neglect cases). Moreover, just under one-fourth (23.8%) of the males and almost one-third (32.3%) of the females were referred for status offenses in this court system during 2000 (Missouri Department of Social Services, 2001). The authors know of other juvenile courts that still handle large numbers of status offense cases (e.g., Honolulu, Las Vegas). More telling, however, are the numbers of status offenders who end up in juvenile correctional facilities, of which more will be said in the next chapter. Suffice it to say at this point that 13 percent of the girls, but only 3 percent of the boys, in juvenile correctional facilities as of 1999 were status offenders; al-

Table 8-1. Juvenile Court Referrals, by Offense and Gender

	Male	Female	Total
Delinquency Cases (1999)*			
Person	282,800	104,300	387,100
Property	537,900	168,300	706,200
Drugs	160,800	30,400	191,200
Public Order	293,000	95,600	388,600
Total	1,274,500	398,600	1,673,100
Status Offenses (1997)**			
Runaway	9,700	14,300	24,000
Truancy	21,600	18,900	40,500
Ungovernable	11,700	9,500	21,200
Liquor Laws	27,700	13,100	40,800
Miscellaneous	22,100	10,000	32,100
Total	92,800	65,800	158,600

SOURCES: *OJJDP Statistical Briefing Book. On-line (ojjdp.ncjrs.org/ojstatbb/asp/
JCSCF_Display.asp).

** Juvenile Court Statistics, 1997. On-line (ncjrs.org/html/ojjdp/jcs_1997). Represents
status offense cases that were "petitioned to court" during 1997, rather than
"referrals to court." Data for 1999 not available at time of this writing (January 2003).

most one-fourth of the girls in private facilities were status offenders compared with only 7 percent of the boys.

National court data also show for 1997 that an almost identical percentage of males and females (48% of the males and 49% of the females) referred to court for delinquency were referred for a property offense. Not surprisingly, the majority of the female property offenders were charged with larceny–theft. Although recent data are incomplete, a 1982 national court study reported that in the index property offense category, 65 percent of the females were charged with shoplifting, compared with only 34.6 percent of the males (Snyder, Hutzler, & Finnegan, 1985: 34, 58). These figures are based upon data from a representative sample of juvenile courts in the United States.

Shelden's longitudinal study (1987), noted earlier, found that males and females differed in significant ways in terms of length of careers and type of offenses committed. The majority of the girls (60.7 percent) had only one contact with the court, compared with 43.3 percent of the boys. Boys were about twice as likely as girls to be "chronic delinquents" (those with five or more referrals to court) and about ten times as likely to be "chronic serious offenders" (the majority of their offenses being felonies). In terms of the overall distribution of offenses, girls were twice as likely as boys to be referred for status offenses and for petty larceny; boys were far more likely than girls to be referred for traditional "male" offenses, such as robbery, aggravated assault, burglary, and grand larceny.

COMPARING GIRLS AND BOYS IN COURT

As related in Chapter 7, studies of the court processing of girls and boys, particularly earlier research analyzing court records and judicial conduct, consistently found that because court officials participated in the double standard of
juvenile justice, girls charged with status offenses were often more harshly
treated than boys or girls charged with crimes (Cohn, 1970; Rogers, 1972;
Chesney-Lind, 1973; Andrews & Cohn, 1974; Kratcoski, 1974; Datesman &
Scarpitti, 1977; Schlossman & Wallach, 1978; Shelden, 1981; Pope & Feyerherm, 1982). Further, as related in Chapter 9, they are also more likely to be
held for long periods in detention centers, and until recently they were overrepresented, relative to percentage of arrests, in both training school and detention center populations (Conway & Bogdan, 1977). Moreover, the pattern
is not confined to the United States.

   Not all research confirms the existence of judicial sexism. Teilmann and
Landry (1981), for example, examined court dispositions of youthful offenders
in several locations, relying heavily on data from a five-state study of services
to status offenders. By controlling for "offense type" and prior record, they
found that "status offenders are consistently given harsher treatment than
delinquent offenders" but that "this is [as]true for boys as it is for girls." From
this, they concluded that treatment within the court was "relatively even-
handed" (Teilmann & Landry, 1981: 47). Several other studies (Dungworth,
1977; Carter, 1979; Cohen & Kluegel, 1979; Clarke & Koch, 1980; Johnson &
Scheuble, 1991) also found little evidence that female status offenders were
more harshly sanctioned than their male counterparts once the effects of a variety of extralegal variables were controlled for.

   Some of the findings of the past decade or so could reflect actual changes
as a result of the deinstitutionalization movement, but that is not the only possible explanation. It may also be that the bias against girls may be less overt.
Mahoney and Fenster (1982) found from courtroom observation that many of
the girls being taken into custody for crimes had actually exhibited behavior
that earlier would have been classified as status offenses. For example, girls who
broke into their parents' homes to take food and clothing to enable prolonga-
tion of their runaway status were being charged with burglary. Such reclassifi-
cation of female status offenders into female criminals occurred during a
period characterized by a "get-tough" attitude toward juvenile crime. Some
observers (Curran, 1984) suggest that the hardening of the public mind has
particularly burdened female offenders because their behavior was being rede-
fined as criminal at precisely the same time that courts were increasingly likely
to process their cases formally and punish them more harshly.

   Other observers, however, have failed to uncover evidence that girls and
boys charged with status offenses are treated equally. Shelden and Horvath
(1986) found that females referred to court for status offenses were more likely
than males referred for the same offenses to receive formal processing (that is,
a court hearing). Girls were also more likely to be detained for status offenses
than boys were (though the differences were not statistically significant).

Mann's (1979) research on runaway youths in the Midwest also found that girls were more likely than boys to be detained and to receive harsher sentences.

Differences in the labels given to the noncriminal behavior of males and females may play a major role in producing harsher treatment for girls. We have seen that girls are far more likely to appear before a court for running away from home or for being ungovernable. As might be expected, the predominantly female status offenses are those that bring on the greatest use of detention, despite the fact that research suggests that male status offenders are more likely to have committed other criminal violations (Boisvert & Wells, 1980).

Datesman and Aickin (1984), examining whether youths charged with status offenses tend to escalate into criminal offenses, also found significant sex differences. In general, the majority of youths charged with status offenses failed to return to court for any offense. Among those who did return, females (particularly white females) were the least likely to appear again before the court for a delinquent offense; it was usually for another status offense (1270–1273; see also Shelden, Horvath, & Tracy, 1989).

Another pattern that may be occurring has been labeled by Feld (1990: 201) as the interaction of "gender and geography." Like other researchers, he found evidence that girls referred to juvenile court in Minnesota were more likely than boys to be detained, particularly for minor and status offenses. But more to the point, he also found evidence that judicial paternalism was less marked in urban courts, which he characterized as more formal and procedural, than in suburban and rural courts. Specifically, in rural juvenile courts larger proportions of females are removed from their homes for minor offenses. He also noted that these courts tended to deal with the smallest proportions of juveniles charged with serious criminal activity and the largest proportion charged with status offenses. Further, although urban courts tended to be more severe in sanctioning, an uncritical embrace of the informal court does not necessarily follow in large part because in "rural juvenile courts female juveniles are processed differently and more severely than are either rural males or female offenders in other settings" (Feld, 1990: 196, 201, 209).

One of the most recent studies of gender and juvenile court processing comes from the American Bar Association (2001). This study found that girls are far more likely to be detained for relatively minor offenses, especially violation of court orders, various misdemeanor charges associated with running away, charges of escape, absconding and AWOL (absent without official leave)," the latter of which suggests that in some situations girls are treated as military personnel who technically are the "property" of those in authority. The report also noted the growing tendency to relabel family conflicts in which girls are involved as "violent" offenses, which impacts minority girls in an especially negative way.

The ABA cited a recent report by the Annie E. Casey Foundation (in its Juvenile Detention Alternative Initiative) which found that girls are more likely than boys to be detained for relatively minor offenses such as public disorder, probation violations, status offenses, and even traffic offenses (29 percent of the girls vs. 19 percent of the boys). Such gender bias was found to be especially evident for violations of probation and parole, where more than half of the girls (54%), but only 19 percent of the boys, were detained. The ABA study concluded that even though the recidivism rate of girls is much lower than that of boys, "the use of contempt proceedings and probation and parole violations make[s] it more likely that, without committing a new crime, girls will return to detention" (American Bar Association, 2001: 20). Specifically, in four sites studied by the Annie E. Casey Foundation, even though girls comprised only 14 percent of the detention population, 30 percent were returned to detention within one year. Among those returned, 53 percent of the girls and 41 percent of the boys were returned for "technical violations" such as violation of probation or parole. Girls who were returned to detention two or three times within a year were far more likely than their male counterparts to be returned on these kinds of violations (for those returned three times, 72 percent of the girls but only 49 percent of the boys were sent back for these violations).

The gendered nature of juvenile arrests continues. As we saw earlier, whereas more than three boys are arrested for every girl, the ratio of serious crimes of violence is about five to one. Over half (59%) of those arrested in 2000 for running away were girls (see Chapter 2). And, as noted in Chapter 2, the number of arrests of both girls and boys for these offenses is increasing. These arrest figures mean a considerable "front-end" pressure on a juvenile justice system that has been told to "divert" and "deinstitutionalize" these youths. Indeed, between 1993 and 1997 the number of male status offenses cases petitioned to juvenile courts increased by 45 percent, while those for females went up by 36 percent. Looking at a longer time frame, between 1988 and 1997 such referrals went up for males by 98 percent and for females by 105 percent (Sickmund, 2000).

More important, it seems increasingly clear that deinstitutionalization may have actually signaled the development of a two-track juvenile justice system—one track for girls of color and another for white girls.

GIRLS, RACE, AND THE NEW
DOUBLE STANDARD OF JUVENILE JUSTICE

Recent research has illustrated the increasing use of detention for girls and the different ways that girls of color are processed through the juvenile justice system. National data indicate that between 1989 and 1998, detentions involving girls increased by 56 percent compared to a 20 percent increase in boys' detentions (Harms, 2002). The increase is most likely related to recent legislation, which has made it easier for girls to be detained for status offenses such as running away (Sherman, 2000). Further, research has illustrated that detention centers are being utilized with girls for a significantly longer duration than with boys, with 60 percent of the girls detained for more than seven days, compared with only 6 percent of the boys (Shorter, Schaffner, Schick, & Frappier, 1996). Quite possibly, this may be related to the lack of gender-specific programs nationally.

Another critical issue is the different ways that girls of color are processed through the juvenile justice system compared to Caucasian girls. Take for example, Bartollas's (1993) study of youth confined in institutional placements in a Midwestern state. His research sampled female adolescents in both public and private facilities. The "state" sample (representing the girls in public facilities) was 61 percent black, while the private sample was 100 percent white. Little difference, however, was found in the offense patterns of the two groups of girls. These findings suggest the development of the two-track juvenile justice system mentioned above.

In a study of investigative reports from one area probation office in Los Angeles, Jody Miller (1994) examined the impact of race and ethnicity on the processing of girls' cases during 1992–1993. Comparing the characteristics of the youth in Miller's group with Schlossman's earlier profile of girls in Los Angeles in the 1950s shows how radically (and racially) different the current girls in the Los Angeles juvenile justice system are from their earlier counterparts. Latinas constituted the largest proportion of the population (43%), followed by white girls (34%) and African American girls (23%) Miller, 1994: 11).

Predictably, girls of color were more likely to be from low-income homes, but this was especially true of African American girls (53 percent were from AFDC families, compared to 23 percent of the white girls and 21 percent of the Latina girls). Most important, Miller found that white girls were significantly more likely to be recommended for a treatment facility rather than a "detention-oriented" placement than either African American or Latina girls. In fact, 75 percent of the white girls were recommended for a treatment facility, compared to 35 percent of the Latinas and only 20 percent of the African American girls (Miller, 1994: 18).

Examining a portion of the probation officers' reports in detail, Miller found key differences in the ways that girls' behaviors were described—reflecting what she called "racialized gender expectations." In particular, African American girls' behavior was often framed as a product of "inappropriate 'lifestyle' choices," while white girls' behavior was described as resulting from low self-esteem, being easily influenced, and the result of "abandonment" (Miller, 1994: 20). Latinas, Miller found, received "dichotomized" treatment, with some receiving the paternalistic care white girls received, while others received more punitive treatment (particularly if they committed "masculine" offenses such as auto theft).

Robinson (1990), in her study of girls in the social welfare (CHINS) and juvenile justice (Department of Youth Services—DYS) systems in Massachusetts, documents the racialized pattern of juvenile justice quite clearly. Her social welfare sample was 74 percent white, and her juvenile justice sample was 53 percent African American or Hispanic. Her interviews document the remarkable similarities of the girls' backgrounds and problems. As an example, 80 percent of those committed to DYS reported being sexually abused, compared to 73 percent of the girls in the social welfare group. The difference between these girls was in the offenses for which they were charged. All the girls in the social welfare system were charged with traditional status offenses (mostly running away and truancy), whereas most of the girls committed to DYS were charged with criminal offenses. Here, however, her interviews reveal clear evidence of bootstrapping. An example is the sixteen-year-old girl who was committed to DYS for "unauthorized use of a motor vehicle." In this instance, Beverly, who is African American, had "stolen" her mother's car for three hours to go shopping with a friend. Previous to this offense she had been a "CHINS" for "running away from home repeatedly." Beverly told Robinson that her mother had been "advised by the DYS social worker to press charges for unauthorized use of a motor vehicle so that Beverly could be sent to secure detention whenever she was caught on the run" (Robinson, 1990: 202).

The American Bar Association study found further racial bias in the processing of girls. The report quoted one girl who called juvenile detention "just another kind of slavery" (American Bar Association, 2001: 16). Nationally, African American male juveniles have an incarceration rate of 969 per 100,000 compared with a rate of only 183 for white juveniles; their rate for drug offenses is about eleven times greater than for white drug offenders. In fact, no matter what the commitment offense is, African American youth are far more likely to be committed to some kind of juvenile institution (Sickmund & Wan, 1999). The ABA study also noted that though in 1985 minority girls were 43 percent of the detention population, by 1995 they comprised 56 percent of the detention population. The report further noted that whereas 70 percent of the white girls were dismissed in court, only 30 percent of African American girls were dismissed (American Bar Association, 2001: 21).

Taken together, these studies suggest that deinstitutionalization pressures may have differentially affected girls depending upon their race. For girls of color, particularly African American girls, bootstrapping may be the response to their acting out, but for white girls a different approach is taken: "transinstitutionalization" into the world of private institutions and placements. In either case, the true intent of the framers of the deinstitutionalization initiative is being subverted.

SUMMARY

This chapter focused on the encounters girls have with the police and the juvenile court. Two stages of police processing were examined: contact with the police on the streets and at the station house. Concerning the former, boys are far more likely to experience contacts with the police. The police are more likely to release a girl than a boy suspected of committing a crime, but are more likely to arrest girls suspected of sex offenses. Girls tend to be overrepresented in arrest statistics for status offenses, especially running away and incorrigibility, in relation to self-reported behavior. Much of this has to do with girls' alleged sexual behavior, which is so often associated (at least from the standpoint of adult authorities) with the two offenses.

One critical variable in police decision making on the streets is a young person's demeanor or attitude. In general, a boy or girl who is hostile or in any way aggressive is the most likely to be arrested. Especially important for girls is whether or not they follow middle-class standards of "proper" behavior.

Police decision making in the station house varies widely throughout the United States. Usually, however, girls are more likely than boys to be referred to court for status offenses. In many jurisdictions police agencies pay very close attention to the sexual behavior of girls while ignoring the identical behavior of boys, and act very paternalistically. Extremely harsh handling of runaways and prostitutes seems to be all too frequent.

Juvenile court statistics show that girls are more likely than boys to be referred to court for status offenses (especially running away and incorrigibility). Boys, in contrast, are more likely to be referred for violent crimes. Property offenses bring large numbers of both girls and boys to court, but for girls the bulk of such offenses are in the larceny–theft category (most are for shoplifting).

Evidence of changes in official responses to girls who appear in the juvenile courts is somewhat mixed. Some studies have found more even-handed treatment in recent years; others have not. The types of status offenses that girls and boys commit seem to account for some of the courts' differential responses: girls typically appear for running away and other offenses that signal that they are beyond parental control, and boys appear for curfew and liquor-law violations. Finally, recent research has specifically identified the need to focus on race as well as gender in the handling of youths. To explore current court responses to these forms of status offenses as well as other forms of delinquency requires consideration of when judges decide to lock youths up in institutions, a topic discussed in the next chapter.

NOTES

1. The authors wish to express their appreciation to Denise Van Rooy, a UNLV student who researched and summarized these cases as part of an independent study class in the fall of 1990. She also summarized *Parham v. J.R.*, discussed in Chapter 9.

2. The term *chivalry* refers to a set of behaviors initially expected of knights in the later medieval period. Gradually, this evolved into an ideal of knighthood that stressed behavior marked by honor, fairness, generosity, and kindliness, especially to foes, the weak, the lowly, and the vanquished. Typically, women and children were included among the weak that a chivalrous knight would be expected to protect.

9

The Contemporary
Juvenile Justice System
and Girls, Part II:
Girls in Institutions

G irls who find their way into the juvenile justice system can be, and
often are, removed from their homes and placed in institutions. The
most common juvenile institutions are detention centers, which are
generally used for short-term incarceration, and training schools, ranches (or
forestry camps and farms), shelters, halfway houses, and group and foster
homes, which are generally used for longer term placement.

Since the early 1970s there has been an intense debate on the institutionalization of young people, particularly those charged with noncriminal status offenses. Previous chapters covered some of the background and the intent of
the Juvenile Justice and Delinquency Prevention Act of 1974, which, among
other things, stressed the great desirability of deinstitutionalizing youths
charged with status offenses. We have also seen that certain elements of this
landmark legislation have come under fire in recent years. This chapter looks
at the situation of girls in juvenile correctional institutions and reviews the impact of federal efforts to deinstitutionalize status offenders on the patterns of
girls' and boys' incarceration.

Table 9-1 Juveniles in Custody in Private and Public Juvenile Correctional Facilities, One-Day Count, 1991 and 1999

	1991			1999		
	Male	Female	Total	Male	Female	Total
Total	77,015	16,717	93,732	94,370	14,567	108,937
	(100%)	(100%)	(100%)	(100%)	(100%)	(100%)
Public Facilities	51,214	6,328	57,542	67,713	9,444	77,157
	(66%)	(38%)	(61%)	(72%)	(65%)	(71%)
Private Facilities	25,801	10,389	36,190	26,626	5,073	31,780
	(34%)	(62%)	(39%)	(28%)	(35%)	(29%)

SOURCE: Office of Juvenile Justice and Delinquency Prevention (1992). *Juveniles Taken into Custody: Fiscal Year 1992* (Washington, DC: U.S. Department of Justice): 31; Office of Juvenile Justice and Delinquency Prevention. "Offense Profile of Juveniles in Residential Placement by Sex, 1999 (Washington, DC: U.S. Department of Justice, 30 October, 2002).

YOUTHS IN INSTITUTIONS: A NATIONAL OVERVIEW

Number of Girls in Institutions

According to a 1999 census of juvenile correctional facilities (confined in detention, correctional, and shelter facilities, the most recent data available), there were a total of 108,937 youths confined. Of these, 14,567 (13%) were females. Females were most likely to be incarcerated in private facilities rather than public institutions, however. In these institutions females constituted 16 percent of those in custody, whereas in public facilities they were 12 percent of the total (see Table 9-1). The total confined (one-day count) in both public and private institutions represents a 16 percent increase over 1991. The total for girls represents a decrease of about 13 percent since 1991, whereas the total for boys constitutes an increase of 23 percent since 1991. This represents a noteworthy drop from the increases reported in earlier editions of this book. Part of the explanation lies in the decrease in the number of girls sent to private institutions, a drop of 51 percent since 1991. The number of girls in public institutions increased, however, by about 49 percent during this time period.

Throughout the 1980s there was an overall increase in youth correctional populations, especially in private facilities. Throughout this period of time there was a rather modest increase in the total number of facilities. Most of these facilities have been described as having an "institutional" environment (Flanagan & McGarrell, 1986: 517; Bureau of Justice Statistics, 1989: 40–41; Jamieson & Flanagan, 1989: 390; Allen-Hagen, 1991: 3; Austin et al., 1995).

Perhaps the most interesting development in juvenile correctional populations has been the decline in those held in private facilities, as noted above, reversing a previous trend. Indeed, in 1991 over 36,000 youths were being held in for-profit institutions, which at that time represented an increase of 15 percent from 1983. The decade of the 1990s, however, witnessed a decline of 13 percent.

The presence of girls in juvenile institutions is an important facet of their experience with juvenile justice. The fact that fewer girls than boys end up in such institutions is one way to look at these numbers. Another way is to look at the numbers of adult women in jails and prisons, whereby a slightly different picture emerges. Essentially, adult women have always been dramatically underrepresented among persons in custody; the same cannot be said about girls. In 1999, for example, adult women constituted 6.6 percent of the persons held in prisons, up from only 3.6 percent in 1976 (Shelden & Brown, 2003: 368). Girls, as we have seen, were about 13 percent of those held in juvenile correctional institutions in 1999. During the early years of the juvenile justice system, girls were an even greater proportion—frequently approaching one-fourth—of those held in juvenile correctional facilities (Cahalan, 1986: 130).

A slightly richer picture of girls in correctional institutions comes from a national snapshot of the offenses for which girls and boys were placed in correctional facilities in 1999. Table 9-2 reveals that girls are still far more likely than boys to be held for status offenses (13% vs. 3%) and for "technical violations" (mainly violations of probation or parole or some sort of court order). This latter category is important for it often represents cases of "bootstrapping" status offenders into "delinquents," thus justifying their incarceration. Fully one-fifth of the girls, but only 12 percent of the boys, fall into this category. Note also that as for crimes against the person, girls are more likely than boys to have committed a "simple assault."

Taken together, the data on girls currently being held in public institutions are clear evidence of tremendous high-level resistance to the notion that youth who have not committed any criminal act should not be held in institutions. Having said this, it would be remiss not to note that the deinstitutionalization movement has reduced the number of girls in detention centers and training schools. It may, though, have simply moved those girls into a private system of institutionalization—the mental health system. We will return to this subject later in this chapter.

Demographic Characteristics of Youths in Institutions

It is clear that the offense backgrounds of girls and boys in juvenile correctional facilities have been vastly different over the years. This quite obviously parallels the differences in offense patterns for those arrested and referred to juvenile court, as we have seen in earlier chapters. Clearly, while the status offense differentiation remains as it always has, one key difference, as noted above, is in terms of so-called "technical violations," which apply disproportionately to girls.

These patterns are similar to those discerned by earlier and more detailed research on youths in custody. In a study of over 1,800 youths in forty-two institutions, Vinter and Sarri (1976: 34–39) found that 54 percent of the females

Table 9-2. Juveniles in Residential Placement, by Sex and Offense, 1999

	Male	Female
Public Facilities		
Delinquent Offenses	99%	84%
Person	37	32
Violent Index	29	18
Other Person	8	14
Property	30	25
Index Property	25	20
Other Property	5	4
Drug	9	6
Public Order	10	8
Technical Violation	12	23
Status Offenses	1	6
Total	100%	100%
Private Facilities		
Delinquent Offenses	93%	76%
Person	32	27
Violent Index	21	9
Other Person	11	17
Property	30	22
Index Property	25	19
Other Property	5	3
Drug	10	7
Public Order	11	6
Technical Violation	10	15
Status Offenses	7	24
Total	100%	100%

SOURCE: OJJDP Statistics Briefing Book. On-line (www.ojjdp.ncjrs.org/pjstatbb/qa178.html), October 30, 2002.

and 27 percent of the males had been committed for status offenses and that most of the status offenses of the girls were running away and incorrigibility. Similarly, a national study of youths in training schools between 1972 and 1974 (Selo, 1979) examined reasons for their incarceration; 39 percent of the girls self-reported status offenses, compared with 18 percent of the boys. Boys were far more likely than girls to be incarcerated for "serious person and property crimes": 72 percent and 32 percent, respectively.

Selo (1979) also found significant differences in offense categories. For example, when girls were committed for drug offenses, it was most often for possession of marijuana or hashish rather than possession of hard drugs or the sale

of drugs, as was the case for boys (Selo, 1979: 152). The difference was significant because 21 percent of the girls and 7 percent of the boys were being held
for drug offenses.

Gender differences were also found in the status offense category. Girls
were disproportionately incarcerated for running away from home: 57 percent
of the female status offenders were incarcerated for that reason. In contrast,
over half the boys were institutionalized because of "school problems," compared to only 16 percent of the girls. This gender-based pattern held for black
status offenders as well (Selo, 1979: 153).

Data from European countries indicate that offense differences parallel
those in the United States. For instance, in Portugal in 1984, 41 percent of the
girl status offenders and only 17 percent of the boy status offenders were
placed in institutions. In England and Wales, of the girls sentenced during
1982, about 60 percent were sentenced for status offenses (specifically, being in
"moral danger" and "beyond control"), compared with only about 15 percent
of the boys. The 1982 figures represent increases from 1978.

Some clear gender differences also emerge between "public" and "private"
facilities. In 1987 girls constituted 14 percent of juveniles held in public institutions, compared with 31 percent in private institutions; another way of looking at this is to say that of girls held in facilities of any sort, 58.6 percent are
held in private facilities. In 1991, girls represented only 11 percent of those in
public institutions, but about 29 percent in private institutions. Altogether, 62
percent of the incarcerated girls were in private facilities (see Table 9-1).

There are major ethnic differences in the populations of these institutions as well; whites constituted about 44 percent of juveniles held in public
institutions in 1987 and 63 percent of those held in private facilities
(Jamieson & Flanagan, 1989: 595); by 1989, whites had fallen to only 39.5
percent of those in public facilities (Allen-Hagen, 1991: 3). Other, more detailed work on this issue suggests that there is a significant interaction between gender and ethnicity in incarceration rates. In addition, where an
increase has occurred in incarceration of youths, it has apparently been in the
incarceration of both male and female minority youths (Krisberg et al.,
1986). In 1982, for example, the ratio of black male incarceration rates to
white male incarceration rates was 4.4:1; Hispanic to white was 2.6:1. For
girls, a similar though less extreme pattern was found: black to white, 2.6:1,
and Hispanic to white, 1.1:1 (16–17).

A study by the National Council on Crime and Delinquency (NCCD) in
the early 1990s examined data on the prevalence rates of juveniles incarcerated in New York. The study showed that African American youths had an
overall 1 in 45 chance of being incarcerated before their eighteenth birthday,
compared with a 1 in 85 chance for Hispanic youths and a 1 in 285 chance
for white youths. African American males had the greatest chance, at 1 in 25,
compared to Hispanic males (1 in 48) and white males (1 in 172). Among females, African Americans had the highest chance of being incarcerated (a 1 in
188 chance), in contrast to Hispanic females (1 in 454) and white females (1
in 1,000). Similar results were found in fifteen other states. Interestingly,

though, there were some wide variations among states. For instance, the chance of an African American male being incarcerated ranged from a high of 13.92 percent (a 1 in 7 chance) in Utah to a low of 3.54 in Louisiana (a 1 in 28 chance). Overall, for all youths, the lowest rate was found in Massachusetts (.56% or 1 in 179 chance) and the highest rate in Ohio (1.55% or 1 in 65 chance). For girls in general, the state with the highest rate was Tennessee (.29% or 1 in 345 chance), while the lowest was found in Massachusetts (.04% or 1 in 2,500 chance). For virtually all states, white females had the lowest chance of being incarcerated and African American females had the highest chance (NCCD, 1993: 6).

There are also major gender differences in the offenses or activities that bring youth into private facilities. The vast majority of girls (87 percent, up from 85 percent in 1987) in private facilities are being held for nondelinquent offenses including status offenses, dependency, neglect, and as a consequence of "voluntary" admissions; less than half the boys (49.3 percent, down from 57.5 percent in 1987) are being held for these reasons, with the remainder being held for criminal offenses (OJJDP, 1992: 39; see also Table 9-2).

In 1991, "voluntary" admissions (juveniles admitted without having been adjudicated in the juvenile court) constituted 26.5 percent of girls' admissions to private facilities and less than 15 percent of boys' admissions; the figures in 1987 were 23.1 percent and 17 percent, respectively. However, it is important to note here that "voluntary" does not necessarily imply that the youths consented to admission; indeed, most of these "voluntary" admissions were not labeled as "self-admitted" but as "referred" admissions (Jamieson & Flanagan, 1989: 596). Parents, in many instances, can "volunteer" their children to these kinds of facilities (Schwartz, Jackson-Beeck, & Anderson, 1984). It should be noted that youths are held in private facilities considerably longer on average than their counterparts in public facilities. It should also be noted that current data on youth in institutions no longer show how many are in the "voluntary" category. We have learned, however, that as of October 1999 an estimated 612 youths (435 delinquents and 177 status offenders) were being held under "diversion agreements" in the country, meaning that they are placed out of their homes into various local community facilities. The gender breakdown is not known from these data (Sickmund, 2003).

In general, these figures show increasing numbers of girls incarcerated in institutions, usually for less serious offenses than boys. This is especially the case for those in private institutions, where such numbers have been on the rise in recent years. Most girls, though, are held in private facilities, where there is an even greater likelihood of their having been committed for a status offense (or no offense at all).

These figures tell us that the deinstitutionalization of status offenders is less than complete, particularly when it comes to girls. The figures also suggest a shift of girls to private facilities. Numbers, though, are often rather sterile. What sorts of girls are in detention centers and training schools? What are the conditions there? And what has happened to the girls shifted from public to private facilities?

CHARACTERISTICS OF GIRLS
IN CORRECTIONAL FACILITIES

According to a 1988 national study of girls in correctional settings conducted by the American Correctional Association (1990), roughly half the girls were white (50.5%), nearly a third were black or partly black (31.7%), 6.2 percent were Hispanic, and 7.7 percent were Native American (American Correctional Association, 1990: 47). Most were between sixteen and seventeen years of age, and 18.6 percent were mothers at the time of their incarceration.

Their backgrounds present a familiar picture. A very large proportion (61.2%) had experienced physical abuse, with nearly half reporting on more than ten occasions. Many had reported the abuse, but the majority said that either nothing changed (29.9%) or that the reporting just made things worse (25.3%). Nearly as many (54.3%) had undergone sexual abuse, and for most it was not an isolated incident; one third said it had happened three to ten times, and 27.4 percent said that it had happened eleven times or more. Most were nine years of age or younger when the abuse began. Again, while most reported the sexual abuse (68.1%), the reporting tended to bring about no change or to make things worse.

The majority had run away from home (80.7%), and of those, 39 percent had run away ten or more times. Over half (53.8%) said they had attempted suicide, and when asked the reason, they said because they "felt no one cared." Many girls reported drug use, particularly alcohol, marijuana, "speed," and cocaine. Half had been arrested ten or more times, and over one third had been incarcerated ten or more times (both figures were far higher than comparable figures in the same study for adult women who were in prison) (30). Girls in correctional establishments reported that their first arrests were typically for running away from home (20.5%) or for larceny–theft (25.0%). The offenses for which they were currently incarcerated were more varied, but the most significant were probation or parole violation (14.6%), aggravated assault (9.5%), larceny–theft (9.0%), and running away (6.5%) (31). The large number of girls incarcerated for probation or parole violation is possibly a measure of new efforts to bootstrap status offenders into delinquents by incarcerating them for these offenses (47–71).

GIRLS IN DETENTION

Although it seemed obvious to some researchers that girls were discriminated against at the point of detention decisions (see Conway & Bogdan, 1977; Chesney-Lind, 1973, 1978), some researchers have disputed the assertion (see Teilmann & Landry, 1981). The dispute involves whether—if the effect of offense is statistically controlled for—girls are still more likely than boys to be detained.

Unfortunately, as noted earlier, such methodologies both obscure and statistically segregate the elements in the juvenile justice system that make girls uniquely vulnerable to harsh sanctions and then conclude that there is no evidence of bias against women. We know that the type of offenses for which girls are arrested—particularly the offenses of running away and ungovernability—increase the likelihood of their detention. The history of girls' detention makes it clear that this pattern has been and is tied to the desire to control girls' sexuality (Odem & Schlossman, 1991).

Much of the logic of girls' detention is explained by the paternalistic ideology of the juvenile justice system. Police and court officials, like good parents, feel the need to "protect" their "daughters"—usually from sexual experimentation or other dangers on the streets. And although arguments about the lack of alternative placements for young people who cannot return home are sometimes advanced, a national study done in the 1970s of the placement of youth found substantial numbers of girls in institutional populations compared with the number of girls in day treatment programs or group homes. Vinter et al. (1976) found that although girls were in the minority overall (constituting 28 percent of the sample), they were proportionally more likely to be found in either training schools or group homes, and boys were more likely to be found in day treatment programs. More recent research by the Youth Law Center in California found girls underrepresented in intermediate programs such as camps because these programs generally exist only for boys (Shauffer & Shotten, 1987: 55). Current national data on the placement of girls on public ranches, on public farms, and in forestry camps show that although the numbers are up, girls in 1985 constituted only 6 percent of those enrolled in this type of program, a proportion unchanged from 1975 (Bureau of Justice Statistics, 1989: 45).

The conditions in the nation's detention facilities are by no means characterized by the protective atmosphere described by proponents of the practice of detaining young women. One review of conditions in these facilities conducted by the American Bar Association in the late 1970s concluded the following:

> We found conditions for young women equally unsuitable: the facilities had cells with only a bed and a blanket and no toilet; limited or no opportunities for recreation; few chances to be in the company of other inmates and long periods behind locked doors. The impressions of one detained girl describe the problem more vividly: I thought I was going crazy for a while just being locked up all the time. . . . I was up on the upper floor because the boys were down below, and I was just locked up in the day and night. And the only time I saw anybody was when they brought my food up to me. (Female Offender Resource Center, 1977: 11)

Besides the jail-like atmosphere that confronts young people held in detention facilities, young women in the past underwent an extra and significant violation of their civil rights: pelvic examinations and, more recently, vaginal searches. Elizabeth Gold (1971: 583) reported that all young women brought before the family court in the early 1970s in New York were subjected to a vaginal smear procedure, even young women brought before the court for nonsexual offenses. Similarly, in Philadelphia each young woman who entered the Youth Study Center during roughly the same period, regardless of age, had to submit to an internal examination. Given the problem of venereal disease among teenagers, this procedure might seem reasonable, but it must be remembered that these examinations took place in an institutional setting and in concert with other entry rituals, and hence were depersonalizing.

One detention center surveyed by the National Council of Jewish women, for example, required all young women to undergo a pelvic examination "to determine if they are pregnant" and at the same time required all detainees to submit to a Cuprex Delouse test, "where a yellow burning substance [is] sprayed on bodies. This is done in a group" (Wakin, 1975: 45). The director of the Philadelphia Youth Study Center was more specific about the administration of the pelvic examination required of all women who entered his institution: "We do put a girl on the table in the stirrups and we do have a smear. . . . We do have a swab. You go in and get a smear." When he was questioned about whether young women who refused to undergo the pelvic examination would be placed in solitary confinement ("medical lock-up"), he responded, "Yes, we may have to" (Schwartz, nd).

At least three lawsuits have been filed on behalf of girls who did not wish to submit to these internal examinations. In one, a young girl was examined internally while she was in a detention center for four days awaiting trial. Her attorney said, "The doctor had reported that she was not a virgin and that she was promiscuous. She did not have venereal disease. This report was sent to [the young girl's parochial] school" (Forer, 1970: 125). The same attorney told of a thirteen-year-old girl who had been arrested and detained after throwing a snowball at a neighbor: "She refused, at intake, to submit to an internal examination and continued to resist this until, after two weeks in solitary confinement, the matrons held her legs and the doctor made the examination" (126). Kenneth Wooden (1976: 121), in his review of juvenile justice systems nationwide, commented as follows:

> Examinations for venereal disease are carried out with outrageous frequency. Young ladies in custody have been known to undergo as many as three and four pelvic exams for the disease. At some facilities, ten- and eleven-year-olds are forced to submit to a vaginal each time they are transferred to a new facility, even though they have not been released between placement. In one town in Louisiana, two detectives complained to me about the county coroner, who forcefully examined all runaways: "You know when he is working because you can hear the young girls screaming at the other end of the hall."

An eloquent expression of the rage young girls feel at a pelvic examination can be found in Gayl Jones's (1980: 128) short essay titled "Asylum" (from a collection of writings of African American women):

> When the doctor coming? When I'm getting examined? They don't say nothing all these white nurses. They walk around in cardboard shoes and grin in my face. They take me in this little room and sit me up on a table

and tell me to take my clothes off. I tell them I won't take them off till the doctor come. Then one of them says to the other, You want to go get the orderly? She might hurt herself. . . . You know, I don't belong here, I start to say, but don't I just watch her standing up there. The doctor will come in a few minutes, she says. I nod my head. They're going to give me a physical examination first. I'm up on the table but I'm not going to take my clothes off. . . . I don't say nothing. I know one thing. He ain't examining me down there. He can examine me anywhere else he want to, but he ain't touching me down there.

From *White Rat: Short Stories*, by Gayl Jones. Copyright © 1971, 1973, 1975, 1977 by Gayl Jones. Reprinted by permission of Random House Inc.

Accounts suggest that blanket administration of pelvic examinations occurred well into the 1970s in various parts of the United States. In the context of entry into detention, it is a degrading experience and probably a violation of the right of privacy. More important, however justified such a procedure might be from a medical standpoint, the routine, and particularly repeated, administration of pelvic examinations and tests for venereal disease and pregnancy also signals that court personnel still tend to equate all female delinquency with sexuality. This point is not simply the product of idle speculation. The practice of administering pelvic examinations has a long history in the juvenile justice system, and the purpose of the examinations in the early years was not obscure in the least (Chesney-Lind, 1971; Odem & Schlossman, 1991). Most recently, justification has shifted from one of concern about venereal disease to a concern about security within facilities. The most controversial aspect of the practice has been the searches, including visual and physical cavity searches, of women and girls in police custody. Instances have included a Chicago high school girl taken into custody for not having a hall pass, a young woman (seven months pregnant) in Dayton, Ohio, wrongly arrested on a void juvenile misdemeanor warrant, and a Cincinnati woman arrested for not having a license for her dog (Satchell, 1982: 2).

Such searches have even been conducted on school grounds (as in the case of a thirteen-year-old girl who underwent a "nude search" after a police sniffer dog behaved as if the girl had drugs in her possession, which she did not) and in private residences (as in the case of two girls, thirteen and fifteen, who were strip-searched by police after they had broken into their father's home looking for marijuana) (Satchell, 1982: 12).

Allegations abound that strip searches are conducted in a degrading and unhygienic fashion and not infrequently in the presence of male officers (Satchell, 1982: 11). Exactly how degrading these searches are can be seen in the comments of a young Honolulu woman who told one of the authors that she will "never forget" the night that she was admitted to the local detention facility in the late 1970s: "She made me go into a cold cement shower stall with cold water with no shower curtain. Then she made me bend over and she stuck her finger in me and then she took the finger and stuck it in my mouth."

The young woman was, at the time, a fourteen-year-old arrested for running away from home. Perhaps because of such conditions and actions, the Honolulu Detention Home has stopped conducting routine cavity searches on admission and has also stopped routine admission of status offenders.

It is unfortunate that most of the large-scale studies of conditions in detention centers were conducted in the early to middle 1970s, so it is unknown whether such examinations are still occurring. There has been a considerable falloff in information about conditions of detention centers, but enough has been learned from selected states to indicate that cause for concern remains.

The main detention center in Honolulu, for example, has been a subject of controversy. In the late 1970s allegations about poor conditions at the facility prompted the chief judge of the jurisdiction to appoint a panel of court officials and public citizens to investigate and recommend changes. The committee's final report concluded that a "lack of physical safety" existed within the facility, inadequate food promoted fights between wards, programs and activities were insufficient, minor and seriously delinquent youths needed to be separated, and the physical plant was in need of repair (Secure Custody Committee Report, Part II, 1981). Many positive changes ensued, but by the mid-1980s many of the same problems as well as new ones surfaced—among them overcrowding and the inappropriate use of the facility to hold status offenders and abused and neglected youths who had run away from placement. In 1987 a consultant said the facility was "badly in need of replacement" and that "pure status offenders" (truants) and "bootstrapped" status offenders (technical violators of a court order) were inappropriately detained. Often, status offenders stayed longer in secure detention than delinquents. Officials maintained that there were not enough available resources, particularly for youths in conflict with their families, repeated runaways, and youths (often girls) at risk of sexual exploitation (DeMuro, 1987: 17).

The Youth Law Center uncovered a disturbing practice in a detention center in a middle-class California community. The center regularly holds youths, both male and female, identified as "disruptive" in a six-by-eight-foot rubber room with a hole in the floor instead of a normal toilet. Youths are now held there for only twenty-four hours, but the Youth Law Center had reports of longer stays before its investigation. If a young person continued to be disruptive in the rubber room, he or she was taken into another room to be stripped and have hands and feet tied with cloth straps to metal rings attached to the edges of a bed. The Youth Law Center had reports of youths restrained in such fashion for four to five hours.

Looking at the rate of detention among girls, the usual pattern persists, and the familiar theme emerges. As noted in Table 9-3, in 1999 four times more girls than boys (8% vs. 2%) were being held for status offenses. Further, girls were much more likely (30% vs. 21%) to be held for "technical violations."

Although somewhat dated, a study of girls committed to or in state care in Virginia in the early 1990s illustrates some of the problems mentioned above, especially the phenomenon of "bootstrapping." This study found that minority girls, who make up about 26 percent of Virginia's population, constitute half of those committed to a secure facility. The most frequent offense type com-

Table 9-3. Juveniles Detained in Public
Facilities, by Offense and Gender, 1999

Most Serious Offense	Males	Females
Person	29%	28%
Violent Crime Index	20	12
Other Person	9	15
Property	27	21
Property Crime Index	22	17
Other Property	5	4
Drug	10	6
Public Order	11	7
Technical Violation	21	30
Status Offenses	2	8
Total	100%	100%

SOURCE: Sickmund, M. and Y. Wan. 2001. "Census of
Juveniles in Residential Placement Databook. On-line
(www.ojjdp.ncjrs.org/pjstatbb/cjrp).

mitted by these girls was misdemeanor offenses, followed by status offenses. Very revealing, though, were the responses of the probation counselors to the query that they rank the reason for the girls' commitments. Most common was "probation violation," followed by "repeated runaway," "self-victimization," and "failure to participate in ordered treatment/service." Far down on the list were "punishment" and "heinous violent crime" (Task Force on Juvenile Offenders, 1991: 2–3).

These patterns have turned up in other countries as well. A study in Canada found that in 1991, "one in four charges laid against young females are against the administration of justice; the rate is one in six for males" (Reitsma-Street, 1993: 445). In Canada, violation of a court order or failure to comply with decisions of the youth administration of justice is described as "offenses against the administration of justice" or, stated more simply, "bootstrapping" Canadian style.

Two studies, both focusing on San Francisco, highlight the double standard treatment of girls within the juvenile justice system. The first comes from a 1996 study specifically focusing on adolescent girls (Schaffner, Shick, & Shorter, 1996). The authors start their report by noting that in the girls' unit of the local juvenile detention center there were 30 placed in a facility equipped to handle 22. This report noted, sadly, that the conclusion of a 1992 report that the needs of adolescent girls are "unexamined, untreated, and invalidated by both the system charged with serving them and by their own community and family support structures" remained true in 1996. The survey by Schaffner, Shick, and Shorter found that between 1990 and 1994 the number of girls in detention went up by 121 percent. Not surprisingly, the percentage of minority girls in out-of-home placements in San Francisco in May 1995 exceeded white girls, as fully 60 percent were African American, while another 16 percent were Hispanic. In short, just over three-fourths of those placed were minorities.

The authors of the study also examined the social context of the offenses these girls were charged with. They noted the special role of drug offenses, noting that many of them got caught up in the "crack" phenomenon during the late 1980s and early 1990s. These girls were heavily recruited by older males to serve as "lookouts" or to handle actual drug sales on the streets. The authors noted also that many of these young girls were the girlfriends of older males and were "convinced to take the physical and legal risks of handling the drugs" because of the perceived lighter penalties the girls would receive. The authors also noted that most of the girls had become involved in gang activity, often in association with their boyfriends. Most of the violent crimes girls were charged with involved males, at least indirectly, as in a case where one girl physically attacked another girl for kissing her boyfriend or "dissin" her boyfriend's gang (Schaffner et al., 1996: 8). Not surprisingly, many of these girls had experienced a great deal of abuse, both within their homes and at the hands of their boyfriends. But instead of receiving much-needed services to address their concerns, the local detention center and institutional placement was the disposition in the majority of their cases.

A more recent study of detention practices in San Francisco reaffirmed the above study (Macallair & Males, 2000). The study found that, despite a "reform" administration dedicated to juvenile justice issues beginning in 1996 (with a $20 million grant from the federal government), juveniles continue to be detained at excessively high rates. For instance, in contrast to a detention rate of 378 per 1,000 bookings in the mid-1980s, detention rates for 1999 were 856 per 1,000 arrests. The average daily population of the local detention center went from 114 between 1984 and 1986 to 124 between 1996 and 1998, with a slight drop to 119 in 1999.

More important for our purposes in this chapter, what fueled these increases more than any other factor was the increase in the detention rates for girls. Whereas in 1988 only 14 percent of those detained were girls, by 1999 the proportion nearly doubled to 24 percent! While the overall proportion of black juveniles declined from 62 percent to 51 percent during this period (although this percentage represented a slight increase from 49 percent in 1992), the proportion of Hispanics more than doubled from 8 percent to 17 percent. The proportion of Asians detained also increased from 10 percent in 1988 to 16 percent in 1999.

All of the above changes took place during a time when serious crime was dropping in the San Francisco area. Total arrests between 1992 and 1999, for instance, decreased by 9 percent, whereas the number detained went up by 18 percent. The number of girls detained went up by 33 percent during this time period, and their detention rate (per 100,000) went up by 54 percent (in contrast, the detention rate for males decreased by 21 percent). The arrest rate for girls increased by 15 percent, compared to a 31 percent decrease in the arrest rate for boys. More dramatically, the largest increases in detention rates were for minority girls. The detention rate for African American girls went up by 107 percent between 1992 and 1999. Hispanic girls saw their detention rate go up by 188 percent, while the rate for Pacific Islander girls increased by 157 percent during this time period. The kinds of crimes that increased the most for girls, as measured by arrests, were robbery, assaults, and drug involvement.

Macallair and Males come right to the point in their conclusion, remarking that "girls of color account for all of San Francisco's juvenile detention booking increase from 1992 to 1999" (2000: 11). They note that while arrests for robbery and assaults for girls increased, boys' arrests for these crimes went down, and further that drug arrests for girls went up but went down for boys. Overall, between 1992 and 1999, violent felonies reported to the police went down by 56 percent, while property crimes declined by 45 percent. Overall juvenile crime rates declined, and it is important to note also that there was a decline in juvenile commitments to both local and state institutions (represented by the Log Cabin Ranch and California Youth Authority, respectively). The authors also came up with the sobering conclusion that despite "reforms" during the administration of Mayor Willie Brown, "it appears a wider pool of lower risk youths were simply absorbed into the system in order to keep juvenile hall [the local detention center] and the rolls of new programs filled. Such a process is known in corrections as net widening" (Macallair & Males, 2000: 15). Such "net widening" has obviously impacted girls and minorities more than white males.

Such concerns are likely of great significance, particularly since national data indicate that between 1989 and 1998, detentions involving girls increased by 56% compared to a 20% increase in boys' detentions (Harms, 2002: 1). This same national study attributed the "large increase" in the detention of girls to "the growth in the number of delinquency cases involving females charged with person offenses" (Harms, 2002:1). Moreover, these detention rates underline the importance of examining racial differences and discrimination. A study by the American Bar Association and the National Bar Association (2001) reported that half of the girls in secure detention in the U.S. are African American and 13% are Latina. White girls account for only one-third of the girls in secure detention although they make up 65% of those in the at-risk population. "Seven of every 10 cases involving white girls are dismissed, compared with 3 of every 10 cases for African American girls" (2001:22).

It appears that in many parts of the country, youths who have committed somewhat minor offenses are still being detained in closed facilities. Studies of the impact of detention on further processing suggest that detention, by itself, has a disturbing self-fulfilling effect. Detained youths tend to be processed further into the juvenile justice system and are more likely to be adjudicated delinquent than youths with similar offense profiles who are not detained (Frazier, Bishop, & Cochran, 1986; McCarthy, 1987).

GIRLS IN ADULT JAILS

The Annual Survey of Jails revealed that in 1991 there were 60,181 juvenile admissions to the nation's jails; 11.5 percent (6,924) of the admissions were of girls (Bureau of Justice Statistics, 1995: 2). During the same period (1991), adult women constituted 9.3 percent of those in jail (Bureau of Justice Statistics,

1995: 2). The figures on girls' admissions to adult jails do, though, represent a 19 percent decrease since 1990, which is encouraging. However, congressional proposals for modifying the "jail removal" mandates of the Juvenile Justice and Delinquency Prevention Act of 1974, if passed, would make it easier for states to jail youths with adults (Coalition for Juvenile Justice, 1996: 4); in fact, the recent re-authorization does increase the amount of time youth in rural areas can be kept in adult facilities from 24 to 48 hours (Doi, 2002:1).

The most recent data show that as of 2001 there were a total of 7,613 juveniles in adult jails, representing a sharp increase of 231 percent since 1990 (U.S. Department of Justice, 2001). The rate (per 100,000 children aged 5–17) was 5.1 in 1990, but 14.8 in 2001, representing an increase of 190 percent. It should be noted, however, that the 2001 numbers represent a decline from a high of 9,458 in 1999 (a rate of 18.3). The gender breakdown is not shown in this source. However, a 2000 report on children in jails found that in 1997 three percent of the 5,400 juveniles were girls (Austin, Johnson, & Gregoriou, 2000).

For this reason, consideration of the specific problems that girls encounter in adult jails is all the more salient. For juveniles in general, there is a far greater risk to their safety and well-being, not just from adults who may be there with them, but from other juveniles as well. More specifically, compared to those held in juvenile detention facilities, children in adult jails are more than seven times more likely to commit suicide, five times more likely to be sexually assaulted, twice as likely to be beaten by a staff member, and about 50 percent more likely to be attacked with a weapon. Moreover, services for such juveniles are rarely available, especially for girls (Sentencing Project, 2000).

A recent report by Human Rights Watch on children in jail in Maryland (1999) found that about 200–300 children are in adult jails on any given day. Between one-half and two-thirds of the children held in Maryland's jails are in the Baltimore City Detention Center, described as a "decaying facility nearly two hundred years old."

On the whole, national data on the offense characteristics of girls in jail are extremely sketchy. Quite often, studies of jail populations require that inmates be incarcerated for a considerable period of time to be counted. One example of this sort of research is a national survey of inmates of local jails that was conducted in 1983 (Bureau of Justice Statistics, 1985a). However, because only seventy-six persons under eighteen qualified for inclusion (and of these only twenty-one were girls), it is impossible to draw firm conclusions. A review of youths in adult jails in Minnesota during 1985 reveals that girls represented 20 percent of the total (Schwartz, Harris, & Levi, 1987: 5). Over one-third of the girls (35.3%) were jailed for status offenses, compared with only 13.8 percent of the jailed boys; 1.6 percent of the girls and 3.7 percent of the boys were in jail for violent index crimes. Most of the boys had been charged with index property crimes (35.8%).

Data on girls incarcerated in 1985 in the jail in Long Beach, California, reveal that girls constituted 28 percent of the 4,511 youths held in that facility. Of these, 16 percent were status offenders, and 21 percent were classified as "dependent youth" (abused and neglected). Data from the Los Angeles jail, which does not hold status offenders but does hold dependent or neglected youths, tell us that in 1985 girls composed 17.8 percent of all admissions of youths under eighteen (Department of Youth Authority, 1986: 12).

More detailed information comes from Kentucky, where girls represented 19.3 percent of the 290 youths admitted to Oldham County Jail during 1982 (*Rita Horn et al. v. Oldham County,* 1983). Only about 2 percent of the girls, but 15.4 percent of the boys, were incarcerated for felonies, and nearly 20 percent of the girls but less than 1 percent of the boys were incarcerated for status offenses. Girls also tended to be younger than boys: only 25 percent were seventeen years of age, compared with half the boys; in fact, 23.2 percent were thirteen or fourteen years of age. Girls remained in this jail about the same length of time as did boys, despite their less serious offenses; 44.9 percent of the boys but only 37.5 percent of the girls stayed just one day.

An earlier study on girls in the jails of Kentucky (Roche & Richart, 1981) covered the late 1970s to the early 1980s. Despite the fact that the jailing of status offenders declined by about 50 percent, the researchers found that over one thousand girls were jailed during the first six months of 1980 (20.8 percent of all jail admissions). Concerning status offenders, 22.6 percent of the girls were placed in jail on such charges, compared with only 5.1 percent of the boys (16). Further, girls were more likely than boys to be jailed on misdemeanor charges (20.9 percent and 8.6 percent, respectively); boys were more likely to be jailed for felonies.

Roche and Richart (1981: 13) also found that girls in jail tended to be younger than their male counterparts; the mean ages were 15.4 and 16.1 years, respectively. Finally, despite their less serious offenses, girls were far less likely than boys to stay in Kentucky jails one day or less; only slightly over a third of the girls but two-thirds of the boys were released after that minimal time. Female status offenders remained in jail for an average of 2.9 days, compared with 2.1 days for those charged with drug or alcohol offenses. Data from several other states tend to confirm the above findings. In Ohio in 1980, for instance, 41.9 percent of the girls and only 15.6 percent of the boys in jail were there for status offenses (*Deborah Doe et al. v. Lloyd W. Burwell et al.,* 1981). In North Dakota and Idaho, girl status offenders also outnumber boys by a wide margin (Community Research Associates, 1983; Arnts, 1986).

Conditions for Girls in Jail

It has long been recognized that adult women in jail are housed under more restrictive and harsher conditions than men. This is doubly true for girls. In the attempt to protect them from contact and abuse from adult inmates, girls, particularly those housed in sexually integrated facilities, are often held in what amounts to solitary confinement (Community Research Associates, 1983: 3).

A chilling example of what can happen to girls placed for even a few days in an adult jail graphically illustrates the problems associated with the holding of girls in such isolation. On August 25, 1984, at 12:30 a.m., fifteen-year-old Kathy Robbins was arrested as a runaway. Handcuffed and taken to the fifty-four-year-old Glenn County (California) Jail, she was refused permission to phone her mother. After being strip-searched and dressed in a jail-issued jump-suit, she was placed in a twelve-by-twelve-foot cell with a solid steel door that had a three-by-six-inch mesh window. It was the male juvenile cell, and she was held there in virtual isolation until her detention hearing on the morning of August 29. At the hearing her probation officer recommended that she be held in custody until September 7; the court ordered that the matter be continued until a later date and that Robbins remain incarcerated at the jail. That afternoon she was found unconscious, hanging from the guardrail of the top bunk bed, and was pronounced dead a few hours later.

Robbins had physical evidence of previous suicide attempts at the time of her jailing. Jailers had denied her all but one short visit with her mother, and they had refused to provide her with reading material brought to the jail by her mother. At the time she was incarcerated, there was space available at a nearby group home, but she was not taken there (*Lillian Robbins v. County of Glenn, California, et al.*, 1985). The suicide grimly highlights both the terrible consequences that can attend the jailing of youths and some of the special problems confronted by girls in jail in the United States. Chief among the latter are isolation and lack of supervision.

Conditions in adult jails are particularly dangerous for girls whose backgrounds of sexual and physical abuse make them more vulnerable to depression and self-destructive behavior (Browne & Finkelhor, 1986). The suicide rate for youths in jail is 4.6 times higher than the suicide rate for youths in the general population; remarkably, it is 7.7 times the rate for youths in juvenile detention centers. The latter figure is particularly striking because youths tend to stay an average of seventeen days in detention centers and only seven days in adult jails (Community Research Associates, 1983: 2). The difference is attributed to the greater degree of supervision in detention centers. The example just given is not an isolated incident; many similar incidents have resulted in lawsuits (e.g., *Johnnie K. et al. v. The County of Curry, New Mexico, et al.*, 1982; Children's Defense Fund, 1976; Wooden, 1976; Soler, 1983).

The Baltimore City Detention Center (see p. 218) is described by Human Rights Watch in the following terms. In this jail, children "spend their days in grim cells lacking direct natural lighting and crawling with cockroaches, rodents, and other vermin. Ineffective heating and poor ventilation offer little relief from the heat of the summer months and the chill of the winter" (Human Rights Watch, 1999: ch. 1, p. 2). Violence in this jail is commonplace and is often supported by some of the guards.

Although there are only a handful of girls (about five to ten on any given day, out of a total of about 150), they are generally held in almost total isolation. These girls are usually housed in Dormitory M of the Women's Detention Center. Although at the time of the visit by researchers from Human Rights Watch the girls were separated from adults, they found that the adult women could be heard very clearly through the walls. The researchers discovered that the girls had to walk by three or four adult dorms every time they go to school, go to the clinic, and go to recreation outside of the dorm. Human Rights Watch described the girls' living area as follows (1999: ch. 4, p. 4):

Within the section [where the girls stay], a series of small single cells, each with a solid metal door fitted with a feeding slot, open onto a passageway. A large fan was placed at one end of the passageway. A minimally furnished dayroom at the other end has two doors with small plexiglass windows. These windows are the only windows in the entire section, meaning that those housed in the section are deprived of natural light altogether. The dayroom has a telephone. A grimy shower is also located in the dayroom, with plastic curtains to afford some small measure of privacy for those using it.

Sometimes the girls are placed in segregation units "for their own protection." The Human Rights Watch study noted that there were the usual metal cells with no exterior windows and the showers leave much to be desired, with only one operational at the time of the researchers' visit. The "workable" shower was described as "in a vile state, its moldy, torn shower curtain dangling from several hooks." Further, "the concrete around the faucets had crumbled away, exposing piping underneath; we observed cockroaches and other vermin crawling in the cracks. Most of these girls are in 'pretrial detention' and are outside of their cells for only one hour each day" (Human Rights Watch, 1999: ch. 4, p. 5).

The problems involved in girls' jail experience have much to do with their doubly disadvantaged status as females and juveniles. Because jails were developed to house adult males, they are woefully ill equipped to house juvenile females. Often, this circumstance results in solitary confinement for girls. The isolation and lack of supervision that can characterize girls' jail experience are particularly risky, given that many of these girls have histories of sexual and physical abuse.

GIRLS IN TRAINING SCHOOLS

The juvenile justice system has a long record of processing and holding females "for their own protection" (Rogers, 1972). The bias was built into the system, and its consequences, in terms of the incarceration of girls, have been dismaying.

Studies of early family-court activity indicated that virtually all the girls who appeared in family courts were charged with immorality or waywardness (Chesney-Lind, 1971; Schlossman & Wallach, 1978; Shelden, 1981; Odem, 1995). More to the point, the sanctions for such misbehavior were extremely severe. For example, in Chicago, where the first family court was founded, half of the girl delinquents but only one-fifth of the boy delinquents were sent to reformatories between 1899 and 1909; family courts elsewhere showed similar patterns well into the 20th century.

Although less dramatic than such proportions, the girls' share of the population of public juvenile correctional facilities suggested by national statistics did increase from 1880 (when girls were 19 percent of the institutionalized population) to 1923 (when girls were 28 percent). By 1950, girls were 34 percent of the total, and in 1960, 27 percent. The comparable figure in 1980 was 19 percent (Cahalan, 1986: 130), and in 1987 about 11 percent (Schwartz, Steketee, & Schneider, 1990).

Recall also that large numbers of reformatories and training schools for girls were established during the early years of the juvenile court as places of "rescue and reform" (Schlossman & Wallach, 1978). The administrators of the early institutions were obsessed with precocious female sexuality, and their intention was to isolate the girls from the boys until the former were of marriageable age and to occupy them in domestic pursuits during their sometimes lengthy incarcerations (Brenzel, 1983). The links between these attitudes and those of juvenile courts some decades later are, of course, arguable, but studies of the environment of training schools conducted in the last few decades do not indicate that major changes have occurred—with the exception of a sharp decline in the number of girls sentenced to these facilities in the late 1970s.

A national survey of training schools conducted in the early 1970s shows the effects of this legacy. Researchers talked to 1,425 youths in sixteen randomly selected institutions in eleven states between 1972 and 1974 as part of the National Assessment of Juvenile Corrections. They found that although the youths had many concerns in common, there were also considerable gender differences in some areas. For example, there was "tremendous dissatisfaction with the quality of food and the availability of snacks when youth were hungry," but the girls were particularly concerned about weight gain due to starches (Selo, 1979: 160). Girls were also more concerned than boys about lack of privacy and about proper medical and dental care.

Researchers also heard from the youths that little attention was given to sex education and contraception while simultaneously excessive attention was given to other aspects of girls' sexual behavior. Selo noted that nurses at one institution urged staff to keep a record of girls' menstrual periods to detect possible pregnancies, and to make sure that if a girl requested a sanitary napkin that "it was for herself." The procedures required that "a girl must undergo a gynecological examination nine days after a truancy" (Selo, 1979: 161).

The national study also found that girls' visitors and correspondence were very severely restricted; this was particularly true for status offenders, who were more likely than criminal offenders to report that their outgoing mail was read. Procedures were different for inspecting girls' and boys' mail: boys' correspondence was monitored "only for the purpose of inspecting for contraband"; girls' correspondence was monitored so that "anything significant" could be discussed with the girl by the social worker (Selo, 1979: 164).

Little difference was found in the searching of personal belongings in this study, and boys were more likely than girls to be personally searched (for example, cavity searches). Punishment for institutional infractions was severe in both male and female institutions, with youths being placed in disciplinary units or rooms for such minor infractions as lending clothes, sleeping in, lying to their group, striking matches, being upset, stealing, and fussing and arguing

(Selo, 1979: 165). Most youths, male and female, felt there were too many rules in institutions and that the punishments were too harsh.

Major differences were ascertained in the perceptions of male and female youths regarding the usefulness of vocational programs. Boys viewed their programs as "much more helpful" than girls did (Selo, 1979: 168). The attitudes were a product, in Selo's view, of the fact that "girls could not participate in these experiences either because there were no programs in the institutions or because the programs were limited to only a few girls." The programs that were available to girls tended to be limited to traditional feminine options such as cosmetology, home economics, and "business education" (generally simple secretarial training). Boys' programs were more varied and included more remunerative fields: graphic arts, electricity, carpentry, and auto mechanics. Consequently, although large numbers of boys and girls faced unemployment after release, finding work was a greater problem for girls. Forty-four percent of the boys but only 36 percent of the girls had jobs waiting for them (Selo, 1979: 168).

Finally, girls in the institutions in the survey were less likely than boys to approve of the changes that the institution was attempting to produce in them, and this was particularly true of female status offenders. Indeed, boys charged with status offenses were the most likely to express approval (42%), followed by boys charged with crimes (36%), girls charged with crimes (26%), and girls charged with status offenses (18%). The opinion of female status offenders was explained by Selo as a product of the fact that they were more likely than the others to regard their institutionalization as "less legitimate: because of their relatively minor delinquency history compared to males." In addition, the girls were apt to resent efforts by the staff to change aspects of their behavior such as "sexual conduct, peer associations, and the use of drugs and alcohol," whereas for boys in general and for criminal offenders, the staff concentrated on criminal behavior alone.

A detailed study conducted in the early 1970s in a New Jersey training school provides a good complement to the national profile. Rogers (1972) found large numbers of girls incarcerated "for their own protection," 71 percent having been found guilty of running away, truancy, being missing overnight, and "sex (UM)" (unmarried mothers, in the school's notations) (224). The Rogers article describes a "campus" of well-tended grounds with cottages scattered about— "a homey enough atmosphere until one notices the bars on the windows" (230).

In the seemingly pleasant atmosphere, girls were subject to considerable restrictions. For example, they were not permitted to receive a daily newspaper because that was deemed "upsetting" literature; they were permitted to write only to "parents and approved relatives," a restriction missing in the boys' facility; and they were locked in their rooms from 8:30 p.m. to 6:00 a.m. and were given a bottle in which to urinate (Rogers, 1972: 230–231). In general, there were many more rules governing girls' behavior than in the comparable male institution, and girls were allowed far fewer opportunities for visits. Boys were allowed home visits during holidays; girls' families had to visit them at the facility (240).

Medical services in the facility were "poor at best" although there was "a great deal of interest in a girl's sexual history and habits" (Rogers, 1972: 235). Sex education was nonexistent because at the time it was against the law to provide it. Girls who were pregnant were seen as "getting what [they] deserved" and at term were encouraged to give the babies up for adoption.

Educational programs at the facility were actually superior to those found in the boys' facility. But although this was in one sense an asset, it actually worked an extra hardship on the girls because it encouraged staff to keep girls at the facility to "complete their educational program"; boys were often released to go home. The programs tended to emphasize traditional feminine pursuits and, at best, traditional occupations: sewing, cooking, cosmetology, laundry work, home economics, cleaning, and gardening. In contrast, boys had access to a print shop, woodworking, small engines, electronics, and auto mechanics (Rogers, 1972: 237). There was no organized recreational program for girls.

Many might hope that such conditions no longer exist in training schools, but this is not the case. Kersten (1989a) studied closed-sections juvenile institutions in Germany between 1983 and 1984 and found many familiar patterns. First, girls were held for quite different offenses than were boys. Half the males but only one-fifth of the females had been committed for criminal offenses. Two-thirds of the girls but only one-third of the boys had been incarcerated for running away, although boys tended to run away from open facilities about as frequently as girls. Girls' facilities, whether closed or "semi-open," were more strictly run than boys'. Open institutions imposed more controls on visits to the girls, more regulations on going out, and so on. Closed institutions held more girls than boys in solitary confinement (14.6 percent and 7.8 percent, respectively). When terms of commitment were completed, girls were more likely than boys to be placed in further institutional education rather than being released.

Kersten comments that because girls are committed "for recorded, feared, or merely supposed prostitution," the institutional milieu is oriented toward "protecting the girl from the street, the customers, and the pimp" and generally toward the "salvation of fallen girls" (Kersten, 1989a: 136). Also present is an almost obsessive concern about homosexuality and constraint on virtually every form of touching so as to suppress this activity. Educational and vocational programs are more closed than such programs for boys and are "a reduced, cheapened, narrow-gauge version of what is possible for boys in institutions" (140).

Interest in conditions in U.S. training schools has fallen so far that no comparable descriptions can be located. A 1988 national study on correctional educational services does, however, illustrate the continued problems that girls have in contemporary training schools (Bergsmann, 1988). The survey of thirty-two states revealed that over half of these states house girls in co-correctional facilities (institutions in which both male and female offenders are incarcerated). This may sound like an advance, but Bergsmann notes that the change came about largely for bureaucratic convenience rather than to address the needs of girls, who have historically been neglected in single-sex facilities.

The study found that traditional education for both males and females was hampered by a lack of coordination between systems; few states transmit educational records to juvenile committal institutions. Vocational programming was still quite gendered, and "vocations that offer high[-]paying wages continue to be offered to males at a higher rate than are offered to females, both within the institution and on study release" (Bergsmann, 1988: 20). For example, twenty-four states offer auto mechanics to males; eight offer it to females. Likewise, welding is offered to males in eleven states and to females in five. By contrast, training in office skills was available to girls in twenty-one states and to boys in eleven; home economics was available to girls in ten states and to boys in six. Health education (including sex education) is apparently a priority in most states, but pregnancy counseling is available in only fifteen states (nine of which restrict it to girls). The study did find a few promising programs, such as Ventura School's Vocational Education Project, which holds a nontraditional job fair at which union, industry, and business representatives make presentations on career and job opportunities.

Although researchers' interest in training schools has fallen off, the problems the schools confront have not. A study conducted by the National Conference on State Legislatures warned that "overcrowding in juvenile correctional facilities is reaching crisis proportions in over half the states." Of the thirty-nine states that responded to the survey, twenty-six reported that overcrowding was a "significant problem; nine states were currently involved in litigation over this problem" (Miller, 1988). Paradoxically, despite a drop in the incarceration of girls, crowding characterizes institutions that house girls. Information collected by the Youth Law Center (1987) on conditions in Ventura School points this up clearly. The school, which once held only girls, now holds 890 juveniles, two-thirds of whom are boys. Yet it is still the main long-term California Youth Authority facility for girls and is chronically overcrowded.

The best and most complete reports on conditions in today's training schools are found in legal documents. Conditions at Ventura School are described in materials pertinent to lawsuits filed by the Youth Law Center—for example, materials that indicate that fewer girls don't mean fewer problems. Indeed, other problems may appear. The characteristics of girls at Ventura School deviate to a considerable degree from the characteristics of incarcerated girls in earlier decades—perhaps reflecting the impact of deinstitutionalization in California. In 1984, for example, the facility held 245 girls whose average age was 18.3 years (girls can be held until the age of 21 in California). They had been incarcerated for more serious offenses than the offenses that drew incarceration before deinstitutionalization. About two-thirds (139) were incarcerated for homicide, robbery, or assault. Kidnapping–extortion, burglary, and drug offenses accounted for 51 commitments, and 55 commitments were for theft, motor vehicle theft, arson, and other offenses (*Rohde v. Rowland J., et al.,* 1986: 6). However, this does not mean that younger girls with minor offense backgrounds are not held in such facilities. Among the first commitments in 1983, 20 percent were under fifteen years of age, 30 percent were fifteen or sixteen years of age, and 51 percent were between seventeen and twenty-one years of age (7).

Lest this profile be taken as typical for the entire country, some data on the population of Hawaii's training schools in 1988 might provide a counterpoint. Girls made up 17.5 percent of the training school population in May 1988 (a figure likely to be higher than that found in states where more aggressive de-institutionalization efforts have been under way). The vast majority of the girls, as well as the boys, were minority-group members (part-Hawaiians accounted for roughly half of both groups), and the girls tended to be about a year younger (15.75 years of age compared with 16.5 for the boys). Further, girls were far more likely to be incarcerated for minor offenses; 57.1 percent of the girls and 31.8 percent of the boys, for example, had been committed for misdemeanors or probation violations. By the way, this profile does not come from a state that has an extraordinarily high incarceration rate (Karraker, Macallair, & Schiraldi, 1988; Karraker, 1988).

Returning to Ventura School, we learn from Youth Law Center legal filings that recreational time for girls was reduced, that pregnant teenagers did not receive adequate medical care or a nutritionally appropriate diet, that girls' meals in general were insufficiently balanced, and that promised parenting classes did not materialize.

The seriousness of the problems of Ventura was exposed by the case of Melissa Pence. Pence was made a ward of the court at the age of fourteen for the misdemeanor offense of obstructing a police officer by giving a false name when questioned. After failing to remain at several placements, she was involuntarily confined at Ventura School at the age of fifteen. By her own account, she had run away "because she feared getting too close to people and had been easily influenced by other residents of the group homes. Her school experience had been generally positive; she planned to finish high school, was bright, and wanted to become a counselor" (*Rohde v. Rowland J., et al.,* 1986: 5).

After a short stay at a cottage for housing middle-adolescent females, Pence was transferred (over her and her grandmother's objections) to a cottage housing older, high-risk, and emotionally disturbed females with violent histories and serious-offense commitments. She became extremely depressed, voiced a desire to die, and said she would never get out of Ventura School. Found hiding in a male inmate's room, she was put on disciplinary lockdown, and her release date was postponed. Pence hanged herself. An autopsy found excessive amounts of benzoylecgonine, ecogonine, methyl ester, and cocaine with a large amount of mephobarbital in her body (the school had a "widespread illicit drug trade" at the time) (*Rohde v. Rowland, J., et al.,* 1986: 12).

There has been a general pattern of institutional neglect when it comes to girls. As one researcher noted, girls in institutions have become the "forgotten few" (Bergsmann, 1989). Institutional practices that are routine in boys' facilities have to be scrutinized for their impact on girls. In particular, there needs to be a sensitivity to the fact that girls' victimization histories make such practices as routine strip searches and isolation extremely risky. It is no surprise that scandals routinely appear after girls are strip-searched. Take the case of a sixteen-year-old runaway who was picked up on a curfew violation in San Francisco. She initially tried to refuse to allow a strip search because she "didn't want to take her clothes off in front of a man." She was then "forcibly strip searched," during which time the male staff member "helped hold the girl down on the floor while a female staffer removed the girl's clothes" (Goldberg, 1996:A1).

Problems also exist in public facilities that have undergone downsizing, where the small number of girls housed is frequently used to deny girls access to services and programs. And, as with adult women inmates in other decades, the small number of girl inmates offers an invitation to new forms of abuse and neglect.

A clear example of these problems surfaced in the year-long investigation of the Lloyd McCorkle Training School for Boys and Girls in Skillman, New Jersey. The training school officially closed in 1992, and all the male inmates and most of the staff were moved out of the facility. Correctional planners were not able to locate a new facility for the girls' unit, so seventeen months later, the facility continued to house about a dozen girls (Rimbach, 1994: 32).

Three girls who agreed to talk to a reporter told stories of sexual assaults from male correctional staff (there were two formal complaints lodged), beatings, extensive use of isolation, and overreliance on "mind-numbing" medications. One girl told of spending eight months in a "stark isolation cell" for infractions such as "cursing at correctional officers," "refusing to go to bed," or speaking to another girl in the next cell. The facility was also routinely transferring girls who turned eighteen to the adult women's prison, while the boys' training school kept boys until age twenty-one.

Journalists investigating the facility also reported extensive use of psychotropic medication; roughly one-third of all the girls who went through the facility in the last year were given medication, compared to no more than about 5 percent of the boys (Rimbach, 1994: 31). A letter from one of the advisory board members, who visited the facility in 1992, provides graphic details of the conditions of the girls' facility:

> During my visit, the girls looked extremely unkempt, they were excessively lethargic, their attitude was very poor, reportedly the majority were on some kind of medication, either tranquilizers or sleeping pills, and were found in "administrative segregation" without even a book to read. Additionally, there were allegations that these girls were not allowed out for the required one hour a day. I was told that one young woman had not had a shower for five days. While I am no expert on juvenile law, I believe that there are several violations going on in this facility. These girls are not being given equal treatment to the boys in the system and they are not being given the physical education required by law. Further, as an enlightened administrator, you should be shocked at the total absence of a program in this facility, particularly as there is specific funding for this program. (Rimbach, 1994: 31)

When asked about these problems, correctional administrators provided an interesting litany of excuses. About the overmedications, administrators noted that "girls come into Skillman from county detention centers already on medication." This administrator continued by noting that girls "usually get so many chances before they are committed, so those who reach Skillman are a pretty disturbed bunch of kids." As to the extensive use of isolation (correctional records showed that each of the eight girls held in 1993 spent an average of thirty days in isolation), the administrator could only suggest that perhaps the girls had come from other facilities to be kept in isolation at Skillman. Yet the record shows that the small facility averages ten disciplinary charges a month. The absence of programming was explained by saying that "the girls have been in transition."

Unfortunately, detailed accounts of youth facilities such as the one above have been extremely scarce in the last few decades. With the increasing "invisibility" of girls in such institutions comes the possibility for extreme correctional neglect and abuse.

The Inmate Subculture and Social System

In discussions of life inside juvenile institutions (most commonly known as training schools), reference must necessarily be made to what is generally referred to as the inmate culture or subculture. Carter (1981: 419) describes inmate girls' culture:

> Inmate culture in a girls reform school is best understood as a complex of meanings through which the girls maintain continuity between their lives inside and outside the institution. . . . The informal world of reform school girls is one of make believe families, homosexual courting relations, and adolescent peer group culture. It is the world of the adolescent girl on the outside, imported into the institution and appropriately modified to fit the formally structured world of the institution. . . .

In one of the most detailed studies ever conducted of training schools for girls, Giallambardo (1974) compared the subcultures of institutions in three geographical locations: the East, Midwest, and West. Each of the 705 girls in the training schools was incarcerated for having committed a crime. In one institution almost 90 percent were classified as PINS (person in need of supervision—mostly runaways and incorrigibles). For the majority, the current commitment was the first placement in the institution. About two-thirds had been in detention facilities or some other local community institution on several occasions, usually for at least two weeks. Giallambardo notes that in this short time girls can become socialized into the inmate culture and that some even begin to develop "kinship ties" that they continue if subsequently committed. Few in the study had been placed on probation more than once before their present commitment, nor had many been placed in foster homes. Giallambardo concluded that the removing of adolescent girls from community settings seems to be the norm rather than the exception, indicating that juvenile courts become rather impatient with such girls.

The backgrounds of the 705 girls indicate that few came from intact families. The most common living arrangement was with the mother only. Over one-third of the families received some form of public assistance, and more than half had five or more children. Few of the parents had graduated from high school.

Each of the three institutions had a clearly defined social arrangement that closely resembled an elaborate "kinship system." In one institution it was called "the racket," in another, the "sillies," and in the third, the "chick business." In all three institutions, Giallambardo found extensive networks of family roles, including a variety of homosexual statuses. Included in the "families" were girls who were clearly homosexual (both within the institution and outside) and those who engaged in homosexual behavior only while incarcerated. Girls who did not participate in homosexual activities were incorporated into families as either "sisters" or "cousins."

Another study of girls in training schools (Propper, 1978) confirmed that homosexuality was a feature of institutional life, although the figures were lower than those reported by Giallambardo (who found that most of her respondents had roles in the family systems described above). The discrepancy may be the product of different methodologies employed and different meanings attached to the behavior the girls admitted. Propper analyzed questionnaire responses from 496 girls held in seven institutions in different parts of the United States. Fourteen percent of the girls reported that they were "going with" or "married to" another girl, and 7 percent had had sexual interactions that went past hugging and kissing (Ibid.: 265).

Propper's work also challenged notions that "deprivation," particularly opportunities to interact with boys, explained this behavioral adaptation (a suggestion that often accompanies arguments for coeducational institutions). She found that rates of homosexuality did not significantly vary at different types of facilities. This is largely a product of the fact that pervasive concern about sexual contact between inmates found at coeducational institutions brought on measures that severely restricted even heterosocial contact between boys and girls. Propper did discover, though, that previous homosexuality played a far more important role than had been thought, noting that it was not the result of the importation of "free world homosexuality." Instead, girls with previous homosexual experiences most frequently had had such experiences in another correctional setting (Propper, 1978: 273).

Similarly, a study by Sieverdes and Bartollas (1982) of six coeducational training schools in the southeast arrived at almost identical conclusions about the inmate social system. Here they found seven different institutional roles, all falling within three broader role categories: aggressive (e.g., "bruiser" and "bitch"), manipulative (e.g., "lady" and "bulldagger"), and passive ("child," "girlfriend," and "asskisser"). The authors found that girls adhered more strongly to their particular inmate groups than did the boys. Also, the girls expressed more satisfaction with institutional life than the boys did, even though they were more victimized than their male counterparts were. The "pseudo-families" within the girls' section of these institutions were less likely to be based upon homosexual alliances than those found in all-girls institutions. It should be noted, however, that 70 percent of the girls were status offenders, who had the most difficult time adjusting to institutional life and who were also the most often victimized.

More recently, research into the subcultures found in institutions for girls and women is looking at the inmates within the context of their past victimizations (Arnold, 1990). That many females in these facilities have come from extremely abusive families might be a strong reason for them to seek to create another family arrangement within which they can find love and acceptance.

Training schools for girls have a mixed history and a murky present. Many girls were held in them during the first half of the century "for their own protection." This legacy was strongly challenged by changes in incarceration policies in the middle and late 1970s. It remains to be seen, though, whether the changes have actually dismantled the courts' historic commitment to the jailing of large numbers of girls in conflict with society and on the streets. Certainly, increases in the numbers of girls held in public detention centers in recent years, coupled with increases in the arrests of girls for status offenses, argue for a possible return of policies that support institutional responses to girls' problems.

As already noted in earlier chapters, race continues to play a significant role in the juvenile justice system. The next section addresses the question of girls and race, noting that there now exists a new "double standard" of juvenile justice.

GIRLS, RACE, AND

INSTITUTIONALIZATION

As noted in Chapter 8, studies of court behavior in recent years have signaled a new form of double standard of juvenile justice—one for white girls and another for girls of color (Robinson, 1990; Miller, 1994).

Evidence of this pattern has also cropped up in studies of institutions. Bartollas (1993) conducted a study of youth confined in juvenile "institutional" placements in a Midwestern state. His research sampled female adolescents in both public and private facilities. The "state" sample (representing girls in public facilities) was 61 percent African American, while the private sample was 100 percent white! However, little difference was found in the offense patterns of the two groups of girls. Seventy percent of the girls in the "state" sample were "placed in a training school as a result of a status offense" (Bartollas, 1993: 473). This state, like many, does not permit youth to be institutionalized for these offenses; however, Bartollas noted that "they can be placed on probation, which makes it possible for the juvenile judge to adjudicate them to a training school." In the private sample only 50 percent were confined for status offenses; the remainder were there for "minor stealing and shoplifting-related offenses." Bartollas also noted that both of these samples of girls had far less extensive juvenile histories than did their male counterparts.

Other evidence, though less direct, points to the development of much the same pattern. As deinstitutionalization has advanced over the last two decades, there was during the 1980s and 1990s a distinct rise in the numbers of youth confined in private as well as public "facilities" or institutions. In comparing public and private facilities, some clear gender and race differences also emerge. Though the majority of the youths in all institutional populations are male, there is a considerable gender difference between youth held in public and private facilities. In 1991, girls constituted 11 percent of those in public institutions, compared to 29 percent in private institutions (Moone, 1993a, 1993b). Another way to look at this is to say that of the girls held in facilities of any sort, over half (62%) are held in private facilities.

There are also major differences in the offenses or activities that bring youth to private facilities. The vast majority of girls (85%) held in private facilities are being held for "nondelinquent" offenses, including status offenses, dependency and neglect, and "voluntary" admissions; for boys, only slightly over half (57%) are held for these reasons, with the rest being held for criminal offenses (Jamieson & Flanagan, 1989: 596).

There are also major ethnic differences in the populations of these institutions. Whites constituted about 40 percent of those held in public institutions in 1989 but 60 percent of those held in private facilities (Krisberg et al., 1991: 57–59). Other, more detailed work on this issue (Krisberg et al., 1986) suggests that there is a significant interaction between gender and ethnicity in incarceration rates. In addition, increases that have occurred in the incarceration of youth have apparently been in the incarceration of minority youth, both male and female. In 1982, for example, the ratio of black male incarceration rates to white male incarceration rates was 4.4 to 1. Hispanic males were incarcerated at a rate 2.6 times that of white males. For girls, a similar though less extreme pattern was found, with black girls being incarcerated at 2.6 times the rate of white girls. A less dramatic difference was seen for Hispanic girls (only 1.1 times the rate of white females) (Krisberg et al., 1986: 16–17).

Other data comparing trends in detention between 1984 and 1988 found a 10 percent increase in detention of nonwhite girls for delinquency offenses, particularly drug offenses (where a fourfold increase in detentions was observed), compared to a drop in white girls' detentions for the same offenses, including drug offenses (Krisberg et al., 1991: 104–105). Turning to detention of girls for status offenses, a far more dramatic drop was seen in the detention of white girls for these offenses (30.5%) than the drop seen for nonwhite girls (7.7%) during the same period.

Detention rates have remained higher for black juveniles over the years. According to 1997 data, the proportion of black juveniles who are detained increased by about 52 percent from 1988, compared to an increase of only 12 percent for all other races. The percentage of all black juveniles referred to court who were detained in 1997 was, however, about the same as in 1988 (27%); however, the percentage of white youths who were detained in 1997 was lower than in 1988, dropping from about 17 percent to 15 percent. Even when considering offense charged, black juveniles are still detained at a higher rate than white juveniles. This was especially true for drug offenses, where black youths constituted 32 percent of all drug cases referred to court, yet they accounted for 55 percent of all drug cases detained. Unfortunately, gender differences according to race are not presented in this report. We have to assume, however, that the detention rates remain higher for black girls than for white girls (Sickmund, 2000).

DEINSTITUTIONALIZATION OR TRANS-INSTITUTIONALIZATION? GIRLS AND THE MENTAL HEALTH SYSTEM

Despite considerable resistance, it is clear that incarceration of young women in public training schools and detention centers across the country fell dramatically after the passage of the Juvenile Justice and Delinquency Prevention Act of 1974. Prior to the act's passage, nearly three-quarters (71%) of the girls and 24 percent of the boys in the nation's training schools were incarcerated for status offenses (Schwartz, Steketee, & Schneider, 1990). Between 1974 and 1979, the number of girls admitted to public detention facilities and training schools dropped by 40 percent. Since then, however, the deinstitutionalization trend has slowed in some areas of the country, particularly at the detention level. Since 1979, the number of girls held in these same public facilities has remained virtually unchanged (U.S. Department of Justice, 1989: 43; Moone, 1993a).

While the trends in public training schools were encouraging, there developed a dramatic growth in the placement of girls in private facilities—up 27 percent between 1979 and 1991 (Moone, 1993a), though in recent years this trend has slowed for reasons that will become clear. Schwartz, Jackson-Beeck, and Anderson (1984 called this the "hidden" private juvenile correctional system where incarcerations (estimated to be about 60 percent female) can be made without accompanying legal procedures and without the consent of the underage youths (since they are under age). Costs are covered by third-party health care insurance plans; indeed the reliance on this funding structure is one reason that the trend has slowed. Health care plans, under new pressure to "manage" costs, began to take a hard look at this practice (see Chesney-Lind and Pasko, 2003). A similar pattern was noted in New Jersey, where deinstitutionalization of female status offenders resulted in "hidden incarceration" rather than freedom because girls referred to the Division of Youth Services are often placed in a "structured environment" for "their own good" (Feinman, 1985: 50). In New Jersey, as elsewhere, girls were more likely to have parents sign a complaint warrant against them than were their male counterparts.

The decision by the Supreme Court in *Parham v. J.R.* (442 U.S. 584, 1979) may have relevance here.[1] This Georgia case involved a neglected child removed from his natural parents at the age of three months. Seven years (and seven foster homes) later, the child was committed to a state hospital upon request by the seventh set of foster parents and a recommendation from the Department of Family Services that he was too retarded and disruptive. (Prior to this commitment, he had been in an outpatient treatment center.) It was reasoned that he "would benefit from the structured environment of the hospital and would enjoy living and playing with the boys of the same age" (Wadlington, Whitebread, & Davis, 1987: 171).

A class action suit was filed on the child's behalf, which charged that Georgia's voluntary commitment procedures for minor children violated the due process clause of the Fourteenth Amendment. The district court agreed with these charges and ruled that the state's procedures in these cases "failed to protect adequately the appellees' due process rights" (Ibid.: 169) and that commitment to any of the eight regional hospitals constitutes a strict deprivation of a child's liberty.

The U.S. Supreme Court reversed the district court's decision, stating that Georgia's "medical fact finding procedures" are "reasonable and consistent with constitutional safeguards" (Ibid.: 181). The Supreme Court rendered its decision, in part, on "the presumption that the state will protect a child's general welfare. . . ." Also, it found "no evidence that the state, acting as guardian, attempted to admit any child for reasons unrelated to the child's need for treatment" (Ibid.: 180).

Adolescent admission rates to private psychiatric hospitals quadrupled between 1980 and 1984, though whether the Supreme Court's decision caused this increase is not known (Weithorn, 1988). *Parham* involved a minor who was already a ward of the state. A commitment requested by a natural parent is another matter altogether, and the Supreme Court expressed this view: "It is possible that the procedures required in reviewing a ward's need for continuing care should be different from those used to review a child with natural parents" (Wadlington, Whitebread, & Davis, 1987: 181).

Yet it appears that when minor children are placed in private psychiatric facilities, there are few judicial safeguards protecting them. It may be that the assumption "parents know best" still prevails.

The clearest problems with private institutions arise in the case of private psychiatric hospitals. A study of the early 1980s found that adolescent admissions to psychiatric units of private hospitals jumped dramatically, increasing fourfold between 1980 and 1984. There has also been a marked shift in the pattern of juvenile mental health incarceration. In 1971, juvenile admissions to private hospitals accounted for 37 percent of all juvenile admissions, but by 1980 this figure had risen to 61 percent. This same study estimated that fewer than one-third of juveniles admitted for inpatient mental health treatment were diagnosed as having severe or acute mental disorders, in contrast to between one-half and two-thirds of adults admitted to these sorts of facilities. A close look by Weithorn at youth in such institutions in Virginia suggests that 36 to 70 percent of the state's psychiatric hospital youth population "suffer from no more than 'acting out' problems and a range of less serious difficulties" (Weithorn, 1988: 773, 783, 788–789). Despite this, juvenile psychiatric patients remain in the hospital approximately twice as long as adults.

These patterns have very clear implications for the treatment of girls, although data on the gender of admissions is regrettably sketchy. The chief concern is that admissions procedures to such private facilities have never been formalized. In addition, the Supreme Court has clearly rejected an attempt to guarantee procedural protections that were extended to adults in *Parham v. J.R.* (442 U.S. 584 [1979]).

While still a cause for concern, the current drop in commitments of youth to private facilities means that girls are less exposed to these sorts of abuses. The reason for this shift, though, has less to do with gender equity and more to do with managed care, which meant that HMOs were less likely to permit lengthy and costly incarceration (Chesney-Lind and Pasko, 2003). Oddly, girls were the likely beneficiaries of this cost-cutting response to out of control medical bills.

Other privately funded programs should also be scrutinized carefully for evidence of gender bias and abuse. An extreme example of this problem turned up in a "tough love" type of "boot camp" in Colorado. Youth in this program complained that counselors "spit in their faces, made them eat their own vomit, challenged them to fight, screamed racial and sexist slurs at them and made them carry human feces in their pockets" (Weller, 1996: 1). Investigators discovered the abuse when two youths were found to have a flesh-eating virus and a girl lost a finger. Youths spent "between two and 12 weeks" at the camp because "their parents had problems with them and wanted them in a regimented environment" (2).

In another case, Mystie Kreimer, a fifteen-year-old resident of a 161-bed youth "shelter and treatment center," died en route to a hospital. Mystie had been placed as a "resident" in one of a "fast growing chain of for-profit congregate care children's facilities" (Szerlag, 1996: 48). Started by a politically connected multimillionaire who launched Jiffy Lube, Youth Services International now operates such homes in ten states. The facility that held Mystie, Forest Ridge, had been investigated by the Iowa Department of Human Services after former staff reported that "teens were frequently physically and emotionally abused by inexperienced youth workers." In addition, a former staff member pled guilty to "sexually exploiting a minor."

Mystie landed at Forest Ridge because she had a "history of substance abuse and sexual adventuring." She entered the facility in March 1995 weighing 145 pounds. When her mother visited her in September, Mystie complained of leg and chest pains. Her mother recalls asking to have her daughter hospitalized but was told by staff at the facility that she was not "sick enough to warrant that kind of medical attention." The mother of another girl reports seeing Mystie lying on a couch and commenting to her daughter that Mystie looked sick. Her daughter replied, "Oh, Mom, she is so sick and they still expect her to do her chores." Mystie died while being transported by helicopter to a Sioux Falls hospital. At the autopsy it was determined that she died of a "massive blood clot in her lung." At the time of her death, she weighed 100 pounds (Szerlag, 1996: 42).

In essence, although the data are far from complete, the evidence seems to point to the incarceration of girls, particularly middle-class white girls, in private hospitals and treatment programs for much the same behavior that, in previous decades, placed them in public institutions. Given the lack of procedural safeguards in these settings, some might even argue that there is greater potential for sexist practices, and even abuse, to flourish in these closed and private settings.

It is apparent that efforts to deinstitutionalize status offenders have had different effects on boys and girls, with boys being the beneficiaries. There are indications that the "relabeling" of female behaviors has occurred in part to get around deinstitutionalization provisions, and, more recently, incarceration of youths in violation of valid court orders has been permitted. Finally, large numbers of girls are incarcerated in facilities that are clearly not meeting their needs for offenses that are far less serious than those of their male counterparts. Even where progress has been made, as is true with increases in private commitments of girls, these trends require careful future monitoring because private facilities are not necessarily an improvement over public facilities. Continued commitment of girls to adult jails and overcrowded training schools is also a matter of great concern. That many of these commitments are still being made, explicitly or implicitly "for girls' protection," is testimony to the durability of the sexual double standard in incarceration. Finally, the use of private hospitals and other privately funded, for-profit programs quite obviously suggests that private profit, rather than real care and treatment of youth, is what matters the most.

SUMMARY

Institutionalization has long been a cornerstone of the juvenile justice system's response to girls' delinquency. Historically, large numbers of girls were incarcerated in both detention and training schools, purportedly for their own protection. The pattern was challenged by the Juvenile Justice and Delinquency Prevention Act of 1974, and the numbers of girls housed in public detention centers and training schools subsequently declined. In recent years, though, we have seen the numbers of youths held in public juvenile facilities, particularly detention centers, begin to climb in a rather dramatic way. National data indicate that between 1989 and 1998, detentions involving girls increased by 56% compared to a 20% increase in boys' detentions (Harms, 2002: 1). Also disturbing are figures indicating that the greatest increases were seen in the incarceration of African American and Hispanic girls. These most recent increases are directly tied to increases in the arrests of girls for "person offenses" which, as we have argued are often "bootstrapped" status offenses, since many involve fights with parents.

Commitments of girls to training schools have dropped, although girls are still more likely than boys to be incarcerated for status and minor offenses. Moreover, there has been a shift of girls into private facilities, where, again, they are held for far less serious offenses than their male counterparts. Large numbers of children, about a fifth of them girls, are still found in adult jails; again, they are often held for status offenses rather than crimes.

Many girls in correctional settings have experienced physical and sexual abuse, and nearly four out of five have run away from home. Not surprisingly, most report that their first arrest was for either running away from home or for larceny–theft. Studies of the conditions in the nation's detention centers and training schools indicate that rather than protecting girls, many such institutions neglect girls' needs and, in some instances, further victimize them.

Deinstitutionalization has also come under fire from those who would re-criminalize status offenses, particularly in the area of detention (see Sherman, 2002). Other areas of concern, such as the hidden system of incarceration in private facilities and mental hospitals that care more about profits than patient well-being, while less a threat than a decade ago, show how robust are the forces that seek to control and punish girls for forms of misconduct we ignore in boys. Rather than retreating from deinstitutionalization (as some have counseled), we have argued that the gains of the movement should be preserved. Indeed, these successes should serve as a basis for a renewed commitment to reduce the number of girls, particularly girls of color, now being held in the nation's detention centers.

NOTE

1. A summary of this case was done by UNLV student Denise Van Rooy and was based upon a review by Wadlington, Whitebread, and Davis, 1987: 169–182.

10

In Their Own Words: Interviews with Girls and Boys on the Margins

ndividuals who spent enormous amounts of time talking to delinquent boys developed early insights into the dynamics of male delinquency. Reviewing the classics in delinquency research reveals how central the work of such individuals as Frederick Thrasher and Clifford Shaw was to the field and how heavily other researchers relied upon their findings. Shaw's work, in particular, often involved the intensive study of only one boy, as in *The Jackroller* (1930), or only a few boys, as in *Brothers in Crime* (1938). However, much of this book so far—and for that matter, much of delinquency research overall—has taken a more quantified view of the lives of delinquents.

This chapter attempts to redress the imbalance to a degree by presenting the results of interviews with girls as well as boys. Listening to their stories is a vital though often neglected task, and particularly essential to the understanding of girls' delinquency; we also focus on the unique ways in which race intersects with gender and class in the lives of girls and boys on the margin.

Only a few studies actually allow girls on the margin to speak about their whole lives and only a very few look specifically at the lives of girls in the juvenile justice system. In the first two editions of this book, material from a study in Hawaii during the mid-1980s was used, in addition to several other studies. In the current edition we present the results of a more recent qualitative study that looks more broadly at issues of gender and ethnicity in Hawaii (see Mayeda, Chesney-Lind, and Koo, 2001 for the complete study). Other research will be cited, including a study of girls being held in California training (Bottcher, 1986) to focus more specifically on girls' issues.

In the following section we bring into focus the complex role of gender and ethnicity in the lives of youth growing up in economically marginalized neighborhoods. Going beyond the stereotype of these youths as "deprived, disadvantaged, deviant, disturbed or dumb" (Gibbs, 1985: 28), it is essential that research be conducted that recognizes the "differences within ethnic and minority groups and within and across socioeconomic status" (Leadbeater & Way, 1996: 2). In this regard, it has become widely accepted that as youths grow into adolescence, they tend to become more conscious of their ethnic identity as it relates to future employment and educational opportunities. Seyfrit et al. (1998) and Ogbu (1991) both found that youth who come from and identify with ethnic groups experiencing social marginalization more often feel the constraints of their social position as they become older.

Gender, like race, also matters in adolescent development, and scholars have noted that youth (both boys and girls) become increasingly aware of their gender identity as they reach adolescence; much research focuses on aesthetic ideals, such as body image. For instance, Mendelson, White, and Mendelson (1996) found that adolescent girls tend to have lower body esteem than adolescent boys due to expectations surrounding "ideal" body appearance. Mendelson, White, and Mendelson also determined that adolescent boys usually rate themselves higher than their female counterparts on scales of athletic competence and physical appearance. Because boys and girls often focus on different ways of achieving self-esteem, it is important to examine the different outcomes that result from these gendered perceptions. As Rierdan and Koff (1997: 620) point out, too often ". . . dissatisfaction with and concern about weight . . . are associated with depressive symptoms in early adolescent girls." A number of studies have also explored direct relationships between youthful ethnic identity, gender identity, and self-esteem. Martinez and Dukes (1991) found significant differences on various self-esteem scores (such as perceived intelligence and satisfaction with self) between youth from different ethnic and gender backgrounds. In addition, Tashakkori (1993: 486) argues that ". . . different types of self-esteem structure (exist), probably based on different perceptual mechanisms, across ethnicity by gender groups." In this regard, Tashakkori contends that people often derive their self-esteem from different sources according to societal expectations.

For example, our research will illustrate the tendency for boys of certain ethnicities to derive their self-concept, and even self-worth, from engaging in delinquent or violent behavior. In this respect, societal race and gender discrimination often influence youth to deviate from acceptable social norms (Chesney-Lind, 1998), frequently leading to disproportionately high rates of incarceration for specific ethnic and gender groups (DeComo, 1998). Thus, understanding youthful delinquency and violence matters when examining ethnic and gender identity development, not in the sense that ethnicity or gender causes crime, but in the sense that social perceptions of ethnicity and gender can persuade behavior.

This part of the chapter presents a study that attempts to further elucidate the relationships between ethnic and gender identity by presenting qualitative data gathered through focus group interviews with at-risk youth in Hawaii.[1] Youth considered "at risk" generally come from poor economic conditions and do not perform well in school (Wood, Hillman, & Sawilowsky, 1996). Most specifically, this study seeks to understand how at-risk youth situate their own ethnic and gender identities within various social spheres, particularly in peer groups and in school. As Marable (2000: B7) states, "A new racial formation is evolving rapidly in the United States, with a new configuration of racialized ethnicity, class, and gender stratification and divisions." In order to specifically explore these stratification lines among at-risk youth, it is important to identify links between racialization, ethnic identity, gender identity, delinquency, and violence.

Price (1999) for instance, reveals different ways that at-risk African American male youth establish their ethnic and gender identities in several key social arenas—namely in school and amongst peers. We hope to build on research like that conducted by Price, by exploring where youth from recent immigrant groups (Filipinos and Samoans) and indigenous youth (Native Hawaiians) position their identities in school and amongst peers. How do youth respond to teachers and peers who label adolescents in ways that reaffirm racialized and gendered stereotypes; in essence, how do youth balance what they think their ethnicity means against what others think their ethnicity means? (Nagel, 1994: 154) We also hope to sketch out some of the "street codes" (Anderson, 2000) that boys and girls from different ethnic groups access in their efforts to craft masculine and feminine identities in economically marginalized communities not unlike those described by Anderson. Like Anderson, we report youths' social experiences, which often circulate around violent campaigns for respect within economically depressed communities of color.

INTERPRETING ETHNICITY AND GENDER IN HAWAII: A CASE STUDY*

Hawaii is one of the most ethnically diverse states in the nation. The largest population groups are Japanese American (20.3%), European American (22.2%), Filipino American (10.0%), and Hawaiian/part-Hawaiian (20.6%); other non-Caucasian ethnic groups comprise the rest of the population (African American, 1.4%; Chinese American, 3.1%; Korean American, .8%;

---

*This section of the chapter relies heavily on a study done by one of the book's authors with David Mayeda and Jennifer Koo (2001).

Puerto Rican, .1%; Samoan/Tongan, .8%). Additionally, 20.6% are of mixed heritage who are not part Hawaiian, or are of other single ethnicities (State of Hawaii Databook, 1997). Although Hawaii is ethnically diverse, it is not without racial or ethnic tensions. Class and ethnic divisions tend to reflect the economic and political power struggles of the state's past as a plantation society and its current economic dependence on mass tourism. In this mix, recent immigrants as well as the descendants of the island's original inhabitants are among the most dispossessed; consequently, youth actively involved in gangs are drawn predominantly from groups that have recently immigrated to the state (Samoans and Filipinos) or from the increasingly marginalized Native Hawaiian population.

Tracing the relationships between adolescents' ethnic and gender identities can be a difficult task in itself. In Hawaii, where nearly one-fifth of all juveniles come from mixed heritage (State of Hawaii Databook, 1997), understanding ethnic and gender identity becomes even more complicated. Critical scholars have noted that popular culture often inaccurately depicts Hawaii as having harmonious ethnic relations, with little or no ethnic tension (Okamura, 1982). Although higher degrees of interracial marriages and multiracial offspring in Hawaii do suggest an increase in tolerance between Hawaii's many ethnic groups, it would be inaccurate to assume that racial discrimination and ethnic identity are not influencing factors on adolescent identity.

Youth from economically marginalized groups in Hawaii face unique challenges based on their particular cultural history and "place" in Hawaii's economic order. Filipino youth and Samoan youth tend to share the stresses of immigration; these include language difficulties, economic marginality, and coping with parenting practices that are customary and effective in the parents' country of origin, but are often at odds with mainstream American norms. Beyond this, though, the cultures are very different. Samoan culture is heavily influenced by the Polynesian value system of collective living, communalism, and social control through family and village ties. In Samoa, though contact with the West has been present for a considerable period, there is still a distinct Samoan culture to be found. Samoan adults drawn from this traditional, communal society often experience cultural shock upon immigration when poverty forces isolation, frustration, and accommodation to a materialistic, individualistic society (Tuana'itau, 1997). As their children begin to feel caught between two very different value systems, and as the village system of social controls weakens, the pressures and problems in Samoan families multiply. Gender relations in traditional Samoan families are heavily regulated by Polynesian traditions of separation, obligation, and male dominance (though girls and women have always found ways to circumvent the most onerous of these regulations) (Linnekin, 1990).

By contrast, Filipino immigrants come from a culture that has already been impacted by centuries of colonialism. As a consequence, the Philippines is a mix and myriad of discrete ethnic cultures that have been reshaped by Spanish and U.S. conquest and occupation. Of the many costs attending colonialism, one of the most insidious is that many Filipinos feel ambivalent about the value of their own culture. In addition, whereas pre-Hispanic women in the Philippines were dynamic and vital members of their ethnic groups, girls in modern Filipino families are impacted by colonial, cultural, and religious (largely Catholic) norms that stress the secondary status of women, girls' responsibility to their families, and a concern for regulating female sexual experimentation (Aquino 1994; Lebra 1991). Boys, on the other hand, are given considerable freedom to roam, though they are expected to work hard, do well in school, and obey their parents. The downward mobility, overemployment, and cultural shock experienced by many adult Filipinos put special strains on the cultural values of filial obligation and strains relationships with both sons and daughters.

Native Hawaiians have much in common with other Native American groups as well as African Americans. Their culture was severely challenged by the death and disease that attended contact with the West in the late 1700s. Until very recently, Hawaiian was a dying language, and many Hawaiians were losing touch with anything that resembled Hawaiian culture. Hawaiians, like urbanized Native Americans and low-income African Americans, have accommodated to poverty by occasionally normalizing early motherhood, higher rates of high school dropout, and welfare dependency for girls, and higher rates of drug dependency, crime, and physical injury for Hawaiian boys. In recent decades, a renaissance of Hawaiian culture, coupled with a vigorous sovereignty movement, has given Hawaiian youth a greater sense of hope (Dougherty, 1992; Dudley, 1990); however, these political shifts have so far failed to address the overwhelming economic marginality of the Native Hawaiian community.

One only needs to glance at the overrepresentation of youth from particular ethnic backgrounds in Hawaii's juvenile justice system to see that this system of ethnic stratification and inequality has dramatic consequences for youth from these communities. For instance, in 1994, although Samoans and Filipinos made up only 1.45% and 11.71% of Hawaii's juvenile population, respectively, they represented 5.42% and 14.92% of all juveniles arrested (Kassebaum et al., 1995: 1–5). Furthermore, statistics have shown that Samoans and Filipinos (juveniles and adults) represent 22% and 36%, respectively, of all identified gang members in Hawaii (Chesney-Lind et al., 1997: 80), percentages much higher than their overall populations would indicate. Finally, Kassebaum et al. (1995) found that Native Hawaiian youth were overrepresented at every decision point of the juvenile justice system. As an example, Native Hawaiian youth accounted for roughly 53% of all youth housed at the state's training school, although they comprise only 31% of the state's juvenile population.

Turning to gender, girls in Hawaii have hardly been shielded from nationally disseminated media images, which encourage young women to pursue virtually unattainable, "ideal" body types—namely thin, voluptuous, and, above all, European. Hawaii's local media have picked up on this reality, stating that more young women of color in Hawaii are actively manipulating their bodies to reach this standard (Infante, 1999). Although Hawaii is one of the only states in the United States where Caucasians do not represent a numerical majority, a trend toward looking more "haole" (Caucasian) and thin is notably evident amongst Hawaii's female population. In terms of gang affiliation and juvenile delinquency, research has asserted that amongst girls in Hawaii, ". . . violence (gang or otherwise) is not celebrated and normative; it is instead more directly a consequence of and a response to the abuse, both physical and sexual, that characterizes their lives at home" (Joe & Chesney-Lind, 1995: 428). Thus, for girls, engaging in delinquent behavior is not a means of gaining popularity and "street elite" status as it often is for boys (Messerschmidt, 1993), but rather a reaction to being ignored in and/or abused by mainstream institutions.

Data presented in this study will show two sides of the same story, as told by the youth themselves. While many youth expressed some internalization of ethnic and gender stereotypes, many youth also displayed a resistance toward the legion of harmful stereotypes cast upon them on a virtually daily basis.[1]

Study Methodology

In December 1997, researchers from the University of Hawaii Youth Gang Project (YGP) and the University of Hawaii Girls' Project began conducting focus groups and small group interview sessions (3 people or fewer) at youth-oriented agencies throughout Oahu (Hawaii's most populated and urban island). The researchers who conducted the focus groups and group interview sessions were both in their mid-twenties; the male researcher was of Japanese and Caucasian ethnicity, and the female researcher was of Korean ethnicity. All but two of the groups were held in urban regions of Honolulu, the state's capital. Youth agencies funded in part by the state's Youth Gang Response System (YGRS) were contacted by the researchers. Practitioners were asked if they knew of high school–aged youth attending their agencies who would be willing to participate in focus groups and small group interview sessions regarding the issues of ethnic and gender identity, racism, and sexism, with the incentive of receiving two free movie passes. In all, thirteen focus group or small group interview sessions were held, the last in May 1998.

The Youth Participants

A total of 58 adolescents participated in the group discussions, 32 male and 26 female. The participants ranged in age from 13 to 21, with a mean age of 15.9 years. Although the youth interviewed represented a wide range of ethnic backgrounds, there was a deliberate effort on the part of researchers to recruit youth from Native Hawaiian, Filipino, and Samoan backgrounds (since these groups are among the most economically marginalized in the islands). As a result, 90% of the youth surveyed were drawn from one of these three groups. As can be seen in Table 10–1, most of the thirteen focus groups were held in "mixed" settings. In other words, the groups usually included participants from different ethnic backgrounds and both genders, though both ethnicity and gender separated some groups. These different group settings provided for a wide variety of responses to the researchers' queries. It was within the groups that were separated by ethnicity that more of the stereotypes of other ethnicities were discussed most freely. Nevertheless, observations about other groups were reflected upon reasonably freely in mixed groupings. Two one-on-one interviews were also conducted, the first with a 26-year-old Samoan male and former gang member who grew up in low-income housing, and the second with a 16-year-old Samoan male, with whom one of the researchers had developed a good rapport.

Though not noted in Table 10-1, many youth participants were bi- or multiracial. For clarity's sake, youth were asked if they tended to identify more with one ethnic group than others. As most participants did, those single ethnic designations will be used throughout this study's text. Unfortunately, using these solitary ethnic markers takes away from Hawaii's unique and rich history of ethnic mixing. However, for the purposes of this study, where specific ethnic stereotypes are discussed, using solitary ethnic designations will be more advantageous.

Focus Group Questions and Session Dynamics

Research has suggested that focus groups are useful because they allow for interaction between the researchers and participants, as well as between participants. Thus, participants can react to one another and build upon different ideas and perspectives (Kent & Felkenes, 1998). A number of strategic measures were applied in order to develop a more relaxed atmosphere and sense of trust between the researchers and youth participants. To begin with, the YGP regularly serves as technical advisors for the state's YGRS. Thus, YGRS counselors are well acquainted with YGP personnel. Prior to conducting the focus groups, counselors (who work with the youth participants on a regular basis) asked youth, who the counselors felt could articulate their feelings on the subjects we were probing, to participate. Counselors also told these youth that all information expressed would be kept confidential and that we could be trusted not to reveal any information which would connect ideas expressed to individual participants.

Upon arriving at the youth facilities, counselors introduced us to the youth participants. In order to ease the atmosphere, we provided food and drinks for participants, and informed them that each participant would receive two movie passes after the focus group session was completed. We explained our affiliation with the YGP and Hawaii Girls' Project, clarified what types of questions we would be asking, and told why we were conducting these focus groups. After the researchers and participants introduced themselves by name, participants were asked if focus group sessions could be tape-recorded (all

Table 10-1. Description of Youth Participants in the Hawaii Study

Agency Participants (ages in parentheses)
Focus Group 1
1 Filipino male (16), 1 Hawaiian female (17), 2 Hawaiian males (18, 15), 1 Samoan female (16)
Focus Group 2
1 Caucasian female (13), 2 Filipino females (16, 14), 1 Japanese female (16)
Focus Group 3
3 Samoan females (16, 14, 14), 3 Samoan males (16, 15, 15)
Focus Group 4
1 Samoan female (16), 5 Samoan males (17, 15, 15, 14, 14)
Focus Group 5
1 African American female (14), 1 Filipino female (13), 2 Filipino males (17, 16), 2 Hawaiian females (15, 15), 1 Japanese female (16)
Focus Group 6
1 African American male (16), 1 Filipino male (16), 1 Hispanic male (14)
Focus Group 7
1 Filipino female (16), 1 Hawaiian female (16)
Focus Group 8
2 Filipino males (16, 15)
Focus Group 9
1 Filipino male (16), 1 Filipino/Hawaiian male (16), 1 Samoan male (17)
Focus Group 10
5 Samoan males (19, 18, 16, 16, 15)
Focus Group 11
1 Hawaiian female (15), 5 Samoan females (18, 17, 15, 15, 15)
Focus Group 12
1 Hawaiian male (17), 5 Samoan males (21, 18, 15, 15, 15)
Focus Group 13
3 Filipino females (18, 18, 18)

groups agreed), understanding that their identities would be kept confidential. Counselors left the room after introductions. Participants were told they did not have to answer any questions if they did not want to and that they could ask us any questions if they desired. No more than two researchers participated in any of the focus group sessions. After these proceedings transpired, focus group sessions began.

Beginning with the researchers, each individual told his or her ethnic background(s) and how they identified in terms of ethnicity. Participants were then asked a series of questions regarding ethnic tension, gang affiliation, scholastic aspirations and expectations, and popular culture (only some of these topics will be addressed in this study). With regard to these issues, participants were asked to compare differences they noticed between different ethnic and gender groups. Researchers clarified to participants that they could share personal information if they desired. However, participants were only asked to describe observations that they had made of their friends, in school, and in their communities.

We developed the questions we would ask youth according to literature on youthful protective factors and inter-ethnic violence. Protective factors are ". . . factors that might lessen the impact of risk, or perhaps spare some high-risk individuals from the deleterious effects of a history of risk . . ." (Grossman et al., 1992: 530). The protective factors that we chose to investigate most vigorously were modes of achieving self-esteem and commitment to school as a means of attaining future success. Recently, these factors have been cited as being extremely important in deterring youthful delinquency (Thornberry et al., 1998). In order to gauge the ethnic and gendered dimensions of self-esteem, typical questions included, "Do you notice that kids from different ethnic groups dress or act differently in school?" As virtually all youth answered "yes" to these types of questions, follow-up questions were asked such as, "How so? Why do you think that is? Do you notice differences between boys and girls too?"

Additionally, in order to explore the issue of commitment to school, we sought out literature that correlates educational experiences with ethnicity. Wood and Clay (1996: 53) found that Native American youth often have an awareness that success in school does not always translate to success in the job market due to societal discrimination. Reyes and Jason (1993: 67) note that high-risk Hispanic students ". . . consistently complained more about their teachers, the school principal, and unfair treatment by these authority figures." Thus, typical questions asked of youth included "Do you notice that kids from different ethnic/gender groups try harder (or try less) in school?" "Why do you think this is?" "Do you feel that teachers treat all students fairly?"

Finally, Joe and Chesney-Lind (1995) found that youth violence and gang affiliation in Hawaii were both racialized and gendered. Other research has documented that gang involvement (in some form) was virtually normative in the neighborhoods we used in this research (Chesney-Lind et al., 1997). Consequently, questions were asked that explored these issues, such as "How about fighting between kids, do you notice that kids from different ethnic groups fight each other, or is fighting more between kids from the same ethnic group? What about girls, do they fight as well? If so, with whom and why?" Though it may be arguable that these types of questions (in regard to self-esteem, commitment to school, and violence) are "loaded," it is crucial to ask these types of critical questions so that youth can problematize their social environments that they so often view as normal. Moreover, in order to fully understand the worlds that these youths regularly negotiate, we sought to explore the role that gangs, delinquency, and violence played in their attempt to establish masculinity and femininity.

For the most part, discussions were free flowing and did not require exten-sive probing by the researchers, though follow-up questioning was necessary to initiate in-depth conversations. Researchers attempted to attain participa-tion from all participants, but obviously some participants were more verbose than others. But ultimately, despite the contentious subject matters being dis-cussed, most focus groups evolved into very casual "talk story" discussions. In Hawaii, the term "talking story" refers to easygoing conversation. It was as-sumed that "talking story" with these youths would yield the most valid data, rather than using a formalized, structured interview procedure, because youth would be more inclined to disclose sensitive information in a relaxed atmos-phere. Most sessions lasted approximately 75 minutes. At the end of focus group sessions, each participant was given two movie passes for his or her ef-forts and assistance. Researchers then transcribed each focus group session in its entirety.

After all focus group sessions were transcribed, researchers analyzed the data using the techniques of grounded theory as defined by Strauss and Corbin (1990). Using open coding procedures, which include "breaking down, exam-ining, comparing, conceptualizing, and categorizing data" (61), various themes were established independently by each author and were cross-checked by each author to ensure reliability of coding. The following data demonstrate how youth from different ethnic and gender groups locate their identities amongst teachers and peers in school, as well as in violent situations in their communities.

Key Findings of the Study

This section details our findings and ensuing discussion. Rather than sepa-rate the results from the discussion, they have been combined for the sake of continuity. Several salient themes that emerged will be expounded upon. The first theme revolves around academics in regard to ethnic stereotypes about scholastic ability, perceived differential treatment from the school sys-tem, and a general lack of opportunity and role models. Issues around eth-nic stereotypes that certain groups were considered violent and gang involved and the corresponding implications are also discussed at length. Lastly, a discussion of ethnic differences in the way females are perceived and treated, and how they, in turn, negotiate these social expectations closes off the section.

"I Thought That One of My
Teachers . . . Was Against Samoans Li'dat."

A frequent stereotype that arose out of focus group discussions was that youth from particular ethnic backgrounds tend to put less effort into aca-demics. In particular, Hawaiian and Samoan youth were tagged with this negative attribute. For instance, an 18-year-old Filipino female participant from Group 13 stated,

. . . I notice that the people I have in my class, like the Samoans, they like kick back, they don't worry, you know what I mean. Like later on they worry when time to find out whether or not they passed . . . but like the Filipinos I had in that class, they like work hard.

Another 16-year-old Filipino female participant from Group 2 stated, "I think [Hawaiians], well, because like I talk to a lot of Hawaiian people, like a lot of them are in my classes, like a lot of them want to get rid of school already." References to Hawaiian and Samoan youth like those above were made quite frequently by non-Polynesian participants in the focus groups.

More to the point, it was not uncommon for Polynesian participants to offer similar statements. A 17-year-old Samoan male from Group 4 made the comment, "Oh, for this one fact . . . for real, see the Filipino kids, they betta than the Samoan kids in school." An 18-year-old Samoan female from Group 11 also stated, ". . . you know Chinese, you know how they say they're so smart . . . you know like Oriental people, like yeah, they're more smart." Thus, in varying degrees, it appears that an internalization of this perceived academic hierarchy exists among some Polynesian youth.

Perhaps the two most unfortunate outcomes emerging from this perceived academic hierarchy are 1) that youth often see a lack of academic effort as a pervasive quality among Polynesian students, failing to acknowledge the many Polynesian students who do work hard and perform well in school, and 2) that academic effort is falsely understood as an innate racial and/or cultural trait. When participants were asked why they felt discrepancies in academic motivation existed, most participants could not offer an immediate explanation, usually placing the blame on parental influence (or lack thereof). Ultimately, such comments point to a "culture of poverty" model, which indirectly suggests that Hawaiian and Samoan parents do not encourage and value educational achievement. However, other comments by participants suggest more probable explanations for these orientations.

The issue of teacher interactions, for example, must be considered. Explaining a time when his class was being punished, a 15-year-old Samoan male from Group 4 stated, ". . . cuz one time we got busted and [the teacher] told all the Filipinos go. All the Polynesian stay, Polynesian students . . . she kept all the Samoans in and let all the Filipinos go." A 15-year-old Samoan female from Group 11 said,

Like um, um teachers. Well, I thought that one of my teachers, yeah, like I thought she was against Samoans li'dat. Most of our Samoans in our class, they all would either fail her class, or they would like barely pass, like D's, you know what I'm saying. That was the highest grade any of the Samoans could get. Like we would ask her for help li'dat and she would ignore us. She would just walk away and she go help, um the other ethnic students li'dat.

Also expressing dissatisfaction with a teacher, this 15-year-old Samoan male from Group 12 stated, "Oh, there one teacher, um, no matter how hard you try, she still hate you, if you Samoan li'dat. . . . Oh, it made me so mad. Like I was the only Samoan in da class. She was always pick on me." Statements such as these, which were made by different participants in separate focus groups, suggest Samoan youth often feel neglected and treated unfairly by their teachers.

How this perceived (and likely real) educational negligence of Polynesian students can affect scholastic effort is seen in the following statement made by the same 15-year-old Samoan female quoted previously.

> Yea cuz like when [the teacher] was, like she said something like that, like our boys, they stop coming class, they cut periods because, you know, no like the way she treat them, so I guess in a way it was pulling them down.

Thus, one factor that is likely to cause a disproportionate amount of Polynesian youth to become "lazy" and more disinterested in school is negative interaction with teachers. Reyes and Jason (1993) investigated success factors associated with academic achievement for Hispanic students, and also found that students who were considered high risk ". . . cited teachers' put-downs of them and their abilities as sources of embarrassment and dissatisfaction" (67). It is also noteworthy to mention here that although 3% (6,221) of Hawaii's public school students are Samoan, only 0.3% (37) of Hawaii's public school teachers are Samoan. In fact, the majority of Hawaii's public school teachers are either Japanese (44%) or Caucasian (25%) (Kreifels, 1999: A-8), the two most economically privileged ethnic groups in Hawaii. Extreme differences in the ethnic and economic backgrounds of teachers and students have been suggested as possible sources of cultural misinterpretation and stereotyping (Burhoe, 1998) and student dropout (Jordan, Lara, & McPartland, 1996).

In addition to being aware of racial obstacles in school, many Polynesian participants also felt limited by their class status. A 15-year-old Hawaiian male from Group 1 stated, "I think [a lot of kids withdraw from school] when they find out their parents won't have enough money to pay for [it]," and went on to say, "The only way I can go college, two ways, if my Mom wins 11 million dollars, or if I go into the army and get the money." In reference to the higher percentages of Japanese students who attend the University of Hawaii, two 15-year-old Samoan males from Group 12 said, "They [Japanese] get da money," and "They get money coming like water." And a 15-year-old Samoan female from Group 11 added, ". . . maybe they have the money . . . I think it's all the money." In fact, these adolescents' perceptions regarding economic opportunity, as it relates to reaching higher education, are reasonably accurate. Research has shown that an increase in family income, particularly during early childhood, increases youths' chances of graduating from high school tremendously (Duncan et al., 1998). Hence, awareness of their class identity and background further limits these adolescents' academic aspirations.

Finally, a lack of role models was cited by one participant as a factor that affected scholastic motivation. In regard to his peers, this 17-year-old male from Group 4 said, "the Laotians, das da ones who always winning the valedictorian. Never see any Samoans. . . .Vietnamese or Laotians, das da key." Furthermore, this same participant demonstrated a perception that Samoans do not hold many prominent positions in Hawaii, outside of his immediate surroundings. Speaking very passionately, this Samoan participant made the following statement.

> . . . the Filipinos on top, like you see, you no see one Samoan governor (other participants laugh). Yea, we had a Hawaiian governor. Nah, Hawaiians you know, hey they see people go college and go places. I tink da guys, da Samoans, they only end up working K-Mart, now our generation, we can see the facts. You know, you know, you hardly see any Samoan businessmen (other participants laugh again), to be honest, das why, but you see planny Filipinos work if they want to.

According to this individual, a perceived lack of high-profile Samoan role models in Hawaii affects Samoan youths' perceptions of opportunity. For Samoan youth, the perceived absence of positive role models in the larger social structure affects youths' perceptions of realistic opportunity. Clearly, this youth's ethnic identity formation includes a sense of structural opposition, with racial obstructions constituting a significant part of his perceptual reality.

Although this was the only participant who made this type of comment regarding role models, other participants indirectly displayed agreement. When this participant stated that there has never been a Samoan governor and very few Samoan businessmen, the other participants (all Samoan) laughed. Thus, associating Samoan ethnicity with positions of high occupational prestige is so unfamiliar for these adolescents that the association is actually humorous. Ideas associating Samoans with high prestige are not realistic for these youths, but are instead hypothetical jokes. As stated previously, research has suggested that socially marginalized youth of color become increasingly aware of structural barriers in society with age (Ogbu, 1991), and that this awareness can negatively affect scholastic performance (Wood & Clay, 1996).

Clearly, the widespread stereotype of Polynesian students as "scholastically lazy" is very problematic and likely the product of educational neglect. We suspect from student comments that there are broader social forces—directly related to race—which in turn influence youths' academic motivation. Perhaps what was most disturbing about these interviews was the extent to which the "scholastically lazy" perception of Polynesian students was normalized among the youth participants. For instance, non-Polynesian youth expressed surprise when Polynesian students demonstrated academic drive and competence. A Filipino participant from Group 13 made the following statement.

> No, there's this [Samoan] girl in my class, she's smart, everything. She works hard, she just got a baby, yeah, and she did the Romeo, no the Macbeth by herself, because she had to go home school yeah, because she's pregnant. And she could do 'em. And I was surprised; everybody was surprised.

Polynesian participants discussed their desire to excel academically despite having to confront the hurdles of racism and classism. The 15-year-old Samoan female from Group 11 who spoke regarding teachers' ill-treatment of Samoan students went on to say of herself, ". . . but like to me, never really matter cuz like if I let her put me down, I'm putting myself down too, you know, so I might as well just go, and just try, you know." These unsettling sentiments suggest that Polynesian youth in Hawaii may face considerable obstacles in their search for an education free from racism.

"But All We da Best in? Violence."

Boys from certain ethnic groups, most notably Samoan and Filipino, are often stereotyped as violent and gang involved. Media constructions of gang violence, in particular, have regularly featured news stories that emphasize the gang problem in Hawaii as dominated by Filipino and Samoan boys (Perrone & Chesney-Lind, 1997). Although these stereotypes are not without foundation (Chesney-Lind et al., 1998), the complexity of gang membership is often lost in these reports, which stress only the most violent and antisocial aspects of gang behavior.

These stereotypes have certainly made headway, however. Males from these two ethnic groups were generally said by many participants to be heavily involved in gangs and frequently engaging in violent forms of behavior. Common statements made of Filipino males by non-Filipinos and some Filipino female participants reflected the widespread perception that Filipino boys carry weapons and are quick to fight: "[Filipinos are] wimps cuz they carry knives, guns . . ."; "But all the Filipino boys, they bring weapons . . . the time when they went fight, the Filipino guys had knives, . . . guns, everything . . ." and "As long as they Filipino . . . they bring one gun." Earlier research has also noted this threatening stereotype that demonizes Filipino males (Okamura, 1982).

Likewise, Samoan males were widely stereotyped by others as violent and prone to stealing. Statements made by participants (mostly by Filipino participants) in regard to Samoan male youth included, ". . . like the Samoans, yeah, they think that Filipinos have a lot of money, so they keep asking us for money . . ."; "Most of us think that, um, the Samoan guys would jack [rob] somebody," and "[Samoans], they jack much, yeah. Then they come back, I just hate it."

Although most Samoan and Filipino boys do not fit the above stereotypes, the involvement of some of these boys in gangs and violence emerged as major themes in these interviews. Again, examining their identity formation process, which is influenced by ethnic and gender labeling, can facilitate understanding of why some of these youths engage in violent behavior. The following statement made by a 17-year-old Samoan male from Group 4 exemplifies this correlation.

> . . . we like be da best. But all we da best in? Violence. You wanna be da best, oh what you wanna be da best in? Violence, violence. But you know das what, das, for me das why I'm proud yeah. People look for me to look da maddest, das why, dat only make us like strike harder. Das what we like you know, about being Samoan.

As this participant suggests, Samoans are expected by others to excel in only one area—violence. Because this external expectation is projected so forcefully, some Samoan boys may internalize it, and actually take pride in their perceived disposition for violence. As Cornell and Hartmann (1998) state, "The identity that others assign to us can be a powerful force in shaping our own self-concepts" (20). When this youth states, "People look for me to look da maddest," we can clearly see how external identification impacts internal identity formation.

Violence between minority boys within an urban context can also be explained as a type of masculine posturing. Messerschmidt (1993: 119) suggests that,

> . . . the personal power struggle with other young, marginalized, racial-minority men is a resource for constructing a specific type of masculinity—not masculinity in the context of a job or organizational dominance but in the context of "street elites" and, therefore[,] in the context of street group dominance.

Thus, when socially marginalized males inhabit the same locales, battles for supremacy (or perceived masculine status) often transpire. A 16-year-old African American male from Group 6 provided additional insight into this area. He described two incidents where groups of Samoan boys attempted to fight him, one of which is transcribed below.

> Like the Samoans, like I remember when I first moved here, [people would say], 'Samoans, they don't like you, they jealous.' The Samoans be hanging out by the bus stop and I'd be walking to class and they'd be, and they say, 'come here,' and I went over there and they tried to start a fight with me, so I stood up to them, right . . . I was like, 'Whatever you're going to do, what's up? I'm right here, I'm not going anywhere,' drop my bag, whatever. And they see like when you stand up to them, they don't really want . . . fight with you.

Here, positioning for a "tough" masculinity is very evident within a lower class, urban context. As African American males are frequently and unfairly feared for their perceived physical prowess and "dangerous" behavior on the mainland United States (Gibbs, 1994), a struggle for "street elite" status provides an additional angle to examining young males' identity development, which includes a perceived need to appear tough.

Ultimately, higher proportions of oppressed minority youth engage in violent behavior in the pursuit of respect, which they feel is unattainable in most acceptable social arenas (Messerschmidt, 1993). The 26-year-old Samoan former gang member interviewed confirms this perspective:

> You know, regardless if you like 'em or not, [Samoans] gonna have, they gonna earn your respect . . . through fear and intimidation. And the only, I mean a lot of the Samoans, they're structured in the family household, but once they leave the house, it's a whole new world because now in the

neighborhood, you tryin' to, you trying to gain status . . . for yourself individually and for the neighborhood. That's how, now that's how gangs start.

Gang affiliation and violent behavior in boys can only be reduced when marginalized youth are assured that respect and success in the classroom are attainable, and that academic success on their part can result in occupational success. In essence, youths' identities should not be constrained by their ethnic backgrounds. Yet at the same time, these youth (both male and female) need to be warned of the challenges they will encounter because of their racialized and gendered positions in society. Stevenson et al. (1997) observe that "those students who have an internalized awareness of racism and their unique cultural heritage will be better prepared to handle life struggles in a race-tense context" (198). This is not to argue that youth should feel limited by their race, class, or gender. They do, however, need to be made consciously aware that because of their current socioeconomic position, and because racism and sexism can hinder social mobility, they will likely face additional social barriers in their efforts to secure educational and occupational mobility.

Furthermore, youth of color, particularly girls, need to see that they have choices, outside of the gang, that offer popularity and employment. In regard to the perceived lack of opportunities available for girls, the 26-year-old respondent stated:

> For females, I think females, they stay in the gang longer than the guys do who are athletes. Guys who excel in athletics, they get the opportunity. But guys who don't excel, those are the guys who gonna be in it with the females for the long run. Cuz that's all the girls know, is know how to live their life, you know, be with that guy and this is how we do it. We wake up, we go to the corner, wait over there, sell our drugs, you know what I mean. . . . That's what they wanna do though. That's what, because again, they feel comfortable in their neighborhood and that's what earns them their status.

These comments reflect a widely held perception that within marginalized communities of color, athletically gifted boys are the only individuals who can expect future success and high public status (see also Hoberman, 1997). The interviewee further demonstrates that too many youths (among nonathletic boys and all girls) do not see mainstream opportunities available, which too frequently leads to gang affiliation and/or juvenile delinquency.

Naturally, it is vital that youth from particular ethnic backgrounds are not tracked solely into athletics. Many Polynesian male participants expressed their exultation in playing football, yet as stated by a 17-year-old Samoan male in a recent newspaper article, this "athletics-only" perception is problematic: "People think if you're Samoan, you're stupid and you steal. . . . Sometimes football is the only time they say you're good" (Kreifels, 1999:A8).

Miller (1998a) has expanded the problematic nature of tracking Polynesians into athletics, noting that Polynesian athletes are often unjustly regarded as more athletic, but less intellectually capable. For instance, Miller quotes two white sports figures, who state, "Polynesian players were naturally superior to us in talent, but a lot of them aren't there (still playing rugby) now because they didn't have the discipline for physical conditioning. They lacked the right kind of mental attitude," (138) and "your typical Polynesian rugby team would just have lost their head in a pressure situation. It was almost as if it was the Polynesian way to do something really stupid . . ." (138). Thus, although athletics offer an avenue of social mobility for some young Polynesian males, competing within this athletic context too often reifies false and inversely related racial stereotypes of athleticism and intelligence. Somehow, if perceived athleticism increases, perceived intelligence in turn decreases, thereby inducing a type of "dumb jock" identity for Polynesian youth.

Here, it is appropriate to highlight the ways in which young African American males and young Polynesian males are similarly stereotyped—as more athletic but less intellectually motivated and able. As early as 1973, Edwards noted the problematic nature of associating African American identity with innate athletic superiority, stating, ". . . by asserting that blacks are physically superior, even well-meaning people at best may be reinforcing some old stereotypes long held about Afro-Americans—to wit, that they are 'little removed from the apes' in their overall evolutionary and cultural development" (Edwards, 1973: 199).

For Polynesian youth as well, making an assumed association between race and athleticism influences an inaccurate ethnic identity grounded in brawn, not brains. Moreover, tracking young males of color primarily into athletics and encouraging a sports fixation (Hoberman, 1997) further tracks these young males of color out of the classroom, where most skills to succeed in professional workplace settings are acquired. Even for young men of color who possess above-average athletic skills and can attend a four-year university through an athletic scholarship, the chances of making a professional career via athletics are still extremely slim. And finally, it is rare that collegiate athletics provide an environment conducive to academic success and graduation for many minority student-athletes (Sperber, 1993).

But Polynesian boys were not the only participants who expressed troublesome aspects of partaking in high school sports. Polynesian girls also enjoyed participating in athletics, but experienced a different set of problems. For instance, one 15-year-old Samoan girl said,

> . . . we never have assemblies for girls. Like our football boys didn't even make, um play-offs. I think, or they only went to first round. Us, we usually went to second round, last year, and like they still don't make one assembly for us. They make one big ol' assembly for the boys. Ah whatevah's . . . all the girls are against it. One time we wanted to do something, but we didn't want to end up getting cut [from the team], yeah, so kind'a didn't do it.

Athletic recognition is very important for boys and girls, yet girls are not provided with equal rewards. This relative absence of positive stimuli in girls' athletics further influences girls of color who are tracked into sports (more so than in academics) to further withdraw from school, fall into delinquency, and enhance an identity grounded in discouragement and gendered inequality.

In terms of direct violence, although participants stated that girls did not fight with one another as much as boys, violence between girls was not reported to be uncommon. What prompted fighting between girls, however, was much different than the type of masculine posturing that often instigated male violence. Focus group participants repeatedly stated that when girls fought with one another, disputes revolved primarily around romantic conflicts involving boyfriends. Female participants said fights between girls begin with rumors and gossip, as stated here by a participant from Group 13, "Yeah, like da kine, you went out with her ex[-boyfriend], that stuff, get mad . . . fist fight the girl." Another 15-year-old female participant from Group 5 also said fighting is prevalent between girls, "if one chick went out with one's ex-boyfriend." These types of "he say, she say" conflicts are not unusual amongst adolescent girls (Anderson, 2000: 311).

Artz (1998) found much of the same pattern in her study of girls' aggression. She linked girls' aggression to patterns of "horizontal violence" found in other powerless groups; here girls mimic the oppressor's behavior (male violence) and beat up similarly situated girls, often on the most specious of pretexts. Artz contends that such female-on-female violence does little to challenge the sexual status quo and becomes a form of tension release that affirms rather than challenges the sex/gender system in high schools.

Artz also noted that the violence was often linked to girls' troubled relations with other girls and with boys. Here, evidence is presented that the "cause" of violence against girls was often their sexual behavior vis-a-vis boys (many of the girls were beaten because they were acting like "sluts," which often means no more than flirting with another girl's boyfriend), and that the audience for much female-on-female violence was boys, who enjoy "watching girls fight" (Artz, 1998: 104). Clearly, these different ways in which gendered behavior influences youthful violence must be accounted for when understanding youthful identity maturation.

When it comes to developing youth violence prevention programs that seek to impress identity formation, it is clear that gender-specific programs must include conflict resolution components that steer boys away from violent behavior as a way to establish masculinity (Connell, 1987). Mitigating violence between girls, on the other hand, would include components that helped girls become less dependent on male approval while also addressing the high levels of victimization found in the histories of violent girls (Artz, 1998).

". . . They Dress as Hoochie Mammas—You Know, Like Hookers."

Labeled identities of youth are frequently racialized and gendered simultaneously, according to the youth we interviewed. Whereas Filipino boys were stereotyped as knife carriers and gang members, Filipino girls were often stereotyped in ways that emphasized their sexuality. Filipino girls were repeatedly tagged with the term "hoochie mamma" by non-Filipino participants, and some Filipino males. For instance, a number of non-Filipino participants made the following comments:

> "You know, the way the girls dress, the way the Filipinos dress, that separates them again, like all the hoochies . . ." "[Filipino] girls, they dress as hoochie mammas—you know, like hookers." "They wear da kine, skanky kine clothes." "[Filipino girls are] like too hoochie out you know. They gotta show off everything."

When asked if all Filipino girls dressed in this manner, one participant stated, "Not all, but most," with the other participants demonstrating agreement. Focus group participants frequently added that girls who dress more provocatively derive much of their self-esteem through their physical appearance and attention from boys. And not surprisingly, Filipino girls were also constructed as more compliant than girls from other ethnic groups, as a female participant from Group 4 stated, "The [Filipino] girls don't want [trouble]. They're scared of everybody."

Because these particular girls were labeled "loose" or "promiscuous," by boys of all ethnicities (including some Filipino boys), they became subject to more sexual harassment and objectification in the way of name-calling, whistling, and other forms of put-downs. For example, a number of Filipino female participants from Group 13 said, ". . . and there was this girl and she was wearing heels and this high skirt and they [boys] was flashing the lights on them . . . like what the hell?"; "[the boys] go 'oohhh' li'dat, or they whistle. . . . It's so gross." Moreover, girls who dress "provocatively" were often said to be "deserving" of such sexist treatment.

Although a minority of girls from all ethnicities may dress in ways that emphasize their sexuality, most focus group participants steadily asserted that Filipino girls specifically were much more apt to dress in this manner than girls from other ethnic groups. Filipino female participants said emphatically, however, that although a slightly higher proportion of Filipino girls may dress in such a way, the majority of Filipino girls do not. Still, these girls were forced to reconcile their own self-defined identities with those that designated them as sexualized objects. In fact, most girls from all ethnic groups do not dress in ways that overly accentuate their sexuality. However, it is apparent that more than a handful of girls (from all ethnicities) do don youthful fashions, which both sexualize and objectify the wearer. The sources of girls' attention to physical appearance are not hard to locate, given the enormous pressure on girls and women to be "pretty" and popular. As Durham (1998: 386) observes

> Through hetero-eroticized beauty ideals, girls are encouraged to cast themselves as objects of male desire while being admonished never to succumb to that desire or to acknowledge their own. Instead, their primary sexual role is culturally defined as bearing the burden of rejecting or accepting male advances without any interrogation or analysis of those advances.

Beauty ideals, she continues ". . . help to socialize girls into roles that historically have been advantageous to men in multiple arenas including the workplace" (Durham, 1998: 386). These interviews also suggested that girls who do not fit male standards of beauty will have higher levels of body shame (McKinley, 1998). While Filipino girls were tagged as dressing in a hypersexual style, Polynesian girls were often said to be somewhat less feminine, because they are sometimes viewed as physically larger and heavier than Asian and Filipina girls. Filipino participants from Group 13 said, for example, "I guess the Samoan girls seem, they act manly, you know like, I don't know, I don't think guys would like to date girls who are tough like that," and "[Samoan girls] look all mean, like most of the girls are bigger than our Filipino guys." In a society that places such high social prestige for women on thinness and smallness, the characterization of girls as big and tough can result in girls feeling socially marginalized and masculinized.

These interviews suggest that girls of different ethnicities experience significant difficulty in their attempts to negotiate the cultural terrain established by a media bent on the construction of images of European American beauty. Essentially, girls of color who can participate in elements of the hypersexual images are constructed as whores (by their own peers), while those young women whose body types make it unlikely that they will be able to participate in mainstream images of beauty are masculinized.

Martinez and Dukes (1991) state that when examining adolescent at-risk factors, "the greatest differences are for female minority group members. Racism and sexism appear to grind them down as they move from junior to senior high school, reflecting, perhaps, cumulative effects" (330). To some extent, the interview results confirm this assertion, as it was the female interviewees who expressed having to oppose both racism and sexism in school and amongst their peers. However, it would be inaccurate to suggest that the girls interviewed were emotionally or psychologically defeated, or "ground down." Conscious of the daily rigors that accompany being a double minority, many of the girls interviewed aired a convincing dissatisfaction with the various forms of discrimination (both racialized and gendered) they were forced to encounter, thereby exhibiting a unique strength rarely acknowledged by others.

Some Concluding Thoughts

This research has documented the ways in which youth in Hawaii experience their own ethnicity and gender, as well as the ways in which youth from economically marginalized neighborhoods view youth from other "have not" ethnic groups. The picture is certainly not consistent with images of racial harmony that were once thought to characterize Hawaii.

Indeed, recent media stories have noted that at some intermediate schools, "Fights occur about three times a month . . . and usually are among students of differing ethnic groups" (Peterson, 1998: A7). Clearly, the racial atmosphere in certain locales is not always convivial; youth stereotype each other and youth are aware of the stereotypes of their own group. They are also keenly aware of the discrimination they experience as a result of holding membership in certain ethnic groups. For some boys of color, there is considerable ambivalence about the fact that athletics is virtually the only way that any of them will achieve prominence in high school. They were also aware that there was very little likelihood that they or their friends would attend college, unless they could play sports and play them well. Certainly, the youth of Polynesian ancestry that we interviewed were well aware that their groups were not known for intellectual achievement, and, indeed, a number knew that they were identified as "violent" by others in their community. Although their social experiences are unique, without question, these youth share many social parallels with other marginalized youth on the mainland, in particular with African Americans. Boys of different ethnicities were also aware of the tensions, sometimes violent, that existed between different nonwhite ethnic groups on their campuses, and the ways in which these tensions ultimately result in youths carrying weapons and joining gangs.

Girls of color are forced to negotiate a terrain that is quite different from that of the boys interviewed. Bombarded by images of white beauty, girls of color seek to either emulate those images (and run the risk of being labeled as "easy" or "whores"), or reject those images of attractiveness, and be subsequently masculinized and stereotyped as "tough" and sometimes "violent." They also face tensions with other girls, often over boys and "rumors," and they, like the boys, experience educational neglect in schools, expressing regret about the fact that their teachers fail to expect much from them—or worse, discriminate against them—because of their ethnicity. Because girls and young women of color must combat being a double minority during a very complicated period in their lives, race theories are incomplete without incorporating the unique impact of gender on the lives of youth of color.

With immigration from numerous regions of Asia, the Pacific, and Latin America still high in many areas of the United States, youth policymakers must be aware that cross-cultural interaction between youth (both American and foreign born) will only increase over time. Therefore, it is important when striving to describe identity development processes in adolescents that scholars advance theoretical paradigms to include complex and multifaceted notions of race and gender. This conceptual framework means incorporating ever-changing immigration patterns, interethnic violence, sexual objectification, notions of class privilege and constraint, and other factors unique to diverse communities. In particular, this study has demonstrated why it is vital that notions of adolescent development seek to capture and document the multiple and complex identities that modern youth craft to deal with their worlds. To capture this world accurately, researchers must be deeply familiar with the many communities youth negotiate as they traverse through this "new configuration of racialized ethnicity, class, and gender stratification" (Marable, 2000) that increasingly characterizes most U.S. cities.

It is rare to find information about how girls in trouble live their lives from day to day. What is it like out there in *their world* (totally different from the academic world, to say the least!)? The next section explores in some detail exactly what this is like, as reported by researcher Jean Bottcher. This section highlights two of the key themes in female as opposed to male delinquency; namely, the experience of sexual abuse and the double standard many girls live under. These two factors are illustrated in a detailed case study of ten young women who were, at the time of the study, wards of the California Youth Authority. The study was conducted by Jean Bottcher, a researcher with the California Youth Authority (Bottcher, 1986).

THE "RISKY" LIVES OF GIRL DELINQUENTS: BOTTCHER'S CALIFORNIA STUDY

Jean Bottcher gathered what she called the "life accounts" of ten young women incarcerated in Ventura School. She used a mixture of personal interviews and information drawn from case files to attempt to understand the context within which their delinquency was exhibited. Two aspects of Bottcher's group distinguish these girls from the young women in Hawaii. First, ethnically, the bulk of the girls Bottcher interviewed were either African American or Hispanic; second, they were incarcerated for more serious offenses than those of the Hawaii girls (see Table 10–2).

The lives of these young women revealed three common themes: independence at an early age, extensive free time, and the inadvertence of their crimes. Bottcher notes that "an unusual riskiness pervaded their lives. On their own with little by way of plan or purpose, their daily lives seemed especially vulnerable to event, to association and to personal need and feeling" (Bottcher, 1986: 13).

The first pattern Bottcher noted is that as early as the age of ten or eleven (but no later than fourteen or fifteen) much of their time was spent on their own. As is true in the vast majority of both male and female delinquent histories, the parents of these young women were simply not there to give them any sort of guidance.

They achieved their independence in one of two ways. First, for some of them, the circumstances of their lives were so grim (poverty, abandonment, violence in the family, etc.) that they had no choice but to leave or else they were "throwaways." Second, some had so little structure from their parents that they simply took their freedom, usually through some form of manipulation. In either case, they had limited choices. One young woman by the name of Diane ran away from home at the age of twelve and never went back. She had experienced a lot of abuse at home (Diane said, "I really don't recall a day when I didn't get hit . . ."), and her mother, to use Diane's words, "liked to go out and drink." An older brother and a sister had left home or were kicked out when they were teenagers, so Diane just followed suit.

Table 10-2 Profile of Girls in Bottcher's California Study

Name	Age at Interview	Last Offense	Ethnicity/Place of Birth
Margarita	16	Kidnap	Hispanic/Nicaragua
Birdie	18	Forcible rape	African American/California
Janet Ann	20	Murder	American Indian/Oklahoma
Carla	18	Battery	Hispanic/Mexico
Le Thi	16	Robbery	Asian/Vietnam
Sad Girl	18	Possession of Hype Kit, missing on parole	Hispanic/California
Diane	17	Assault with a deadly weapon	African American/California
Rose	21	Prostitution	African American/ Puerto Rican/New York
Perline	20	Robbery	White/California
Roberta	16	Missing on parole, drugs	Hispanic/California

SOURCE: Bottcher, Jean. *Risky Lives: Female Versions of Common Delinquent Life Patterns* (Sacramento: California Youth Authority, 1986): 12–13.

When Perline was just five years old, her mother left and ran off with a boyfriend. By the time she was in the sixth grade, she left her father and went to live with her mother and stepfather. Perline eventually dropped out of school while in the tenth grade. At the age of fifteen, Perline asked her mother if she could live with her boyfriend. Her mother said no, but Perline decided to do it anyway in defiance of her mother.

As stated earlier, at a young age these women began to spend a lot of time on their own, without any sort of adult supervision. They began by cutting school, usually beginning in junior high or middle school (the majority liked elementary school, but like most delinquents and many nondelinquents, had trouble adjusting to junior high or middle school). They began to use school merely as a place to gather and plan the day's activities, which consisted mostly of just "having fun" and "hanging out," which eventually evolved into using drugs and consuming alcohol. Not surprisingly, most found school an alienating experience and just dropped out, and in most cases got suspended at least once.

They were never alone, as they always gravitated toward a group of similarly situated friends, especially a boyfriend. In time, their friends became their home and family. Perline's case was typical. As already mentioned, she took off and went to live with her boyfriend, Harold, when she was around fifteen. As Bottcher writes,

She was in love with Harold and he wanted her to live with him. . . .
In retrospect, she can still remember a few good times—but not many.
When Harold was not drinking, it was fun to be with him. But when
he got back to drinking he was very difficult and violent. Eventually

Harold got into drug dealing and both Harold and Perline got hooked on drugs. . . . She left Harold briefly . . . but she returned and shortly discovered that Harold had planned to do a robbery with her and two of his friends. He threatened to leave her if she didn't go along. . . . (Bottcher, 1986: 25)

Others were attached to groups of friends—a "gang," their "homegirls" and "homeboys," and similar groupings. However, their so-called "friends" too often let them down after crimes were committed; ironically, if anyone came to help out during these times (and few did), it was usually members of their original family.

Most of the time they spent was rather boring. Their daily lives seemed random, casual and idle, but there nevertheless "was an undertone of anxiety that pervaded their lives. They moved from one tight spot, one dilemma, to another. Or they did practically nothing" (28–29). They moved around a lot, and whatever they did was usually done without much planning, usually on the spur of the moment. Here's how one young woman, named Rose, spent a typical day:

. . . I stayed awake all night and slept in the day. . . . I'd get up around four in the afternoon. I'd clean the room, change the sheets, do everything I had to do. . . . I would do my hair, take my shower, iron my clothes, get ready to go out and make some money, or else go out and find somebody to buy me some drugs. . . . Or just go out to eat. Or go see my sister and Pineapple and Charlie. . . . I always found something to do. I was always looking for a way to get some money. . . . (29)

Most survived by turning tricks or, as they say in street slang, having "dates." Roberta describes her daily life as follows:

You would get up sometimes six in the morning, and go out and sit in front of the motel and wait for . . . tricks. Like men going to work and stuff. You know, try to stop them, ask them if they want a date. And then after . . . I'd say about ten, then you would go on about your business. Like go down to the clubs or something and get high, drink. But I don't drink, so I just sit there and trip. . . . Or else stand out in front of the club and talk . . . until about noontime. And then you would go back down there. . . . You would try to catch some tricks during the lunch hour. And then go back down there and do the same thing again until about six in the evening. Try to catch some tricks. And then if you don't, then you just go down there and trip (31–32).

Others in the group Bottcher studied spent time at the homes of friends or relatives. They mostly talked, listened to music, smoked marijuana, and drank liquor.

Few had any concrete plans. For them, events "just happened." Perline noted that "I didn't know what I wanted, what I wanted to be. There were no real long-term goals, no real short-term goals . . . my life just fell in places. It happened" (33). The crimes they got involved in were part of a more general lifestyle that simply evolved in no particular way. For the most part, crime was merely one among other methods of surviving. The bulk of their crimes were attempts to secure property (mostly shoplifting, and some burglaries) for the purpose of selling the goods to a fence. Bottcher writes that most of these young women were actually or more self-consciously living a life of crime. They seemed just as helpless about their arrests. But their arrests, as their lives of crime, appeared so often random and unextraordinary. Day after day, crimes and other things just happened. Life was unplanned and dreary. Why did Birdie commit a purse snatch? "I just seen this lady," she said, "and I took her purse. . . . That was that." (36)

Even though her respondents were doing time for kidnapping, forcible rape, murder, robbery, and assault with a deadly weapon, Bottcher reports that "for many of these young women, crime came as a shock to them. They seemed genuinely caught off guard by the event—totally surprised" (34). Her respondents, too, seemed to drift into criminal behavior largely because their lives were falling apart, they had difficult home situations, or they had left home. They also tended to locate their problems elsewhere, often with their families.

SUMMARY

The girls and boys whose lives have been summarized in this chapter had much in common. First, most were from lower income families. In most cases, both parents held jobs that were highly sex typed and of lower status. Although the girls admitted involvement in a variety of crimes, all of them entered the criminal justice system for offenses typical of female offenders (status offenses). The interviews in the California study made it apparent that the girls did not define themselves as delinquents and, in fact, believed the delinquent label unjustified, particularly because of the offenses for which they were being charged and held.

The girls' family environments were highly unstable, with frequent divorces, separations, and deaths. Relationships with parents or stepparents were strained at best; most girls described being unable to communicate with one or both. Family life was also characterized by high degrees of violence and abuse. Most girls had been severely beaten and, in many cases, sexually abused. Ongoing maltreatment and family disharmony have apparently led to lowered self-esteem and provoked feelings of being unloved and unworthy. Motivated by anger, neglect, and frustration, many directly linked their unrest and problems with the law to their family situations.

Outside the home, the girls faced many dilemmas with their peers, aspirations, and sexuality. Turmoil in the family further complicated outside relationships and heightened the problems. Added to this, low family incomes made it impossible to gain status through typical white, middle-class means. In seeking recognition and popularity, they engaged in behaviors calculated to enhance their standing with peers. Although the behaviors had the potential to eventuate in deleterious consequences (for example, complications with the police and more family strife), the girls saw the "bad girl" image as one of the few options available to them.

The girls expressed traditional attitudes toward the place of men and women in society and approval of such arrangements. They aspired to jobs typically occupied by females, wanted to be married, and anticipated large families. Further, they saw men as strong and assertive, women as passive and nonviolent. The attitudes influenced relationships with romantic partners, for the girls allowed themselves to be abused and bullied. The nature of the girls' family environments, coupled with their limited perceptions of male and female roles, fostered and reinforced low self-esteem and alienation. The girls sought to escape from their problems by selectively reminiscing about the past and fantasizing about the future. Ironically, they saw their less-than-ideal boyfriends as their rescuers through marriage. Marriage was also perceived as bringing an end to loneliness. The fantasies offered hope and a sense of assurance that things would somehow get better.

Girls in the juvenile justice system have been and are survivors as well as victims. Forced to cope with daunting and shocking conditions, they manage accommodations at tremendous cost to themselves. Their behaviors may puzzle us until we understand their predicaments. Their delinquencies are, in fact, attempts to pull themselves out of their dismal circumstances.

NOTE

1. This is taken from a study called "'Talking Story' with Hawaii's Youth: Confronting Violent and Sexualized Perceptions of Ethnicity and Gender" researched and written by David Tokiharu Mayeda, Meda Chesney-Lind, and Jennifer Koo between 1997 and 1998.

11

Programs for
Girls in Trouble

"For years people have assumed that all you have to do to make a
program designed for boys work for girls is to paint the walls pink
and take out the urinals."

MARIAN DANIEL, FEMALE INTERVENTION TEAM, BALTIMORE, MARYLAND, 1996

Girls in trouble, particularly those in the juvenile justice system, share
many problems with their male counterparts. They are likely to be
poor, to have come from disrupted and violent families, and to be
having difficulties in school. In addition, they confront sexual abuse, sexual assaults, unplanned pregnancies, and adolescent motherhood. Girls who live in
poor and violent communities face the greatest challenges to growing up op-
timally. Structural inequality and institutional racism impede girls of marginalized backgrounds from obtaining quality education and employment, accessing
resources, and developing positive life choices. Lack of opportunity increases
despair and the possibility of engaging in self-destructive behavior (Ms. Foundation, 1993). Sometimes perceived economic necessity leads girls to actually
commit crime (see Chapter 5). A survey of girls in training schools by the
American Correctional Association (1990) found that 9 percent of the girls
broke laws specifically because of economic pressures and an additional 9 percent did so to pay for drugs.

Academic failure is another salient risk factor related to youth involvement in delinquency. The American Correctional Association (1990) found that 78 percent of female juvenile offenders had neither completed high school nor obtained a GED. A staggering 12 percent had not even gone beyond elementary school. Of the proportion that did attend school, 29 percent were enrolled in a vocational or technical program. Another study that focused on the educational backgrounds of incarcerated adult women found that almost half (46%) had been expelled from school, while 28 percent had repeated a grade and 26 percent had been placed in a special class (e.g., learning disabilities, etc.; Acoca and Austin, 1996).

Research also indicates that girls, in general, are seven times more likely than boys to drop out of school for family reasons, such as needing to care for siblings, elderly relatives, as well as perhaps their own children (Fine & Zane, 1989). The American Correctional Association (1990) found that 27 percent of the girl offenders dropped out of school because they were pregnant, while 20 percent dropped out because they were parents and needed to care for their kids. Clearly, programming geared toward school success needs to be an integral part of services to at-risk girls.

Substance abuse is another prominent characteristic of girls at risk. The American Correctional Association's study found that 60 percent of the girls in training schools need substance abuse treatment at intake and that more than half are addicted to more than one drug. The survey also reported that almost half of the girls took drugs (34%) or drank alcohol (11%) as a form of self-medication to make themselves feel better. In addition, the majority stated that they used alcohol (50%) and marijuana (64%) regularly. Of the girls who are substance-dependent, most first started using drugs (including alcohol) between the ages of 12 and 15. Although models that delineate the relationship between delinquency and substance abuse have largely involved adolescent males, evidence for females also indicates that substance abuse is highly correlated with disruptive behavior (Girls, Incorporated, 1996).

As was mentioned in an earlier chapter, rates of sexual abuse are exceedingly high among at-risk girls. Girls in the juvenile justice system have experienced particularly outrageous levels of abuse; over 60 percent have been physically abused and 54 percent sexually abused, according to the American Correctional Association survey (1990). Estimates of the general population of girls indicate that at least one-third will suffer some form of abuse before they reach adulthood (Benson, 1990). As we have already noted, there is a strong link between victimization and subsequent delinquent behavior.

Girls often respond to such abuse by fighting back, "acting out," and running away from home. As noted in Chapter 3, studies show that more than 70 percent of girls on the streets run away to flee violence in their homes. One consequence is that these girls are at further risk of victimization and often resort to prostitution, petty theft, and drug dealing just to survive. The American Correctional Association survey noted that more than 80 percent of the girls ran away from home at least once, and an amazing 50 percent ran away six or more times.

As noted in Chapters 3 and 6, girls in general are subjected to problems of self-esteem. Recall the survey by the American Association of University Women (1992) that showed that girls at age nine had higher self-concepts than they did by their adolescent years. Such negative self-images coincide with their risk for distorted body images, eating disorders, and chronic dieting, often leading to high levels of stress and problems. Two large studies have shown that girls are twice as likely as boys to experience depression (Allgood-Merton et al., 1990; Whitaker et al., 1990). One of these studies linked girls' depression to dissatisfaction with their physical appearance. Girls also make more suicide attempts than boys (Pipher, 1994; Miller, 1994). In essence, girls are in grave jeopardy of not developing and maintaining psychological resilience.

The NCCD study of girls in the California juvenile justice system (see Chapter 6) found extensive problems within their families, general academic failure and serious health problems (both physical and mental). Speaking of family problems, the study found that over half of the girls had mothers who had been arrested, some of whom had been incarcerated. Almost half (46%) said their fathers had been incarcerated (a common experience among male delinquents, too). Many of these girls had already borne children and an alarming 83 percent had been separated from their infants during the first three months of the children's lives, while more than half "had not had a single visit with their child or children while in detention or placement (Acoca, 1999: 6).

Not surprisingly, academic failure and other serious problems at school were common in their lives. More than 90 percent had been suspended, expelled, repeated a grade, and/or were placed in a "special" classroom. Fully 85 percent had been suspended or expelled, and the median age at which this occurred was 13. Many said that dropping out of school seemed the only sensible solution, as they continually experienced sexual harassment, racism, problems with peers, and lack of attention on the part of adult professionals (Acoca, 1999).

The vast majority (88%) had experienced many different types of health problems and more than half (53%) said they needed psychological services (probably an underestimate, as many are reluctant to admit such problems). Not surprisingly, about one-quarter had considered suicide, while one-fifth had experienced psychiatric hospitalization. Moreover, 29 percent of the girls had been pregnant at least once and 16 percent were pregnant while they were in custody. Of those who were pregnant while in custody, 23 percent had miscarried (Acoca, 1999). A study of girl offenders in Baltimore arrived at almost identical findings (most had been abused, 14 percent were pregnant while in detention, about a third had serious health problems, etc.; Daniel, 1999).

Programming for girls in the juvenile justice system needs to take into consideration girls' unique situations and their special problems in a gendered society. Traditional delinquency treatment strategies, employed in both preventive and intervention programs, have been shaped largely by commonsense assumptions about what youths (generally boys) need. Sometimes girls will benefit from these assumptions and sometimes not. This chapter first discusses a variety of approaches, with an eye toward problems that girls might encounter in programs based on the approaches. We also review some of the problems of existing youth-serving programs and how girls are generally shortchanged. Next, an ideal program is presented, and then several promising programs are reviewed.

We are sad to report that, as in the previous two editions of this book, readers may be disappointed if they expect to learn of many innovative, effective programs. As reported in the NCCD California study noted above, there is a "paucity of services targeting female juvenile offenders." This was the identical conclusion of a national survey by OJJDP in 1998 (Greene, Peters, & Associates, 1998), which indicated that there were just a few successful programs, most of which are very small and have little funding (Acoca, 1999: 9). Many evaluations of particular approaches do not deal with gender issues, and frequently the evaluated programs do not even serve girls. Further, programs that have been evaluated are often run in training schools—not the best setting to try out a particular strategy. Moreover, evaluations of most programs tend to show that even the most determined efforts to help often yield poor results. Of course, the last two points may be related; programs in closed institutional settings are at a disadvantage and consequently tend to be less effective (Lipsey, 1990). Readers also might hope to see a more extensive consideration of promising, community-based programs for girls, but these have been few and far between.

It might be fruitful to review briefly the general problems associated with the establishment of programs for girls. Before the 1970s (and the second wave of feminism), there was little specific public concern over uniquely female problems such as wife battering and sexual assault, and even less concern over girls' problems (Gordon, 1988). Instead of girls' victimization, it was girls' sexuality that was seen as a problem. The typical response to girls' sexuality was to insist they return to their dysfunctional families and, if they ran from these settings, to place them in foster homes or, alternatively, in institutions "for their own protection."

As noted above, programs for troubled young women in general (and delinquents in particular) have had low funding priority. A report in the mid-1970s noted that "girls' organizations receive only $1.00 of every $4.00 that corporate foundations donate to youth agencies." The Law Enforcement Assistance Administration revealed in 1975 that only 5 percent of federally funded juvenile delinquency projects were directed at girls, and that only 6 percent of all local monies for juvenile justice was spent on girls (Female Offender Resource Center, 1977: 34). A survey of most program evaluations done since 1950 located reports on some 443 delinquency programs; of these, 34.8 percent were exclusively male and 42.4 percent served principally males. Only 2.3 percent of the delinquency programs served only girls, and 5.9 percent served "some males," meaning that most participants were girls (Lipsey, 1990: 58). A review of seventy-five private foundations in 1989 revealed that funding "targeted specifically for girls and women hovered around 3.4 percent" (Valentine

Foundation, 1990: 5). Finally, a 1993 study of the San Francisco Chapter of the National Organization for Women found that only 8.7 percent of the programs funded by the major city organizations funding children's and youth programs "specifically addressed the needs of girls" (Siegal, 1995: 18). Not surprisingly, then, a 1995 study of youth participation in San Francisco after-school or summer sports programs found that only 26 percent of the participants were girls (Siegal, 1995: 20). Both the NCCD California study and the study by OJJDP (both published in 1998) arrived at the same conclusion, which tempts us to conclude: "what else is new?" or perhaps "girls don't matter much."

What are the specific needs of young women in general, and of those who come in contact with the juvenile justice system either as victims or offenders? The most desperate need of many young women is to find the economic means of survival. Whereas females today are still being socialized to believe that their security lies in marriage and motherhood, surveys of teenage mothers indicate that approximately 90 percent receive no financial aid from the fathers of their children (Davidson, 1983: ix; Acoca, 1999). Recent federal welfare legislation has hit teen mothers especially hard as benefits have been cut back, while they are required to live with an adult or stay in school in order to receive benefits. This places a heavy burden on those teens who have experienced abuse in their families and also on those who have dropped out of school because of various learning disabilities. And in many cases, these girls are being forced to establish who the father is in order to receive benefits, which may in turn force them into unwanted marriages (Hoke, 1998; Quigley, 1998; Wald, 1998).

Likewise, a study of homeless youths in Waikiki, about half of whom were girls, discovered that their most urgent needs are housing, jobs, and medical services (Iwamoto, Kameoka, & Brasseur, 1990). A survey conducted in a very poor community in Hawaii (Waianae) revealed that pregnant and parenting teens saw medical care for their children, financial assistance, and child care as their major needs. Social workers in the same community, by contrast, saw parenting classes as paramount, followed by child care, educational and vocational opportunities, and family planning (Yumori & Loos, 1985: 16–17). These findings suggest that though youths understand that economic survival is their most critical need, this is not always the case among persons working with them.

TRADITIONAL APPROACHES

A variety of approaches have been used to deal with delinquent youths—both males and females. In previous editions of this book we reviewed in some detail several of these approaches, such as casework, academic education, and family, individual, and group therapy, among others. Evaluations of these and other approaches have not found very many successes, as noted in a 1970s review by Romig (1978), a meta-analysis by Lipsey (1990),[1] and a review by Dryfoos (1990).

One of the most traditional approaches has been the "casework" approach, also known as the social-work approach, which involves diagnosis, recommendations, and direct services (Romig, 1978: 7). Romig's general conclusion seems just as relevant today: he wrote that an approach based on only diagnosis and recommendations is "doomed to failure from the start" (1978: 7). Casework, which appends a direct-service component to diagnosis and recommendations, apparently fails to add much unless continued access to the service is guaranteed and there is follow-up to ensure that youths can increasingly provide the service for themselves. One might join to Romig's concerns the necessity for casework and services to be delivered by persons who are sensitive to gender issues and culturally aware. Services that are not tailored to the needs of youths in a multicultural society will not be as helpful to a young population that is increasingly nonwhite in composition. Evaluations by subsequent researchers have not found much success (Altschuler & Armstrong, 1984; Karraker, Macallair, & Schiraldi, 1988; Stroul & Friedman, 1988; Lipsey, 1990).

Many programs have stressed improving the educational levels of offenders. Such a focus is clearly appropriate because, according to some estimates, 85 percent of the youths who appear in court are illiterate (Dryfoos, 1990: 99). Over the years delinquency prevention and intervention programs have employed a variety of strategies to improve the academic performance of youngsters labeled as delinquent or predelinquent. Such programs include improving reading, writing, and mathematical skills, and some have among their goals the earning of a high school diploma or a general equivalency diploma (GED).

More optimistic news seems to be coming from delinquency prevention programs that have an educational focus. Specifically, the successes of Head Start and other innovative preschool programs have been connected to later academic success and fewer contacts with the police (Schweinhart, 1987; Dryfoos, 1990: 132–133). Altered after-school curricula and structures also appear to be somewhat successful. Some programs have developed an array of behavior modification programs aimed at teaching problem-solving skills as well as training modules to impart a wide variety of social skills. These have been reported to produce at least short-term successes in the reduction of "antisocial behavior and improved academic achievement" (Dryfoos, 1990: 135). However, other researchers are less sanguine, noting that social skills learned in classroom role playing are not likely to apply to the real-life situations that high-risk youths may find themselves confronting (Henggler, 1989).

Most educational programs have been structured without specific attention to the manner in which the lives of girls and boys, particularly during middle adolescence, are constructed. This occurs despite evidence that at this age, girls and boys exist in two separate school cultures (girls' far more adult and teacher oriented, boys' far more group and peer oriented) (Block, 1984). Educational and social skills programs should be reviewed to ensure that the developmental needs and deficits of girls, in addition to those of boys, are being addressed (Crombie, 1988). For example, girls need to be encouraged to work cooperatively in large groups; boys need additional training in the development and maintenance of intimate, dyadic relationships.

Finally, school programs for youth at risk should have as their general aim the "upgrading of the quality of education, particularly for disadvantaged children" (Dryfoos, 1990: 139). It is increasingly clear that the educational opportunities in poor communities, particularly for children in the early years, should be enriched. That said, the notion that bad schooling causes delinquency needs to be avoided because there is considerable evidence, particularly regarding girls, that problems in school may be caused by problems at home.

One of the most common approaches in delinquency prevention is known generally as *diversion*, which attempts to address the problem *outside* the formal juvenile justice system. This topic is discussed next.

JUVENILE DIVERSION

Diversion involves using programs outside the juvenile justice system to reduce or eliminate offenders' contacts with the system. The programs may take the form of school, probation supervision in lieu of detention, drug treatment in a day program, and remedial education, among many other possibilities. Diversionary programs have a strong theoretical background, which is based firmly on "labeling" principles (see Chapter 5). These principles have evolved from Tannenbaum, who initially wrote in 1938 on the "dramatization of evil," and Becker's notion that social groups create deviance by labeling acts as "deviant" and treating those so labeled as "outsiders," and Lemert's classic statements about labeling leading to "secondary deviance" (Tannenbaum, 1938; Lemert, 1951; Becker, 1963). Thus, the legal interaction by the juvenile justice system may actually perpetuate crime or delinquency by processing cases that might otherwise be ignored, normalized in their original settings, or better dealt with in more informal settings within the community.

One of the most immediate responses to the labeling perspective was the President's Commission on Law Enforcement and Administration of Justice report that called for the creation of "Youth Services Bureaus" to develop alternative programs for juvenile offenders in local communities and many different programs for adult offenders. The establishment of these Youth Services Bureaus began a move toward diverting youths, especially status offenders and other nonserious delinquents, from the juvenile court. These bureaus were quickly established in virtually every community regardless of size (President's Commission on Law Enforcement and Administration of Justice, 1967).

It should not be surprising that conflicting expectations, findings, and conclusions would emerge from such a widespread, disjointed, and complicated social experiment. There are many studies which show that diversion programs are successful in reducing subsequent deviance. These findings are balanced at least equally, however, by findings of no impact. There are, additionally, reports that find diversion programs to have detrimental properties (Polk, 1995).

Proponents of diversion programs cite numerous studies such as the diversion project in Colorado that involved comparisons between an experimental group of diverted youths and a control group that received regular processing within the juvenile justice system. The diversion program administered individual, parental, and/or family counseling to the diversion cases, resulting in significantly lower recidivism rates (Pogebrin, Poole, & Regoli, 1984; see also Frazier & Cochran, 1986).

The most successful diversion projects have been those that provide more intensive services, which is consistent with Dryfoos's findings that successful programs involve more comprehensive services (Dryfoos, 1990). Especially important is the use of experienced youth workers. For example, a project in St. Louis found that the most experienced youth workers were able to bring about greater behavioral changes on the part of their youths, while the inexperienced youth workers did not (Feldman, Caplinger, & Wodarskil, 1983).

The issue of increased or decreased recidivism rates is coupled with the concerns over prejudice, discrimination, civil rights violations, and "net widening." The issue of "net widening" has perhaps received the most attention. Ideally, a true "diversion" program (and the original concept behind diversion) seeks to take those who would ordinarily be processed within the juvenile justice system and place them into some alternative program. So, for instance, if normally you would have 1,000 youths processed within the system, a true diversion would be to take, say, 300 of these youths and place them in some alternative. Essentially, "net widening" would occur if (using these same numbers) the alternative programs would be serving 300 that would not have heretofore been part of the 1,000 normally processed. Thus, instead of having 1,000 youths being dealt with (300 in diversion programs and 700 within the juvenile justice system), you have instead a total of 1,300 being processed (1,000 + 300). In this example, you have a "net gain" or a "net widening" of 300 youths.

Lundman (2001: 125–148) examined several evaluations of diversion programs. Included were the Sacramento County Diversion Program (around 1,500 youths), several other California programs (around 2,500 youths), and the National Evaluation of Diversion programs in four states (about 2,500 youths). The programs included boys and girls. With few exceptions, the experimental groups (that is, children receiving the special treatment included within the diversion programs) did not differ significantly from the control groups in terms of recidivism. But it was also found that the recidivism rates of status offenders were almost identical for those diverted and those not diverted. Thus, diversion of status offenders at least does no greater harm. Because girls are far more likely to have committed status offenses and minor crimes, perhaps diversion is especially suitable for them.

Lundman also reports on two follow-up evaluations, one known as the National Evaluation of Diversion Programs, covering four locations (Kansas City; Memphis; Orange County, Florida; and New York City). Youths were randomly selected to one of three comparison groups: (1) release with no services; (2) release with diversion services; or (3) further penetration into the juvenile justice system. Follow-up was done in 6 and 12 months. The results showed that there were no differences in recidivism rates among the three groups after both 6 months and 12 months. What is significant here is the fact that literally doing nothing (no services, no further penetration into the system) was just as effective as providing services or further punishment!

Finally, Lundman reported on yet another follow-up evaluation, the Youth Enhancement Program (YEP) in Pennsylvania, which was undertaken in the early 1990s. The main attention of this program was on the overrepresentation of minorities in secure state facilities (75 percent of those incarcerated were minorities, even though they represented only 12 percent of the total youth population). The evaluation design was "quasi-experimental" in that participation in one of several types of services was voluntary on the part of the juvenile offenders. Out of a total of 191 who were referred for this program, 83 (43.5%) chose not to participate (and they were the "control group"). The remaining youths who volunteered were split into two groups: one that spent less than 30 hours in the various services provided during the course of one year and another group that spent at least 30 hours in such services (Lundman, 2001: 142). The main goal of the program was to improve school performances and reduce the recidivism rates, especially for minority youth. A variety of existing community services was used, provided by such organizations as Girls, Incorporated; Boys Clubs; and Camp Curtain YMCA.

The results showed little overall improvement in school performance among each of the three groups. However, the results showed that the control group had the highest arrest rate after two years (50.6%), while the "low attendance" group had a recidivism rate of 41.3 percent and the "high attendance" group had the lowest recidivism rate (25.8%). The program also did an effective job at keeping minority youths away from further trouble. The most important conclusion that we can take from this study is that the more youths participate in the various services that are offered, the greater the chance they will succeed.

Most diversion programs have typically used such methods as individual counseling, casework, and work experience as their major treatment modes. None of these types of treatments has worked notably well in other settings, so it is little wonder that they have done no better in diversion programs; rigorous evaluations of diversion programs consistently turn up mixed results (Gibbons & Blake, 1976; Decker, 1985). Additional concerns about diversion programs have surfaced in connection with girls' experiences with them. Specifically, researchers who reviewed these efforts believe that rather than serving as an alternative to formal processing, they have actually widened the net of intervention (Blomberg, 1978; Klein, 1980; Decker, 1985). Alder makes the point that this was more directly a problem for girls than for boys. She notes that girls constitute 40 percent of the participants in diversion programs but only about 25 percent of offense cases in the courts. Moreover, girls are referred for less serious offenses or in some instances no offense at all but simply "personal problems, family difficulties, school problems and the like" (Alder,

1984: 402–404). Alder also uncovered indications that girls with no prior offense records were far more likely than boys to be referred to diversion programs, even though many of the boys had previous arrests. These findings suggest that many girls currently in diversion programs would have been released in times past. At a minimum, she points out, these programs may be unnecessarily monitoring girls who have not committed crimes but are simply having problems with their parents or their schools.

Probation is one of the most common forms of diversion. Developed as an early alternative to incarceration, it has been one of the most common dispositional alternatives of the juvenile court since its founding in 1899. Basically, probation involves supervision of a delinquent within the community. Probation officers are expected to help their "clients" with problems, and they are also supposed to enforce the "conditions of probation" (rules and regulations). The two mandates make the role of probation officer an often contradictory one (Lundman, 2001).

Other kinds of probation programs did not yield significant differences between groups assigned to regular probation and groups assigned to special programs, such as day care treatment and group counseling (Romig, 1978: 129–132). Similarly, Lipsey reported that enhanced probation or parole services had extremely modest effects on recidivism (3%). Only slightly more effective were release programs, 5 percent; reduced caseloads, 4 percent; and probation with restitution, 4 percent. Romig (1978: 133) concluded that regular probation is just as successful as all the more expensive programs, if not more so. He declared that probation programs should have the following ingredients: indigenous probation aides who are empathetic and who set individualized and specific treatment goals for youth, involvement of family, aides to monitor school attendance, active use of the community, and a variety of treatment approaches (137).

One very unique diversion, known as the Detention Diversion Advocacy Project, was begun in San Francisco in the early 1990s and has since spread to other locations, such as Washington, DC and Philadelphia. We now turn to a more detailed look at this program.

THE DETENTION DIVERSION ADVOCACY
PROJECT (DDAP)

The original Detention Diversion Advocacy Project (DDAP) was begun in 1993 by the Center on Juvenile and Criminal Justice (CJCJ) in San Francisco, California. The program's major goal is to reduce the number of youths in court-ordered detention and provide them with culturally relevant community-based services and supervision. Youths selected are those that are likely to be detained pending their adjudication. DDAP provides an intensive level of community-based monitoring and advocacy that is not presently available in most programs.

Disposition case advocacy is the concept that describes the type of approach being used in this program. This method has been defined as "the efforts of lay persons or nonlegal experts acting on behalf of youthful offenders at disposition hearings" (Macallair, 1994: 84). Clients are primarily identified through referrals from the public defender's office, the probation department, community agencies, and parents. Admission to DDAP is restricted to youths currently held, or likely to be held, in secure detention. The youths selected are those deemed to be "high risk" in terms of their chance of engaging in subsequent criminal activity. The selection is based upon a risk assessment instrument developed by the National Council on Crime and Delinquency. The target population is those whose risk assessment scores indicate that they would ordinarily be detained. This is what Miller has termed the "deep-end" approach (Miller, 1998a).

This is very important, for by focusing on detained youth the project ensures that it remains a true diversion alternative, rather than "net widening." Youths are screened by DDAP staff to determine if they are likely to be detained and whether they present an acceptable risk to the community.

Client screening involves gathering background information from probation reports, psychological evaluations, police reports, school reports, and other pertinent documents. Interviews are conducted with youths, family members, and adult professionals to determine the types of services required. Once a potential client is evaluated, DDAP staff presents a comprehensive community service plan at the detention hearing and requests that the judge release the youth to DDAP custody.

Because the project deals only with youths who are awaiting adjudication or final disposition, their appropriateness for the project is based on whether they can reside in the community under supervision without unreasonable risk and their likelihood of attending their court hearings. This is similar in principle of what often occurs in the adult system when someone is released on bail pending his or her court hearings (e.g., arraignments, trial).

The primary goal of the project is to design and implement individualized community service plans that address a wide range of personal and social needs. Case managers locate services that address specific linguistic or medical needs. Along with the youth's participation, the quality and level of services is monitored by DDAP staff. It should be noted that the purpose of multiple collaborations is to ensure that the project is able to represent and address the needs of the various communities within San Francisco in the most culturally appropriate manner. Because ethnicity, race, and community have historically fragmented youth services in San Francisco, a more unified approach is being tried with DDAP in that it has become a neutral site within the city staffed by representatives from CJCJ and several other community-based service agencies.

Shelden conducted an evaluation of this program, which consisted of comparing a group of youths referred to DDAP with a similarly matched control group that remained within the juvenile justice system (Shelden, 1999). The results showed that after a three-year follow-up, the recidivism rate for the DDAP group was 34 percent, compared to a 60 percent rate for the control group. Detailed comparisons holding several variables constant (e.g., prior record, race, age, gender, etc.) and examining several different measures of recidivism (e.g., subsequent commitments, referrals for violent offenses) showed that the DDAP youths still had a significantly lower recidivism rate.

How does this type of program relate to girls? Were there any significant differences in outcomes based upon gender? The next section explores these and other questions.

Gender Differences

Girls comprised a total of 105 subjects (19.4%), while boys comprised 437 of the total subjects. Among the DDAP cases, girls constituted a total of 43 (representing 41 percent of all girls in both samples and 16 percent of all DDAP cases).

As noted in Table 11–1, though there were some important differences, for the most part males and females did not differ very much. The differences included referral age, risk scores, the nature of prior offenses, and subsequent petitions. Girls were more likely than boys to be younger (about one-third of the girls were 14 or younger, compared with 18.5 percent of the boys), and they were more likely to have low risk scores (38 percent vs. 28 percent for the boys), which may be related to the nature of previous offenses for girls. The prior offenses for girls were significantly more likely to be of a minor nature (mostly shoplifting and status offenses).

Boys and girls did not differ in terms of race, whether or not they had any prior referrals and prior out-of-home placements. Recidivism rates did not vary according to gender, no matter how this was defined. Thus, both boys and girls were about equally likely to be serious recidivists (see definition above), have two or more subsequent referrals, have at least one subsequent out-of-home placement, and have a subsequent referral for a violent crime (most of these, incidentally, were simple assaults).

As noted in Table 11–2, when looking at girls only and comparing the DDAP group with the control group, we find few statistically significant differences. However, what is noteworthy is that the control group did have a somewhat higher overall recidivism rate (48 percent vs. 30 percent) and a slightly higher rate of serious recidivism. What was statistically significant was that the DDAP group was more likely to have high risk scores than the control group (78.8 percent vs. 53.2 percent). This may have something to do with the fact that the DDAP girls were more likely to have had previous out-of-home placements (one-third did, compared to only 13 percent of the control group). What is important to note here is the fact that so many of these girls had only minor prior offenses (31%), although girls referred for minor offenses were no more likely than boys with similar charges to receive out-of-home placements. The majority of those receiving placements had been charged with a serious offense.

Another significant finding was that the control group was far more likely to have two or more subsequent referrals (43.5 percent vs. 11.6 percent). In other words, while the overall recidivism rates were not statistically significant

Table 11–1. Comparing Gender with Selected Variables

	Male (n=437)	Female (n=105)	Significance
DDAP	52.2%	41.0%	
Control	47.8	59.0	p. <.05
Referral Age			
14 and under	18.5%	32.4%	
15 and older	81.5	67.6	p. <.01
Race			
White	13.0%	11.4%	
Black	52.6	62.9	
Other	34.3	25.7	ns
Risk Scores			
Low (under 10)	27.5%	37.9%	
High (10 or more)	72.5	62.1	p. <.05
Prior Referrals	64.1%	59.0%	ns
Nature of Priors			
Serious Violence	43.2%	35.5%	
Serious Other	42.1	33.9	
Minor (including status)	14.7	30.6	p. <.05
Prior Placements	21.5%	21.0%	ns
Recidivism Rate:			
Total	48.7%	41.0%	
Serious Recidivist	35.5	31.4	
Minor Recidivist	13.3	9.5	ns
Two or More Subsequent Referrals	32.7%	30.5%	ns
Subsequent Placements	21.5%	19.0%	ns
Subsequent Referrals, Violent Crime	18.1%	12.4%	ns
Subsequent Petitions	37.8%	26.7%	p. <.05

(including no differences as far as serious and minor recidivists are concerned), it appears that the DDAP girls had only one subsequent appearance in court, if they returned at all.

Table 11–3 shows a comparison of the DDAP and control group for boys only. As with girls, one of the most significant relationships concerned risk scores and prior placements. For the DDAP group the risk scores were considerably higher, as 85 percent had scores of 10 or higher, compared with only 61 percent of the control group. Viewed somewhat differently, the control group was twice as likely to have low risk scores. Nevertheless, the recidivism rates were considerably higher for the control group. The total recidivism rate was 35 percent for the DDAP group and 64 percent for the control group; the serious recidivism rate for the control group was double that for the DDAP group.

Table 11–2. Comparison of DDAP and Control Groups, Girls Only (n=105)

	DDAP	Control	Significance
Prior Referrals	55.8%	61.3%	ns
Nature of Priors			
Serious Violence	16.3%	24.2%	
Serious Other	25.6	16.1	
Minor (including status)	14.0	21.0	ns
Prior Placements	32.6%	12.9%	p. <.05
Risk Scores			
Low (under 10)	21.2%	46.8%	
High (10 or more)	78.8	53.2	p. <.05
Recidivism Rate			
Total	30.2%	48.4%	
Serious Recidivist	23.3	37.1	
Minor Recidivist	7.0	11.3	ns
Two or More Subsequent Referrals	11.6%	43.5%	p. <.001
Subsequent Placements	18.6%	19.4%	ns
Subsequent Referrals, Violent Crime	11.6%	12.9%	ns
Subsequent Petitions	20.9%	30.6%	ns

Table 11–3. Comparison of DDAP and Control Groups, Boys Only (n=437)

	DDAP	Control	Significance
Prior Referrals	64.5%	63.6%	ns
Nature of Priors			
Serious Violence	24.6%	32.1%	
Serious Other	28.9	25.8	
Minor (including status)	11.4	7.7	ns
Prior Placements	26.3%	16.3%	p. <.05
Risk Scores			
Low (under 10)	14.9%	38.8%	
High (10 or more)	85.1	61.2	p. <.001
Recidivism Rate			
Total	35.1%	63.6%	
Serious Recidivist	23.7	48.3	
Minor Recidivist	11.4	15.3	p. <.001
Two or More Subsequent Referrals	14.9%	52.2%	p. <.001
Subsequent Placements	18.0%	25.4%	ns
Subsequent Referrals, Violent Crime	8.8%	28.2%	p. <.001
Subsequent Petitions	24.1%	52.9%	p. <.001

Other indications of recidivism further point to the differences between the two groups. First, the control group boys were more than three times as likely as the DDAP group to have two or more subsequent referrals. Second, the control group was significantly more likely to be referred on a charge of violence and to have subsequent petitions. Third, although not statistically significant, the control group was slightly more likely to have subsequent placements.

A comparison of boys and girls revealed literally no significant differences in terms of socio-demographic variables. For instance, while 76 percent of the girls came from single-parent families (mostly female-headed), so did 72 percent of the boys. There was a small difference in school attendance, but not statistically significant (55 percent of the boys and 45 percent of the girls were attending at the time of the referral to DDAP). Though girls were slightly more likely to have been either suspended or expelled from school (36 percent vs. 29 percent of the boys), this relationship was not statistically significant. There was virtually no difference between boys and girls as far as drug use was concerned, as just over half of each group had used drugs at least once (55 percent of the boys and 52 percent of the girls). There was a slight difference in the proportion living in poverty (49 percent of the girls vs. 39 percent of the boys), but this was not statistically significant. Also, no racial differences existed and there were no significant neighborhood differences.

Although there were some significant gender differences when considering both samples together, when looking closely at girls and boys separately, it appears that the impact of the DDAP program was greater for boys than for girls. Indeed, the recidivism rates among the boys were significantly different for the DDAP and control groups. DDAP boys fared much better than control group boys. Although girls in the control group did have a higher recidivism rate (48 percent vs. 30 percent), this relationship was not statistically significant. This could stem from the relatively small number of girls in the total sample ($n = 105$). On the other hand, control group girls were far more likely to have two or more subsequent referrals. Thus, while the DDAP girls were not likely to be prevented from returning to the court once, the extent to which they remained within the system (measured by the total number of subsequent referrals) was diminished as a result of their participation in the program.

However, the far greater impact of the DDAP program for the boys does raise some concerns. It could be because of the relatively short supply of programs that address the unique needs of girls. A 1996 report on programs for girls in San Francisco noted that while women and girls are the fastest growing segment of the juvenile justice population in that city, they "are all but invisible in terms of programs and statistics" (Schaffner et al., 1996: 1). Apparently not much has changed in San Francisco since a 1992 study concluded that, after a survey of 154 service providers, the needs of young women in the juvenile justice system are "unexamined, untreated, and invalidated by both the system charged with serving them and by their own community and family support structures" (Delinquency Prevention Commission, 1992: 3). This same report further noted that "These institutions fail to develop a diversity of placement options for girls, to encourage and contract with community-based programs targeting the needs of girls, even to collect information on who the girls are, what they need, and what worked to meet such needs" (Ibid.: 8).

There may be several reasons for the apparent success of the DDAP program. From the data collected here and information from previous research, three reasons seem of paramount importance.

First, the caseloads of the DDAP caseworkers are extremely low in comparison to those of normal probation officers. The DDAP workers average about ten cases each. Regular probation officers in major urban areas have caseloads ranging from 50 to 150. Smaller caseloads typically result in more intensive supervision, and more intensive supervision means that the caseworker is constantly "on top of things" with regard to his or her clients. Indeed, with small caseloads, caseworkers can spend more "quality time" with their clients in the field (e.g., in their homes, on the street corners, at school), rather than spending endless hours in an office doing paperwork, talking on the phone, and doing other bureaucratic chores.

Second, DDAP is a program that is "out of the mainstream" of the juvenile justice system; that is, it is a true "alternative" rather than one of many bureaucratic extensions of the system. This means that normal bureaucratic restrictions do not generally apply. For instance, the qualifications for being a caseworker with DDAP are not as strict as you might find within the juvenile justice system (e.g., age restrictions, educational requirements, arrest records, "street" experience, etc.). From casual observations of some of these caseworkers, at least one researcher was impressed with their dedication to and passion about helping youth. Moreover, the backgrounds of these workers were similar to the backgrounds of some of their clients (e.g., similar race, neighborhood of origins, language, etc.).

Third, the physical location of DDAP seemed to observers "user friendly" and lacked the usual "macho" appearance of the formal system. There are no bars, no concrete buildings, no devices for screening for weapons as one enters the building, no "cells" for "lockdown," etc. Further, the DDAP workers are not "officers of the court" with powers of arrest and bearing the usual accoutrements of such occupations (e.g., badges, guns).

There could also be a possible fourth explanation, though one we can only speculate on at this time because we lack the data to draw such a conclusion. It could be that given the low caseloads, DDAP caseworkers are more likely than regular probation officers to be "on top of the case," that is, be in constant contact with the youth and thus be able to "nip in the bud" potential problems. Also, if some police officers, when facing a possible arrest situation, learn that the youth is a DDAP case (presuming the officer knows about DDAP), they may be in a position to contact the caseworker, who might be able to show that the situation could be handled without a formal arrest. We have no way of knowing whether or not this occurs with any degree of regularity. Even if it did, such a procedure may be a positive sign; youths from more privileged backgrounds are often treated this way by the police, if it is believed that someone in authority can "handle" the youth informally. Significant adults in their lives have made a significant difference in the lives of many youths.

Though certainly not a "magic bullet," DDAP has much promise. It remains to be seen if such a program can adapt to the needs of girls, but we suspect that it can, provided the appropriate services are made available.

FOSTER CARE AND GROUP HOMES

Foster care is defined as a "24-hour substitute care for children placed away from their parents or guardians and for whom the State agency has placement and care responsibility" (National Clearinghouse, 2001). Foster homes have long been held up as a form of residential treatment that allows young people to grow up in a familylike setting and that has the potential to prevent further delinquent behavior. In a twelve-year follow-up of boys placed in foster homes, McCord, McCord, and Thurber (1968) discovered that youths placed in such settings were involved in significantly more criminal behavior than boys not so placed. These negative findings sounded early warnings in regard to foster care.

In 1980, Congress approved sweeping reforms under the Adoption Assistance and Child Welfare Act that, in part, recognized that too many young people were being uprooted from their families only to embark upon the foster care circuit. States receiving federal foster care dollars were required to develop a permanent plan for placement in the least restrictive and most familylike setting available. There is some evidence that the law had the desired effect, at least initially. The number of youths in foster care dropped from 500,000 in 1977 to 263,000 in 1982. The mean length of stay was also falling (Sullivan, 1988a: B3). Since this time the numbers have been climbing, hitting a high mark of an estimated 568,000 as of September 1999 (National Clearinghouse, 2001). The median age of children in foster care was 10.1 years. More were racial minorities (64%), with African American children constituting the largest category at 42 percent; whites constituted 36 percent of the total. The gender breakdown was 52 percent males and 48 percent females. The specific breakdown of placements in foster care was as follows: 48 percent in family foster homes, 26 percent in relative foster homes, 17 percent in group homes or institutions, and the remainder in other types of homes. It should be noted that the actual total of foster homes is not known, although 38 states reported a total of 133,503 homes as of the end of 1998 (National Clearinghouse, 2001).

There are concerns that within foster homes, young people are being maltreated. The most recent estimate by the National Clearinghouse on Child Abuse and Neglect is that around 1.5 percent of all children who were maltreated in 1999 were victimized by "substitute care providers." Although a small percentage, this figure translates to around 12,390 children out of an estimated 826,000 maltreated in 1999 (National Clearinghouse, 1999). In a landmark civil rights class action suit (*G. L. v. Zumwalt 1983*), a federal court approved a consent decree mandating specific widespread improvements in the policies and practices of the entire foster care system of a major metropolitan area. The attorneys who brought the case had found that 29 percent in a study sample of 194 foster children in Jackson County, Missouri, had been in four or more homes in less than five years, that 31 percent had had four or more case-workers, and that for 74 percent of the foster children, there was no record of face-to-face caseworker visits during the past year.

The attorneys also documented abuse and neglect in foster homes and found that in all but 3 percent of the homes in the study, the foster parents had received no training (Mushlin, Levitt, & Anderson, 1986: 146–147). Such con-ditions are not unique to Missouri (see, for example, Prescott, 1981; Glave, 1987). As a longtime observer of foster care, Congressman George Miller said, "We are in the situation now where we are underwriting a system of abuse. Amnesty International ought to take a look at these kids" (Sullivan, 1988a: B3).

Scandals continue to be uncovered in not just the foster care system, but the entire system that deals with abused and neglected children. A recent case in Newark, New Jersey, is illustrative. According to a *New York Times* story, a seven-year-old African American boy was found dead in the basement of a home where he was placed by the New Jersey Division of Youth and Family Services (Jones & Kaufman, 2003). Further investigation discovered a national pattern of overworked caseworkers. In the Newark case, it was found that the caseworker who was in charge of this particular boy had a caseload of 107. The average caseload was 35, with many having caseloads in excess of 70, and one having 147 cases. The Child Welfare League has recommended a caseload of no more than 17. Not surprisingly, turnover is quite high (in Newark 65 per-cent of the caseworkers have less than two years of experience). In this partic-ular case, the boy was left with his twin brother and another sibling (both severely malnourished and being treated at a local hospital at the time this story appeared). They had been placed under the temporary care of a cousin while their mother was serving time in a local jail. The mother had been un-der investigation for 11 allegations of child abuse and neglect during the pre-vious decade, including leaving the children alone for extended periods of time (Jones & Kaufman, 2003).

The *New York Times* story goes on to note that in New Jersey there are 1,300 caseworkers who handle about 39,000 allegations of abuse and neglect each year, of which around 8,000 are substantiated. Around 11,000 were in foster care at the time. The story also noted many previous deaths of children within the state. Between 1997 and 1999, for instance, there were 39 deaths of children by abuse or neglect (Jones & Kaufman, 2003).

Still another recent case, this time in Chicago, Illinois, further illustrates some of the problems with the foster care system. In Illinois, whose youth welfare system was seen as a model for the nation as a whole, six adults were arrested on charges of child abuse and 12 children were taken to emergency shelters. While on a drug raid, the police found a three-year-old boy "chained by the neck to a bed in a foster home where they also found cocaine, cannabis and unregistered firearms" (Wilgoren, 2003). In another case in Chicago, the police found six children (including two girls) in a basement, with no food, nor even a toilet, and just a quilt and a few pillows to cover a concrete floor. Cook County public guardian Patrick Murphy quipped that "Child welfare today is basically run the same way it was run in the 1890s. They try to do too much and as a result, they end up doing too little." According to the story in the *New York Times*, experts debated whether these two cases were symptomatic of a larger problem or simply aberrations (Wilgoren, 2003).

How effective are group homes? Lipsey (1990) asserted that youths in such placements show a reduction of 8 percent in delinquency recidivism when compared with youths in other programs. But what is unclear from Lipsey's meta-analysis is how comparison groups were established for the studies he reviewed. In Romig's review (1978) of group home programs, youths in such facilities were often compared to youths in even less restrictive settings (usually living at home). His assessment of the eight studies he reviewed was that youths in these settings typically did no better than those in control groups. In five of the eight programs, in fact, the youths in the halfway houses did worse upon follow-up. This outcome he attributed to the reliance of these facilities upon counseling interventions, most notably individual counseling, that have proved to be ineffective in open settings.

Although group home placements are clearly more desirable than institutional placements, concerns remain about their use in response to girls' problems. A study by Simone (1985) of three group homes in Ohio found that over a four-year period, 41 percent of the girls "failed," compared with 30 percent of the older boys and 20 percent of the younger boys. This was despite the fact that girls had far less serious offense profiles; 85 percent of the girls had been placed in the group homes because of a status offense or a probation violation, compared with 47 percent of the older boys. After failing, girls were more likely than boys to go on to a more restrictive environment (81 percent and 61 percent), and boys were more likely to be officially emancipated or released to their homes (360–361). Simone concludes that even group homes are generally not prepared to deal with girls and their problems.

More recently, a survey in Los Angeles conducted by the *Los Angeles Times* arrived at some sobering conclusions about that city's foster care system (*Los Angeles Times*, 2002). It was revealed that about 40 percent of those placed within the county's welfare system eventually drop out of school. The study noted that while state law requires that welfare agencies come up with specific plans for these children, most such plans are "boilerplate that swamped social workers have slapped together on the run." Although there are some success stories in the Los Angeles area, the report notes that "too many of the 50,000 children in public care in Los Angeles remain caught between a bad family and a fate that is potentially worse."

THE IDEAL PROGRAM

What would the ideal program for girls include? There are no easy answers to this, particularly since the literature evaluating programs is quite lean, and especially so in regard to programs for girls. Further, a fair number of components of model programs rely on family-strengthening strategies; these need to be reviewed with care, given the gendered nature of family life and girls' special problems within the family.

Lipsey's meta-analysis reported on a wide variety of programs and listed reductions in recidivism ranging downward from 50 percent. He categorized programs into groups run by juvenile justice agencies and those run by outside agencies. In summarizing the findings, he wrote that "more structured and focused treatments" (for example, employment, behavioral, skill oriented) and multimodal treatments seem to be more effective than "less structured focused approaches" such as counseling. He also said that although some reductions were close to being ratifications of the "nothing works" school of thought, some interventions showed considerable promise. He also declared that programs built on a deterrence model of justice and that included such elements as "shock incarceration" and the "scared straight" program were counterproductive, actually showing increased delinquent behavior among participants.

Romig (1978: 113), after reviewing many rehabilitation programs for delinquents, provided several ingredients of his ideal program. Perhaps the most important is employees who are genuinely empathetic toward young people. He recommended that behavior modification techniques be limited to simple behaviors and that contingency contracting be used when youths set their goals. The goals of rehabilitation should be as specific as possible. For instance, if education is a goal, the program should culminate in the awarding of a diploma or certificate. Job training should support educational training and should include job advancement skills and career decision-making skills. Further, there should be a follow-up after job placement. If individual counseling is used, it should get input from the youngsters about their problems, and specific behavioral goals should be arrived at. The new behaviors taught should be practiced and evaluated.

Finally, if the family is the unit of intervention, the program should focus on improving communication. Particularly important here is the need to include some forms of parental training. Romig's advisory comments were supported by Lipsey's positive findings concerning behavior programs that showed success in both juvenile justice and public settings (12 percent and 10 percent reductions in recidivism).

Dryfoos (1990) suggested that "programs should have broader goals than delinquency prevention per se" and that they should have multiple components because no one component has proved to be a "magic bullet." She also stressed the need for early intervention and the importance of allowing schools to play an integral role because the characteristics of safe and orderly schools are well understood. Moreover, programs should stress "institutional rather than individual change." Dryfoos qualified her last point by adding that intensive, individual attention with "personalized planning" is important to success in work with high-risk youth. If the effort is undertaken, "treatment integrity" (carrying out a program as designed) must be maintained, and because program benefits tend to become diluted after intervention stops, continuity of effort is important (146). But what of programs directed at girls? During our interview with Lois Lee, director of the program Children of the Night, we asked what she would include in an ideal program. Although her seven ingredients apply to programs for runaway girls and prostitutes, most have relevance for programs for other delinquents and youth in trouble (and some are really philosophical points about working with young people in trouble on the streets).

First, "Don't throw them out." In other words, let them know that if they want your help you will not turn them away. Many have come from abusive and dysfunctional families and have already experienced abandonment, and some have been literally thrown out of their homes. Second, "Don't allow them to fail." In other words, give them some sense of accomplishment (finding a job, getting a GED, improving their self-concepts, turning in their pimp, leaving their pimp, and so on). They have already experienced too many failures in life. Third, "Don't leave them to their own resources." In other words, with the limited resources they possess, they have already failed and have proved that they need help. They need other resources. Left on their own, they will no doubt return to the life that they have been living. Fourth, the ideal program should have a hotline, preferably around the clock. After all, crises do not obey an 8-to-5 or 9-to-6 Monday–Friday schedule. Fifth, "Don't try to rescue them." In other words, don't always try to stop them from doing what you know will be a mistake. There are times when people simply have to learn the hard way. Sixth, change their relationship with the police. They must be convinced that ultimately the police will be on their side if they are being victimized or if they have a serious problem and want or need help. Seventh, and perhaps most important, in working with young people in trouble, try to understand their sub-culture—their value system, lifestyle, and the like. Such understanding precludes shock at what one hears and sees, and mitigates a tendency to patronize troubled youngsters or to discredit their beliefs and impose your own value system.

SHORTCHANGING GIRLS: PATTERNS WITHIN YOUTH-SERVING PROGRAMS

Because the majority of delinquency prevention programs are co-ed, the specific needs of girls are either shortchanged or simply ignored because of the population of boys who outnumber them. Programs that are single-sex within the juvenile justice system provide far more options for boys than for girls. In fact, a list of "potentially promising programs" identified by the Office of Juvenile Justice and Delinquency Prevention cites 24 programs specifically for boys in contrast to only 2 programs specifically for girls (Girls, Incorporated, 1996). Ironically, one program geared for incarcerated teen fathers has no counterpart for incarcerated teen mothers.

Often programs tend to miss the "at-risk" years for girls. A comprehensive survey of 112 individual youth-oriented programs (for both delinquent and nondelinquent youth) showed that less than 8 percent provided services to girls between the ages of 9 and 15, the crucial determining years of adolescence and the years when self-esteem plummets (American Association of University Women, 1992). Rather, services and programs tended to serve girls younger than the age of 9 and those between 14 and 21 years of age.

Moreover, the few programs available for girls often tend to address single issues, such as teen pregnancy and mothering, although occasionally other problems such as substance abuse or gang behavior are included. This pattern is largely a result of issue-specific funding initiatives, but it means that girls' often interconnected and overlapping problems get ignored. Similarly, programs tend to be more intervention oriented ("reactive") rather than preventive, concentrating more on girls who are already in trouble than on girls who are at risk of getting into trouble (Ms. Foundation for Women, 1993).

Unfortunately, at-risk youth possess high degrees of overlap in services needed; thus, girls who are drug addicts may also have histories of being abused, suicidal tendencies, academic difficulties, and/or be in need of gainful employment. Patterns of multiple service needs are unfortunately increasing just as public funding to meet these needs has proportionately decreased. (As of this writing—fall 2002—national priorities are dominated by the "war on terrorism" and related concerns in the post-9/11 era.) Ultimately, at-risk youth's multiple needs point to the necessity of more comprehensive programming than is available within any single program or system. Some research has suggested the need for inter-agency, inter-disciplinary collaborations to address these needs (Arella, 1992).

The Ms. Foundation for Women found that most programs for girls typically respond to the outcome or symptoms of girls' distress, rather than addressing the underlying structural problems of inequality and poverty that affect so many girls. Also, few programs address the special problems that girls of color experience. Likewise, programs geared specifically to the needs of lesbian and bisexual girls and those with disabilities are virtually nonexistent. In general, programs do not provide services within a context that acknowledges the realities of sexism, racism, classism, and heterosexism as problematic forces in their lives. Thus, little is offered in the way of giving girls the information and support needed to fathom and combat these mechanisms of multiple marginality (Ms. Foundation for Women, 1993).

ARE GENDER-SPECIFIC
PROGRAMS NECESSARY?

Despite the mounting evidence that girls have rather severe problems, youth programs have in the main ignored the needs of girls (or assumed that programs crafted to meet the needs of boys will also work for girls); some would contend that the jury is still out on the need for gender-specific programming. Indeed, there appears to be a belief in some quarters that within the juvenile justice system, gender-specific programming is not necessary. In a General Accounting Office study, the results of a national survey of chief probation officers were reported (the chiefs are mostly males, we should note). The report noted that though these juvenile court officials felt that "insufficient facilities and services were available to status offenders," they also believed that status offenders do not need gender-specific services, "except for gynecological services and pre-natal care." They also reported that these same high-level court administrators did not feel that "any significant gender bias concerns" emerged in the treatment of female and male status offenders (GAO, 1995: 3–4).

This perspective on girls' delinquency, and lack of interest in the special needs of girls, is both ironic and yet consistent with the juvenile justice system's checkered past with reference to the treatment of girls. Although currently the court is embracing and valorizing equal treatment largely as a way to justify current practices and avoid change, early court history reveals just the reverse. Indeed, a careful reading of the situations of girl and women offenders reveals that whether we are in a legal and social environment that supports "equal treatment" or one that argues for "special treatment," girls and women tend to be the losers.

PROGRAMMING AS IF GIRLS MATTERED: GETTING PAST GIRLS WATCHING BOYS PLAY SPORTS

As we have already noted, programming for girls in the juvenile justice system needs to take into consideration their unique situations and their special problems. Traditional delinquency treatment approaches have been shaped mostly by commonsense assumptions about what youths—mostly boys—need. Sometimes girls will benefit from these assumptions, sometimes they will not. As noted at the start of this chapter, "for years people have assumed that all you have to do to make a program designed for boys work for girls is to paint the walls pink and take out the urinals" (Marian Daniel, quoted in Girls, Incorporated, 1996: 34).

Lack of Validated Gender-Specific Programs: Programming and the "Forgotten Few"

A good snapshot of where we are nationally on girls' issues and programming can be seen from a brief overview of the activities of 23 states that successfully applied for challenge grant funds from the Office of Juvenile Justice and Delinquency Prevention. This review indicates that most states are in the very early stages of understanding the needs of girls in their systems. As a result, of the states where information was available (21), virtually all (95%) used some of these funds to gather data on the characteristics and needs of the girls in their systems. Slightly over a third (38%) funded a specific new program for girls or expanded an existing program that seemed successful. (We emphasize "seemed" to make the point that many a program is started because, from someone's perspective, it "feels" good or they have a "gut feeling" it will work; many continue, with no evidence of effectiveness, because it "seems to work.") About a quarter (28%) of the states held either a conference and/or undertook special training on girls' needs, and slightly under a quarter (23%) formed special committees. Finally, only ten percent of the states indicated that their committees were involved in the crafting of specific legislation and/or system policy changes (Chesney-Lind et al., 1998).

Among other needs that programs for girls should address are the following: dealing with the physical and sexual abuse in girls' lives (from parents, boyfriends, pimps, and others); the threat of HIV/AIDS; dealing with pregnancy and motherhood; drug and alcohol dependency; confronting family problems; vocational and career counseling; managing stress; and developing a sense of efficacy and empowerment. Many of these needs are universal and should be part of programs for all young people (Schwartz & Orlando, 1991), but they are particularly important for young women.

A good example of the synergy between understanding the dimensions of girls' problems and the crafting of evaluations of programs with this information in mind comes from the work of Sibylle Artz and Ted Riecken. Their review of the outcomes of thirteen individual anti-violence initiatives in Canadian schools shows the importance of focusing on gender and the desirability of establishing interventions that are gender specific (Artz & Riecken, 1997). Moreover, their research reminds us that both girls and boys have a gender, and that both could benefit from attention to the specific ways that masculinity and femininity work in the lives of young people. Employing pre- and post-tests of self-reported violence of both student and parent participants as well as school-based data on the same, the researchers quickly concluded that "one size does not fit all" in violence prevention.

Specifically, the researchers found that "boys are far less [likely] than girls to participate in student groups that promote violence prevention" and that "boys are less likely than girls to adopt the anti-violence messages of their schools' violence prevention programs" (Artz & Riecken, 1997: 296). Girls, even those with a history of violence, were more likely to see violence as problematic and to change as a result of intervention (particularly interventions based on skills-based programs and positive reinforcement). General "consciousness raising" was found to be ineffective with both sexes. Finally, males tended to be reached only when men participate in violence prevention efforts and when fathers (not mothers) condemn bullying (Artz & Riecken, 1997: 298).

Violence

Even though girls were being reached by the messages in the generic curriculum, the researchers noted that anti-violence curricula needed to be expanded to include sexual and domestic abuse because virtually no programs cover these issues. Other work by these researchers, based on in-depth interviews as well as self-report data, indicate that violent girls were much more likely than nonviolent girls to have histories of abuse and current experiences with abusive boyfriends. Girls' violence often tends to be a mimicking of the male violence in their lives (they come from homes with dominating and abusive fathers). Girls fight with other girls either to excite boys and get their attention, or they fight in order to be seen to be as good as boys (Artz, 1998).

Finally, Artz concludes that the prevention of girls' violence means recognizing that "the two kinds of violence against women, male-to-female and female-to-female, have their origins in the same belief systems." That is, a system of sexual inequality that valorizes male violence as a means of exerting power and influence and has girls growing up "seeing themselves through the eyes of males" (Artz, 1998: 204).

Running Away, Education, and Trauma

Another important issue unique to girls is that of running away. Any successful program for girls must address their needs for safe housing, and in some instances, legal emancipation. Economic support for these choices is also clearly desirable and available in some parts of Canada and Australia, but sadly unlikely, given the current hostility in the United States to young women living independently (see Alder, 1986).

At-risk girls have severe emotional problems, and significant numbers may have educational disabilities (Dryfoos, 1990; Hugo & Rutherford, 1992; Girls, Incorporated, 1996; Belknap et al., 1997). Thus, programming for female adolescents should invariably address academic difficulties. The educational neglect of young minority women, particularly African Americans, must be addressed (Orenstein, 1994; Arnold, 1995). Likewise, any program that encourages girls to succeed in the traditionally male-dominated subjects of math and science is likely to bolster self-esteem, school performance, and even career prospects (Sadker & Sadker, 1994).

Many at-risk girls have had histories of trauma, which set the stage for substantial problems with depression, self-image, and attempted suicide. One researcher stated the gender bias in our society very succinctly by noting that "no one will demand and obtain intervention for her because in our country it is more often slashed tires, not slashed wrists, that are noticed" (Wells, 1994: 4). Indeed, automobiles (and their parts) often seem to be more valued than human beings, especially women. Programming for young women should address, without labeling them as pathological, histories of sexual and physical abuse. Girls' problems with substance abuse, which are substantial (Howell & Davis, 1992), should be informed by the understanding that often, for girls, polydrug use is a way of self-medicating.

Peers and the Importance of Age

Negative peer influence is one of the major causative factors in delinquency. Most girls join negative peer groups or even gangs so that they feel like they "belong" and are accepted somewhere (Girls, Incorporated, 1996). Indeed, almost half (45%) of girls in the juvenile justice system report feeling little or no love or acceptance while growing up (American Correctional Association, 1990). Consequently, girls, particularly delinquent girls, need the positive influence and support of new peers and adult mentors that will encourage them to break or renegotiate bonds with people who have been harmful influences. Thus, ready access to a broad network of adult mentors and peer counselors sensitive to the girls-specific issues and problems should be made available.

Girls seem to prize connectedness and relationships with other people more than boys do (Gilligan, 1982). In this respect, a relational approach that emphasizes trust and relationship building with positive female role models would be highly beneficial. However, trust can only be developed when girls perceive their programs as being "safe" spaces where they do not have to fear condemnation. This entails creating an atmosphere that allows girls to express their thoughts and emotions freely and appropriately.

Similarly, program staff must be affirmative by acknowledging the worth of each girl despite her attitude or background. Girls' programs also need to create separate time and space for girls, apart from boys, so that issues related to sexism will not be overshadowed by boys' more disruptive behavior.

Programs for at-risk girls should ideally begin before adolescence, by age 9 or 10, and continue through the rest of adolescence. This is consistent with research that suggests that earlier preventive approaches are the most effective (Ms. Foundation for Women, 1993). Likewise, programs, particularly those that are issue-specific, need to provide transition and after-care services that support young women in maintaining the progress they have made.

Recreation: Beyond Cheerleading

Many at-risk girls may engage in delinquent behavior simply because there is little else to occupy their free time. Unfortunately, all too often these programs end up being "girls watching boys play sports." Structured recreation should consist of varied activities, including sports, leadership opportunities, programs and projects, arts and crafts, community service, ethnic and culturally oriented activities, dances, and social events. These provide a great way for girls to learn new skills, develop responsibility, increase self-esteem and self-confidence, befriend other girls, and, most importantly, have fun. Additionally, time and energy spent on rewarding activities dissuades girls from wanting to engage in delinquent or self-defeating behavior in the first place. Girls already embedded within the juvenile justice system frequently state that had they had opportunities to engage in meaningful, interesting activities, they probably would not have fallen into the system. In the words of one girl at the Hawaii Youth Correctional Facility, having "something to do, like a job or something" could have helped her to be delinquency-free. Likewise, another girl in the same facility stated that "if you're smart and strong enough and keep busy, you can stay out of trouble" (Chesney-Lind et al., 1998: 45).

Programs should invariably work to empower girls. This entails building on girls' innate strengths, skills, and creativity to develop their voices and their abilities to assert themselves. In this respect, girls need to be able to identify positively with themselves and each other. They also need the opportunity to aid in the design, implementation, and evaluation of programs that are geared for their benefit. Similarly, programs should continually reevaluate their effectiveness and remain flexible to change.

Quality programming for at-risk girls entails a commitment to positive youth development. To this end, young women, rather than being in need of "fixing," need to be "empowered" through effective prevention- and intervention-oriented approaches. This ultimately entails respecting female development processes and celebrating the uniqueness of girls and women.

In the remaining pages of this chapter we will provide brief summaries of some specific programs that have been established during the past couple of decades to address at-risk girls.

PROGRAMS FOR GIRLS

In the pages that follow we rely heavily on several sources that provide reviews of programs for girls, especially *Prevention and Parity: Girls in Juvenile Justice* (Girls, Incorporated, 1996). Few of these programs have been subjected to rigorous evaluation, so as you read, judge elements of the programs against what we currently know about effective and ineffective strategies for working with troubled girls. The section concludes by suggesting some policy implications that emerge from the review.

Children of the Night

Children of the Night is a program begun in 1979 in southern California to aid young prostitutes, the majority of whom are girls who have run away from abusive homes. The current director, Lois Lee, started it while she was a graduate student in sociology at UCLA studying the relationships between prostitutes and their pimps in the Los Angeles area. Lee asked herself, "Why would a girl stand on a street corner and do something deplorable, then give all the money she earned to a pimp?" Soon she began to offer her apartment as a temporary shelter to the young males and females who wanted to escape the life.[2]

Children of the Night relies heavily on volunteers and obtains funding from a variety of sources, including individuals and foundations. The program consists of: (1) a twenty-four-hour hotline (1-800-551-1300) for those who want someone to talk to or to get off the streets and away from pimps; (2) a walk-in center in Hollywood that provides medical aid, clothing, crisis intervention, and referrals for housing, drug counseling, schools, jobs, and foster home placement, among other things; (3) free professional counseling by volunteer psychologists and psychiatrists; (4) an outreach component whose trained volunteers walk the streets distributing informational materials to potential clients and engaging in on-the-spot counseling; and (5) a "turn-in-a-pimp" component that entails cooperation among the youths, the agency, the police, and the court system (the aim here is to obtain court testimony against pimps to assist in the prosecution of individuals who otherwise might go free because of lack of evidence).

Since the program opened, more than 10,000 girls and boys (roughly 40 percent of the total have been males) have gone through the program, with an estimated 80 percent having been successful (i.e., not returned to the streets). Virtually all had experienced sexual and other forms of abuse within their families. Almost all were under eighteen, the majority under sixteen. About one-third were eligible for existing shelter programs because they had no place to live. Over half came because no other resources were available to them. The most positive feature of the program is its provision of direct, emergency services. Serving as a broker for services, as many programs do, may also be effective, but only if young people are able to access and use the services. The counseling component is clearly sensitive to the abuse backgrounds of the street youth, but is not an adequate substitute for educational and realistic employment programming.

NATIONAL PROGRAMS OF GIRLS, INCORPORATED[3]

Girls, Incorporated (formerly the Girls Clubs of America) recently published a summary of the existing "state of the art" as far as programs for girls are concerned. Its report (Girls, Incorporated, 1996) begins its summary with a look at its own national program, which sponsors affiliates and outreach programs at more than nine hundred program sites (more information can be found on the Web site: www.girlsinc.org).

Girls, Incorporated sponsors three types of programs that are most significantly linked to those who are "at risk" of getting into trouble. These programs are offered "through a network of 1,000 sites nationwide and are facilitated by trained professional staff." Funding for the various programs comes from several major foundations, such as the Lilly Endowment, W. K. Kellogg Foundation, Nancy Reagan Foundation, David and Lucile Packard Foundation, Annie E. Casey Foundation, and the W. T. Grant Foundation. Among the programs are the following:

Friendly PEERsuasion. This program provides assistance to help young women avoid substance abuse "by providing accurate information, practicing refusal skills and developing healthy, fun ways to reduce stress and teaching what they have learned to younger children."

Preventing Adolescent Pregnancy. This program attempts to build the skills needed to resist pressure to use harmful substances such as tobacco, alcohol, and various drugs. It also includes "age-appropriate components that encourage parent–daughter communication about sexuality and provide girls with the information and skills they need to postpone sexual activity without losing friends, engage girls in life planning and provide access to health care, including reproductive health care." Girls who go through the program assume roles as "Peersuaders" for younger girls.

Operation SMART. This is a program that helps build skills and interests in science, math, and "relevant technologies" in order to "encourage young women to persist in these areas vital to everyday life and interesting, well-paying careers."

Preventing Adolescent Pregnancy. This program helps girls avoid early pregnancy through fostering communication skills, providing health education, and helping them plan for the future through four age-appropriate components known as "Growing Together," "Will Power/Won't Power," "Taking Care of Business" and "Health Bridge." The first two of these components have been translated into Spanish.

Media Literacy. This unique program helps girls think critically about the power of the media and how manipulative it can be, and especially its effects on girls and women.

Project Bold. This program helps girls develop strategies for self-defense (including physical techniques) and helps them seek out and talk with caring adults about the problem of violence.

Economic Literacy. This is a program that gets to the heart of one of the most important issues facing any young person, but especially young women—namely, financial concerns. Included in this program (which starts as early as six years of age) are such basic problems as money management, investments, how money affects people both locally and globally, and how to develop skills to be financially self-sufficient.

Local Programs Sponsored by Girls, Incorporated

A program in Minneapolis is known as The City, Inc. Community Intervention for Girls provides a comprehensive range of services, addressing such issues as substance abuse, employability, parenting, and urban poverty. Two specific programs within this grouping include *Kupona Ni'Uhuru* (which means "healing is freedom") and *Oshki Bug* (meaning "new leaf"), both based upon healing practices of African American and Native American cultures. These two cultures represent the majority of girls served by The City, Inc. Included within these programs are alternative schools for girls who cannot attend regular public schools and a group home for those who need more intensive attention.

A program in Baltimore known as the *Female Intervention Team* (FIT) supervises and provides various treatment services for adjudicated delinquent girls or those in need of services. The founder of this program, Marian Daniel, wanted to design a program to "make it look as if girls might want to come." They have an "infant and toddler" program to help young women learn good parenting skills. They also provide family counseling and tutoring, recreation activities, and close monitoring by FIT "case managers" who, by using the "case management approach," are able to provide more intensive services than do regular probation officers.

The *Harriet Tubman Residential Center* in Auburn, New York, is another program sponsored by Girls, Inc. and one of those that responded to our questionnaire. The girls in this program have been adjudicated in juvenile court. What we find most interesting about this program is that it is research based. That is, the program description includes a review of the literature on the problem of female delinquency in addition to research on developmental theory (quoting some of the same research cited earlier in Chapter 5 of this book). Therefore, this program focuses on women's issues and development and tries to offer services that relate to these issues. The program description includes four specific "outcome objectives": (1) self-management (this includes such things as personal hygiene and developing responsibility for one's own physical well-being); (2) relationship building (includes interacting with peers and parents, and developing an understanding of nonviolent methods of solving problems); (3) empowerment and self-direction (focuses on such issues as academics, vocational development, and independent living); and (4) future orientation (includes setting personal goals and a sense of future direction). The program takes into account the differences between the way boys and girls develop and how they view their surrounding world (e.g., boys tend to be "task oriented" whereas girls focus on "building relationships").

The *P.A.C.E. Center for Girls, Inc.* (P.A.C.E. stands for Practical, Academic, Cultural, Educational) is a program located in Jacksonville, Florida. This program is a "gender-sensitive, non-profit, non-residential, community-based program providing comprehensive education and therapeutic intervention services to troubled girls." The program focuses on at-risk girls between the ages of twelve and eighteen. Begun in 1985, it now has been replicated in several other locations, including Bradenton, Orlando, Miami, and Tallahassee.

Also included among the P.A.C.E. programs is the *Escambia Bay Marine Institute,* a nonresidential program for both male and female adjudicated offenders, especially those with problems at school. These youths have been unsuccessful in the more traditional school settings and they are placed in this program when they have been recommended for expulsion by the school board. The program offers "accelerated remedial education, vocational and employability skills training, and personal/group/family counseling in a motivating environment with a caring and skilled staff" (www.escambia.k12.fl.us/alted.djj_programs.htm).

The P.A.C.E. program takes a holistic approach and focuses on providing such services as life management skills, community service, counseling, and self-esteem building. It offers both day programs and after-care services. It provides a fully accredited high school program that works toward a high school diploma and also gives those who want it an opportunity to enroll in college-preparatory classes while developing career plans and building self-esteem. P.A.C.E. also has programs (e.g., through counseling and life management assistance) that address pregnancy and drug abuse, cultural awareness, and responsible health choices, and encourage involvement and volunteerism in the community (by requiring each girl in the program to participate in at least two different community service projects). P.A.C.E. also provides after-care and placement services.

The Department of Justice and OJJDP praised the P.A.C.E. program as a model program rated much higher than any other. P.A.C.E. is cited by the OJJDP publication *What Works: Promising Interventions in Juvenile Justice* (OJJDP, 1994: 5). The University of Florida does yearly evaluations, and thus far the outcomes have been very positive, showing a success rate of 78 percent.

A unique program is the *Marycrest Euphrasia Center*, located in Independence, Ohio. Funded by the Ohio Department of Youth Services, this is one of the few residential centers licensed for female offenders who are mothers and who can have their children live with them while they are in the program. Most are African American, ranging in age from thirteen to twenty-one, and have been convicted of a felony. *Marycrest* has been operating for 125 years; the *Euphrasia Center* is only two years old. It provides these young women with a curriculum that includes health services, individual and group counseling, family therapy, substance abuse therapy, parent effectiveness training, regular high school educational classes, job readiness and vocational training, and an on-site nursery. It has also developed an evaluation methodology to monitor the program (Girls, Incorporated, 1996: 36–37).

Another rather unusual program, one that targets a specific Asian American group called the Hmong, is known as Peem Tsheej Nthais Hluas (which translates as Struggle for Success for Young Women). Located in St. Paul, Minnesota, the program focuses on keeping families intact and helping girls (who are the first generation of their families to grow up in this country) live in two different cultures while giving them support for educational and vocational choices. More specifically, the program is an intervention program that was originally founded as a diversion to gang involvement. It has been expanded to include any Hmong girl either directly involved in the juvenile justice system or seriously at risk of becoming involved. Culturally based activities are part of the program, in addition to job referrals, employment training, and educational support. There is a day program and a drop-in center, both of which are highly visible in the community and easily accessible (Girls, Incorporated, 1996: 37–38). These are just a few of several promising programs that have developed in recent years. A complete summary of all these programs is well beyond the scope of this book. A partial listing of these and other programs can be found in the report of Girls, Incorporated (1996) and on its Web site.

POLICY IMPLICATIONS AND FUTURE DIRECTIONS

Programming for girls in the juvenile justice system is exceedingly challenging. First, effective delinquency intervention programs, even for boys, are very scarce. A careful reading of the literature reveals that there is no universal curative for male delinquency. To this rather bleak situation is added the female dimension:

the forces that bring girls into the juvenile justice system present challenges and issues that service providers are only now acknowledging.

It is clear that if deinstitutionalization of youths is still a societal goal, then sound criticisms of the movement must be addressed. One major and often repeated concern is that youngsters released from detention centers and other institutional settings end up on the streets, where they become victims of a criminal subculture that knows only too well how to prey on their vulnerabilities. The failure of the deinstitutionalization movement to anticipate this problem can be attributed, in retrospect, to girls' invisibility within the juvenile justice system. Their low profile meant that programming for them never happened. The very limited number of dollars targeted for girls' programming during the 1970s demonstrates this very clearly. Upon release from facilities, the girls were simply referred to systems and service providers whose understanding of girls' lives, problems, and delinquency was minimal at best.

During that same decade, however, a few experiments in programming for girls were undertaken. Some, as this chapter has related, used traditional methods, though modified by the insights of feminism. Others, and particularly efforts in subsequent years, were and are more ambitious. Certain themes emerge from the small number of innovative programs. First, if counseling is to be included—and it should be part of a solid program for girls—it must be sensitive to issues such as sexual abuse, rape (including date rape), violence in teenage sexual relationships, and the special problems that girls face (particularly those who are parents) in housing and employment. Second, the program should go past counseling per se to the areas of skill building, particularly in the employment area. Third, the program should meet the needs of girls who cannot safely return to their families. In this regard, we should focus on the urgent need for teens to have access to medical, dental, educational, and housing resources. As a society, we have been reluctant to provide long-term, stable solutions to the problems of teens in conflict with their families. The consequence has been a paucity of effective services for an estimated 133,500 runaway and 59,200 throwaway youths (Finkelhor, Hotaling, & Sedlak, 1990: 4), many of whom are girls.

Some of the more recent programs reviewed here show even more promise, especially since they are becoming more culturally sensitive and aware of the special needs of girls. The new programs address some of the most pressing needs of young women in trouble and at risk, such as help with problems of physical and sexual abuse, drug involvement, the HIV virus, pregnancy and parenting issues, and many more. The authors are pleased to find such innovative programs have emerged in recent years and hope that they will continue to spread.

SUMMARY

Much more work must be done to support the fundamental needs of girls on the margin. We must do a better job of recognizing that they need less "programming" and more support to live on their own because many cannot or will not return home. Programs that specifically target the housing and employment requirements of youths while also providing them with the specific skills they need to survive on their own are emerging. These often include a built-in caseworker or service broker, as well as counseling components. Many girls require specialized counseling to recover from the ravages of sexual and physical victimization, but research cautions that approaches that rely simply on the provision of counseling services are not likely to succeed.

Additionally, innovative programs must receive the same sort of regular and extended financial underwriting generally accorded their institutional counterparts. A careful reading of the descriptions of innovative programs reveals that many rely on federal funds or private foundation grants; the same reading reveals that pitifully few go on for any length of time. To survive and thrive, they must be able to count on stable funding.

There is no shortage of work to be done to understand how to better serve the young women who find themselves in the juvenile justice system. What research we do have, both on girls' problems and on girls' experiences with the juvenile justice system, suggests that gender has long played a role in this system, whether officially recognized or not.

The challenge that confronts us is whether we can take what we know about girls' development, the different ways culture impacts gender development, and the ways in which girls' problems evolve into female delinquency and craft programming responses to this. Clearly, much more research is needed to fully understand all of the topics covered here, and that research should be used to inform both policy and practice.

What scant research we possess suggests that gender-specific programming may allow us to better serve a population that is generally ignored in a justice system that tends to respond to agitated victims and egregious crimes. Lacking a powerful constituency, we have in the past been left with a pattern of "throwaway services for throwaway girls" (Wells, 1994: 4). We can and should do better than this for tomorrow's women.

Programs must be continuously scrutinized to guarantee that they are serving as genuine alternatives to girls' incarceration rather than simply functioning to extend the social control of girls. The tendency of programs to become more "security" oriented in response to girls' propensity to run away must also be resisted (Schwartz & Orlando, 1991). Indeed, a component of successful programming for girls is advocacy and ongoing monitoring of the closed institutions. If nothing else can be learned from the rocky history of nearly two decades of efforts to decarcerate youths, it is an appreciation of how fraught with difficulty these efforts are and how easily their gains can be eroded. We also note the spread of more programs for girls that specifically target some of their special needs, such as in the areas of abuse and pregnancy.

Admittedly, the jury is still out and will be out for some time regarding the necessity and effectiveness of gender-specific services, but that girls deserve equitable (not equal) treatment and services is undeniable. Perhaps the best case we have seen for girls' programming is made by a poem written by a young woman in a girls' program in the juvenile justice system in Chicago. It is also a reminder about the humanity, energy, and talent that girls in our systems can offer the world if we can help develop those undeniable talents so girls can go boldly forward into the world that awaits them. The poem is from Anetra (1995) and it is from a source called "Girls Talkin' . . . Poetry":

Boys Can't Talk Girl Talk

Boys can't talk girls talk
because you talk about things
boys shouldn't know
or have no right to know
but maybe they need to know?
or do they?
Boys can't talk girls talk
because women and men are different
but men need to know some things
about women in order to have a
relationship or do they?
Boys can't talk girls talk
because boys would take all of
the attention away from girls and
would demand it for themselves,
it is their security or our insecurity
no more
what ever it is
boys can't talk girls talk

NOTES

1. "Meta-analysis" is a more quantified approach in summarizing research results drawn from different studies. It allows greater precision in determining the effectiveness of particular intervention techniques. In addition to this strength, Lipsey's analysis also includes a review of 443 studies of delinquency treatment programs.

2. For additional information on Children of the Night, see its Web site: http://childrenofthenight.org. The information about this program is taken from this Web site and from an interview (done by Shelden in October 1988) with the director and founder of the program, Dr. Lois Lee.

3. The following information is taken from the Web site: www.girlsinc.org. More detailed descriptions of the programs mentioned here are found within this Web site.

12

Conclusions

This book has attempted to put girls and their problems at the center of any discussion of their delinquency and has taken a hard look at their experiences with the juvenile justice system. Several questions regarding conventional assumptions about the causes of delinquency in girls have been raised. We have also been critical about the quality of the juvenile justice accorded girls. Much needs to be done before we can fully appreciate the dynamics involved in girls' delinquency, and, perhaps more important, much has to be done to ensure that girls experience true justice when they appear in juvenile courts.

Although female delinquency differs from male delinquency, some research, particularly that based on self-report studies, suggests that there are more similarities than previously imagined in female and male delinquency. In essence, most delinquency is trivial, and the differences between the deviance of boys and girls are not pronounced. Discussions of delinquency that focus on very serious violent offenses tend to exaggerate the gender differences in delinquency because males are more likely to commit these offenses.

The evidence also suggests that female delinquency has changed little in the past two decades. Both official arrest statistics and self-report data support the notion that what changes we have seen in girls' misbehavior have been in minor and traditionally female offenses. Girls are still arrested and referred to court primarily for minor property offenses and status offenses. Cohort studies indicate that lately more girls are being arrested, but there is little or no evidence that during a period characterized by much discussion about the need for changes in girls' and women's situations, there was any major change in girls' criminal behavior. Finally, while arrest statistics in the last decade seem to indicate major changes in the arrests of girls for violent offenses, we argue that much of this is explained by three related factors: rediscovery of minor forms of violence that girls have always reported in self-report data and relabelling of girls' status offenses as person offenses (particularly family arguments that might involve minor altercations or even girls defending themselves in physical assaults). The best self-report data, in fact, show that girls' involvements in fighting actually declined in the nineties.

There is also less support than some imagine for the belief that African American girls are markedly more delinquent than white girls. Differences certainly exist, but they tend to appear more often in official statistics; self-report studies show white girls to be actually slightly more delinquent than black girls, although there are differences in the types of delinquency that the two groups commit. On the other hand, racial differences in victimization are clear: African American girls are more likely than white girls to be the objects of violent crimes.

In total, studies of female and male delinquency, like studies of other forms of gender differences, tend to make more of dissimilarities than of similarities. Both are interesting from a theoretical standpoint, but to date only the gender difference in the commission of violent crime has garnered attention. Also of interest is the fact that although girls commit many offenses, only some of these offenses, notably status offenses, tend to result in their arrest.

Examination of the offenses that typically bring girls into the juvenile justice system highlights the fact that girls' delinquencies are shaped by their unique problems in a society that gives women, particularly girls, very little power and few options, and even fewer legal rights. These burdens become heavier when compounded by poverty, abusive families, and membership in a minority group.

Status offenses have always been closely identified with female delinquency. Running away from home and being "unmanageable" or "incorrigible" have long been seen as typical female offenses. The prevalence of status offenses in girls' delinquency, we have argued, stems in part from a parental desire to control the behavior of girls. The obvious gender bias appears when referrals to juvenile court are compared with self-report studies that show that boys and girls are about equally likely to commit status offenses. The bias is even more troubling when one considers that persistent status offense behavior in girls, notably running away, appears to be linked to abuse, especially sexual abuse, within the home.

Running away very often leads girls to commit a variety of crimes in order to survive, among them prostitution. Girls who join the ranks of street youths often end up in the world of prostitution, where their abuse continues at the hands of pimps and customers alike. Even more tragic is the situation of girls enmeshed in international prostitution; the extreme powerlessness of girls in impoverished Asian societies has resulted in their wholesale sexual commodification.

Shoplifting has consistently been the most common property offense committed by girls. From the few available studies, it appears that although both sexes are about equally likely to shoplift, girls are more likely to be detected by store personnel, arrested by the police, and referred to juvenile court. Items stolen by girls are of lesser value than those stolen by boys, and girls are more apt to be amateurs. Most of the items girls steal are for personal use and may be linked to their desire to conform to a standard of female beauty and appearance that is otherwise inaccessible to poor girls.

Gang delinquency among girls, often featured prominently in the news, has consistently been less frequent and less serious than the delinquency exhibited by boys in gangs. Current research is rectifying the previous neglect of girl gangs, filling in gaps and explaining the roles played by gender as well as race in girls' involvement in gangs. Clearly, girls are in gangs, but it is less clear that such involvement signals any *new* kind of female delinquency, since work done on girls in gangs in previous decades also found more involvement than the gang stereotype would allow. In the main, girls are involved in gangs for many of the same reasons boys are, but their gender also colors their gang involvement in particular ways. A reflection of the deteriorating social conditions of inner-city ghettos, gangs provide what the surrounding environment does not: status, recognition, and protection.

In listening to the words of girls and young women in the juvenile justice system, we reinforce our awareness of the role that girls' problems play in their delinquency. Also made apparent is the failure of current systems to deal with their difficulties. The girls we interviewed, as well as those interviewed by other researchers, were from poor families, and most are members of minority groups. They also came from families that have multiple problems, not the least of which, from the girls' standpoints, had high levels of physical violence and sexual abuse.

The girls admitted involvement in a variety of crimes, yet the great majority were drawn into the juvenile justice system for offenses typical of female offenders: status offenses. The girls did not identify strongly with their "delinquent" identities but were quite resentful of the label—particularly in view of the offenses for which they were being charged and held.

Girls in our society face many dilemmas pertaining to peers, aspirations, and sexuality. Turmoil in the home complicates outside relationships and heightens the problems experienced by normal teenagers in their pursuit of peer approval. Added to this, low-income backgrounds make it impossible to gain status through typical middle-class means. In seeking recognition and popularity, many girls turn into "bad girls" who party, fight, and take drugs to achieve status in the eyes of their peers. Such a route to approval has drawbacks (for example, it attracts police attention and aggravates strife at home), but many girls see it as one of the few options available.

That these delinquent acts are somehow related to an increased awareness of the women's movement is a notion easily dismissed. These girls express highly traditional, approving attitudes toward the place of men and women in society. They aspire to careers most typically followed by females, want to be married, and anticipate large families. They see a dichotomy between male and female behavior: men are strong and assertive; women are passive and nonviolent. Such attitudes influence relationships with romantic partners as the girls (holding true to their perceived roles) seem resigned to abuse by their partners.

The nature of delinquent girls' family environments, coupled with their limited perceptions of men and women in society, fosters and reinforces low self-esteem and alienation. The message given by family, friends, and boyfriends to these girls tells them that they are bad and that their poor treatment is justified and deserved.

The girls seek to escape from their problems by selectively reminiscing about the past and fantasizing about the future. Ironically, they see their boyfriends as rescuing them from their present difficulties. Marriage and family life are perceived as a means of escape to stability and as a way to end their loneliness. The girls cannot psychologically afford to acknowledge the actual character and resources of their boyfriends. The fantasies enable the hope of a better life to come.

Girls, in short, experience a childhood and adolescence heavily colored by their gender. It is simply not possible to discuss their problems, their delinquency, and what they encounter in the juvenile justice system without considering gender in all its dimensions. Girls and boys do not inhabit the same worlds, and they do not have the same choices. This is not to say that girls do not share some circumstances and qualities with boys (notably class and race), but even the manner in which these affect the daily lives of young people is heavily mediated by gender.

A truly inclusive delinquency theory must await more information about girls' lives. Essentially, too little is known about girls' development now to formulate this sort of grand theory. This can be gathered from the complexity of findings delineated in earlier chapters. Sometimes the long-standing male theories seem to apply, but more often it's "Yes, but." Yes, youth being in groups often leads to delinquency, but if we are talking about girls' groups, that may not be so. Yes, school failure contributes to delinquency of boys, but sometimes it is more important in the delinquency of girls. We need to conduct more basic research on girls' lives before we can sketch out a delinquency theory that is sensitive to the context of patriarchy. Such a theory would also account for the role played by social institutions, particularly the institutions charged with the social control of youth—the juvenile justice system.

The historic commitment of the juvenile justice system to parental authority and the system's direct involvement in the enforcement of the sexual double standard have posed enormous problems for girls. Girls' complaints about even gross forms of parental abuse of authority (for example, sexual and physical abuse) were, until recently, routinely ignored by police and court authorities. For this reason, statutes originally devised to protect young people criminalized the survival strategies of girls who could not stay at home. When girls ran away (some from abusive homes), parents were able to join with public agencies to enforce their return. If runaways persisted in refusing to stay at home, they were incarcerated.

Young women on the run are, after a time, driven by the very statutes designed to protect them into the life of escaped convicts. Unable to enroll in school or take jobs to support themselves because they fear detection, they take to the streets and, in order to survive, engage in panhandling, petty theft, and occasional prostitution.

Because young girls (but not necessarily young boys) are defined as sexually desirable—and, in fact, more desirable than their older sisters due to the double standard of aging (Bell, 1984)—their lives on the streets and their survival strategies take on unique shapes heavily influenced by patriarchal values. It is no accident that girls fleeing abusive homes or who are on the streets because of profound poverty become involved in criminal activities that exploit their sexual-object status. They have little else of value to trade and are encouraged to use this "resource." Certainly, the criminal subculture views them from this perspective (Miller, 1986; Arnold, 1990).

On a more theoretical level, perhaps girls' delinquency is placed in a context relative to sexual behavior precisely because women's struggle against patriarchal control over their sexual capital has historically been central to the maintenance of patriarchy (Lerner, 1986). Young women's possession of more of this capital relative to older women has been one reason for the excessive concern that both families and official agencies of social control have exhibited about youthful female defiance.

Societal ambivalence about teenage women's sexuality has also surfaced with a vengeance in public debates about young women's access to abortion, teen motherhood, and, most recently, welfare benefits. Clearly, as a society, we are still extremely concerned about monitoring the sexual behavior of girls but have far less interest in that of males (many of whom are adults) who are involved with these pregnancies (Males, 1994: 8). Clearly, as a society, we are still uncomfortable with young women's sexual agency, and we will go to rather extreme lengths (even institutionalization) to punish those girls who violate the traditional societal demand that girls (but not boys and men) must remain sexually passive and "pure."

Most recently, the policing of girl's sexuality appears to have taken a back seat to the controlling of girl's aggression and violence. Certainly, we have seen dramatic arrests of girls for person offenses, and more to the point, steep increases in the detention of girls for these offenses. A closer look at these trends, though, reveals that much of this increase is likely due to the "relabeling" of girl's status offenses as crimes of violence. This pattern of "bootstrapping" has a long tradition in juvenile justice, and this current trend, like its earlier counterparts, permits the incarceration of girls who should otherwise be diverted from the juvenile justice system.

In short, supporters of diversion and deinstitutionalization were never prepared for the political significance of allowing girls to escape abusive families;

in fact, these policies were crafted with little or no attention to unique situation of girls. Hence, the proponents of deinstitutionalization were blindsided by horror stories about victimized youth, youthful prostitution, and youthful involvement in pornography, to say nothing about even more angry parental and policymaker efforts to recriminalize status offenses. No surprise, then, that those critical of deinstitutionalization all routinely neglected the unpleasant reality that most of these behaviors were often in direct response to earlier victimization, often by parents, that official agencies ignored (Office of Juvenile Justice and Delinquency Prevention, 1985).

The justice system's historic silence and lack of concern about girls' victimization as well as the current political manipulation of girls' problems must also be placed within the context of patriarchy. What is really at stake in current efforts to roll back deinstitutionalization is not protection of youth so much as it is the control of young women and their sexuality. Court officials and policy makers still believe girls should be under control; this opinion, rather than addressing their real problems with their families, motivates today's influential criticisms of deinstitutionalization. The lack of official interest in the establishment of viable alternative living situations for girls who cannot remain with their parents is also evidence on this point.

Indeed, much more work should be done to support the fundamental needs of girls on the margin. We must recognize that they need less "programming" and more support to live on their own. Programs that fill housing and employment requirements while also providing youths skills to survive on their own are emerging. These often include a built-in caseworker or service broker and counseling components. Many girls need specialized counseling to recover from sexual and physical victimization, but research cautions that approaches that rely only on counseling services are not likely to succeed.

Additionally, innovative programs must receive the same sort of stable funding generally accorded programs of long standing in the institutions. Many innovative programs have relied on federal funds or private foundation grants, and very few have survived for any length of time. A dependable source of money enables operational well-being.

Programs must also be regularly scrutinized to guarantee that they are serving as genuine alternatives to incarceration rather than merely functioning to extend the social control of girls. The tendency of these programs to become more security oriented in response to girls' propensity to run away must also be resisted. Indeed, a component of successful programming for girls must be advocacy and continuous monitoring of closed institutions. If nothing else can be learned from the rocky history of nearly two decades of efforts to decarcerate young people, it is an appreciation of how fraught these efforts are with difficulty and how easily their gains can be eroded.

In sum, this book has argued that the extensive theoretical and programmatic focus on disadvantaged boys and their problems has meant that girls' victimization and its relationship to girls' crime have been systematically ignored. Also missed has been the central role played by the juvenile justice system in the sexualization of girls' delinquency and the criminalization of girls' survival strategies. Further, it has been argued that the official actions of the juvenile justice system should be understood as major elements in girls' oppression because these actions have historically served to reinforce the obedience of all young women to patriarchal authority, no matter how abusive and arbitrary.

On a more programmatic level, while those who oppose deinstitutionalization mounted a strong effort to erode the basic mandates of the Juvenile Justice and Delinquency Prevention Act of 1974 and attempted specific attention to girls' programming, they did not wholly succeed. In fact, the current reauthorization of the JD Act retains a concern about bootstrapping, and it also provides continued funding for gender specific services. Still, state level efforts to erode the JD Act persist, and although girls' victimization is often used to support such a view, a look at the juvenile justice system's treatment of young women in trouble makes it clear that, for them, such an approach would be a disaster. Instead, girl advocates should continue to build on the excellent start on girl's programming that the earlier Challenge Grant funding initiated, and, in particular, address the growing threat posed by the increasing numbers of girls been held in detention.Continued commitment of girls to adult jails and overcrowded training schools is also a matter of concern and testimony to the durability of the sexual double standard in girls' incarceration. In short, eternal vigilance is necessary to assure that the numbers of girls in training schools do not start climbing again. We should certainly hope that the new millennium will bring a fresh and more enlightened approach to girls' troubles than the approach of the last century, which was deeply flawed by malign neglect at best and rank sexism at worst. We can and should do better for this century's girls.

Bibliography

Acoca, L. 1999. "Investing in Girls: A 21st Century Challenge." *Juvenile Justice* 6: 3–13

Acoca, L., and K. Dedel. 1998. *No Place to Hide: Understanding and Meeting the Needs of Girls in the California Juvenile Justice System*. San Francisco: National Council on Crime and Delinquency.

Acoca, L., and J. Austin. 1996. *The Crisis: Women in Prison*. San Francisco: National Council on Crime and Delinquency.

Adams, S. 1959. *Effectiveness of the Youth Authority Special Treatment Program: First Interim Report*. Sacramento: California Youth Authority.

Adams-Tucker, C. 1982. "Proximate Effects of Sexual Abuse in Childhood." *American Journal of Psychiatry* 193: 1252–1256.

Adler, C. M. 1998. "'Passionate and Willful' Girls: Confronting Practices." *Women and Criminal Justice* 9: 81–101.

Adler, F. 1975. *Sisters in Crime*. New York: McGraw-Hill.

Adler, P., S. J. Kless, and P. Adler. 1992. "Socialization to Gender Roles: Popularity Among Elementary School Boys and Girls." *Sociology of Education* 65 (July): 169–187.

Adolescent Female Subcommittee. 1994. *Needs Assessment and Recommendations for Adolescent Females in Minnesota*. St. Paul: Minnesota Department of Corrections.

Adoption Assistance and Child Welfare Act 1980: PL96-272, June 17, 1980. 94 Stat. 500.

Ageton, S. 1983. "The Dynamics of Female Delinquency, 1976–1980." *Criminology* 21: 555–584.

Albelda, R., N. Folbre, and the Center for Popular Economics. 1996. *The War on the Poor*. New York: The New Press.

Alder, C. 1984. "Gender Bias in Juvenile Diversion." *Crime and Delinquency* 30: 400–414.

———. 1986. "Unemployed Women Have Got It Heaps Worse." *Australian and New Zealand Journal of Criminology* 19: 210–224.

———. 1987. "Girls, Schooling and Trouble." Unpublished manuscript

———. 1995. "Delinquency Prevention with Young Women." Paper presented at the Delinquency Prevention Conference, Terrigal, New South Wales.

Alexander, B. 1998. "Hatch Quarterbacks Sneak Play for Youth Crime Bill." *Youth Today*, October, pp. 46–47.

Allen-Hagen, B. 1988. *Children in Custody: Public Juvenile Facilities, 1987.* Washington, DC: U.S. Department of Justice.

————. 1991. *Children in Custody 1989.* Washington, DC: U.S. Bureau of Justice Statistics, U.S. Government Printing Office.

Altonn, H. 1982. "55 Women Prisoners 'Home' at Olomana." *Honolulu Star-Bulletin*, Nov. 10.

Altschuler, D. M., and L. Armstrong. 1984. "Intervening with Serious Juvenile Offenders: A Summary of a Study on Community-Based Programs." In *Intervening with Violent Offenders*. San Francisco: National Council on Crime and Delinquency.

Amaro, H. 1995. "Love, Sex, and Power: Considering Women's Realities in HIV Prevention." *American Psychologist* 50: 437–447.

Amaro, H., and M. Agular. 1994. "Programa Mama: Mom's Project: A Hispanic/Latino Family Approach to Substance Abuse Prevention." Center for Substance Abuse Prevention, Mental Health Services Administration.

American Association for University Women (AAUW). 1992. *How Schools Are Shortchanging Girls.* Washington, DC: AAUW Educational Foundation.

American Bar Association. 2001. *Justice by Gender.* Chicago: American Bar Association.

American Correctional Association. 1990. *The Female Offender: What Does the Future Hold?* Washington, DC: American Correctional Association.

Anderson, E. 1977. "A Comparison of Male and Female Adolescents' Attachment to Parents and Differential Involvement with Marijuana." *International Review of Modern Sociology* 7: 213–223.

Anderson, E. 2000. "The code of the streets." In R.D. Crutchfield, G.S. Bridges, J.G. Weis, and C. Kubrin (eds.) *Crime Readings* (2nd ed.). Boston: Pine Forge Press.

Andrews, R. H., and A. H. Cohn. 1974. "Ungovernability: The Unjustifiable Jurisdiction." *Yale Law Journal* 83: 1383–1409.

Anetra, N. 1995. "Girls Talkin'...Poetry." Chicago: Chicago Girls Project, Dec. 19.

Aquino, B. 1994. *Filipino Women and Political Engagement.* The Office for Womens' Research, working paper series. Volume Two (1993–1994) Honolulu: University of Hawaii, Manoa.

Arakawa, L. 1999. "Racial sensitivity programs urged." *The Honolulu Advertiser*, Jan. 20, B1.

Arella, L. 1993. "Multiservice Adolescent Programs: Seeking Institutional Partnership Alternatives." *Journal of Youth and Adolescence* 22: 283–295.

Aries, P. 1962. *Centuries of Childhood.* New York: Knopf.

Arnold, R. 1989. "Processes of Criminalization: From Girlhood to Womanhood." In M. B. Zinn and B. T. Dill (eds.), *Women of Color in American Society.* Philadelphia: Temple University Press.

————. 1990. Personal communication with authors.

————. 1995. "The Processes of Victimization and Criminalization of Black Women." In B. R. Price and N. Sokoloff (eds.), The Criminal Justice System and Women. New York: McGraw-Hill.

Arnts, D. 1986. *Detention of Juveniles in Local Jail Facilities.* Report by the Office of the Attorney General, State of Idaho, Boise.

Artz, S. 1998. *Sex, Power and the Violent School Girl.* Toronto: Trifolium Books.

Artz, S. 2000. "Considering Adolescent Girls' Use of Violence: A Researcher's Reflections on Her Inquiry." *The B.C. Counsellor*, 22 (1).

Artz, S., Blais, M., & Nicholson, D. 2000. *Developing Girls' Custody Units.* Unpublished report. British Columbia Crime Trends

Artz, S., and T. Riecken. 1997. "What, So What, Then What?: The Gender Gap in School-Based Violence and Its Implications for Child and Youth Care Practice." *Child and Youth Care Forum* 26 (4): 291–303.

Austin, J., B. Bloom, and T. Donahue. 1992. *Female Offenders in the Community: An Analysis of Innovative Strategies and Programs.* National Council on Crime and Delinquency. Washington DC: National Institute of Corrections.

Austin, J., B. Krisberg, R. DeComo, S. Rudenstine, and D. Del Rosario. 1995. *Juveniles Taken into Custody: Fiscal Year 1993.* Washington, DC: Office of Juvenile Justice and Delinquency Prevention.

Austin, J., and J. Irwin. 2001. *It's About Time: America's Incarceration Binge* (3rd ed.). Belmont, CA: Wadsworth.

Austin, J., K. D. Johnson, and M. Gregoriou. 2000. *Juveniles in Adult Prisons and Jails: A*

National Assessment. Washington, DC: U. S. Department of Justice.

Barlow, H. 1987. *Introduction to Criminology*. Boston: Little, Brown.

Bartollas, C. 1993. "Little Girls Grown Up: The Perils of Institutionalization." In C. Culliver (ed.), *Female Criminality: The State of the Art*. New York: Garland Press.

———. 2003. *Juvenile Delinquency* (6th ed.) Boston: Allyn and Bacon.

———, and S. J. Miller. 2001. *Juvenile Justice in America* (3rd ed.). Upper Saddle River, NJ: Prentice-Hall.

Baskin, D., and J. Fagan. 1993. "The Political Economy of Female Violent Street Crime." *Fordham Urban Law Journal* 20: 401–417.

Bearrows, T. 1987. "Status Offenders and the Juvenile Court: Past Practices, Future Prospects." In F. Hartmann (ed.), *From Children to Citizens, Vol. 2: The Role of the Juvenile Court*. New York: Springer-Verlag.

Becker, H. S. 1963. *Outsiders: Studies in the Sociology of Deviance*. New York: Free Press.

Belknap, J., M. Dunn, and K. Holsinger, 1997. "Moving toward Juvenile Justice and Youth-Serving Systems That Address the Distinct Experience of the Adolescent Female." Cincinnati, OH: Gender Specific Services Work Group.

Bell, I. P. 1984. "The Double Standard: Age." In J. Freeman (ed.), *Women: A Feminist Perspective*. Palo Alto, CA: Mayfield.

Bennett, W. J., J. DiIulio, Jr., and J. P. Walters. 1996. *Body Count: Moral Poverty and How to Win America's War Against Crime and Drugs*. New York: Simon and Schuster.

Benson, P. L. 1990. *The Troubled Journey: A Portrait of 6th-12th Grade Youth*. Minneapolis: Search Institute.

Bergsmann, I. R. 1989. "The Forgotten Few: Juvenile Female Offenders." *Federal Probation* 53: 73–78.

Beyette, B. 1988. "Hollywood's Teen-age Prostitutes Turn Tricks for Shelter, Food." *Las Vegas Review-Journal*, Aug. 21.

Bishop, D. M., and C. E. Frazier. 1992. "Gender Bias in Juvenile Processing: Implications of the JJDP Act." *Journal of Criminal Law and Criminology* 82: 1162–1186.

Bjerregard, B., and C. Smith. 1993. "Gender Differences in Gang Participation, Delinquency, and Substance Abuse." *Journal of Quantitative Criminology* 4: 329–355.

Bjorkqvist, K., and P. Niemela, 1992. "New Trends in the Study of Female Aggression." In Bjorkqvist, K. & P. Niemela, (eds.). In *Of Mice and Women: Aspects of Female Aggression*. San Diego: Academic Press.

Bjorkqvist K., K. Osterman, and A. Kaukiainen. 1992. "The Development of Direct and Indirect Aggressive Strategies in Males and Females." In *Of Mice and Women: Aspects of Female Aggression*. San Diego, Academic Press.

Black, T., and C. Smith. 1981. *A Preliminary National Assessment of the Number and Characteristics of Juveniles Processed in the Juvenile Justice System*. Washington, DC: U.S. Department of Justice.

Blaylock, J. 2001. "A Living Hell: A Cultural Perspective on Child Prostitution in the Far East." On-line (www.ageofconsent.com/comments/alivinghell.htm).

Block, J. H. 1984. *Sex Role Identity and Ego Development*. San Francisco: Jossey-Bass.

Blomberg, T. 1978. "Diversion from Juvenile Court: A Review of the Evidence." In F. Faust and P. Brantingham (eds.), *Juvenile Justice Philosophy* (2d ed.). St. Paul: West.

Bloom, B. 1996. Triple Jeopardy: Race, Class, and Gender as Factors in Women's Imprisonment. Ph.D. diss., University of California-Riverside.

Blume, J. M. 1990. "Status of Court-Ordered Detention of Juvenile Status Offenders." Paper presented at the annual meeting of the American Society of Criminology.

Boisvert, M. J., and R. Wells. 1980. "Towards a Rational Policy on Status Offenders." *Social Work* 25: 230–234.

Boritch, H., and J. Hagan. 1990. "A Century of Crime in Toronto: Gender, Class and Patterns of Social Control, 1859–1955." *Criminology* 28: 567–599.

Bortner, M. A. 1988. *Delinquency and Justice: An Age of Crisis*. New York: McGraw-Hill.

Bottcher, J. 1986. *Risky Lives: Female Versions of Common Delinquent Life Patterns*. Sacramento: California Youth Authority.

Bowker, L. 1976. *Drug Use at a Small Liberal Arts College*. Palo Alto, CA: R and E Research Associates.

———. 1978. *Women, Crime and the Criminal Justice System*. Lexington, MA: Lexington Books.

———, and M. Klein. 1983. "The Etiology of Female Juvenile Delinquency and Gang Membership: A Test of Psychological and

Social Structural Explanations." *Adolescence* 13: 739–751.

Bownes, D., and R. L. Albert. 1996. "State Challenge Activities." OJJDP Juvenile Justice Bulletin (Sept.). Washington, DC: U.S. Department of Justice.

Boyer, D., and J. James. 1982. "Easy Money: Adolescent Involvement in Prostitution." In S. Davidson (ed.), *Justice for Young Women.* Seattle: New Directions for Young Women.

Boyle, P. 1999. "Youth advocates gear up to fight over the fine points." *Youth Today*, July/August, pp. 46–47.

Bremner, R. H. (ed.). 1970. *Children and Youth in America.* Cambridge: Harvard University Press.

Brennan, T. 1980. "Mapping the Diversity Among Runaways: A Descriptive Multivariate Analysis of Selected Social Psychological Background Conditions." *Journal of Family Issues* 1: 189–209.

Brener, N. D., T. R. Simon, E. G. Krug, and R. Lowry. 1999. "Recent Trends in Violence-Related Behaviors Among High School Students in the United States." *Journal of the American Medical Association* 282: 330–446.

Brenzel, B. 1975. "Lancaster Industrial School for Girls: A Social Portrait of a 19th Century Reform School for Girls." *Feminist Studies* 3: 40–53.

———. 1983. *Daughters of the State.* Cambridge: MIT Press.

Brown, W. K. 1977. "Black Female Gangs in Philadelphia." *International Journal of Offender Therapy and Comparative Criminology* 21: 221–228.

Browne, A., and D. Finkelhor. 1986. "Impact of Child Sexual Abuse: A Review of Research." *Psychological Bulletin* 99: 66–77.

Budnick, K. J., and E. Shields-Fletcher, (1998). *What about girls?* (OJJDP Publication No. 84). Washington, DC: U.S. Department of Justice

Burhoe, J.C. 1998. "Characteristics of Cultural Adaptation and the Emergence of New Identities Among Southeast Asian Refugees in the United States." Paper presented at the Annual Meeting of the Association of Asian American Studies, Honolulu, HI, June.

Burbeck, T. 1978. "Sex Discrimination in the Disposition of Incarcerated Juveniles." Ann Arbor: University of Michigan, Department of Sociology.

Bureau of Criminal Information and Analysis. 1999. *Report on arrests for domestic violence in California, 1998.* Sacramento: State of California, Criminal Justice Statistics Center.

Bureau of Justice Statistics. 1983. *Report to the Nation on Crime and Justice.* Washington, DC: U.S. Department of Justice.

———. 1985a. *Jail Inmates, 1984.* Washington, DC: U.S. Department of Justice.

———. 1985b. *The Crime of Rape.* Washington, DC: U.S. Department of Justice.

———. 1986a. *Children in Custody: 1982/83 Census of Juvenile Detention and Correctional Facilities.* Washington, DC: U.S. Department of Justice.

———. 1986b. *Children in Custody.* Washington, DC: U.S. Department of Justice.

———. 1986c. *Survey of Inmates of Local Jails, 1983.* Washington, DC: U.S. Department of Justice.

———. 1987a. *Prisoners in 1986.* Washington, DC: U.S. Department of Justice.

———. 1987b. *Jail Inmates, 1985.* Washington, DC: U.S. Department of Justice.

———. 1988. *Survey of Youth in Custody, 1987.* Washington, DC: U.S. Department of Justice.

———. 1989. *Children in Custody, 1975–1985.* Washington, DC: U.S. Department of Justice.

———. 1990. *Jail Inmates, 1989.* Washington, DC: U.S. Department of Justice.

———. 1990b. *Prisoners in 1989.* Washington, DC: U.S. Department of Justice.

———. 1994. *Criminal Victimization in the United States, 1973–92 Trends.* Washington, DC: U.S. Department of Justice.

———. 1995. *Prisoners in 1994.* Washington, DC: U.S. Department of Justice.

Burgess, E. W. 1928. "The Growth of the City." In R. E. Park, E. Burgess, and R. D. McKenzie (eds.), *The City.* Chicago: University of Chicago Press.

Bursik, R., J. D. Merten, and G. Schwartz. 1985. "Appropriate Age-Related Behavior for Male and Female Adolescents: Adult Perceptions." *Youth and Society* 17: 115–130.

Butts, J. A., H. N. Snyder, T. A. Finnegan, A. L. Aughenbaugh, and R. S. Poole. 1994. *Juvenile Court Statistics, 1991.* Pittsburgh: National Center for Juvenile Justice, Office of Juvenile Justice and Delinquency Prevention.

————. 1996. *Juvenile Court Statistics, 1993.* Washington, DC: Office of Juvenile Justice and Delinquency Prevention.

Cahalan, M. W. 1986. *Historical Corrections Statistics in the United States, 1950–1984.* Washington, DC: U.S. Department of Justice.

Cain, M. (ed.). 1989. *Growing Up Good: Policing the Behavior of Girls in Europe.* London: Sage.

————. 1990. "Towards Transgression: New Directions in Feminist Criminology." *International Journal of the Sociology of Law* 18 (1): 1–18.

Cameron, M. 1953. *Department Store Shoplifting.* Ph.D. diss., Indiana University.

————. 1964. *The Booster and the Snitch.* New York: Free Press.

Campagna, D. S., and D. L. Poffenberger. 1988. *The Sexual Trafficking in Children.* Dover, MA: Auburn House.

Campbell, A. 1981. *Girl Delinquents.* New York: St. Martin's Press.

————. 1984a. *The Girls in the Gang.* Oxford: Basil Blackwell.

————. 1984b. "Girls' Talk: The Social Representation of Aggression by Female Gang Members." *Criminal Justice and Behavior* 11: 139–156.

————. 1990. "Female Participation in Gangs." In G. R. Huff (ed.), *Gangs in America.* Newbury Park, CA: Sage.

————. 1993. *Men, Women, and Aggression.* New York: Basic Books.

Canter, R. J. 1981. *Family Correlates of Male and Female Delinquency.* Boulder, CO: Behavioral Research Institute.

————. 1982. "Sex Differences in Self-Report Delinquency." *Criminology* 20: 373–393.

Carey, A. 1995. *Taking the Risk Out of Democracy.* Chicago: University of Illinois Press.

Carmen, A., and H. Moody. 1985. *Working Women.* New York: Harper.

Carter, B. 1981. "Reform School Families." In L. Bowker (ed.), *Women and Crime in America.* New York: Macmillan.

Carter, T. 1979. "Juvenile Court Dispositions: A Comparison of Status and Non-Status Offenders." *Criminology* 17: 341–359.

Castro, L. A. 1981. "Venezuelan Female Criminality." In F. Adler (ed.), *The Incidence of Female Criminality in the Contemporary World.* New York: New York University Press.

CBS. 1992. "Girls in the Hood." *Street Stories,* Aug. 6.

Centers for Disease Control. 2000. *Youth Risk Behavior Surveillance—United States, 1999.* CDC Surveillance Summaries. U.S. Department of Health and Human Services. Atlanta: Centers for Disease Control.

Cernkovich, S., and P. Giordano. 1979. "A Comparative Analysis of Male and Female Delinquency." *Sociological Quarterly* 20: 131B145.

Champion, D. 2001. *The Juvenile Justice System* (3rd ed.). Upper Saddle River, NJ: Prentice-Hall.

Chesler, P. 1972. *Women and Madness.* New York: Doubleday.

Chesney-Lind, M. 1971. "Female Juvenile Delinquency in Hawaii." Master's thesis, University of Hawaii.

————. 1973. "Judicial Enforcement of the Female Sex Role." *Issues in Criminology* 8: 51–70.

————. 1977. "Judicial Paternalism and the Female Status Offender: Training Women to Know Their Place." *Crime and Delinquency* 23: 121–130.

————. 1978. "Young Women in the Arms of the Law." In L. Bowker (ed.), *Women, Crime and the Criminal Justice System.* Lexington, MA: Lexington Books.

————. 1986. "Women and Crime: The Female Offender." *Signs* 12: 78–96.

————. 1987. "Girls and Violence: An Exploration of the Gender Gap in Serious Delinquent Behavior." In D. Crowell, I. Evans, and C. O'Donnell (eds.), *Childhood Aggression and Violence.* New York: Plenum.

————. 1988. "Girls and Deinstitutionalization." *Criminal Justice Abstracts* 20: 144–165.

————. 1993. "Girls, Gangs and Violence: Reinventing the Liberated Female Crook." *Humanity and Society* 17: 321–344.

————. 1999. "Media Misogyny: Demonizing 'Violent' Girls and Women." In J. Ferrel & N. Websdale (eds.), Making trouble: Cultural representations of crime, deviance, and control (pp. 115–141). New York: Aldine.

Chesney-Lind, M., and B. Bloom. 1999. "Feminist Criminology: Thinking About Women and Crime." In B. Maclean (ed.), *Thinking Critically About Crime.* Vancouver: Press Gang.

Chesney-Lind, M., M. Brown, D. Mayeda, D. Kwack, P. Perrone, D. Kato, N. Marker, and S. Hookano. 1997. *Risk, Delinquency, & Gangs in Hawaii: Neighborhood and Agency Profiles.* Honolulu: University of Hawaii at Manoa, Social Science Research Institute

Chesney-Lind, M., N. Marker, H. Reyes, Y. Reyes, and A. Rockhill. 1992. "Gangs and Delinquency in Hawaii." Paper presented at the Annual Meeting of the American Society of Criminology, New Orleans, November.

Chesney-Lind, M., D. Mayeda, N. Marker, V. Paramore, and S. Okamoto. 1998. *Trends in Delinquency and Gang Membership: An Interim Report to the Hawaii State Legislature.* Honolulu: University of Hawaii at Manoa, Social Science Research Institute.

Chesney-Lind, M., D. Mayeda, V. Paramore, S. Okamoto, and N. Marker. 1999. *Delinquency and Gangs in Hawaii: Volume 1: Prevalence.* Honolulu: University of Hawaii at Manoa, Social Science Research Institute.

Chesney-Lind, M., and S. K. Okamoto. 2001. "Gender Matters: Patterns in Girls' Delinquency and Gender Responsive Programming." *Journal of Forensic Psychology Practice,* 1(3), 1–28.

Chesney-Lind, M., and V. Paramore. 2001. "Are Girls Getting More Violent?: Exploring Juvenile Robbery Trends." *Journal of Contemporary Criminal Justice* 17(2):142–166.

Chesney-Lind, M., and L. Pasko. 2003. "Jailing Girls." Paper presented at the Hawaii Sociological Association Meeting, February 15, Honolulu, Hawaii.

Chesney-Lind, M., A. Rockhill, N. Marker, and H. Reyes. 1994. "Gangs and Delinquency: Exploring Police Estimates of Gang Membership." *Crime, Law and Social Change* 21: 210–228.

Chesney-Lind, M., and N. Rodriguez. 1983. "Women Under Lock and Key." *Prison Journal* 63: 47–65.

Chesney-Lind, M., R. G. Shelden, and K. Joe. 1996. "Girls, Delinquency and Gang Membership." In R. Huff (ed.), *Gangs in America,* 2d ed. Thousand Oaks, CA: Sage.

Children's Bureau. Department of Health, Education and Welfare. 1967. *Statistics on Public Institutions for Delinquent Children, 1965.* Washington, DC: U.S. Government Printing Office.

Children's Defense Fund. 1976. *Children in Adult Jails.* Washington, DC: U.S. Government Printing Office.

Chilton, R., and S. Datesman. 1987. "Gender, Race and Crime: An Analysis of Urban Arrest Trends, 1960–1980." Paper presented at the annual meeting of the American Sociological Association, New York.

Chomsky, N. 1989. *Necessary Illusions: Thought Control in Democratic Societies.* Boston: South End Press.

———. 1994. *Keeping the Rabble in Line.* Monroe, ME: Common Courage Press.

———. 1996. *Powers and Prospects: Reflections on Human Nature and the Social Order.* Boston: South End Press.

Clarke, S. H., and G. C. Koch. 1980. "Juvenile Court: Therapy and Crime Control, and Do Lawyers Make a Difference?" *Law and Society Review* 14: 263–308.

Cloward, R. A., and L. E. Ohlin. 1960. *Delinquency and Opportunity.* New York: Free Press.

Coalition for Juvenile Justice. 1996. "Comparison of the JJDPA and House and Senate Reauthorization Bills." Washington, DC: Coalition for Juvenile Justice, pp. 1–8.

Cohen, A. 1955. *Delinquent Boys: The Culture of the Gang.* New York: Free Press.

Cohen, L. E., and J. R. Kluegel. 1979. "Selecting Delinquents for Adjudication." *Journal of Research in Crime and Delinquency* 16: 143–163.

Cohen, S. 1972. *Folk Devils and Moral Panics: The Creation of the Mods and Rockers.* London: London, MacGibbon and Kee.

Cohn, Y. 1970. "Criteria for the Probation Officer's Recommendation to the Juvenile Court." In P. G. Garbedian and D. C. Gibbons (eds.), *Becoming Delinquent.* Chicago: Aldine.

Community Research Associates. 1983. *Juvenile Suicides in Adult Jails: Findings from a National Survey of Juveniles in Secure Detention Facilities.* Washington, DC: U.S. Department of Justice.

Connell, R. W. 1987. *Gender and Power.* Palo Alto, CA: Stanford University Press.

———. 1990. "The State, Gender, and Sexual Politics: Theory and Appraisal." *Theory and Society* 19: 507–544.

———, and D. Hartmann. 1998. *Ethnicity and Race: Making Identities in a Changing World.* Thousand Oaks, CA: Pine Forge Press.

Constantinople, A. 1973. "Masculinity-Femininity: An Exception to a Famous Dictum?" *Psychological Bulletin* 80: 389–407.

Conway, A., and C. Bogdan. 1977. "Sexual Delinquency: The Persistence of a Double Standard." *Crime and Delinquency* 23: 131–135.

Corrado, R., I. Cohen, and C. Odgers. 1998. "Teen Violence in Canada." In R. Sommers and A. Hoffman (eds.) *Teen Violence: A Global Perspective*. San Diego, CA: Greenwood.

Corrado, R., C. Odgers, and I. Cohen. 1999. "Girls in Jail: Custody or Care?" In R. Roesch, R. Corrado and R. Dempster (eds.) *Psychology in the Courts: International Advances in Knowledge*. New York: Harwood Academic Press.

Corrado, R., C. Odgers, and I. Cohen. 2000. "The Incarceration of Female Young Offenders: Protection for Whom?" *Canadian Journal of Criminology*, April, 189–207.

Costello, J. C., and N. L. Worthington. 1981–82. "Incarcerating Status Offenders: Attempts to Circumvent the Juvenile Justice and Delinquency Prevention Act." *Harvard Civil Rights-Civil Liberties Law Review* 16: 41–81.

Cowan, G., and C. D. Hoffman. 1986. "Gender Stereotyping in Young Children: Evidence to Support a Concept Learning Approach." *Sex Roles* 14: 211–224.

Cowie, J., V. Cowie, and E. Slater. 1968. *Delinquency in Girls*. London: Heinemann.

Crain, R. M. 1996. "The Influence of Age, Race, and Gender on Child and Adolescent Multidimensional Self-Concept." In B. A. Brackan (ed.), *Handbook of Self-Concept: Developmental, Social and Clinical Considerations*. New York: Wiley.

Criminal Justice Newsletter. 1990. "Hawaii Shows Mixed Results in Shift to Community Sanctions." June 1: 7–8.

Criminal Justice Statistics Center. 1999. *Crime in Hawaii: 1998*. Honolulu: Department of the Attorney General.

Crick, N. R., and J. K. Grotpeter. 1995. "Relational Aggression, Gender, and Social-Psychological Adjustment." *Child Development*, 66, 710–722.

Crites, L. (ed.). 1976. *The Female Offender*. Lexington, MA: Lexington Books.

Crittenden, D. 1990. "You've Come a Long Way, Moll." *Wall Street Journal*, Jan. 25: A14.

Crombie, G. 1988. "Gender Differences: Implications for Social Skills Assessment and Training." *Journal of Clinical Child Psychology* 17: 116–120.

Cugini, M. 1997. "Teen Prostitution." College Park, MD: Advocates for Children, College Park Scholars, on-line (http"//www.wam.umd.edu/~stwright/ac/papers97/Cugini-acl.html).

Cullen, F., K. Golden, and J. Cullen. 1979. "Sex and Delinquency." *Criminology* 7: 301–310.

Curran, D. 1984. "The Myth of the New Female Delinquent." *Crime and Delinquency* 30: 386–399.

Curry, G. D. 1998. "Female Gang Involvement." *Journal of Research in Crime and Delinquency* 35: 100–118.

Curry, G. D., R. A. Ball, and R. J. Fox. 1994. *Gang Crime and Law Enforcement Recordkeeping*. Washington, DC: National Institute of Justice.

Curry, G. D., R. J. Fox, R. A. Ball, and D. Stone. 1992. *National Assessment of Law Enforcement Anti-Gang Information Resources: Draft 1992 Final Report*. West Virginia University: National Assessment Survey.

Curtis, C. 1987. "Gender Bias in Discretionary Decision Making in the Criminal Justice System: An Application of a New Model." Paper presented at the annual meeting of the Western Society of Criminology, Las Vegas.

Daly, K. 1988. "The Social Control of Sexuality: A Case Study of the Criminalization of Prostitution in the Progressive Era." In S. Spitzer and A. T. Scull (eds.), *Research in Law, Deviance, and Social Control*, vol. 9. Greenwich, CT: JAI Press.

———. 1994. *Gender, Crime and Punishment*. New Haven: Yale University Press.

Daly, K., and M. Chesney-Lind. 1988. "Feminism and Criminology." *Justice Quarterly* 5: 497–538.

Daniel, M. D. 1999. "The Female Intervention Team." *Juvenile Justice* 6: 14–20.

Dannefer, D., and R. K. Schutt. 1982. "Race and Juvenile Justice Processing in Court and Police Agencies." *American Journal of Sociology* 87: 1113–1132.

Datesman, S., and M. Aickin. 1984. "Offense Specialization and Escalation Among Status Offenders." *Journal of Criminal Law and Criminology* 75: 1246–1275.

Datesman, S., and F. Scarpitti. 1977. "Unequal Protection for Males and Females in the Juvenile Court." In T. N. Ferdinand (ed.), *Juvenile Delinquency: Little Brother Grows Up*. Newbury Park, CA: Sage.

Datesman, S., F. Scarpitti, and R. M. Stephenson. 1975. "Female Delinquency: An Application of Self and Opportunity Theories." *Journal of Research in Crime and Delinquency* 66: 107–132.

Davidson, S. (ed.). 1982. *Justice for Young Women*. Seattle: New Directions for Young Women

———. (ed.). 1983. *The Second Mile: Contemporary Approaches in Counseling Young Women*. Tucson, AZ: New Directions for Young Women.

Davidson, W., and R. Redner. 1988. "The Prevention of Juvenile Delinquency: Diversion from the Juvenile Justice System." In R. Price, E. Cowen, R. Orion, and J. Ramos-McKay (eds.), *14 Ounces of Prevention*. Washington, DC: American Psychological Association.

Davis, C., R. Estes, and V. Schiraldi. 1996. *"Three Strikes": The New Apartheid*. San Francisco: Center on Juvenile and Criminal Justice, March.

Davis, N. 1999. *Youth Crisis*. Westport, CT: Praeger.

Dawley, D. 1973. *A Nation of Lords: The Autobiography of the Vice Lords*. Garden City, NY: Anchor Books.

Day, L., J. Maltby, and D. Giles. 2000. "Psychological Predictors of Self-Reported Shoplifting." *Psychology, Crime and Law* 6: 77–79.

Deborah Doe et al. v. Lloyd W. Burwell et al. 1981. Plantiffs' Memorandum in Support of Motion for Class Certification. Filed in U.S. District Court for Southern District of Ohio. Civil Action No. C-1-81-416.

Decker, S. H. 1985. "A Systematic Analysis of Diversion: Net Widening and Beyond." *Journal of Criminal Justice* 13: 207–216.

DeComo, R. E. 1998. "Estimating the prevalence of juvenile custody by race and gender." *Crime and Delinquency*, 44 (4), 489–506.

DeFleur, L. B. 1975. "Biasing Influences on Drug Arrest Records: Implications for Deviance Research." *American Sociological Review* 40: 88–101.

DeJong, A. R., A. R. Hervada, and G. A. Emmett. 1983. "Epidemiologic Variations in Childhood Sexual Abuse." *Child Abuse and Neglect* 7: 155–162.

DeKeseredy, W. 2000. *Women, Crime and the Canadian Criminal Justice System*. Cincinnati: Anderson.

Delinquency Prevention Commission. 1992. "Findings and Recommendations on the Needs of Women and Girls in the Justice System." San Francisco: Come Into the Sun Coalition, Commission on the Status of Women.

Dell'Olio, J., and P. Jacobs. 1991. "The Child, Inc. of Delaware Experience." In I. Schwartz and F. Orlando (eds.), *Programming for Young Women in the Juvenile Justice System*. Ann Arbor, MI: Center for the Study of Youth Policy.

de Mause, L. (ed.). 1974. *The History of Childhood*. New York: Psychohistory Press.

Dembo, R., L. Williams, and J. Schmeidler. 1993. "Gender Differences in Mental Health Service Needs Among Youths Entering a Juvenile Detention Center." *Journal of Prison and Jail Health* 12: 73–101.

Dembo, R., S. C. Sue, P. Borden, and D. Manning. 1995. "Gender Differences in Service Needs Among Youths Entering a Juvenile Assessment Center: A Replication Study." Paper presented at the Annual Meeting of the Society of Social Problems, Washington, D.C.

DeMuro, P. 1987. "Hawaii's Juvenile Justice System: Opportunity for Reform." Honolulu: Hawaii Department of Corrections. Mimeo.

Deng, X., and L. Zhang. 1998. "Correlates of Self-Control: An Empirical Test of Self-Control Theory." *Journal of Crime and Justice* 21: 89–110.

Department of Youth Authority. 1986. *The 1985 Jail Report: Minors Detained in California Jails and Lockups in 1985*. Sacramento: State of California.

Deschenes, E., J. Rosenbaum, and J. Fagan. 1990. "Gender Differences in Delinquency and Drug Use." Paper presented at the annual meeting of the American Society of Criminology, Baltimore.

Dimenstein, G. 1994. "Little Girls of the Night." *NACLA Report on the Americas* 27: 29–35.

Dobash, R. E., and R. Dobash. 1979. *Violence Against Wives*. New York: Free Press.

Doi, D. 2002. "Reauthorization Update." Memorandum to the Coalition for Juvenile Justice. October 10.

Domhoff, G. W. 1998. *Who Rules America? Power and Politics in the Year 2000*. 3d ed. Mountain View, CA: Mayfield.

Donziger, S. (ed.). 1996. *The Real War on Crime.* New York: Harper Perennial.

Dore, M., M. Young, and D. M. Pappenfort. 1984. "Comparison of Basic Data for the National Survey of Residential Group Care Facilities." *Child Welfare* 68: 485–495.

Dougherty, M. 1992. *To Steal a Kingdom.* Waimanalo, Hawaii: Island Style Press.

Douglas, J. W., J. M. Ross, W. A. Hammond, and D. G. Mulligan. 1966. "Delinquency and Social Class." *British Journal of Criminology* 6: 294–302.

Druckman, J. M. 1979. "A Family-Oriented Policy and Treatment Program for Female Juvenile Status Offenders." *Journal of Marriage and the Family* 41: 627–636.

Dryfoos, J. G. 1990. *Adolescents at Risk: Prevalence and Prevention.* New York: Oxford University Press.

Dudley, M.K. 1990. *A Call for Hawaiian Sovereignty.* Honolulu: Na Kane O Ka Malo Press.

Duncan, G., J. Yeung, J. Brooks-Gun, and J. Smith. 1998. "How much does childhood poverty affect the life chances of children?" *American Sociological Review,* 63, 406–423.

Dungworth, T. 1977. "Discretion in the Juvenile Justice System." In T. N. Ferdinand (ed.), *Juvenile Delinquency: Little Brother Grows Up.* Newbury Park, CA: Sage.

Durham, M. 1998. "Dilemmas of Desire: Representations of Adolescent Sexuality in Two Teen Magazines." *Youth and Society,* 29 (3), 369–389.

Durkheim, E. 1951. *Suicide.* New York: Free Press.

Eaton, M. 1986. *Justice for Women?* Milton Keynes: Open University Press.

Edelbrock, C. 1980. "Running Away from Home: Incidence and Correlates Among Children and Youth Referred for Mental Health Services." *Journal of Family Issues* 1: 210–228.

Edwards, A. 1973. "Sex and Area Variations in Delinquency Rates in an English City." *British Journal of Criminology* 13: 121–137.

Edwards, H. 1974. *Sociology of Sport.* Homewood, IL: Dorsey Press.

Ehrhart, J. K., and B. R. Sandler. 1987. *Looking for More Than a Few Good Women in Traditionally Male Fields.* Washington, DC: Project on the Status and Education of Women.

Elder, G. H. 1969. "Appearance and Education in Marriage Mobility." *American Sociological Review* 34: 519–533.

Elikann, P. 1999. *Superpredators: The Demonization of Our Children by the Law.* Reading, MA: Perseus.

Elliott, D. 1993. *Youth Violence: An Overview.* Philadelphia: Center for the Study of Youth Policy.

Elliott, D., and H. L. Voss. 1974. *Delinquency and Dropout.* Lexington, MA: Lexington Books.

Elliott, D., H. L. Voss, D. Huizinga, and B. Morse. 1987. "A Career Analysis of Serious Violent Offenders." In I. Schwartz (ed.), *Violent Juvenile Crime: What Can We Do about It?* Minneapolis: Hubert Humphrey Institute of Public Affairs.

Empey, L. T. (ed.). 1979. *The Future of Childhood and Juvenile Justice.* Charlottesville: University Press of Virginia.

———. 1982. *American Delinquency.* Homewood, IL: Dorsey Press.

Enloe, C. 1983. *Does Khaki Become You?* Boston: South End Press.

Esbensen, F., P. Deschenes, and L. T. Winfree. 1999. "Differences Between Gang Girls and Gang Boys." *Youth and Society* 31: 27–53.

Facella, C. A. 1983. Female Delinquency in a Birth Cohort. Ph.D. diss., University of Pennsylvania.

Fagot, B. 1984. "The Child's Expectations of Differences in Adult Male and Female Interactions." *Sex Roles* 11: 593–600.

Faludi, S. 1991. *Backlash: The Undeclared War Against Women.* New York: Crown.

Farmer, H. S. 1985. "The Role of Typical Female Characteristics in Career Achievement Motivation." *Youth and Society* 16: 315B334.

Farnworth, M. 1984. "Male-Female Differences in Delinquency in a Minority Group Sample." *Journal of Research in Crime and Delinquency* 21: 191–212.

Farrington, D. 1999. "Measuring, Explaining, and Preventing Shoplifting: A Review of British Research." *Security Journal* 12: 9–27.

Faust, F., and P. Brantingham. 1979. *Juvenile Justice Philosophy,* 2d ed. St. Paul: West.

Federal Bureau of Investigation. 1965, 1971, 1975, 1976, 1981, 1985, 1986, 1987, 1988, 1989, 1993, 1995, 1997, 2001. *Crime in the United States.* Washington, DC: U.S. Department of Justice.

Federle, K. H. 1990. "The Abolition of the Juvenile Court: A Proposal for the Preservation of Children's Legal Rights." *Journal of Contemporary Law* 16: 23–51.

Feinman, C. 1980. *Women in the Criminal Justice System.* New York: Praeger.

———. 1985. "Criminal Codes, Criminal Justice and Female Offenders: New Jersey as a Case Study." In I. L. Moyer (ed.), *The Changing Roles of Women in the Criminal Justice System.* Prospect Heights, IL: Waveland.

Feld, B. C. 1988. "The Juvenile Court Meets the Principle of Offense: Punishment, Treatment and the Difference It Makes." *Boston University Law Review* 68: 821–915.

———. 1990. "Justice by Geography: Urban, Suburban, and Rural Variations in Juvenile Justice Administration." *The Journal of Criminal Law and Criminology* 82: 156–210.

———. 1998. *Bad Kids: Race and the Transformation of the Juvenile Court.* New York: Oxford University Press.

Feldman, R. A., T. E. Caplinger, and J. S. Wodarski. *The St. Louis Conundrum.* Englewood Cliffs, N.J.: Prentice-Hall, 1983.

Felice, M., and D. R. Offord. 1971. "Girl Delinquency: A Review." *Corrective Psychiatry and Journal of Social Therapy* 17: 18–33.

Female Offender Resource Center. 1977. *Little Sisters and the Law.* Washington, DC: American Bar Association.

Figueria-McDonough, J. 1984. "Feminism and Delinquency." *British Journal of Criminology* 24: 325–342.

Figueria-McDonough, J., W. Barton, and R. Sarri. 1981. "Normal Deviance: Gender Similarities in Adolescent Subcultures." In M. Warren (ed.), *Comparing Male and Female Offenders.* Newbury Park, CA: Sage.

Finckenauer, J. O. 1984. *Juvenile Delinquency and Corrections.* New York: Academic Press.

Fine, M., and N. Zane. 1989. "Bein' Wrapped Too Tight: When Low-income Women Drop Out of High School." In L. Weis, E. Farrar and H. G. Petrie (eds.), *Dropouts from Schools: Issues, Dilemmas and Solutions.* Albany, NY: SUNY Press.

Finkelhor, D. 1978. *Social Forces in the Formulation of the Problem of Sexual Abuse.* Durham: University of New Hampshire, Family Violence Program.

———. 1982. "Sexual Abuse: A Sociological Perspective." *Child Abuse and Neglect* 6: 95–102.

Finkelhor, D., and L. Baron. 1986. "Risk Factors for Child Sexual Abuse." *Journal of Interpersonal Violence* 1: 43–71.

Finkelhor, D., G. Hotaling, and A. Sedlak. 1990. *Missing, Abducted, Runaway, and Throwaway Children in America: Executive Summary.* Washington, DC: U.S. Department of Justice.

Fishman, L. T. 1995. "The Vice Queens: An Ethnographic Study of Black Female Gang Behavior." In M. Klein, C. Maxson, and J. Millers (eds). *The Modern Gang Reader* (pp. 83–92). Los Angeles: Roxbury.

Flanagan, T. J., and E. F. McGarrell. 1986. *Sourcebook of Criminal Justice Statistics, 1985.* Washington, DC: U.S. Department of Justice.

Flaste, R. 1977. "Is Juvenile Justice Tougher on Girls Than Boys?" *New York Times*, Sept. 6.

Flowers, R. B. 1987. *Women and Criminality.* New York: Greenwood.

Fo, W. S. O., and C. R. O'Donnell. 1975. "The Buddy System: Effect of Community Intervention on Delinquent Offenses." *Behavior Therapy* 6: 522–524.

Folbre, N., and the Center for Popular Economics. 1995. *The New Field Guide to the U.S. Economy.* New York: The New Press.

Fones-Wolf, E. 1994. *Selling Free Enterprise.* Indianapolis: University of Indiana Press.

Fordam, S. 1993. "'Those Loud Black Girls': (Black) Women, Silence, and Gender Passing in the Academy." *Anthropology and Education* 24(1): 3–32.

Forer, L. 1970. *No One Will Listen.* New York: John Day.

Frazier, C. E., and D. Bishop. 1990. "Gender Bias in Juvenile Justice Processing: Implications of the JJDP Act." Paper presented at the annual meeting of the Academy of Criminal Justice Sciences, Denver.

Frazier, C. E., D. Bishop, and J. C. Cochran. 1986. "Detention of Juveniles: Its Effects on Subsequent Juvenile Court Processing Decisions." *Youth and Society* 17: 286–305.

Frazier, C.E., and J. K. Cochran. "Official Intervention, Diversion from the Juvenile Justice System, and Dynamics of Human Services Work: Effects of a Reform Goal Based on Labeling Theory." *Crime and Delinquency* 32 (1986), pp. 157–176.

Freedman, E. 1981. *Their Sisters' Keepers.* Ann Arbor: University of Michigan Press.

Frey, K. S. 1979. "Differential Teaching Methods Used with Girls and Boys of Moderate and High Achievement Levels." Paper presented at the annual meeting of the Society for Research in Child Development, San Francisco.

Fuentes, A., and B. Ehrenreich. 1983. *Women in the Global Factory.* Boston: South End Press.

Fujimoto, L., and H. Altonn. 1990. "Molokai Rescue Raises Old Fears About Program." *Honolulu Star Bulletin,* Dec. 12.

G. L. v. Zumwalt. 1983. 564 Supp. 1030 (W.D. Mo., 1983).

Gay, J. 1985. "The 'Patriotic' Prostitute." *The Progressive* (February): 34–36.

Geller, G. 1981. "Streaming of Males and Females in the Juvenile Justice System." Paper presented at the Canadian Psychological Association annual meeting, Toronto.

———. 1984. "The Medicalization of Female Delinquency." Paper presented at the American Society of Criminology annual meeting, Cincinnati.

Gelsthorpe, L. 1986. "Towards a Skeptical Look at Sexism." *International Journal of the Sociology of Law* 14: 125–152.

General Accounting Office. 1978. *Removing Status Offenders from Secure Facilities: Federal Leadership and Guidance Are Needed.* Washington, DC: General Accounting Office.

———. 1995. *Juvenile Justice: Minimal Gender Bias Occurring in Processing Non-Criminal Juveniles.* Washington, DC: Letter Report.

Giallambardo, R. 1974. *The Social World of Imprisoned Girls.* New York: Wiley.

Gibbons, D., and G. Blake. 1976. "Evaluating the Impact of Juvenile Diversion Programs." *Crime and Delinquency* 22: 411–420.

Gibbons, D., and M. J. Griswold. 1957. "Sex Differences Among Juvenile Court Referrals." *Sociology and Social Research* 42: 106–110.

Gibbs, J. 1994. "Anger in Young Black Males: Victims or Victimizers?" In R. Majors and J. Gordon (eds.), *The American Black Male: His Present Status and His Future.* Chicago: Nelson-Hall.

Gibbs, J. T. 1985. "City Girls: Psychosocial Adjustment of Urban Black Adolescent Females." *Signs* 2 (2): 28–36.

Gilfus, M. 1988. *Seasoned by Violence / Tempered by Love.* Ph.D. diss., Brandeis University.

———. 1992. "From Victims to Survivors to Offenders: Women's Routes of Entry and Immersion into Street Crime." *Women and Criminal Justice* 4: 63–89.

Gilligan, C. 1982. *In a Different Voice: Psychological Theory and Women's Development.* Cambridge: Harvard University Press.

Gilligan, C., J. V. Ward, J. M. Taylor, and B. Bardige (eds.). 1988. *Mapping the Moral Domain.* Cambridge: Harvard University, Center for the Study of Gender, Education and Human Development.

Gilligan, C., N. P. Lyons, and T. J. Hammer. 1990. *Making Connections: The Relational Lives of Girls at Emma Willard School.* Cambridge: Harvard University Press.

Giordano, P. 1978. "Girls, Guys and Gangs: The Changing Social Context of Female Delinquency." *Journal of Criminal Law and Criminology* 69: 126–132.

Giordano, P., S. Cernkovich, and M. Pugh. 1986. "Friendships and Delinquency." *American Journal of Sociology* 5: 1170–1202.

Girls, Inc. 1996. *Prevention and Parity: Girls in Juvenile Justice.* Indianapolis: Girls Incorporated National Resource Center.

Glaser, D. 1974. "Remedies for the Key Deficiency in Criminal Justice Evaluation Research." *Journal of Research in Crime and Delinquency* 11: 144–154.

Glave, J. 1987. "Police Say Girl Sexually Abused in Three Homes." *Philadelphia Inquirer,* Feb. 8: A26.

Glueck, S., and E. Glueck. 1934. *Five Hundred Delinquent Women.* New York: Knopf.

Gold, S. 1971. "Equal Protection for Juvenile Girls in Need of Supervision in New York State." *New York Law Forum* 17: 570–91.

Goldberg, L. 1996. "Juvenile Hall Strip Search of Girls Spurs Questions." *San Francisco Examiner,* Feb. 16: A1.

Goldman, N. 1969. "The Differential Selection of Juvenile Offenders for Court Appearances." In W. Chambliss (ed.), *Crime and the Legal Process.* New York: McGraw-Hill.

Golley, L. 1983. "For Sale: Girls." *Southeast Asia Chronicle,* April.

Gordon, L. 1988. *Heroes in Their Own Lives.* New York: Viking.

Gori, K. 1993. "Cry of the Innocents: The Story of a Chinese Girl Sold into Prostitution in Thailand." *Far Eastern Economic Review*, Sept. 9: 36–38.

Greene, Peters and Associates. 1998. *Guiding Principles for Promising Female Programming: An Inventory of Best Practices.* Washington, DC: Office of Juvenile Justice and Delinquency Prevention.

Greenwood, P., and F. Zimring. 1985. *One More Chance: The Pursuit of Promising Intervention Strategies for Chronic Juvenile Offenders.* Santa Monica, CA: Rand Corporation.

Gropper, N., and M. Froschl. 2000. "The Role of Gender in Young Children's Teasing and Bullying Behavior." *Equity and Excellence in Education*, 33: 48–56.

Grosser, G. 1952. *Juvenile Delinquency and Contemporary American Sex Roles.* Ph.D. diss., Harvard University.

Grossman, F.K., J. Beinashowitz, L. Anderson, M. Sakurai, L. Finnin, and M. Flaherty. 1992. "Risk and Resilience in Young Adolescents." *Journal of Youth and Adolescence*, 21: 529–550.

Hagan, F. E. 1987. *Introduction to Criminology.* Chicago: Nelson-Hall.

Hagan, J. 1989. *Structural Criminology.* New Brunswick: Rutgers University Press.

Hagan, J., A. R. Gillis, and J. Simpson. 1985. "The Class Structure of Gender and Delinquency: Toward a Power-Control Theory of Common Delinquent Behavior." *American Journal of Sociology* 90: 1151–1178.

Hagedorn, J. M. 1998. *People and Folks: Gangs, Crime and the Underclass in a Rustbelt City.* (2nd ed.) Chicago: Lakeview Press.

Hancock, L. 1981. "The Myth That Females Are Treated More Leniently Than Males in the Juvenile Justice System." *Australian and New Zealand Journal of Sociology* 16: 4–14.

———, and M. Chesney-Lind. 1982. "Female Status Offenders and Justice Reforms: An International Perspective." *Australian and New Zealand Journal of Criminology* 15: 109–122.

Hanson, K. 1964. *Rebels in the Streets: The Story of New York's Girl Gangs.* Englewood Cliffs, NJ: Prentice-Hall.

Hare-Mustin, R. T. 1983. "An Appraisal of the Relationship Between Women and Psychotherapy." *American Psychologist* 38: 593–601.

Harms, P. 2002. *Detention in delinquency cases, 1989–1998.* (OJJDP Fact Sheet No. 1). Washington, DC: U.S. Department of Justice.

Harper, G., and L. Robinson. "Pathways to Risk Among Inner-City African American Adolescent Females: The Influence of Gang Membership." *American Journal of Community Psychology* 27: 383–404.

Harris, A. 1977. "Sex and Theories of Deviance." *American Sociological Review* 42: 3–16.

Harris, M. G. 1988. *Cholas: Latino Girls and Gangs.* New York: AMS Press.

———. 1997. "Cholas, Mexican-American Girls, and Gangs." In Mays, ed., *Gangs and Gang Behavior.* Chicago: Nelson-Hall.

Harrison, P., Maupin, J. and G. L. Mays. 2001. "Teen Court: An Examination of Processes and Outcomes." *Crime and Delinquency* 47: 243–264.

Hartman, F. 1987. "The Current System: Structure and Operations." In M. Moore (ed.), *From Children to Citizens. Vol. 1, The Mandate for Juvenile Justice.* New York: Springer-Verlag.

Hawes, J. 1971. *Children in Urban Society.* New York: Oxford University Press.

Hayes, R. 1996. "1996 Retail Theft Trends Report: An Analysis of Customer Theft in Stores." On line (http://webspirs3.silverplatter.com/cgi-bin/customers)

Heimer, K. 1995. "Gender, Race, and Pathways to Delinquency." In J. Hagen and R. D. Peterson (eds.), *Crime and Inequality.* Stanford: Stanford University Press.

Henggler, S. 1989. *Delinquency in Adolescence.* Newbury Park, CA: Sage.

Herman, E., and N. Chomsky. 1988. *Manufacturing Consent: The Political Economy of the Mass Media.* New York: Pantheon.

Herman, J. L. 1981. *Father-Daughter Incest.* Cambridge: Harvard University Press.

Hill, G. D., and M. P. Atkinson. 1988. "Gender, Familial Control, and Delinquency." *Criminology* 26: 127–150.

Hindelang, M. J. 1979. "Sex Differences in Criminal Activity." *Social Problems* 27: 143–156.

Hindelang, M. J., T. Hirschi, and J. Weis. 1981. *Measuring Delinquency.* Newbury Park, CA: Sage.

Hirschi, T. 1969. *Causes of Delinquency.* Berkeley: University of California Press.

Hoberman, J. 1997. *Darwin's Athletes: How Sport Has Damaged Black America and Preserved the Myth of Race.* New York: Houghton Mifflin Company.

Hoffman, T. 1981. "Sex Discrimination in Oregon's Juvenile Justice System." Paper presented at the Oregon Psychological Association, Newport, Oregon, May.

Hoke, C. 1998. "State Discretion Under New Federal Welfare Legislation: Illusion, Reality, and a Federalism-Based Constitutional Challenge." *Stanford Law and Policy Review* 9: 115–130.

Honolulu Star Bulletin. 1989. "U.N. Petitioned to Help Death Row Woman, 19." Mar. 4.

———. 1990. "Judge Allows State Suit Against Therapy Program." Dec. 11.

Horowitz, A. V., and H. R. White. 1986. "Gender Role Orientations and Styles of Pathology Among Adolescents." Paper presented at the American Society of Criminology, Atlanta.

Horowitz, D. L. 1977. *The Courts and Social Policy.* Washington, DC: Brookings Institution.

Horowitz, R., and A. E. Pottieger. 1991. "Gender Bias in Juvenile Justice Handling of Seriously Crime-Involved Youths." *Journal of Research in Crime and Delinquency* 28: 75–100.

Howard, B. 1996. "Congress Debating Juvenile Justice Act's Mandates: To Stay or Go?" *Youth Today* (July/August): 22.

Howell, J. C. 1998. *Youth Gangs: An Overview.* Office of Juvenile Justice and Delinquency Prevention. Washington, DC: U.S. Department of Justice.

Howell, N., and S. P. Davis. 1992. "Special Problems of Female Offenders." *Corrections Compendium* 12: 1, 5–20.

Huff, R. (ed.). 1990. *Gangs in America.* Newbury Park, CA: Sage.

———. 1993. "Gangs in the United States." In A. P. Goldstein and C. R. Huff (eds.), *The Gang Intervention Handbook.* Champaign, IL: Research Press.

———. (ed.). 1996. *Gangs in America.* (2nd ed.) Newbury Park, CA: Sage.

Hugo, K. E., and R. B. Rutherford, Jr. 1992. "Issues in Identifying Educational Disabilities Among Female Juvenile Offenders." *Journal of Correctional Education* 43: 124–127.

Huizinga, D. 1994. Personal communication with the authors.

Huizinga, D. 1997. *Over-Time Changes in Delinquency and Drug-Use: The 1970s to the 1990s.* Boulder, CO: University of Colorado, Research Brief.

Human Rights Watch. 1999. *No Minor Matter: Children in Maryland's Jails.* New York: Human Rights Watch. On-line (www.hrw.org/reports/1999/maryland/Maryland.htm).

Hurst, H. 1975. "Juvenile Status Offenders." Speech delivered to the New Mexico Council on Crime and Delinquency, Albuquerque, June 20.

Hyde, J. S. 1985. *Half the Human Experience.* Lexington, MA: Heath.

Ikeda, L., M. Chesney-Lind, and K. Kameoka. 1985. *The Honolulu Anti-Truancy Drive: An Evaluation.* Honolulu: Youth Development and Research Center.

Immarigeon, R. 1987. "Few Diversion Programs Are Offered Female Offenders." *Journal of the National Prison Project* 12: 9–11.

Infante, E. M. 1999. "Borrowed Beauty: 'Euro' Look Still Standard of Beauty for Most Women." *The Honolulu Advertiser*, February 7, E1, 3.

In re Gault. 1967. 387 U.S. 1.

Iwamoto, J. J., K. Kameoka, and Y. C. Brasseur. 1990. *Waikiki Homeless Youth Project: A Report.* Honolulu: Catholic Services to Families.

James, J. 1976. "Motivations for Entrance into Prostitution." In L. Crites (ed.), *The Female Offender.* Lexington, MA: Lexington Books.

James, J., and W. Thornton. 1980. "Women's Liberation and the Female Delinquent." *Journal of Research in Crime and Delinquency* 20: 230–244.

Jamieson, K. M., and T. Flanagan (eds.). 1989. *Sourcebook of Criminal Justice Statistics-1986.* Washington, DC: U.S. Department of Justice.

Jankowski, M. S. 1991. *Islands in the Street: Gangs and American Urban Society.* Berkeley, CA: University of California Press.

Janus, M., F. X. Archambault, S. Brown, and L. Welsh. 1995. "Physical Abuse in Canadian Runaway Adolescents." *Child Abuse and Neglect* 19: 433–447.

Jappler, V. E., M. Blumberg, and G. W. Potter. 1996. *The Mythology of Crime and Criminal Justice*, 2d ed. Prospect Heights, IL: Waveland Press.

Jensen, G., and K. Thompson. 1990. "What's Class Got to Do with It? A Further Examination of Power-Control Theory." *American Journal of Sociology* 95: 1009–1023.

Jensen, G., and R. Eve. 1976. "Sex Differences in Delinquency." *Criminology* 13: 427–448.

Joe, K., and M. Chesney-Lind. 1995. "'Just Every Mother's Angel': An Analysis of Gender and Ethnic Variations in Youth Gang Membership." *Gender and Society* 9: 408–431.

Johnnie K. et al. v. The County of Curry, New Mexico, et al. 1982. *Plaintiffs' Memorandum in Support for Motion for Class Certification.* Filed in the U.S. District Court for the District of New Mexico. No. CIV 81–0914 M.

Johnson, D. R., and L. K. Scheuble. 1991. "Gender Bias in the Disposition of Juvenile Court Referrals: The Effects of Time and Location." *Criminology* 29: 677–699.

Johnson, W. T., R. E. Petersen, and L. E. Wells. 1977. "Arrest Probabilities for Marijuana Users as Indicators of Selective Law Enforcement." *American Journal of Sociology* 83: 681–699.

Jones, G. 1980. "Asylum." In M. H. Washington (ed.), *Midnight Birds.* New York: Anchor.

Jones, H. E. 1938. "The California Adolescent Growth Study." *Journal of Educational Research* 31: 561–567.

Jones, R. L., and L. Kaufman. 2003. "Caseworker Overload Cited in Newark Boy's Death." *New York Times*, January 8, A24.

Jordan, W. J., and Lara, J., and McPartland, J. M. 1996. "Exploring the Causes of Early Dropout Among Race-Ethnic and Gender Groups." *Youth & Society*, 28: 40–61.

Jurjevich, R. M. 1968. *No Water in My Cup: Experiences and a Controlled Study of Psychotherapy of Delinquent Girls.* New York: Libra.

Juvenile Justice Coordinating Council, State of Hawaii. 1984. *The Status of Status Offenders.* Honolulu: November 5. Mimeo.

Karraker, N. 1988. Personal communication with M. Chesney-Lind.

Karraker, N., D. E. Macallair, and V. Schiraldi. 1988. *Public Safety with Care: A Model Juvenile Justice System for Hawaii.* San Francisco: National Center on Institutions and Alternatives.

Kassebaum, G. 1994. *Criminal justice and Hawaiians in the 1990's.* Honolulu: Alu Like, Inc.

Katz, A., and L. H. Teitelbaum. 1977. "PINS Jurisdiction, the Vagueness Doctrine and the Rule of Law." In L. H. Teitelbaum and A. R. Gough (eds.), *Beyond Control: Status Offenders in the Juvenile Court.* Cambridge, MA: Ballinger.

Katz, P. 1979. "The Development of Female Identity." In C. Kopp (ed.), *Becoming Female: Perspectives on Development.* New York: Plenum.

Kaufman, J. G. and C. S. Widom. 1999. "Childhood Victimization, Running, Away and Delinquency." *Journal of Research in Crime and Delinquency* 36: 347–370.

Keiser, R. L. 1969. *The Vice Lords: Warriors of the Streets.* New York: Holt, Rinehart and Winston.

Kelly, D. M. 1993. *Last Chance High: How Girls and Boys Drop In and Out of Alternative Schools.* New Haven: Yale University Press.

Kelly, F. J., and D. J. Baer. 1968. *Outward Bound Schools as an Alternative to Institutionalization for Adolescent Delinquent Boys.* Boston: Fandel Press.

Kent, D., and G. Felkenes. 1998. *Cultural Explanations for Vietnamese Youth Involvement in Street Gangs.* Westminister, CA: United States Department of Justice.

Kersten, J. 1989a. "The Institutional Control of Girls and Women." In M. Cain (ed.), *Growing Up Good.* London: Sage.

———. 1989b. "Patterns of Violence in Juvenile Institutions: A Gender-Specific Perspective." Paper presented at the American Society of Criminology annual meeting, Reno.

Ketchum, O. 1978. "Why Jurisdiction Over Status Offenders Should Be Eliminated from Juvenile Courts." In R. Allinson (ed.), *Status Offenders and the Juvenile Justice System.* Hackensack, NJ: National Council on Crime and Delinquency.

Kett, J. F. 1977. *Rites of Passage: Adolescence in America, 1790 to the Present.* New York: Basic Books.

Kitchen, D. B. 1995. *Sisters in the Hood.* Unpublished Ph.D. dissertation, Western Michigan University.

Klein, D. 1973. "The Etiology of Female Crime." *Issues in Criminology* 8: 3–30.

Klein, M. 1980. "Deinstitutionalization and Diversion of Juvenile Offenders: A Litany of Impediments." In N. Morris and M. Tonry (eds.), *Crime and Justice: An Annual Review of Research, vol. 1.* Chicago: University of Chicago Press.

Klein, M., and C. Maxson. 1989. "Street Gang Violence." In M. E. Wolfgang and N. A. Weiner (eds.), *Violent Crime, Violent Criminals*. Newbury Park, CA: Sage.

Komorosky, M. 1953. *Women in the Modern World*. Boston: Little, Brown.

Konopka, G. 1966. *The Adolescent Girl in Conflict*. Englewood Cliffs, NJ: Prentice-Hall.

————. 1983. *Young Girls: A Portrait of Adolescence*. New York: Hayworth Press.

Koopman, C., M. Rosario, and M. J. Rotheram-Borus. 1994. "Alcohol and Drug Use and Sexual Behavior Placing Runaways at Risk for HIV Infection." *Addictive Behaviors* 19: 95–103.

Koroki, J., and M. Chesney-Lind. 1985. *Everything Just Going Down the Drain: Interviews with Female Delinquents*. Report 319. Honolulu: Youth Development and Research Center.

Kratcoski, P. C. 1974. "Delinquent Boys and Girls." *Child Welfare* 5: 16–21.

Kratcoski, P. C., and J. E. Kratcoski. 1975. "Changing Patterns in the Delinquent Activity of Boys and Girls." *Adolescence* 10: 83–91.

Kreifels, S. 1999. "Racism in Hawaii's Public Schools: Is Trouble Brewing?" *Honolulu Star-Bulletin*, April 23, A1, 8, 9.

Krisberg, B., and J. Austin. 1993. *Reinventing Juvenile Justice*. Newbury Park, CA: Sage.

Krisberg, B., R. DeComo, N. C. Herrera, M. Steketee, and S. Roberts. 1991. *Juveniles Taken into Custody 1990*. San Francisco: National Council on Crime and Delinquency.

Krisberg, B., and I. Schwartz. 1983. "Re-Thinking Juvenile Justice." *Crime and Delinquency* 29: 381–397.

Krisberg, B., I. M. Schwartz, P. Litsky, and J. Austin. 1985. *The Watershed of Juvenile Justice Reform*. Minneapolis: Hubert Humphrey Institute of Public Affairs.

Krisberg, B., I. M. Schwartz, G. Fishman, Z. Eisikovits, and E. Guttman. 1986. *The Incarceration of Minority Youth*. Minneapolis: Hubert Humphrey Institute of Public Affairs.

Krohn, M. D., J. P. Curry, and S. Nelson-Kilger. 1983. "Is Chivalry Dead?" *Criminology* 21: 417–439.

Kuhn, D., S. Nash, and L. Brucken. 1978. "Sex Role Concepts of Two and Three Year Olds." *Child Development* 49: 445–451.

Kunstel, M., and J. Albright. 1987. "Prostitution Thrives on Young Girls." *CJ International* 3: 9–11.

Kurtz, P. D., Kurtz, G. L., and S. V. Jarvis. 1991. "Problems of Maltreated Runaway Youth." *Adolescence* 26: 543–555.

Ladner, J. A. 1971. *Tomorrow's Tomorrow: The Black Woman*. New York: Doubleday.

LaFave, W. 1969. "Arrest: The Decision to Take a Suspect into Custody." In L. M. Friedman and S. Macaulay (eds.), *Law and the Behavioral Sciences*. Indianapolis: Bobbs-Merrill.

LaFromboise, T. D., and B. Howard-Pitney. 1995. "Suicidal Behavior in American Indian Female Adolescents." In S. Canetto and D. Lester (eds.), *Woman and Suicidal Behavior*. New York: Springer.

Lagerspetz, K. M. J., and K. Bjorkqvist. (1994). Indirect Aggression in Boys and Girls. In L. R. Huesmann (ed.), *Aggressive behavior: Current perspectives* (pp. 131–150). New York: Plenum Press.

Laidler, K. A., and G. Hunt. 1997. "Violence and Social Organization in Female Gangs." *Social Justice* 24: 148–169.

Lanier, M. M., and S. Henry. 1998. *Essential Criminology*. Boulder, CO: Westview Press.

Lappe, F. M., J. Collins, and C. Fowler. 1977. *Food First: Beyond the Myth of Scarcity*. Boston: Houghton Mifflin.

Laub, J., and M. J. McDermott. 1985. "An Analysis of Serious Crime by Young Black Women." *Criminology* 23: 81–98.

Lauderback, D., J. Hansen, and D. Waldorf. 1992. "'Sisters Are Doin' It for Themselves': A Black Female Gang in San Francisco." *The Gang Journal* 1: 57–72.

Leadbeater, B. J., and N. Way. 1996. *Urban Girls: Resisting Stereotypes, Creating Identities*. New York: New York University Press.

Lebra, J. 1991. *Women's Voices in Hawaii*. Niwot, CO: University Press of Colorado.

Lee, F. R. 1991. "For Gold Earrings and Protection, More Girls Take the Road to Violence." *New York Times*, Nov. 25: A1.

Lemert, E. 1951. *Social Pathology*. New York: McGraw-Hill.

————. 1967. *Human Deviance, Social Problems and Social Control*. Englewood Cliffs, NJ: Prentice-Hall.

Lenze, I. 1979. "Tourism Prostitution in Asia." *ISIS International Bulletin* 13: 4–21.

Lerner, G. 1986. *The Creation of Patriarchy*. New York: Oxford University Press.

Lerner, P. M., J. B. Orlos, and J. R. Knapp. 1976. "Physical Attractiveness, Physical Effectiveness and Self-Concept in Late Adolescents." *Adolescence* 11: 314–326.

Leslie, C., et al. 1993. "Girls Will Be Girls." *Newsweek*, Aug. 2: 44.

Lewis, N. 1992. "Delinquent Girls Achieving a Violent Equality in D.C." *Washington Post*, Dec. 23: A1, A14.

Lillian Robbins v. County of Glenn, California, et al. 1985. *Amended Civil Rights Complaint for Damages*. Filed in the U.S. District Court for the Eastern District of California. No. CIVS-85–0675 RAR.

Linnekin, J. 1990. *Sacred Queens and Women of Consequence*. Ann Arbor: University of Michigan Press

Lipsey, M. 1992. "Juvenile Delinquency Treatment: A Meta-analytic Inquiry in the Variability of Effects." In T. A. Cook et al. (eds.), *Meta-Analysis for Explanation: A Casebook*. New York: Russell Sage.

Lipsey, M. W. 1990. *Juvenile Delinquency Treatment: A Meta-analytic Inquiry into the Variability of Effects*. New York: Russell Sage Foundation (Research Synthesis Committee).

Little, A. 1965. "The 'Prevalence' of Recorded Delinquency and Recidivism in England and Wales." *American Sociological Review* 30: 260–263.

Lo, L. 1994. "Exploring Teenage Shoplifting Behavior: A Choice and Constraint Approach." *Environment and Behavior* 26: 613–639.

Loeb, R. C., and L. Horst. 1978. "Sex Differences in Self- and Teachers' Reports of Self-Esteem in Preadolescents." *Sex Roles* 4: 779–788.

Lombroso, C., and W. Ferrero. 1895. *The Female Offender*. New York: Philosophical Library.

Loper, A. B., and D. G. Cornell. 1995. "Homicide by Girls." Paper presented at the annual meeting of the National Girls Caucus, Orlando, Florida.

Lorber, J. 1994. *Paradoxes of Gender*. New Haven: Yale University Press.

Los Angeles Times, 2003. "L.A.'s Parent of Last Resort: Forging Strong Adults from Hard-Knock Kids." December 24 (editorial pages).

Lott, B. 1987. *Women's Lives: Themes and Variations in Gender Learning*. Pacific Grove, CA: Brooks/Cole.

Loy, P., and S. Norland. 1981. "Gender Convergence and Delinquency." *Sociological Quarterly* 22: 275–283.

Lundman, R. 2001. *Prevention and Control of Juvenile Delinquency*, 3rd ed. New York: Oxford University Press.

Macallair, D. 1990. "ACLU's Demands Trigger Change in Hawaii's Juvenile System." *National Prison Project Journal* (Spring): 5–6.

———. 1994 "Disposition Case Advocacy in San Francisco's Juvenile Justice System: A New Approach to Deinstitutionalization." *Crime and Delinquency* 40: 84–95.

———, and M. Males 2000. *An Analysis of San Francisco Juvenile Justice Reforms During the Brown Administration*. San Francisco: Center on Juvenile and Criminal Justice.

Maccoby, E. 1966. *The Development of Sex Differences*. Palo Alto, CA: Stanford University Press.

Macfarlane, J. W. 1971. "The Berkeley Studies: Problems and Merits of the Longitudinal Approach." In M. C. Jones et al. (eds.), *The Course of Human Development*. Waltham, MA: Xerox College Publishers.

Macleod, C. 1974. "Street Girls of the 70s." *The Nation*, April 20.

Magee, A., and P. Sherwell. 1996. "For Girls, Few Choices—All Bad: Seamstress, Servant, or Prostitute?" *World Press Review* 43: 12–14.

Maguire, K., and A. L. Pastore (eds.). 1994. *Sourcebook on Criminal Justice Statistics, 1993*. Washington, DC: U.S. Department of Justice, Bureau of Justice Statistics.

Mahoney, A. R., and C. Fenster. 1982. "Female Delinquents in a Suburban Court." In N. Rafter and E. Stanko (eds.), *Judge, Lawyer, Victim, Thief*. Boston: Northeastern University Press.

Males, M. 1994. "Bashing Youth: Media Myths About Teenagers." *Extra* March/April: 8–11.

———. 1996. "Wild in Deceit: Why Teen Violence Is Poverty Violence in Disguise." *Extra* 9: 7–9.

———. 1999. *Framing Youth: Ten Myths About the Next Generation*. Monroe, ME: Common Courage Press.

———, and A. Shorter. 2001. "To Cage and Serve." Unpublished Manuscript.

Mann, C. 1979. "The Differential Treatment Between Runaway Boys and Girls in Juvenile Court." *Juvenile and Family Court Journal* 30: 37–48.

———. 1984. *Female Crime and Delinquency*. University, AL: University of Alabama Press.

Marable, M. 2000. "We Need New and Critical Study of Race and Ethnicity." *The Chronicle of Higher Education*, February 25, B4–B7.

Marini, M. M. 1978. "Sex Differences in the Determination of Adolescent Aspirations: A Review of Research." *Sex Roles* 4: 723–753.

Marinucci, C., S. Winokur, and G. Lewis. 1994. "Ruthless Girlz." *San Francisco Examiner*, Dec. 12: A1.

Martinez, R., and R. L. Dukes. 1991. "Ethnic and Gender Differences in Self-Esteem." *Youth and Society*, 22: 318–338.

Marx, K. 1963. *The 18th Brumaire of Louis Bonaparte*. New York: International Publishers.

Maslow, A. H. 1951. *Motivation and Personality*. New York: Harper & Row.

Masson, J. M. 1984. *The Assault on Truth*. New York: Penguin.

Mauer, M., and T. Huling. 1995. *Young Black Americans and the Criminal Justice System: Five Years Later*. Washington, DC: The Sentencing Project.

Mayer, J. 1994. "Girls in the Maryland Juvenile Justice System: Findings of the Female Population Taskforce." Presentation to the Gender Specifics Services Training. Minneapolis, MN.

Mawby, B. 1980. "Sex and Crime: The Results of a Self-Report Study." *British Journal of Sociology* 31: 526–543.

May, D. 1977. "Delinquent Girls Before the Courts." *Medical Science Law Review* 17: 203–210.

———. 1978. "Juvenile Shoplifters and the Organization of Store Security: A Case Study in the Social Construction of Delinquency." *International Journal of Criminology and Penology* 6: 137–160.

May, T., M. Hough, and M. Edwards. 2000. "Sex Markets and Drug Markets: Examining the Links." *Crime Prevention and Community Safety* 2: 25–41.

Mayeda, D. T., M. Chesney-Lind, J. Koo. 2001. "Talking Story with Hawaii's Youth: Confronting Violent and Sexualized Perceptions of Ethnicity and Gender." *Youth and Society* 33: 99–128.

McArthur, L. 1996. "Nepal Women Caught in Trafficking Rings." *Off Our Backs* 26: 7–8.

McCarthy, B. 1985. "An Analysis of Detention." *Juvenile and Family Court Journal* 36: 49–50.

———. 1987. "Preventive Detention and Pretrial Custody in the Juvenile Court." *Journal of Criminal Justice* 15: 185–200.

McCord, J., W. McCord, and E. Thurber. 1968. "The Effect of Foster Home Placement in the Prevention of Adult Anti-social Behavior." In J. R. Stratton and R. Terry (eds.), *Prevention of Delinquency*. New York: Macmillan.

McCormack, A., M. Janus, and A. Burgess. 1986. "Runaway Youths and Sexual Victimization: Gender Differences in an Adolescent Runaway Population." *Child Abuse and Neglect* 10: 387–395.

McDermott, M. J., and S. J. Blackstone. 1994. "White Slavery Plays of the 1910's: Fear of Victimization and the Social Control of Sexuality." Paper presented at the annual meeting of the American Society of Criminology, Miami.

McEachern, A. W., and R. Bauzer. 1967. "Factors Related to Disposition in Juvenile Police Contacts." In M. W. Klein (ed.), *Juvenile Gangs in Context*. Englewood Cliffs, NJ: Prentice-Hall.

McGarrell, E., and T. J. Flanagan. 1985. *Sourcebook on Criminal Justice Statistics, 1984*. Washington, DC: U.S. Department of Justice.

McKinley, N. 1998. "Gender Differences in Undergraduates' Body Esteem: The Mediating Effect of Objectified Body Consciousness and Actual/Ideal Weight Discrepancy." *Sex Roles*, 39 : 113–123.

McNaught, S. 1999. "Gangsta Girls." *The Boston Phoenix*. May 20–27.

McRobbie, A., and J. Garber. 1975. "Girls and Subcultures." In S. Hall and T. Jefferson (eds.), *Resistance Through Rituals: Youth Subculture in Post-War Britain*. New York: Holmes and Meier.

Media Monitor. 1994. "Crime Down, Media Coverage Up." 3: January/February.

Meichenbaum, D. H., K. S. Bowers, and R. R. Ross. 1969. "A Behavioral Analysis of Teacher Expectancy Effect." *Journal of Personality and Social Psychology* 3: 306–316.

Meier, E. 2000. "Legislative Efforts to Combat Sexual Trafficking and Slavery of Women and Children." *Pediatric Nursing*, May.

Meiselman, K. 1978. *Incest*. San Francisco: Jossey-Bass.

Mendelson, B.K., White, D.R., and Mendelson, M.J. 1996. "Self-esteem and body esteem: effects of gender, age, and weight." *Journal of Applied Developmental Psychology*, 17, 321–346.

Mendez, D. 1996. "More and More Girls Joining Violent Male Gangs." *The Seattle Times*. Oct. 27: A7.

Mennel, R. 1973. *Thorns and Thistles: Juvenile Delinquents in the U.S., 1820–1940*. Hanover, NH: University Press of New England.

Merton, R. K. 1938. "Social Structure and Anomie." *American Sociological Review* 3: 672–682.

Messerschmidt, J. 1986. *Capitalism, Patriarchy and Crime*. Totowa, NJ: Rowman and Littlefield.

———. 1987. "Feminism, Criminology, and the Rise of the Female Sex 'Delinquent', 1880–1930." *Contemporary Crises* 11: 243–262.

———. 1996. *Masculinities and Crime*. Lanham, MD: Rowman and Littlefield.

Meyer, H. J., E. F. Borgatta, and W. C. Jones. 1965. *Girls at Vocational High: An Experiment in Social Work Intervention*. New York: Sage.

Miller, E. 1983. "A Cross-Cultural Look at Women and Crime: An Essay Review." *Contemporary Crises* 7: 59–70.

———. 1986. *Street Woman*. Philadelphia: Temple University Press.

Miller, E., and G. S. Graczkowski. 1985. "Gender, Sex and Money: A Comparative Analysis of Female Heterosexual and Male Homosexual Prostitution." Paper presented at the annual meeting of the American Society of Criminology, San Diego.

Miller, G. 1988. "Overcrowded Youth Correctional Facilities Top State Agendas." Testimony presented to the House of Representatives (Mar. 17). Congressional Record 134(33).

Miller, J. 1994. "Race, Gender and Juvenile Justice: An Examination of Disposition Decision-Making for Delinquent Girls." In M. D. Schwartz and D. Milovanovic (eds.), *The Intersection of Race, Gender and Class in Criminology*. New York: Garland Press.

———. 1998a. *Last One Over the Wall: The Massachusetts Experiment in Closing Reform Schools*

(2nd ed.). Columbus, OH: Ohio State University Press.

———. 1998b. "Up it Up: Gender and the Accomplishment of Street Robbery." *Criminology* 36: 37–65.

———. 2001. *One of the Guys: Girls, Gangs, and Gender*. New York: Oxford University Press.

Miller, P.B. 1998. "The Anatomy of Scientific Racism: Racialist Responses to Black Athletic Achievement." *Journal of Sport History*, 25: 119–151.

Miller, W. B. 1958. "Lower Class Culture as a Generating Milieu of Gang Delinquency." *Journal of Social Issues* 14: 5–19.

———. 1975. *Violence by Youth Gangs and Youth Groups as a Crime Problem in Major American Cities*. Washington, DC: U.S. Department of Justice.

———. 1980. "The Molls." In S. K. Datesman and F. R. Scarpitti (eds.), *Women, Crime, and Justice*. New York: Oxford University Press.

"Minority Views: The Act's Core Mandates Should Be Maintained." 1996. Appended to the Juvenile Justice and Delinquency Prevention Act Reauthorization (H.R. 3876), House Economic and Educational Opportunities Committee, September 16, 1996.

Minow, M. 1987. "The Public Duties of Families and Children." In F. X. Hartmann (ed.), *From Children to Citizens, Vol. 2: The Role of the Juvenile Court*. New York: Springer-Verlag.

Missouri Department of Social Services. 2001. *Missouri Juvenile Court Annual Report, Calendar Year 2000*. Jefferson City, MO: Missouri Department of Social Services.

Monahan, T. P. 1970. "Police Dispositions of Juvenile Offenders." Phylon 31: 91–107.

Money, J., J. L. Hampson, and J. G. Mapson. 1957. "Imprinting and the Establishment of Gender Role." *AMA Archives of Neurology and Psychology* 77: 333–336.

Moone, J. 1993a. *Children in Custody: Public Facilities*. Washington, DC: Office of Juvenile Justice and Delinquency Prevention.

———. 1993b. *Children in Custody: Private Facilities*. Washington, DC: Office of Juvenile Justice and Delinquency Prevention.

Moore, J.W. 1978. *Homeboys: Gangs, Drugs, and Prisons in the Barrio of Los Angeles*. Philadelphia: Temple University Press.

———. 1991. *Going Down to the Barrio: Homeboys and Homegirls in Change*. Philadelphia: Temple University Press.

———. 1993. "Gangs, Drugs, and Violence." In S. Cummings and D. Monti (eds.), *Gangs: The Origins and Impact of Contemporary Youth Gangs in the United States*. Albany: SUNY Press.

Moore, J. W., D. Vigil, and J. Levy. 1995. "Huisas of the Street: Chicana Gang Members." *Latino Studies Journal* 6: 27–48.

Moore, J. W., and J. Hagedorn. 1996. "What Happens to the Girls in the Gang?" In C. R. Huff (ed.), *Gangs in America*, 2d ed. Thousand Oaks, CA: Sage.

Morash, M. 1986. "Gender, Peer Group Experiences, and Seriousness of Delinquency." *Journal of Research on Crime and Delinquency* 23: 43–67.

Morash, M., and M. Chesney-Lind. 1991. "A Re-Formulation and Partial Test of the Power Control Theory of Delinquency." *Justice Quarterly* 8: 347–377.

Morash, M., and T. Bynum. 1996. *Findings from the National Study of Innovative and Promising Programs for Women Offenders*. East Lansing: School of Criminal Justice, Michigan State University.

Morris, A. 1987. *Women, Crime and Criminal Justice*. New York: Basil Blackwell.

Morris, R. 1963. Comparison of Female and Male Delinquency. Ph.D. dissertation, University of Michigan.

———. 1964. "Female Delinquency and Relational Problems." *Social Forces* 43: 82–89.

———. 1965. "Attitudes Toward Delinquency by Delinquents, Nondelinquents and Their Friends." *British Journal of Criminology* 5: 249–265.

Moselina, L. 1981. "Olongopo's R and R Industry: A Sociological Analysis of Institutionalized Prostitution." *Ang Makatao: Official Publication of the Asian Social Institute* (January-June): 5–34.

Mouzakitas, C. M. 1981. "An Inquiry into the Problem of Child Abuse and Juvenile Delinquency." In R. J. Hunner and Y. E. Walkers (eds.), *Exploring the Relationship Between Child Abuse and Delinquency*. Montclair, NJ: Allanheld, Osmun.

Ms. Foundation for Women, National Girls Initiative. (1993). *Programmed Neglect, Not Seen, Not Heard: Report on Girls Programming in the United States*. New York: Ms. Foundation for Women

Mulligan, D. G., J. W. Douglas, W. A. Hammond, and J. Tizard. 1963. "Delinquency and Symptoms of Maladjustment." *Proceedings of the Royal Society of Medicine* 56: 1083–1086.

Mushlin, M. B., L. Levitt, and L. Anderson. 1986. "Court Ordered Foster Care Reform: A Case Study." *Child Welfare* 65.

Naffine, N. 1987. *Female Crime: The Construction of Women in Criminology*. Sydney, Australia: Allen and Unwin.

———. 1989. "Toward Justice for Girls." *Women and Criminal Justice* 1: 3–19.

Nagel, J. 1994. "Constructing ethnicity: Creating and recreating ethnic identity and culture." *Social Problems* 41: 152–176.

National Advisory Committee for Juvenile Justice and Delinquency Prevention. 1984. *Serious Juvenile Crime: A Redirected Effort*. Washington, DC: U.S. Department of Justice.

National Clearinghouse on Child Abuse and Neglect Information. 2001. *Foster Care National Statistics*. Washington, DC: U. S Department of Health and Human Services, on-line (www.calib.com/nccanch/pubs/factsheets/foster.cfm).

———. 2002. *National Child Abuse and Neglect Data System Summary of Key Findings From Calendar Year 2000.*. Washington, DC: U. S Department of Health and Human Services, on-line (www.calib.com/nccanch/pubs/factsheets/canstats.cfm).

National Council on Crime and Delinquency. 1993. *The Juveniles Taken into Custody Research Program: Estimating the Prevalence of Juvenile Custody by Race and Gender, 1993*. San Francisco: National Council on Crime and Delinquency.

National Institute of Justice. 1985. *Prosecution of Child Sexual Abuse: Innovations in Practice*. Washington, DC: U.S. Department of Justice.

National Institute of Mental Health. 1977. *Study of Females in Detention*. King County, Washington.

NBC. 1993. "Diana Koricke in East Los Angeles." World News Tonight, March 29.

Nettler, G. 1984. *Explaining Crime*, 3d ed. New York: McGraw-Hill.

Nguyen, N. T. nd. "Prostitution in Japan: A Young Body Worth a Profit." On-line (www.public.iastate.edu/~rhetoric/105H17/nnguyen/cof.html).

Norland, S., N. Shover, W. E. Thornton, and J. James. 1979. "Intrafamily Conflict and Delinquency." *Pacific Sociological Review* 22: 223–237.

Norland, S., R. C. Wessel, and N. Shover. 1981. "Masculinity and Delinquency." *Criminology* 19: 421–433.

Nye, F. I. 1958. *Family Relationships and Delinquent Behavior*. New York: Wiley.

Nye, F. I., and C. Edelbrock. 1980. "Some Social Characteristics of Runaways." *Journal of Family Issues* 1: 147–150.

Odem, M. E. 1995. *Delinquent Daughters: Protecting and Policing Adolescent Female Sexuality in the United States, 1885–1920*. Chapel Hill: University of North Carolina Press.

Odem, M. E., and S. Schlossman. 1991. "Guardians of Virtue: The Juvenile Court and Female Delinquency in Early 20th Century Los Angeles." *Crime and Delinquency* 37: 186–203.

O'Donnell, C. R., and W. S. O. Fo. 1976. "The Buddy System: Mediator—Target Locus of Control and Behavioral Outcome." *American Journal of Community Psychology* 4: 161–166.

O'Donnell, C., T. Lydgate, and W. S. O. Fo. 1979. "The Buddy System: Review and Follow-up." Child Behavior Therapy 1 (Summer): 161–169.

Office of Juvenile Justice and Delinquency Prevention (OJJDP). 1985. *Runaway Children and the Juvenile Justice and Delinquency Prevention Act: What Is the Impact?* Washington, DC: U.S. Government Printing Office.

———. 1986. *America's Missing and Exploited Children*. Washington, DC: U.S. Government Printing Office.

———. 1992. *Arrests of Youth 1990*. Washington, DC: U.S. Government Printing Office.

———. 1994. *What Works: Promising Interventions in Juvenile Justice*. Washington, DC: U.S. Government Printing Office.

Ogbu, J.U. 1991. "Low School Performance as an Adaptation: The Case of Blacks in Stockton, California." In M.A. Gibson and J.U. Ogbu (eds.), *Minority status and schooling: A comparative study of immigrant and involuntary minorities*. New York: Garland Publishing.

Okamura, J. 1982. "Ethnicity and Ethnic Relations in Hawaii." In A. Cohen (ed.), *Urban Ethnicity*. Singapore: Maruzen Asia.

Olson, L., E. Liebow, F. Mannino, and M. Shore. 1980. "Runaway Children Twelve Years

Later: A Follow Up." *Journal of Family Issues* 1: 165–188.

Opinion Research Center. 1982. *Public Attitudes Toward Youth Crime: National Public Opinion Pool*. Minneapolis: Hubert Humphrey Institute of Public Affairs.

Orenstein, P. 1994. *Schoolgirls*. New York: Doubleday.

O'Reilly, A. 1993. "Child Prostitution: The Next Push for Human Rights." *Human Rights* 20: 30–31.

Ostner, I. 1986. "Die Entdeckung der Madchen: Neue Perspecktiven fur die." Kolner-Zeitschrift-fur *Soziologie und Sozialpsychologie* 38: 352–371.

Otten, L. A. 1985. *A Comparison of Male and Female Delinquency in a Birth Cohort*. Ph.D. diss., University of Pennsylvania.

Ouston, J. 1984. "Delinquency, Family Background, and Educational Attainment." *British Journal of Criminology* 24: 2–26.

Owen, B., and B. Bloom. 1995. "Profiling Women Prisoners." *The Prison Journal* 75: 165–185.

Owens, L. 1996. "Sticks and Stones and Sugar and Spice: Girls' and Boys' Aggression in Schools." *Australian Journal of Guidance and Counseling* 6: 45–55.

Owens, L. 1997. "Teenage Girls: Voices of Aggression." Paper presented at the 20th International School Psychology Colloquium, Melbourne, Australia, July 15–19, 1997.

Pagelow, M. D., and L. W. Pagelow. 1984. *Family Violence*. New York: Praeger.

Parham v. J.R. 1979. 442 U.S. 584.

Peacock, C. 1981. *Hand Me Down Dreams*. New York: Schocken.

Perrone, P., and M. Chesney-Lind. 1997 "Media Representations of Gangs and Delinquency: Wild in the Streets?" *Social Justice*, 2 (4), 96–117.

Perschler-Desai, V. 2001. "Childhood on the Market: Teenage Prostitution in Southern Africa." *African Security Review* 10, on-line (www.iss.co.za.Pubs/ASR/10/No4/Perschler.html).

Peterson, K. 1998. "Students Feel Safer in Hawaii." *The Honolulu Advertiser*, A1, 7, October 14.

Phelps, R. J., M. McIntosh, V. Jesudason, P. Warner, and J. Pohlkamp. 1982. *Wisconsin*

Juvenile Female Offender Project. Madison: Youth Policy and Law Center, Wisconsin Council on Juvenile Justice.

Pipher, M. B. 1994. *Reviving Ophelia: Saving the Selves of Adolescent Girls.* New York: Putnam.

Pisciotta, A. W. 1982. "Saving the Children: The Promise and Practice of Parens Patriae, 1838–98." *Crime and Delinquency* 28: 410–425.

———. 1983. "Race, Sex, and Rehabilitation: A Study of Differential Treatment in the Juvenile Reformatory, 1825–1900." *Crime and Delinquency* 29: 254–268.

Platt, A. M. 1969. *The Child Savers.* Chicago: University of Chicago Press.

Pleck, J. 1981. *The Myth of Masculinity.* Cambridge: MIT Press.

Poe-Yamagata, E., and J. A. Butts. 1995. *Female offenders in the juvenile justice system.* Pittsburgh: National Center for Juvenile Justice.

Pogrebin, L. C. 1981. *Growing Up Free.* New York: Bantam Books.

Pogebrin, M. R., E. D. Poole, and R. M. Regoli. 1984. "Constructing and Implementing a Model Juvenile Diversion Program." *Youth and Society* 15: 305–324

Polk, K. 1995. "Juvenile Diversion: A Look at the Record." In P. M. Sharp and B. W. Hancock (eds.), *Juvenile Delinquency.* Englewood Cliffs, NJ: Prentice-Hall.

Pollak, O. 1950. *The Criminality of Women.* New York: Barnes.

Pollak, O., and A. S. Freidman (eds.). 1969. *Family Dynamics and Female Delinquency.* Palo Alto, CA: Science and Behavior Books.

Pope, C., and W. Feyerherm. 1982. "Gender Bias in Juvenile Court Dispositions." *Social Service Research* 6: 1–16.

Portillos, L., and M. Zatz. 1995. "Not to Die For: Positive and Negative Aspects of Chicano Youth Gangs." Paper presented at the American Society of Criminology meeting, Boston, November.

Powers, J. L., J. Eckenrode, and B. Jaklitsch. 1990. "Maltreatment Among Runaway and Homeless Youth." *Child Abuse and Neglect* 14: 87–98.

Prescott, P. 1981. *The Child Savers.* New York: Knopf.

President's Commission on Law and Administration of Justice. 1967. *The Challenge of Crime in a Free Society.* Washington, DC: U.S. Government Printing Office.

Presser, H. 1980. "Sally's Corner: Coping with Unmarried Motherhood." *Journal of Social Issues* 36: 107–129.

Pressly, C. 1984. "Police Are Now Picking Up Under-Age Visitors." *Honolulu Star Bulletin,* June 16.

Price, J.N. 1999. "Schooling and Racialized Masculinities: The Diploma, Teachers, and Peers in the Lives of Young, African American Men." *Youth & Society,* 31: 224–263.

Project on Equal Education Rights (PEER). *Computer Equity Report. 1984. Sex Bias at the Computer Terminal-How Schools Program Girls.* Washington, DC.

Propper, A. 1978. "Lesbianism in Female and Coed Correctional Institutions." *Journal of Homosexuality* 3: 265–274.

Province of British Columbia. 1978. *Youth Services in Juvenile Justice.* Victoria: Information Services, Corrections Branch.

Quicker, J. C. 1974. "The Chicana Gang: A Preliminary Description." Paper presented at the annual meeting of the Pacific Sociological Association, San Jose.

———. 1983. *Homegirls: Characterizing Chicano Gangs.* San Pedro, CA: International University Press.

Quigley, W. P. 1998. "Backwards into the Future: How Welfare Changes in the Millennium Resemble English Poor Law of the Middle Ages." *Stanford Law and Policy Review* 9: 101–114.

Quinney, R. 1970. *The Social Reality of Crime.* Boston: Little, Brown.

———. 1977. *Class, State and Crime.* New York: Longman.

Quinney, R., and J. Wildeman. 1991. *The Problem of Crime,* 3d ed. New York: Longman.

Rabban, M. L. 1950. "Sex Role Identification in Young Children in Two Diverse Social Groups." *Genetic Psychological Monographs* 42: 81–158.

Rafter, N. H. 1990. *Partial Justice: Women in State Prisons, 1800–1935,* 2d ed. New Brunswick, NJ: Transaction Books.

Rankin, J. H. 1980. "School Factors and Delinquency: Interaction by Age and Sex." *Sociology and Social Research* 64: 420–434.

Rausch, S. 1983. "Court Processing Versus Diversion of Status Offenders: A Test of Deterrence and Labeling Theories." *Journal of Research in Crime and Delinquency* 20: 39–54.

Ray, D. 2002. Official letter sent to Claudia MacMullin, American Bar Association, March 20.

Reckless, W. C. 1961. *The Crime Problem*, 3d ed. New York: Appleton-Century-Crofts.

Redfering, D. L. 1973. "Durability of Effects of Group Counseling with Institutionalized Delinquent Females." *Journal of Abnormal Psychology* 82: 85–86.

Reich, J. W., and S. E. Guitierres. 1979. "Escape/Aggression Incidence in Sexually Abused Juvenile Delinquents." *Criminal Justice and Behavior* 6: 239–243.

Reid, T. 2001. "Teen Prostitution in My City?" On-line (www.youthcommunication-vox.org).

Reiner, I. 1992. *Gangs, Crime and Violence in Los Angeles: Findings and Proposals from the District Attorney's Office.* Arlington, VA: National Youth Gang Information Center.

Reiss, A. 1951. "Delinquency as the Failure of Personal and Social Controls." *American Sociological Review* 16: 196–207

Reiss, A. J. 1986. "Why Are Communities Important in Understanding Crime?" In A. J. Reiss and M. Tonry (eds.), *Communities in Crime.* Chicago: University of Chicago Press.

Reitsma-Street, M. 1999. "Canadian Youth Court Charges and Dispositions for Females Before and After Implementation of the Young Offenders Act." *Canadian Journal of Criminology* (October): 437–458.

Rendleman, D. R. 1979. "Parens Patriae: From Chancery to the Juvenile Court." In F. L. Faust and P. J. Brantingham (eds.), *Juvenile Justice Philosophy*, 2d ed. St. Paul, MN: West.

Reyes, O., and L. A. Jason. 1993. "Pilot Study Examining Factors Associated with Academic Success for Hispanic High School Students." *Journal of Youth and Adolescence*, 22: 57–71.

Rhode v. Rowland, J., et al. 1986. Civil Action No. CV-85–8130 AWT (BX). Second Amended Civil Rights Complaint for Damages. Filed in the U.S. District Court, Central District of Calif.

Rhodes, J. E., and K. Fischer. 1993. "Spanning the Gender Gap: Gender Differences in Delinquency Among Inner-City Adolescents." *Adolescence* 28: 879–889.

Ribach, L. 1971. "Juvenile Delinquency Laws: Juvenile Women and the Double Standard." *UCLA Law Review* 19: 313–342.

Rice, R. 1963. "A Reporter at Large: The Persian Queens." *New Yorker*, Oct. 19.

Rich, A. 1976. *Of Women Born: Motherhood as Experience and Institution.* New York: Norton.

Richards, P., and C. R. Tittle. 1981. "Gender and Perceived Chances of Arrest." *Social Forces* 51: 1182–1199.

Rierdan, J., and E. Koff. 1997. "Weight, Weight-Related Aspects of Body Image, and Depression in Early Adolescent Girls." *Adolescence* 32: 615–624.

Rimbach, J. 1994. "Bad Prison: Tools at Skillman: Medication, Isolation." *Delinquent Justice: A Special Reprint.* New Jersey: The Record: 21–40.

Rita Horn et al. v. Oldham County, Kentucky, et al. 1983. Motion for Class Certification. Filed in the U.S. District Court for the Western District of Kentucky, Civil Action No. C-83–0208–LB.

Roberts, A. R. 1987. *Runaways and Non-Runaways.* Chicago: Dorsey Press.

Roberts, S. 1972. "Crime Rate of Women up Sharply Over Men's." *New York Times*, June 13: 72.

Robinson, L. S. 1996. "Touring Thailand's Sex Industry." *The Nation* 257: 492–497.

Robinson, R. 1990. *Violations of Girlhood: A Qualitative Study of Female Delinquents and Children in Need of Services in Massachusetts.* Ph.D. Diss., Brandeis University.

Roche, S., and D. Richart. 1981. *A Comparative Study of Young Women and Men in Kentucky Jails.* Louisville: Kentucky Youth Advocates.

Rogers, K. 1972. " 'For Her Own Protection': Conditions of Incarceration for Female Juvenile Offenders in the State of Connecticut." *Law and Society Review* (Winter): 223–246.

Romig, D. 1978. *Justice for Our Children: An Examination of Juvenile Delinquent Rehabilitation Programs.* Lexington, MA: Lexington Books.

Rosenbaum, J. 1989. "Family Dysfunction and Female Delinquency." *Crime and Delinquency* 35: 31–44.

Rosenberg, M. 1965. *Society and the Adolescent Self-Image.* Princeton, NJ: Princeton University Press.

Rosenblum, K. 1980. "Female Deviance and the Female Sex Role: A Preliminary Investigation." In S. Datesman and F. Scarpitti (eds.), *Women, Crime and Justice.* New York: Oxford University Press.

Rossi, A. 1973. *The Feminist Papers: From Adams to Beauvoir*. New York: Columbia University Press.

Rotherman-Borus, M. J. 1993. "Suicidal Behavior and Risk Factors Among Runaway Youths." *American Journal of Psychiatry* 150: 103–107.

Rothman, D. 1971. *The Discovery of the Asylum*. Boston: Little, Brown.

Rothman, R. A. 1999. *Inequality and Stratification: Race, Class, and Gender*. 3d ed. Upper Saddle River, NJ: Prentice- Hall.

Rothman, S. M. 1978. *Woman's Proper Place: A History of Changing Ideals and Practices, 1870 to the Present*. New York: Basic Books.

Rubin, L. 1976. *Worlds of Pain: Life in the Working Class Family*. New York: Basic Books.

Rush, F. 1980. *The Best Kept Secret: Sexual Abuse of Children*. New York: McGraw-Hill.

Russell, A., and L. Owens. 1999. "Peer Estimates of School-Aged Boys' and Girls' Aggression to Same- and Cross-Sex Targets." *Social Development* 8: 364–379.

Russell, A., and C. Trainor. 1984. *Trends in Child Abuse and Neglect: A National Perspective*. Denver: American Humane Association.

Russell, D. E. 1984. *Sexual Exploitation: Rape, Sexual Abuse and Workplace Harassment*. Newbury Park, CA: Sage.

———. 1986. *The Secret Trauma: Incest in the Lives of Girls and Women*. New York: Basic Books.

Ryan, T. 1988. "Manila's Street Children Lead a Tragic Life." *Honolulu Star Bulletin*, Sept. 26: A3.

Sachs, A. 1994. "The Last Commodity: Child Prostitution in the Developing World." *World Watch* 7: 24–31.

Sadker, M. and D. Sadker. 1994. *Failing at Fairness*. New York: Charles Scribner's & Sons.

Salmelainen, P. 1995. "The Correlates of Offending Frequency: A Study of Juvenile Theft Offenders in Detention." *Criminal Justice Abstracts* (www://webspirs3.silverplatter.com/cgi-bin/customers/c74431/c74431.cgi.)

Sampson, R. 1985. "Sex Differences in Self-Reported Delinquency and Official Records: A Multiple Group Structural Modeling Approach." *Journal of Quantitative Criminology* 1: 345–368.

Sampson, R., and J. Laub. 1993. "Structural Variations in Juvenile Court Processing: Inequality, the Underclass, and Social Control." *Law and Society Review* 27: 285–311.

Sandberg, D. N. 1985. "The Abuse-Delinquency Connection and Juvenile Court Responsibility." *Justice for Children* 1: 10–11.

Sandhu, H. S., and D. E. Allen. 1969. "Female Delinquency: Goal Obstruction and Anomie." *Canadian Review of Sociology and Anthropology* 5: 107–110.

Santiago, D. 1992. "Random Victims of Vengeance Show Teen Crime." *The Philadelphia Inquirer*, Feb. 23: A1.

Sarasalo, E., B. Bergman, and J. Toth. 1998. "Repetitive Shoplifting in Stockholm, Sweden: a Register Study of 1802 Cases." *Criminal Behavior and Mental Health* 8: 256–265.

Sarri, R. 1978. "Juvenile Law: How It Penalizes Females." In L. Crites (ed.), *The Female Offender*. Lexington, MA: Lexington Books.

Satchell, M. 1982. "When Strip-Search Is Shameful." *Parade*, June 13: 8–12.

———. 2000. "Fighting the Child Sex Trade." *U. S. News and World Report*. May 8.

Schaffner, L., S. Shick, and A. D. Shorter. 1996. *Out of Sight, Out of Mind: The Plight of Adolescent Girls in the San Francisco Juvenile Justice Center*. San Francisco: Center on Juvenile and Criminal Justice.

Schiraldi, V., and M. Soler. 1998. *The Will of the People? The Public's Opinion of the Violent and Repeat Juvenile Offenders Act of 1997*. Washington, DC: Justice Policy Institute.

Schlossman, S. 1977. *Love and the American Delinquent: The Theory and Practice of "Progressive" Juvenile Justice*. Chicago: University of Chicago Press.

Schlossman, S., and S. Wallach. 1978. "The Crime of Precocious Sexuality: Female Delinquency in the Progressive Era." *Harvard Educational Review* 48: 65–94.

Schur, E. 1971. *Labeling Deviant Behavior*. New York: McGraw-Hill.

———. 1984. *Labeling Women Deviant*. New York: Random House.

Schwartz, I. M. 1980. *Juvenile Justice: Before and After the Onset of Delinquency*. Washington, DC: U.S. Department of Justice.

———. 1989. *(In)Justice for Juveniles: Rethinking the Best Interests of the Child*. Lexington, MA: Lexington Books.

———. n.d. "The Kids Nobody Wants." Paper distributed by the Philadelphia Program for Women and Girl Offenders.

Schwartz, I. M., G. Fishman, R. Hatfield, B. Krisberg, and Z. Eisikovits. 1986. *Juvenile*

Detention: The Hidden Closets Revisited. Minneapolis: Hubert Humphrey Institute of Public Affairs.

Schwartz, I. M., L. Harris, and L. Levi. 1987. *The Jailing of Juveniles in Minnesota.* Minneapolis: Hubert Humphrey Institute of Public Affairs.

Schwartz, I. M., M. Jackson-Beeck, and R. Anderson. 1984. "The 'Hidden' System of Juvenile Control." *Crime and Delinquency* 30: 371–385.

Schwartz, I. M., and F. Orlando (eds.). 1991. *Programming for Young Women in the Juvenile Justice System.* Ann Arbor, MI: Center for the Study of Youth Policy.

Schwartz, I. M., M. Steketee, and V. Schneider. 1990. "Federal Juvenile Justice Policy and the Incarceration of Girls." *Crime and Delinquency* 36: 503–520.

Schweinhart, L. 1987. "Can Preschool Programs Help Prevent Delinquency?" In J. Q. Wilson and G. C. Loury (eds.*), From Children to Citizens, Vol. 3, Families, Schools, and Delinquency Prevention.* New York: Springer-Verlag.

"Secure Custody Committee Report, Part II." 1981. Honolulu: Family Court, First Circuit. Mimeo.

Seligson, T. 1986. "Are They Too Young to Die?" *Parade,* Oct. 19: 4–7.

Selo, E. 1979. "The Cottage Dwellers: Boys and Girls in Training Schools." In L. Crites (ed.*), The Female Offender.* Lexington, MA: Lexington Books.

Senate Judiciary Committee (Majority Staff). 1990. "Ten Facts About Violence Against Young Women." Washington, DC: U.S. Student Association.

Sentencing Project. 2000. "Prosecuting Juveniles in Adult Court: An Assessment of Trends and Consequences." Washington, DC: The Sentencing Project, Briefing/Fact Sheets. On line (www.sentencingproject.org/brief/juveniles)

Seyfrit, C.L., L.C. Hamilton, C.M. Duncan, and J. Grimes. 1998. "Ethnic Identity and Aspirations Among Rural Alaska Youth." *Sociological Perspectives,* 41: 343–365.

Shannon, L.W. 1982. *Assessing the Relationship of Adult Criminal Careers to Juvenile Careers.* Washington, DC: U.S. Department of Justice.

Shauffer, C., and A. Shotten. 1987. "Legal Challenges to the Treatment of Young Women in the Juvenile Justice System." In Youth Law Center (ed.), *Working with Young Women.* San Francisco: Youth Law Center.

Shaw, C. 1930. *The Jackroller.* Chicago: University of Chicago Press.

———. 1938. *Brothers in Crime.* Chicago: University of Chicago Press.

Shaw, C., and H. McKay. 1931. *Social Factors in Juvenile Delinquency.* Chicago: University of Chicago Press.

———. 1942. *Juvenile Delinquency in Urban Areas.* Chicago: University of Chicago Press.

Shelden, R. G. 1976. *Rescued from Evil: Origins of Juvenile Justice in Memphis, Tennessee, 1900-1917.* Ph.D. diss., Southern Illinois University, Carbondale.

———. 1981. "Sex Discrimination in the Juvenile Justice System: Memphis, Tennessee, 1900–1917." In M. Q. Warren (ed.), *Comparing Male and Female Offenders.* Newbury Park, CA: Sage.

———. 1982. *Criminal Justice in America: A Sociological Approach.* Boston: Little, Brown.

———. 1987. "The Chronic Delinquent: Gender and Racial Differences." Paper presented at the annual meeting of the American Society of Criminology, Montreal.

———. 1999. *Detention Diversion Advocacy: an Evaluation.* Washington, DC: U. S. Department of Justice, Office of Juvenile Justice and Delinquency Prevention. Juvenile Justice Bulletin.

———. 2001. *Controlling the Dangerous Classes: A Critical Introduction to the History of Criminal Justice.* Boston: Allyn and Bacon.

———. 2002. "If You Build it, They Will Come." *Las Vegas Mercury* (November 28). Also, on-line (www.cjcj.org).

Shelden, R. G., and W. B. Brown. 1997. "The Crime Control Industry and the Management of the Surplus Population." Paper presented at the Western Society of Criminology annual meeting, Honolulu, Hawaii, February.

———. 2003. *Criminal Justice in America: A Critical Review.* Boston: Allyn and Bacon.

Shelden, R. G., and M. Chesney-Lind. 1991. "Gender and Race Differences in Delinquent Careers." *Juvenile and Family Court Journal* 44: 73–90.

Shelden, R. G., and J. Horvath. 1986. "Processing Offenders in a Juvenile Court: A Comparison of Male and Female Offenders." Paper presented at the annual meeting of the Western Society of Criminology, Newport Beach, California.

Shelden, R. G., J. Horvath, and S. Tracy. 1989. "Do Status Offenders Get Worse? Some Clarifications on the Question of Escalation." *Crime and Delinquency* 35: 202–216.

Shelden, R. G., T. Snodgrass, and P. Snodgrass. 1993. "Comparing Gang and Non-Gang Offenders: Some Tentative Findings." *The Gang Journal* 1: 73–85.

Shelden, R. G., S. Tracy, and W. Brown. 2004. *Youth Gangs in American Society*, 3rd ed. Belmont, CA: Wadsworth.

Sherman, F. 2002. "Promoting Justice in an Unjust System. Part Two." *Women, Girls, & Criminal Justice*. Vol 3, No. 5, August/September. pp. 65–80.

Sherman, F. 2000. "What's in a Name? Runaway Girls Pose Challenges for the Justice System." *Women, Girls and Criminal Justice*, 1: 19–20, 26.

Sherry, A., M. Lee, and M. Vatikiotis. 1995. "For Lust or Money." *Far Eastern Economic Review* 158: 22–24.

Shoemaker, D. J. 1990. *Theories of Delinquency*, 2d ed. New York: Oxford University Press.

Shorter, A. D., L. Schaffner, S. Schick, and N. S. Frappier. 1996. *Out of Sight, Out of Mind: The Plight of Girls in the San Francisco Juvenile Justice System*. San Francisco: Center for Juvenile and Criminal Justice.

Short, J. F. 1990. "Gangs, Neighborhoods, and Youth Crime." *Criminal Justice Research Bulletin* 5. Houston, TX: Sam Houston State University, Criminal Justice Center.

Short, J. F., and F. Strodbeck. 1965. *Group Process and Gang Delinquency*. Chicago: University of Chicago Press.

Shover, N., S. Norland, J. James, and W. Thornton. 1979. "Gender Roles and Delinquency." *Social Forces* 58: 162–175.

Sickmund, M. 2000. *Offenders in Juvenile Court, 1997*. Washington, DC: Office of Juvenile Justice and Delinquency Prevention.

———, and Y. Wan. 1999. "Census of Juveniles in Residential Placement Databook." On-line (www.ojjdp.ncjrs.org/ojstatbb/cjrp/index.asp).

———. 2003. Personal communication with author Shelden.

Sidel, R. 1996. *Keeping Women and Children Last*. New York: Penguin.

Siegel, L., and J. Senna. 2000. *Juvenile Delinquency* (7th ed.). Belmont, CA: Wadsworth.

Siegal, N. 1995. "Where the Girls Are." *San Francisco Bay Guardian*, Oct. 4: 19–20.

Sieverdes, C. M., and C. Bartollas. 1982. "Social Roles, Sex, and Racial Differences." *Deviant Behavior* 5: 203–218.

Sikes, G. 1997. *Eight Ball Chicks: A Year in the Violent World of Girl Gangsters*. New York: Anchor Books.

Silbert, M., and A. Pines. 1981. "Sexual Child Abuse as an Antecedent to Prostitution." *Child Abuse and Neglect* 5: 407–411.

Silvern, L. E. 1978. "Masculinity-Femininity in Children's Self-Concepts: The Relationship to Teachers' Judgements of Social Adjustment and Academic Ability, Classroom Behaviors, and Popularity." *Sex Roles* 6: 929–949.

Simon, R. 1975. *Women and Crime*. Lexington, MA: Lexington Books.

———. 1981. "American Women and Crime." In L. Bowker (ed.), *Women and Crime in America*. New York: Macmillan.

Simone, M. V. 1985. "Group Home Failures in Juvenile Justice: The Next Step." *Child Welfare* 64: 4.

Simons, M. 1994. "The Littlest Prostitutes." *New York Times Magazine*, Jan. 16: 30.

Simons, R. L., M. G. Miller, and S. M. Aigner. 1980. "Contemporary Theories of Deviance and Female Delinquency: An Empirical Test." *Journal of Research on Crime and Delinquency* 20: 42–57.

Simons, R. L., and L. B. Whitbeck. 1991. "Sexual Abuse as a Precursor to Prostitution and Victimization Among Adolescent and Adult Homeless Women." *Journal of Family Issues* 12: 361–379.

Simpson, S., and L. Ellis. 1995. "Doing Gender: Sorting out the Caste and Crime Conundrum." *Criminology* 33: 47–81.

Singer, S. I., and M. Levine. 1988. "Power-Control Theory, Gender and Delinquency: A Partial Replication with Additional Evidence on the Role of Peers." *Criminology* 26: 627–648.

Smart, C. 1976. *Women, Crime and Criminology: A Feminist Critique*. London: Routledge and Kegan Paul.

———. 1982. "The New Female Offender: Reality or Myth." In B. R. Price and N. J. Sokoloff (eds.), *The Criminal Justice System and Women*. New York: Clark Boardman.

Smith, D. A. 1979. "Sex and Deviance: An Assessment of Major Sociological Variables." *Sociological Quarterly* 27: 183–195.

Smith, D. E. 1992. "Whistling Women: Reflections on Rage and Rationality." In W. K. Carroll et al. (eds.), *Fragile Truths: 25 Years of Sociology and Anthropology in Canada*. Ottawa: Carleton University Press.

Smith, D. L. 1980. *Young Female Offenders: Analysis of Differential Handling Based on Sex*. Pittsburgh: National Center for Juvenile Justice.

Smith, L. S. 1978. "Sexist Assumptions and Female Delinquency." In C. Smart and B. Smart (eds.), *Women, Sexuality and Social Control*. London: Routledge and Kegan Paul.

Smothers, R. 1990. "Atlanta Sets a Curfew for Youths, Prompting Concern on Race Bias. *New York Times*, Nov. 21: A1.

Snell, T. L., and D. C. Morton. 1994. *Women in Prison*. Washington, DC: Bureau of Justice Statistics, Special Report.

Snyder, H. 1990. *OJJDP Update on Statistics: Growth in Minority Detentions Attributed to Drug Law Violators*. Washington, DC: U.S. Department of Justice.

Snyder, H., T. A. Finnegan, E. H. Nimick, M. H. Sickmund, D. P. Sullivan, and N. J. Tierney. 1989. *Juvenile Court Statistics, 1985*. Washington, DC: U.S. Department of Justice.

Snyder, H., J. L. Hutzler, and T. A. Finnegan. 1985. *Delinquency in the United States, 1982*. Pittsburgh: National Center for Juvenile Justice.

———. 1987. *Delinquency in the United States, 1983*. Pittsburgh: National Center for Juvenile Justice.

Snyder, H., and M. Sickmund. 1999. *Juvenile Offenders and Victims: 1999 National Report*. Washington, DC: Office of Juvenile Justice and Delinquency Prevention.

Soler, M. 1983. "Prepared Statement." Hearing to Inquire into the Continued Detention of Juveniles in Adult Jails and Lock-ups. Hearings Before the Subcommittee on Juvenile Justice, Senate Committee on the Judiciary.

Sommers, I., and D.R. Baskin. 1993. "The Situational Context of Violent Female Offend-ing." *Journal of Research on Crime and Delinquency* 30:136–162.

Sowles, R. C., and J. H. Gill. 1970. "Institutional and Community Adjustment of Delinquents Following Counseling." *Journal of Consulting and Clinical Psychology* 34: 398–402.

Sperber, M. 1993. "Myths about College Sport." In D.S. Eitzen (ed.), *Sport in Contemporary Society: An Anthology*. New York: St. Martin's Press.

Staff. 1995. "Rape for Profit: Trafficking of Nepali Girls/ Women to India's Brothels." *WIN News* 21: 46–47.

Stanford v. Kentucky. 1989. 57 U.S.L.W. 4973.

Staples, B. 1980. Personal communication with authors.

State of Hawaii Databook: the Department of Business, Economic Development and Tourism. 1997. Honolulu: Hawaii State Department of Health.

Steffensmeier, D., and E. Allan. 1995. "Criminal Behavior: Gender and Age." In J.F. Sheley, *Criminology* (2nd ed.). Belmont, CA: Wadsworth.

Steffensmeier, D. J. 1978. "Crime and the Contemporary Woman: An Analysis of Changing Levels of Female Property Crime, 1960–1975." *Social Forces* 57: 566–584.

———. 1980. "Sex Differences in Patterns of Adult Crime, 1965–1977." *Social Forces* 58: 1080–1109.

Steffensmeier, D. J., and M. D. Harer. 1987. "Is the Crime Rate Really Falling? An Aging U.S. Population and Its Impact on the Nation's Crime Rate, 1980–1984." *Journal of Research in Crime and Delinquency* 24: 23–48.

Steffensmeier, D. J., and R. H. Steffensmeier. 1980. "Trends in Female Delinquency: An Examination of Arrest, Juvenile Court, Self-Report, and Field Data." *Criminology* 18: 62–85.

Steinem, G. 1992. *Revolution from Within*. Boston: Little, Brown.

Stevenson, H., J. Reed, P. Bodison, and A. Bishop. 1997. "Racism Stress Management: Racial Socialization Beliefs and the Experience of Depression and Anger in African American Youth." *Youth & Society*, 29: 197–222.

Stratton, J. G. 1975. "Effects of Crisis Intervention Counseling on Predelinquent and Misdemeanor Juvenile Offenders." *Juvenile Justice* 26: 7–18.

Strauss, A., and Corbin, J. 1990. *Basics of Qualitative Research: Grounded Theory, Procedures and Techniques*. Newbury Park, CA: Sage.

Streib,V. L. 1991. "The Juvenile Death Penalty Today." Mimeo.

Streib,V. L., and L. Sametz. 1988. "Capital Punishment of Female Juveniles." Paper presented at the annual meeting of the American Society of Criminology, Chicago.

Stroul, B. A., and R. M. Friedman. 1988. "Principles for a System of Care." *Children Today* (July–August): 11–15.

Sturdevant, S. 1988. "American Friends Service Committee Conference on Women's Labor as Prostitutes Around U.S. Military Bases in the Southern Part of Korea, Japan, Okinawa, and the Philippines." Naha, Okinawa, July 1–4. Mimeo.

Sullivan, C. 1988a. "America's Troubled Children: The Harm in Foster Care." *Christian Science Monitor*, Sept. 27: B1, B8.

———. 1988b. "Out of 'the System' and onto the Streets." *Christian Science Monitor*, Sept. 30: B2, B8.

Sullivan, P. M., and J. F. Knutson. 2000. "The Prevalence of Disabilities and Maltreatment Among Runaway Children." *Child Abuse and Neglect* 24: 1275–1288.

Sussman, A. 1977. "Sex-Based Discrimination and the PINS Jurisdiction." In L. E. Teitelbaum and A. R. Gough (eds.), *Beyond Control: Status Offenders in the Juvenile Court*. Cambridge, MA: Ballinger.

Sutherland, E., and D. Cressey. 1978. *Criminology*, 10th ed. Philadelphia: Lippincott.

Suttles, G. 1968. *The Social Order of the Slum*. Chicago: University of Chicago Press.

Sutton, J. R. 1988. *Stubborn Children: Controlling Delinquency in the United States, 1640–1981*. Berkeley: University of California Press.

Swaim, F. F., and B. A. Bracken. 1997. "Global and Domain-Specific Self-Concepts of a Matched Sample of Adolescent Runaways and Nonrunaways." *Journal of Clinical and Child Psychology* 26: 397–403.

Szerlag, H. 1996. "Teen's Death Probed at YSI Iowa Center." *Youth Today* (February): 42, 48.

Tannenbaum, F. 1938. *Crime and the Community*. New York: Columbia University Press.

Tappan, P. 1947. *Delinquent Girls in Court*. New York: Columbia University Press.

Tashakkori, A. 1993. "Gender, ethnicity, and the structure of self-esteem: an attitude theory approach." *The Journal of Social Psychology*, 133: 479–488.

Task Force on Juvenile Female Offenders. 1991. *Young Women in Virginia's Juvenile Justice System: Where Do They Belong?* Virginia: Department of Youth and Family Services.

Tasker, R. 1994. "Dirty Business: A Spate of Child Sex Cases Highlights a National Concern." *Far Eastern Economic Review* 157: 23–24.

Taylor, A. J. 1967. "An Evaluation of Group Psychotherapy in a Girls' Borstal." *International Journal of Group Psychotherapy* 17: 168–177.

Taylor, C. S. 1990. *Dangerous Society*. East Lansing, MI: Michigan State University Press.

———. 1993. *Girls, Gangs, Women, and Drugs*. East Lansing, MI: Michigan State University Press.

Teilmann, K., and P. Landry. 1981. "Gender Bias in Juvenile Justice." *Journal of Research in Crime and Delinquency* 18: 47–80.

Teitelbaum, L. E., and A. R. Gough (eds.). 1977. *Beyond Control: Status Offenders in the Juvenile Court*. Cambridge, MA: Ballinger.

Teitelbaum, L. E., and L. J. Harris. 1977. "Some Historical Perspectives on Governmental Regulation of Children and Parents." In L. E. Teitelbaum and A. R. Gough (eds.), *Beyond Control: Status Offenders in the Juvenile Court*. Cambridge, MA: Ballinger.

Terry, R. M. 1970. "Discrimination in Handling of Juvenile Offenders by Social Control Agencies." In P. Garabedian and D. Gibbons (eds.), *Becoming Delinquent*. Chicago: Aldine.

Thomas, W. I. 1928. *The Unadjusted Girl*. Boston: Little, Brown.

Thompson v. Oklahoma. 1988. 108 S. Ct. 2687.

Thornberry, T. P., Krohn, M. D., Lizotte, A. J., Smith, C. A., and Porter, P. K. 1998. *Taking Stock: An Overview of Findings from the Rochester Youth Development Study*. Washington DC: American Society of Criminology.

Thorne, B. 1994. *Gender Play: Girls and Boys in School*. New Brunswick, NJ: Rutgers University Press.

Thornton, W., and J. James. 1979. "Masculinity and Delinquency Revisited." *British Journal of Criminology* 19: 225–241.

Thornton, W., J. James, and W. G. Doerner. 1987. *Delinquency and Justice*. Glenview, IL: Scott, Foresman.

Thrasher, F. 1927. *The Gang*. Chicago: University of Chicago Press.

Tiet, Q. Q., G. A. Wasserman, R. Loeber, L. S. McReynolds, and L. S. Miller. 2001.

"Developmental and sex differences in types of conduct problems." *Journal of Child and Family Studies,* 10: 181–197.

Toby, J. 1957. "Social Disorganization and Stake in Conformity: Complementary Factors in Predatory Behavior of Hoodlums." *Journal of Criminal Law, Criminology and Police Science* 48: 12–17.

Tracy, P. E., and K. Kempf-Leonard. 1996. *Continuity and Discontinuity in Criminal Careers.* New York: Plenum Press.

Tracy, P. E., M. E. Wolfgang, and R. M. Figlio. 1985. *Delinquency in Two Birth Cohorts.* Washington, DC: U.S. Department of Justice.

Treanor, B. 2003 "Oy Vey, Pitty OJJ." *Youth Today,* March, pp. 24–25.

Tremblay, R. E. 2000. "The Development of Aggressive Behavior During Childhood: What Have We Learned in the Past Century." *International Journal of Behavioral Development* 24: 129–141.

Trounson, R. 1981. "Child Sexual Abuse: All in the Family." *Los Angeles Times,* Oct. 22.

Truax, C., D. Wargo, and L. Silber. 1966. "Effects of Group Psychotherapy with High Adequate Empathy and Nonpossessive Warmth upon Female Institutionalized Delinquents." *Journal of Abnormal Psychology* 71: 267–274.

Trumbull, M. 1995. "Washington State Gets Tough on Runaway Teens." *Christian Science Monitor* (May 31), p. 1.

Tuana'itau, F. 1997. "Culture, Drugs, Violence and Crime." Paper presented at Fa'a Samoa Conference, Honolulu, HI.

U.S. Bureau of the Census. 1985. *Statistical Abstract of the United States: 1986.* Washington, DC: U.S. Government Printing Office.

U.S. Department of Health and Human Services. 1986. *Child Abuse and Neglect: An Informed Approach to a Shared Concern.* Washington, DC: National Center on Child Abuse and Neglect.

U.S. Department of Justice. 1998. *Addressing Community Gang Problems: A Practical Guide.* Washington, DC: Office of Juvenile Justice and Delinquency Prevention.

U. S. Department of Justice. 2001. *Sourcebook of Criminal Justice Statistics 2001.* On-line. (www.albany.edu/sourcebook)

U.S. House of Representatives, Committee on Education and Labor. 1980. *Juvenile Justice Amendments of 1980.* Washington, DC: U.S. Government Printing Office.

U.S. House of Representatives. 1992. *Hearings on the Reauthorization of the Juvenile Justice and Delinquency Prevention Act of 1974.* Hearings Before the Subcommittee on Human Resources of the Committee on Education and Labor. One Hundred and Second Congress, Serial No. 102–125. Washington, DC: U.S. Government Printing Office.

U.S. Senate, Committee on the Judiciary. 1981. *Reauthorization of the Juvenile Justice and Delinquency Prevention Act of 1974.* Washington, DC: U.S. Government Printing Office.

U.S. Statutes at Large. Ninety-Sixth Congress, 2d sess. 1980. Public Law 96–509, December 8, 1980. Washington, DC: U.S. Government Printing Office.

Valentine Foundation and Women's Way. 1990. "A Conversation About Girls." Bryn Mawr, PA: Valentine Foundation.

Vedder, C. B., and D. B. Somerville. 1970. *The Delinquent Girl.* Springfield, IL.: Charles C. Thomas.

Vetter, L. 1985. "Stability and Change in the Enrollment of Girls and Young Women in Vocational Education, 1971–1980." *Youth and Society* 16: 335–356.

Vinter, R. D., and R. Sarri (eds.). 1976. *Time Out: A National Study of Juvenile Correctional Programs.* Ann Arbor: University of Michigan.

Visher, C. A. 1983. "Gender, Police Arrest Decisions, and Notions of Chivalry." *Criminology* 21: 5–28.

Visher, C. A., and J. A. Roth. 1986. "Participation in Criminal Careers." In A. Blumstein et al. (eds.), *Criminal Careers and Career Criminals, Vol. 1.* Washington, DC: National Academy Press.

Vold, G. B., and T. J. Bernard. 1986. *Theoretical Criminology,* 3d ed. New York: Oxford University Press.

Wadlington, W., C. H. Whitebread, and S. M. Davis. 1987. *Children in the Legal System.* Mineola, NY: Foundation Press.

Wadsworth, M. 1979. *Roots of Delinquency.* New York: Barnes and Noble.

Wakin, E. 1975. *Children Without Justice.* New York: National Council of Jewish Women.

Wald, M. S. 1998. "Symposium Introduction." *Stanford Law and Policy Review* 9: 1–4.

Walker, L. J. 1984. "Sex Differences in the Development of Moral Reasoning: A Critical Review." *Child Development* 55: 677–691.

Walters, D. R. 1975. *Physical and Sexual Abuse of Children*. Bloomington: Indiana University Press.

Warren, J. K., F. A. Gary, and J. Moorhead. 1994. "Self-reported Experiences of Physical and Sexual Abuse Among Runaway Youths." *Perspectives in Psychiatric Care* 30: 23–28.

Washington Post. 1994. "Study: Many Under 18 Raped." *Honolulu Advertiser*, June 23: A10.

Weis, J. G. 1976. "Liberation and Crime: The Invention of the New Female Criminal." *Crime and Social Justice* 6: 17–27.

Weisfeld, C. C. 1986. "Female Behavior in Mixed-Sex Competition: A Review of the Literature." *Developmental Review* 6: 278–299.

Weithorn, L. A. 1988. "Mental Hospitalization of Troublesome Youth: An Analysis of Skyrocketing Admission Rates." *Stanford Law Review* 40: 773–838.

Weitzman, L. 1984. "Sex-Role Socialization: A Focus on Women." In J. Freedman (ed.), *Women: A Feminist Perspective*. Palo Alto, CA: Mayfield.

Weller, R. 1996. "Teens Returned to Parents After Claiming Abuse by Camp Counselors." Associated Press, July 11: 1–2.

Wells, R. H. 1990. "The YWCA of Portland, Oregon's Girls Emancipation Program." In J. Henly (ed.), *Girls' Programming*. Ann Arbor: University of Michigan, Center for Youth Policy.

———. 1991. "Help Girls Create Independent Futures." In I. Schwartz and F. Orlando (eds.), *Programming for Young Women in the Juvenile Justice System*. Ann Arbor: University of Michigan, Center for Youth Policy.

———. 1994. "America's Delinquent Daughters Have Nowhere to Turn for Help." *Corrections Compendium*, November, pp. 4–6.

Werner, E. E., and R. S. Smith. 1982. *Vulnerable, But Invincible: A Longitudinal Study of Resilient Children and Youth*. New York: McGraw-Hill.

Whitbeck, L. B., D. R. Hoyt, and K. A. Ackley. 1997. "Familes of Homeless and Runaway Adolescents: A Comparison of Parent/Caretaker and Adolescent Perspectives on Parenting, Family Violence, and Adolescent Conduct." *Child Abuse and Neglect* 22: 108–125.

Widom, C. S. 1988. "Child Abuse, Neglect and Violent Criminal Behavior." Unpublished manuscript.

———. 2000. "Cycle of Violence." Washington, DC: National Institute of Justice, on-line.

Widom, C. S., and M. A. Ames. 1994. "Criminal Consequences of Childhood Sexual Victimization." *Child Abuse and Neglect* 18: 303–318.

Wilgoren, J. 2003. "'Illinois Miracle' Disputed After Child Abuse Cases." *New York Times*, January 28, A14.

Wolfgang, M. E., R. M. Figlio, and T. Sellin. 1972. *Delinquency in a Birth Cohort*. Chicago: University of Chicago Press.

Wood, P., and C. Clay. 1996. "Perceived Structural Barriers and Academic Performance Among American Indian High School Students." *Youth & Society*, 28: 40–61.

Wood, P., S. Hillman, and S. Sawilowsky. 1996. "Locus of Control, Self-Concept, and Self-Esteem Among At-Risk African American Adolescents." *Adolescence*, 31: 597–604.

Wooden, K. 1976. *Weeping in the Playtime of Others*. New York: McGraw-Hill.

Yorkin, N. 1982. "The Story of Sheri, 12, a Prostitute." *Los Angeles Herald Examiner*, Aug. 4.

Youth Law Center. 1987. *Working with Young Women in the Juvenile Justice System*. San Francisco.

Yumori, W. C., and G. P. Loos. 1985. "The Perceived Service Needs of Pregnant and Parenting Teens and Adults on the Waianae Coast." Working Paper. Kamehameha Schools/Bishop Estate.

Zatz, M. 1985. "Los Cholos: Legal Processing of Chicano Gang Members." *Social Problems* 33: 13–30.

Ziedenberg, J., and V. Schiraldi. 1997. "The Risks Juveniles Face When They Are Incarcerated with Adults." San Francisco: Center on Juvenile and Criminal Justice.

Zinn, H. 1990. *The Politics of History*, 2d ed. Urbana, IL: University of Illinois Press.

Index

AAUW (American Association of University Women), 132–133, 265
A.A. v. Rolle, 187
Abuse/neglect. *See also* Physical abuse; Sexual abuse
  in foster homes, 279–281
Acoca, L., 54
Adjudication, 195
Adler, Freda, 126–127
Adler, P., 136
Adolescent Girl in Conflict, The (Konopka), 105
Adoption Assistance and Child Welfare Act (1980), 279
Adult jails
  conditions for girls in, 219–221
  statistics on girls in, 217–219
Ageton, S., 24
Aggression
  gender and, 57–59
  "ideology of familial patriarchy" and, 58–59
  indirect aggression, 57
  trauma and, 57–58
Aickin, M., 24–25, 199
AIDS/HIV
  gang initiation and, 81
  in Mozambique, 50

prostitution and, 44–45, 47, 49
runaways and, 42
Albright, J., 47
Alcohol-related offenses, 11, 188
Alder, C., 152, 271–272
Allen, D.E., 123
American Association of University Women (AAUW), 132–133, 265
American Bar Association
  gender bias study, 199–200
  racial bias study, 202, 217
American Correctional Association, 38, 264
American Humane Association Child Protection Division, 144
Anderson, E., 123, 239
Anderson, R., 232
Andrews, R.H., 36, 173
Annie E. Casey Foundation, 199, 200
Anomie, 109–110
Anthony, Susan B., 167
Anti-Slavery Project, 47
Ariès, P., 159
Arrest data
  by crime/gender (2000), 10
  gender and, 9–18, 200
  girls' share, 13
  rank order/gender, 12

Arrest data *(continued)*
self-report surveys vs., 53–54, 55
trend/gender, 14
Artz, S., 54, 58, 59, 61–62, 147, 254, 286–287
Asia and prostitution, 46–49
Assault, increase, 11, 13–16, 54
"Asylum" (Jones), 212–213
Athleticism
gender and, 253–254
perceived intelligence and, 252–253

Ball, R.A., 68
Baron, L., 145
Bartollas, C., 201, 229–230
Becker, H.S., 269
Bergsmann, I.R., 224–225
Bernard, Jessie, 98
Bishop, D., 176, 192
Bjerregaard, 68
Blais, M., 59, 147, 148
Block, J.H., 123, 140–141, 142
Blondheim v. State, 187–188
Blume, J.M., 176–177
Boot camps, 234
Boyer, D., 43, 44, 45
Brazilian Center for Childhood and Adolescence, 49
Brener, N.D., 53
Brennan, T., 41
Brenzel, B., 169
Brothers in Crime (Shaw), 237
Brown, W.K., 80
Burgess, A., 41, 146
Bursik, R., 141
Bush Administration, 159, 180–181

Cain, Maureen, 98
California Youth Authority study, 258–262
Campagna, D.S., 43, 44
Campbell, A.
gangs, 66, 70, 73–74, 80, 83, 86, 89–90, 94, 138
shoplifting, 33
Canter, R.J., 19–20, 53, 122
Capitalism
crime and, 119, 120, 129
morality and, 110
Carter, B., 228
Cartographic School of criminology, 107
Causes of Delinquency, The (Hirschi), 2
CDC (Centers for Disease Control), 52–53

Center on Juvenile and Criminal Justice (CJCJ), San Francisco, 272
Centers for Disease Control (CDC), 52–53
Cernkovich, S., 19, 20, 21, 22, 26, 127
Chesney-Lind, M.
gangs, 68, 72, 78, 80, 82, 85, 245
physical/sexual abuse, 39
robbery, 60–61
Chicago School of sociology, 107, 108
Children of the Night, 44, 45, 46, 179, 283, 289–290
Children of the Night Web site, 296n2
Children's Hospital High Risk Project, Los Angeles, 44
Children's Protection and Young Offender's Act (South Australia/1979), 174
"Child-saving movement," 121, 163–169
Child Welfare League, 280
CHINS (children in need of supervision), 34
Cholas gang, 87, 94
City, Inc. Community Intervention for Girls, 291
Class, State, and Crime (Quinney), 119
Clay, C., 245
Cloward, Richard, 111–112
Cohen, Albert, 2, 113–114
Cohen, I., 56–57, 147–148
Cohen's "culture of the gang," 113–114
Cohn, A.H., 36, 173
Concentric zone model, city life, 108
Connell, R.W., 129
Control theory, 115–116
"Convergence" theory, 27–28
Corbin, J., 246
Cornell, D.G., 54–55
Cornell, R.W., 251
Corrado, R., 56–57, 147–148
County of Curry, New Mexico, et al., Johnnie K. et al. v., 220
County of Glenn, California, et al., Lillian Robbins v., 220
Cowie, J., 103–104
Cowie, V., 103–104
Crime and social reality, 117–118
Crime control industry, 120
Crime in the United States: Uniform Crime Reports (FBI), 9, 10
Criminality of Women, The (Pollak), 102
Criminology (Sutherland), 115
Critical/Marxist theory, 118–121
Crouse, Mary Ann, 162–163